Second Edition

RANDOM

PERSONAL

COMPUTER

DICTIONARY

D0462735

Second Edition

RANDOM HOUSE
PERSONAL
COMPUTER
DICTIONARY

PHILIP E. MARGOLIS

RANDOM HOUSE
New York

The first edition of this book was published by Random House in 1991.

Library of Congress Cataloging-in-Publication Data

Margolis, Philip E.
    Random House personal computer dictionary/
Philip E. Margolis .—2nd ed.
        p. cm.
    ISBN 0—679—76424—0
    1.Microcomputers—Dictionaries.   I. Title.
QA76.15.M37 1996
004.16'03—dc20
        95-45508
        CIP

Book design © REM Studio, Inc.
Illustrations by Jared Schneidman Design Inc.
Desktop publishing by Philip E. Margolis

Typeset and printed in the United States of America
9 8 7 6 5 4 3 2 1

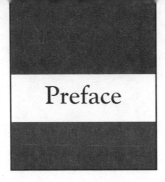

Preface

Like any complex discipline, computer science has its own specialized vocabulary. But what makes "computerese" different is that we come face to face with the language every day. It's not like law where you can hire a lawyer each time you need someone to translate a piece of legal gibberish. Imagine hiring a computer consultant every time you came across an incomprehensible passage in a computer manual!

There's not much hope that *computerese* will go away; the precision allowed by technical terms cannot be reproduced with parochial words. If you use computers (by choice or by necessity), you must bite the bullet and learn the terminology. This dictionary is designed to help you do this as painlessly as possible.

In the preface to the first edition, I remarked ruefully that many of the definitions would be out of date before the ink was dry. Alas, my prediction proved even truer than I anticipated. In producing this second edition, I have had to update nearly every definition, and add several hundred new terms.

Of course, my forecast of obsolescence is as true today as it was in 1991. The technology of personal computers, and the vocabulary to describe it, is a galloping target. Thankfully, the basic concepts have not changed—a bit is a bit and a byte is still a byte.

Many people helped me produce this book. In particular, I want to rethank my three technical reviewers for the first edition—Peter Darnell, Paul Hayslett, and Doug McGlathery—who made innumerable and invaluable suggestions. Obviously, any flaws that remain are my own. And I want to thank my editor, Enid Pearsons, who shepherded both the first edition and this new edition through the publishing maze.

PHILIP E. MARGOLIS
ROCKPORT, MASSACHUSETTS, 1995

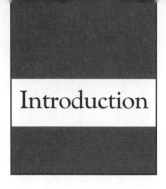

Introduction

Few things are more frustrating than looking up a word and finding that the definition contains ten new mysterious terms. I have tried to avoid these circular definitions as much as possible, although sometimes they're unavoidable. I have at least refrained from using terms that are not included in this dictionary. In addition, most of the definitions include cross references to lead you to more information about a particular topic.

The following list organizes terms into broad categories. If you are interested in learning about a particular area of computer science, you might start by looking up the terms in the appropriate category. You can start with any term and the cross references will lead you to related terms.

ARTIFICIAL INTELLIGENCE

artificial intelligence
expert system
fuzzy logic
handwriting recognition

neural network
pattern recognition
robotics
voice recognition

BUSES AND ADAPTERS

accelerator board
adapter
ADB
add-in
add-on
address bus
AT bus
bus
controller

DIP
DIP switch
DSP
edge connector
EIDE
EISA
expansion board
expansion bus
expansion slot

IRQ
ISA bus
jumper
local bus
Micro Channel architecture
NuBus
PC card

PCI
PCMCIA
plug-and-play
PnP
printed circuit board
slot
VL-Bus

COMMUNICATIONS

acoustic coupler
asynchronous
AT command set
auto-answer
auto-redial
bandwidth
baseband transmission
baud
Bell 103
Bell 212A
Binary File Transfer
bps
CCITT
channel
checksum
codec
communications
communications protocol
communications software
direct-connect modem
even parity
external modem
FAX machine
FAX modem
frame
full duplex
Group 3 protocol
Group 4 protocol
half duplex
handshaking
Hayes compatible

host
internal modem
Kermit
MNP
modem
noise
null-modem cable
odd parity
on-board modem
parity
parity checking
polling
POTS
protocol
remote
remote control
RS-232C
RS-422 and RS-423
serial
SIG
stop bit
synchronous
sysop
telecommuting
terminal emulation
UART
upload
Xmodem
Ymodem
Zmodem

DATA STORAGE

access time
archive
backup
bad sector
bay
Bernoulli disk drive
CD-I
CD-R drive
CDROM
CD-ROM player
cluster
compact disc
corrupted
cylinder
DAT
defragment
density
disk
disk cache
disk controller
disk drive
disk optimizer
double-density disk
double-sided disk
drive bay
erasable optical disk
FDHD
floppy disk
format
fragmentation
half height
hard card
hard disk
hard disk drive
hard disk type
head
head crash
helical-scan cartridge
high-density disk

IDE interface
interleaving
lossless compression
lossy compression
low-level format
magneto-optical (MO) drive
mass storage
media
MFM
microfloppy disk
mount
MTBF
optical disk
optimize
park
partition
platter
quad-speed CD-ROM drive
QIC
RAM disk
read-only
removable hard disk
RLL
SCSI
sector
seek time
sequential access
single-density disk
ST-506 interface
SuperDrive
tape
tape drive
tpi
track
volume
Winchester disk drive
worm
write-protect

DISPLAY MONITORS & VIDEO ADAPTERS

8514/A
active-matrix display
alignment
analog monitor
aspect ratio
autosizing
backlighting
bitblt
CGA
codec
color depth
color monitor
composite video
convergence
CRT
digital monitor
display screen
dot pitch
dual-scan display
EGA
electroluminescent display
ELF emission
fixed-frequency monitor
flat-panel display
flat technology monitor
gas-plasma display
genlock
graphics accelerator
graphics coprocessor
graphics mode
gray scaling
Hercules graphics
intelligent terminal
interlacing
LCD

MCGA
MDA
monochrome
multifrequency monitor
multiscanning monitor
non-interlaced
NTSC
paper-white display
passive-matrix display
pixel
plasma display
resolution
reverse video
RGB monitor
screen flicker
screen saver
scroll
smart terminal
Supertwist
SVGA
terminal
Texas Insruments Graphics
    Architecture
TFT
TI 34010
touch screen
true color
TTL monitor
VDT radiation
VESA
VGA
video adapter
video standards
XGA

GRAPHICS

aliasing
antialiasing
autotracing

Bézier curves
bit map
bit-mapped graphics

block graphics
BMP
CAD
CAD/CAM
CADD
CAE
CGM
character mode
CIE color model
clip
color depth
crop
dithering
draw program
DVI
DXF
EPS
fill
fractal
GEM
graphics based
graphics file formats
gray scaling
handle
HPGL
IGES
image editor
image enhancement
jaggies
line art

mask
monitor
monochrome
morphing
object-oriented graphics
page-white display
paint program
palette
PCX
PGA
photo illustration
PIC
PICT file format
plot
plotter
polyline
presentation graphics
quickdraw
ray tracing
rendering
resolution
scale
text mode
TIFF
true color
vector graphics
video capture
video mode
video standards
WMF

HARDWARE (MISCELLANEOUS)

architecture
chassis
chip
CMOS
connector
device
DIN connector
DIP
hardware

LED
male connector
motherboard
NiCad battery pack
port
power supply
reset button
surge protector
UPS

INPUT DEVICES

antistatic mat
AT keyboard
bus mouse
carpal tunnel syndrome
CCD
digital camera
digitizing tablet
Dvorak keyboard
enhanced keyboard
extended keyboard
F1, F2...F15
flatbed scanner
grabber
input device
IrDA
joystick

keyboard
light pen
membrane keyboard
mouse
numeric keypad
optical scanner
pointing device
pointing stick
puck
QWERTY keyboard
scan
serial mouse
stylus
touchpad
trackball
TWAIN

INTERNET AND ONLINE SERVICES

access code
America Online
Archie
ARPANET
BITNET
bulletin board system (BBS)
chat
conference
connect time
cyber
cyberspace
e-mail
emoticon
FAQ
flame
forum
FTP
gopher
home page
HTML

Information Highway
Mosaic
netiquette
newbie
newsgroup
PPP
Prodigy
service provider
SLIP
TCP/IP
thread
URL
USENET
user group
virtual reality
WAIS
web page
web site
World Wide Web

MEMORY

access time
cycle time
DRAM
dynamic RAM
EDO DRAM
EEPROM
EPROM
flash memory
interleaved memory
main memory
memory
non-volatile memory

page mode memory
PRAM
PROM
RAM
RAM cache
ROM
SIMM
SRAM
virtual memory
volatile memory
VRAM

MICROPROCESSORS

Alpha Processor
ALU
chip
CISC
clock speed
coprocessor
CPU
CPU time
integrated circuit
Intel microprocessors
microprocessor
Motorola microprocessors

OverDrive
PGA
pipelining
primary cache
register
RISC
secondary cache
semiconductor
SIP
ULSI
wait state
zero insertion force (ZIF) socket

MULTIMEDIA

3DO
animation
CD-R drive
CD-ROM player
Cinepak
Indeo
JPEG
motion-JPEG
MPC
MPEG

multimedia
multimedia kit
PhotoCD
QuickTime
sound card
video capture
videoconferencing
Video for Windows
virtual reality

NETWORKS

access code
AppleTalk
ARCnet
broadband ISDN
broadband transmission
broadcast
chat
client/server architecture
coaxial cable
connectivity
diskless workstation
e-mail
Ethernet
FDDI
fiber optics
gateway
groupware
heterogeneous network
ISDN
local-area network
local-area wireless network
    (LAWN)
LocalTalk

NetBIOS
NetWare
network
network interface card
network operating system
NSFnet
node
peer-to-peer architecture
public carrier
router
server
star network
TCP/IP
token-ring network
topology
TOPS
traffic
twisted-pair cable
Tymnet
videoconferencing
voice mail
wide-area network
workgroup computing

OPERATING SYSTEMS AND ENVIRONMENTS

A/UX
AIX
ANSI.SYS
ASCII file
autoexec.bat
AUX
background
BAK file
batch file
batch processing
BIOS
boot
cdev
Chooser
clipboard

COM file
command language
command processor
compound document
CONFIG.SYS
configuration file
Control Panel
control program
cooperative multitasking
CP/M
cross-platform
DDE
demand paging
desk accessory
directory

distributed processing
DOS
embedded object
environment
event
EXE file
executable file
execute
expanded memory
extended memory
extension
external command
file
file allocation table
file management
filename
Finder
folder
hidden file
high memory
internal command
launch
LIM memory
load
loader
MAPI
memory resident
multi-user
Multifinder
multiprocessing
multitasking
multithreading
native
NetWare
network operating system
NextStep

OLE
OpenDoc
operating environment
operating system
OS/2
paging
parallel processing
parent directory
path
pathname
pipe
PnP
pop-up utility
process
real time
redirection
resource
root directory
segment
swap
swap file
System folder
systems software
task switching
thread
time sharing
transaction processing
TSR
Unix
utility
virtual memory
Windows NT
Windows 95
working directory
Xenix

PORTABLE COMPUTING

battery pack
docking station
hand-held computer
laptop computer

NiMH battery pack
notebook computer
palmtop
PC card

PCMCIA
PDA
pen computer
portable

slate PC
sleep mode
subnotebook computer

PRINTERS

carriage
cartridge
color printer
continuous-form paper
cps
daisy-wheel printer
dot-matrix printer
draft mode
draft quality
font cartridge
form feed
friction feed
HP-compatible printer
imagesetter
ImageWriter
impact printer
ink-jet printer
laser printer
LaserWriter
LCD printer
letter quality
line printer
Linotronic
LPT
near letter quality

non-impact printer
offset printing
page description language
page printer
paper feed
PCL
pin
PostScript
ppm
printer
printer driver
printer engine
raster image processor (RIP)
resident font
RIP
sheet feeder
smoothing
soft font
solid ink-jet printer
spooler
thermal printer
toner
tractor feed
typesetter

PROGRAMMING

absolute address
Ada
address
address space
algorithm
AND operator
ANSI character set

API
argument
arithmetic expression
array
assembler
assembly language
assign

authoring tool
base address
BASIC
benchmark
beta test
binary
binary file
bind
bomb
Boolean expression
Boolean logic
Boolean operator
bug
C
C++
call
character string
class
COBOL
code
compiler
component software
conditional
constant
contiguous
copy protection
data structure
data type
debug
debugger
declare
double precision
dummy
dynamic variable
encryption
exclusive OR
expression
filter
floating-point number
FORTRAN
function
garbage in, garbage out
glitch
GW-BASIC

hack
hacker
handwriting recognition
hardwired
hexadecimal
high-level language
inclusive OR operator
interpreter
invoke
iteration
kludge
library
link
linker
LISP
listing
loop
low-level language
machine language
macro
mask
modula-2
module
nesting
NOR operator
NOT operator
object
object code
object oriented
object-oriented programming
octal
offset
operand
operator
optimize
OR operator
Pascal
patch
precedence
procedure
program
programming language
property
recursion

relational operator
relative address
reserved word
reverse engineering
routine
runtime error
scientific notation
script
semantics
simulation
software

source code
stack
statement
static variable
subscript
system call
systems analyst
tree structure
tweak
variable
XOR operator

SPREADSHEETS AND DATABASE MANAGEMENT SYSTEMS

absolute cell reference
aggregate function
area chart
audit trail
automatic recalculation
bar graph
browse
built-in function
cell
column
column graph
comma-delimited
data dictionary
data processing
database
database management system
dBASE
distributed database
export
field
fixed length
flat-file database
formula
fourth-generation language
hypercard
Hypertext
import

join
key
legend
line graph
Lotus 1-2-3
manual recalculation
ODBC
online service
pie chart
query
query by example
query language
range
recalculate
record
relational database
relative cell reference
report
report writer
scatter diagram
spreadsheet
SQL
table
three-dimensional spreadsheet
variable-length record
variable length

TYPES OF COMPUTERS

Amiga
Apple Computer
AT
clone
computer
diskless workstation
home computer
IBM PC
Macintosh computer

mainframe
minicomputer
PC
personal computer
PowerPC
subnotebook computer
supercomputer
workstation

USER INTERFACES

active
alert box
Apple key
associate
box
branch
button
character based
check box
choose
click
collapse
command driven
Control key combination
cursor
cursor position
desktop
dialog box
double click
drag
drag-and-drop
floating
graphical user interface (GUI)
GUI

highlight
hot key
hot spot
I-beam pointer
icon
insertion point
menu
menu bar
menu driven
Microsoft Windows
modifier key
moving-bar menu
overlaid windows
pointer
pop-up window
push-button
radio buttons
scroll bar
shift clicking
shortcut key
tear-off menu
tiled windows
title bar
window

WORD PROCESSING AND DESKTOP PUBLISHING

alignment

anchor

annotation
ascender
baseline
boilerplate
boldface
bullet
camera-ready
caps
CIE color model
clip art
CMYK
color management system (CMS)
color matching
color separation
·continuous tone
Courier font
crop marks
cut
descender
desktop publishing
dingbat
drop cap
editor
electronic publishing
embedded command
even header
feathering
fixed pitch
flow
flush
font
font family
footer
forced page break
greeking
gutter
halftone
hanging indent
hard return
header
HTML
hyphenation
imagesetter
insert mode

justification
justify
kerning
landscape
layout
leader
leading
left justify
Linotronic
mail merge
margins
micro-justification
microspacing
monospacing
odd header
offset printing
orphan
outline font
page break
page layout program
pagination
Pantone Matching System (PMS)
pica
pitch
portrait
preview
process colors
proportional font
proportional pitch
ragged
redlining
repaginate
replace
rich text format (RTF)
rule
ruler
sans serif
scalable font
screen shot
search and replace
· serif
service bureau
SGML
soft return

spell checker
spot color
strikeout
style
style sheet
text wrap
thumbnail
TrueType

typeface
typesetter
vertical justification
widow
word processing
word wrap
WYSIWYG

A

abort: To end a program or function before it has finished naturally. The term *abort* refers to both requested and unexpected terminations. For example, many applications let you abort a search or a print job by pressing a specified abort key. On the other hand, programs can abort unexpectedly for any of the following reasons:

- bugs in the software
- unexpected input that the program cannot handle
- hardware malfunction

When a program aborts, you are usually returned to the operating system shell level. Contrast *abort* with *crash*, which makes the entire system, including the operating system, unusable.

➠ See also *bomb; crash; hang; shell.*

absolute address: A fixed address in memory. The term *absolute* distinguishes it from a *relative address*, which indicates a location by specifying a distance from another location (see Figure 1 at *address*). Absolute addresses are also called *real addresses* and *machine addresses*.

➠ See also *address; relative address.*

absolute cell reference: In spreadsheet applications, a reference to a particular cell or group of cells that does not change, even if you change the shape or size of the spreadsheet, or copy the reference to another cell. For example, in Lotus 1-2-3 and other spreadsheet programs, the cell reference "A3" is an absolute cell reference that always points to the cell in the first column and third row. In contrast, the reference "A3" is a *relative cell reference* that initially points to the cell in the first column and third row, but may change if you copy the

1

reference to another cell or change the shape and size of the spreadsheet in some other way. Absolute cell references are particularly useful for referencing constant values (i.e., values that never change).

⇒ See also *constant; relative cell reference; spreadsheet.*

accelerator board: A type of *expansion board* that makes a computer faster by adding a faster CPU or FPU. Accelerator boards provide a relatively inexpensive way to increase the performance of a computer.

There are many accelerator boards for Macintoshes and PCs. For example, a 486 *accelerator board* contains an Intel 80486 microprocessor. By adding it to an older PC with a 286 or 386 processor, you can effectively turn the computer into a 486 PC.

Note, however, that adding an accelerator board to a computer affects only the speed of the CPU (and sometimes main memory). This may not have a large effect on your applications if the limiting factors are the speed of the disk drive or the bus. If you want to increase performance of an old computer, you are probably better off buying a modern disk drive or adding extra memory.

Most modern computers are designed to accept simpler upgrades. Built into the motherboard is a socket in which the CPU sits. It is usually possible simply to remove the CPU and replace it with a faster model. This is particularly easy if the socket is a zero insertion force (ZIF) socket.

⇒ See also *bus; coprocessor; CPU; expansion board; floating-point number; FPU; graphics accelerator; Intel microprocessors; main memory; microprocessor; motherboard; PC; RAM; ZIF socket.*

access: (v) (1) To use. For example, programs can *access memory*, which means they read data from or write data to main memory. A user can access files, directories, computers, or peripheral devices.

(2) More specifically, *access* often means to read data from or write data to a mass storage device. The time it takes to locate a single byte of information on a mass-storage device is called the *access time.*

⇒ See also *access time; byte; mass storage; memory; random access; read; write.*

(n) (1) The act of reading data from or writing data to a storage device.

(2) A privilege to use computer information in some manner. For example, a user might be granted *read access* to a file, meaning that the user can read the file but cannot modify or delete it. Most operating systems have several different types of access privileges that can be granted or denied to specific users or groups of users.

access code: Same as password, a series of characters and numbers that enables a user to access a computer.

➠ See also *access; log on; password.*

accessory slot: Same as *expansion slot.*

access time: The time a program or device takes to locate a single piece of information and make it available to the computer for processing. DRAM *(dynamic random access memory)* chips for personal computers have access times of 50 to 150 nanoseconds (billionths of a second). Static RAM (SRAM) has access times as low as 10 nanoseconds. The access time of memory should be fast enough to keep up with the CPU. If not, the CPU will waste a certain number of clock cycles, which makes it slower.

Table 1
TYPICAL ACCESS TIMES FOR DIFFERENT COMPUTER DEVICES

DEVICE	TYPICAL ACCESS TIMES
static RAM (SRAM)	10–50 nanoseconds
dynamic RAM (DRAM)	50–150 nanoseconds
EPROM	55–250 nanoseconds
read-only memory (ROM)	55–250 nanoseconds
Hard Disk Drive	9–30 milliseconds
Erasable Optical	19–200 milliseconds
CD-ROM	100–800 milliseconds
DAT tape drive	about 20 seconds
QIC tape drive	about 40 seconds
8 mm tape drive	40–500 seconds

Note, however, that reported access times can be misleading because most memory chips, especially DRAM chips, require a pause between back-to-back accesses. This is one reason why SRAM is so much faster than DRAM, even when the reported access times are equivalent; SRAM requires fewer refreshes, so the pause between back-to-back accesses is smaller. A more important measurement of a chip's speed, therefore, is its cycle time, which measures how quickly two back-to-back accesses can be made.

Access time is also frequently used to describe the speed of disk drives. Disk access times are measured in milliseconds (thousandths of a second), often abbreviated as *ms*. Fast hard disk drives for personal computers boast access times of about 9 to 15 milliseconds. This means that the drive can make about 500 data accesses per second. Note that this is about 200 times slower than average DRAM.

The access time for disk drives (also called the *seek time*) refers to the time it actually takes for the *read/write head* to locate a sector on the disk. This is an average time since it depends on how far away the head is from the desired data. The performance of disk drives can be improved through special techniques such as *caching* and *interleaving*.

➡ See also *access; cycle time; clock speed; CPU; disk cache; interleaving; wait state.*

accounting software: A class of computer programs that perform accounting operations. The simplest accounting programs, sometimes called *personal finance managers,* are single-entry systems that automate check writing and record keeping.

Double-entry systems include functions for general ledger, accounts receivable, and accounts payable. More sophisticated systems also support functions for payroll, inventory, invoicing, and fixed assets. Some high-end systems even support sales analysis and time billing.

ACM: Abbreviation of the *Association for Computing Machinery,* an organization composed of U.S. computer professionals. Founded in 1947, the ACM publishes information relating to computer science, holds seminars, and creates and promotes computer standards.

acoustic coupler: A device onto which a telephone handset is placed to connect a computer with a network. The acoustic coupler might also contain a modem, or the modem could be a separate device.

Popular in the 1970s, acoustic couplers are no longer widely used. Nowadays, telephones connect directly to a modem via modular telephone connectors. This produces better connections than acoustic couplers and avoids the problems produced by irregularly shaped telephones. Still, acoustic coupler modems are useful in some situations, such as in hotel rooms where the telephone cable is anchored to the wall. Modems that do not use an acoustic coupler are sometimes called *direct-connect modems*.

➡ See also *modem; network*.

active: Refers to objects currently being displayed or used. For example, in graphical user interfaces, the *active window* is the window currently receiving mouse and keyboard input. In spreadsheet applications, the *active cell* is the cell, usually highlighted, in which data can be entered or modified. The *active program* is the program currently running. When you enter a command, it usually applies only to the active elements.

➡ See also *cell; graphical user interface; spreadsheet; window*.

active-matrix display: A type of flat-panel display in which the screen is refreshed more frequently than in conventional passive-matrix displays. The most common type of active-matrix display is based on a technology known as *TFT (thin film transistor)*. The two terms, *active matrix* and *TFT*, are often used interchangeably.

➡ See also *flat-panel display; LCD; TFT*.

Ada: A high-level programming language developed in the late 1970s and early 1980s for the United States Defense Department. Ada was designed to be a do-everything language, from business applications to rocket guidance systems. One of its principal features is that it supports *real-time* applications. In addition, Ada incorporates modular techniques that make it easier to build and maintain large systems. Since 1986, Ada has been the mandatory development language for most U.S. military applications.

Ada is named after Augusta Ada Byron (1815–52), daughter of Lord Byron, and Countess of Lovelace. She helped Charles Babbage develop programs for the *analytic engine*, the first mechanical computer. She is considered by many to be the world's first programmer.

➡ See also *high-level language; modular architecture; real time*.

adapter: (1) The circuitry required to support a particular device. For example, *video adapters* enable the computer to support graphics monitors, and *network adapters* enable a computer to attach to a network. Adapters can be built into the main circuitry of a computer or they can be separate add-ons that come in the form of expansion boards.

➠ See also *controller; expansion board; video adapter.*

(2) Short for *video adapter.*

ADB: MAC Abbreviation of *Apple Desktop Bus*, a type of communications pathway built into all versions of the Apple Macintosh computer since the SE. It is used to connect low-speed input devices such as the keyboard and mouse. ADB ports are designated with the icon. A single ADB port can support as many as 16 simultaneous input devices.

➠ See also *bus; interface; Macintosh computer; port.*

add-in: (1) A component you can add to a computer or other device to increase its capabilities. Add-ins can increase memory or add graphics or communications capabilities to a computer. They can come in the form of expansion boards, cartridges, or chips. The term *add-in* is often used instead of *add-on* for chips you add to a board that is already installed in a computer. In contrast, *add-on* almost always refers to an entire circuit board.

(2) A software program that extends the capabilities of larger programs. For example, there are many Excel add-ins designed to complement the basic functionality offered by Excel. In the Windows environment, add-ins are becoming increasingly common thanks to OLE 2.0.

➠ See also *add-on; cartridge; expansion board; OLE.*

add-on: Refers to a product designed to complement another product. For example, there are numerous *add-on boards* available that you can plug into a personal computer to give it additional capabilities. Another term for *add-on board* is *expansion board.*

Add-on products are also available for software applications. For example, there are add-on report generation programs that attach to popular database products such as dBASE, giving them additional report generation and graphics capabilities.

The terms *add-on* and *add-in* are often, but not always, used synonymously. The term *add-in* can refer to individual chips you can insert into boards that are already installed in your computer. *Add-on*, on the other hand, almost always refers to an entire circuit board, cartridge, or program.

➡ See also *add-in; cartridge; expansion board; expansion slot; printed circuit board.*

add-on board: Same as *expansion board.*

address: (1) A location of data, usually in main memory or on a disk. You can think of computer memory as an array of storage boxes, each of which is one byte in length (Figure 1). Each box has an address (a unique number) assigned to it. By specifying a memory address, programmers can access a particular byte of data. Disks are divided into *tracks* and *sectors,* each of which has a unique address. Usually, you do not need to worry about addresses unless you are a programmer.

➡ See also *absolute address; base address; disk; machine address; main memory; memory; offset; relative address; sector; track.*

(2) A name or token that identifies a network component. In local area networks (LANs), for example, every node has a unique address. On the Internet, every file has a unique address called a *URL.*

➡ See also *URL.*

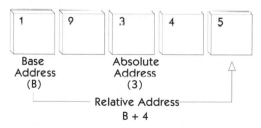

Figure 1: *Memory Addresses*

address bus: A collection of wires connecting the CPU with main memory that is used to identify particular locations (addresses) in main memory. The width of the address bus (that is, the number of wires) determines how many unique memory locations can be addressed. Modern PCs and Macintoshes have 24 address lines, which enables them to access 16MB (megabytes) of main memory.

➠ See also *address; bus; CPU; main memory.*

address space: The set of all legal addresses in memory for a given application. The address space represents the amount of memory available to a program. Interestingly, the address space can be larger than physical memory through a technique called *virtual memory.*

➠ See also *address; main memory; memory; virtual memory.*

Adobe PostScript: See *PostScript.*

aggregate function: A function that performs a computation on a set of values rather than on a single value. For example, finding the average or mean of a list of numbers is an aggregate function.

All database management and spreadsheet systems support a set of aggregate functions that can operate on a set of selected records or cells.

➠ See also *database management system; function; spreadsheet.*

AI: Abbreviation of *artificial intelligence.*

AIX: Acronym for *Advanced Interactive eXecutive,* a version of UNIX produced by IBM. AIX runs on a variety of computers, including PCs and workstations.

➠ See also *UNIX.*

alert box: A small box that appears on the display screen to give you information or to warn you about a potentially damaging operation. For example, it might warn you that the system is deleting one or

more files. Unlike dialog boxes, alert boxes do not require any user input. However, you need to acknowledge the alert box by pressing the Enter key or clicking a mouse button to make it go away.
Alert boxes are also called *message boxes*.

➡ See also *box; dialog box; graphical user interface; window.*

algorithm: A formula or set of steps for solving a particular problem. To be an algorithm, a set of rules must be unambiguous and have a clear stopping point. Algorithms can be expressed in any language, from natural languages like English or French to programming languages like FORTRAN (Figure 2).

We use algorithms every day. For example, a recipe for baking a cake is an algorithm. Most programs, with the exception of some artificial intelligence applications, consist of algorithms. Inventing elegant algorithms—algorithms that are simple and require the fewest steps possible—is one of the principal challenges in programming.

➡ See also *artificial intelligence; program; programming language.*

alias: (1) An alternative name for an object, such as a variable, file, or device. On Macintoshes, you can assign aliases for files, which allows you to have icons for the same file in different folders. Windows provides the same functionality but does not use the term *alias*.

➡ See also *device; file; name; variable.*

aliasing: (1) In computer graphics, the process by which smooth curves and other lines become jagged because the resolution of the graphics device or file is reduced.

➡ See also *antialiasing; jaggies; resolution.*

(2) In digital sound, aliasing is a static distortion resulting from a low sampling rate–below 40 kilohertz (Khz).

alignment: (1) When used to describe text, *alignment* is the arrangement

Recipe
CHOCOLATE CAKE

4 oz. chocolate	3 eggs
1 cup butter	1 tsp. vanilla
2 cups sugar	1 cup flour

Melt chocolate and butter. Stir sugar into melted chocolate. Stir in eggs and vanilla. Mix in flour. Spread mix in greased pan. Bake at 350° for 40 minutes or until inserted fork comes out almost clean. Cool in pan before eating.

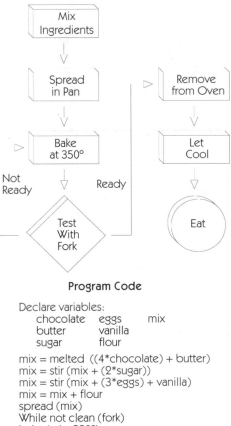

Program Code

```
Declare variables:
    chocolate    eggs       mix
    butter       vanilla
    sugar        flour

mix = melted ((4*chocolate) + butter)
mix = stir (mix + (2*sugar))
mix = stir (mix + (3*eggs) + vanilla)
mix = mix + flour
spread (mix)
While not clean (fork)
bake (mix, 350°)
```

Figure 2: *Algorithms*

of text or graphics relative to a margin. For example:

flush left alignment means that text is lined up along the left margin.	*flush right alignment* lines up text along the right margin.
centered alignment means that text is aligned around a midpoint.	*justified alignment* means that text lines up along both margins.

➠ See also *justification; margins.*

(2) In reference to graphical objects, *alignment* describes their relative positions. Most draw programs support an align command that allows you to align two or more objects so that their tops, bottoms, sides, or middles are aligned.

➠ See also *draw program.*

Alpha Processor: A RISC processor developed by Digital Equipment Corporation used in their line of workstations.

➠ See also *RISC; workstation.*

alphanumeric: Describes the combined set of all letters in the alphabet and the numbers 0 through 9 (Table 2). It is useful to group letters and numbers together because many programs treat them identically, and differently from punctuation characters. For example, most operating systems allow you to use any letters or numbers in file-names but prohibit many punctuation characters. Your computer manual would express this rule by stating: "Filenames may be composed of alphanumeric characters."

Sometimes additional characters are considered alphanumeric. For example, on IBM mainframes the characters @, #, and $ are considered alphanumeric characters.

➠ See also *special character.*

Alt key: PC Short for *Alternate key*, the Alt key is like a second Control key. Not all computer keyboards have an Alt key, but it is standard on

Table 2
ALPHANUMERIC, PUNCTUATION, AND SPECIAL CHARACTERS

ALPHANUMERIC CHARACTERS

a -z
A-Z
0 -9

PUNCTUATION CHARACTERS

;	semicolon
:	colon
,	comma
"	double quote
'	single quote
#	number sign or pound sign
/	slash
\	backslash
*	asterisk or star
^	caret
.	period, point, or dot
@	at sign
&	ampersand
~	tilde
!	bang or exclamation mark
-	dash
=	equal sign
—	em dash
–	en dash
...	ellipsis

SPECIAL CHARACTERS

Esc
Tab

all PCs. You use it in the same fashion as the Control key—holding it down while you press another key. For example, an instruction to use the Alt+P combination means that you should hold the Alt key down while pressing and then releasing the P key. The meaning of any Alt key combination depends on which application is running.

MAC On Macintoshes, the equivalent key is called the *Option key.*

➠ See also *ASCII; control character; keyboard; Option key.*

ALU: Abbreviation of *arithmetic logic unit,* the part of a computer that performs all arithmetic computations, such as addition and multiplication, and all comparison operations. The ALU is one component of the CPU (central processing unit).

➡ See also *CPU*.

America Online: A popular online service. It is often abbreviated as *AOL*.

➡ See also *online service*.

American National Standards Institute: See *ANSI*.

American Standard Code for Information Interchange: See *ASCII*.

Amiga: A family of personal computers produced by Commodore Business Machines. Amigas are powerful personal computers that have extra microprocessors to handle graphics and sound generation. They also have built-in MIDI interfaces for connecting to synthesizers and other electronic musical devices. Like older Apple Macintosh computers, the Amiga line of computers is built around the Motorola 680x0 line of microprocessors. Amiga computers, however, are not compatible with Macintoshes because they use different operating systems. Nor are they compatible with PCs.

➡ See also *graphics; microprocessor; MIDI; personal computer*.

analog: Almost everything in the world can be described or represented in one of two forms: *analog* or *digital*. The principal feature of analog representations is that they are continuous. In contrast, digital representations consist of values measured at discrete intervals (Figure 3).

Digital watches are called *digital* because they go from one value to the next without displaying all intermediate values. Consequently, they can display only a finite number of times of the day. In contrast, watches with hands are analog, because the hands move continuously around the clock face. As the minute hand goes around, it not only touches the numbers 1 through 12, but also the infinite number of points in between.

Early attempts at building computers used analog techniques, but accuracy and reliability were not good enough. Today, almost all computers are digital.

➠ See also *digital.*

Analog   Digital

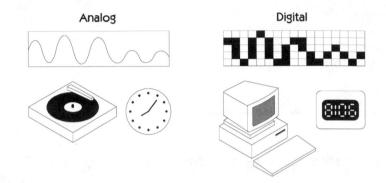

Figure 3: *Analog vs. Digital*

analog monitor: The traditional type of color display screen that has been used for years in televisions. In reality, all monitors based on CRT technology (that is, all monitors except *flat-panel displays*) are analog. Some monitors, however, are called *digital monitors* because they accept digital signals from the video adapter. EGA monitors, for example, must be digital because the EGA standard specifies digital signals. Digital monitors must nevertheless translate the signals into an analog form before displaying images. Some monitors can accept both digital and analog signals.

Most analog monitors are designed to accept signals at a precise frequency. They are therefore called *fixed-frequency monitors.* However, a special type of monitor, called a *multiscanning* or *multisync monitor*, automatically adjusts itself to the frequency of the signals being sent to it. A third type of monitor, called a *multifrequency monitor*, is designed to accept signals at two or more preset frequency levels.

➠ See also *analog; CRT; digital; digital monitor; monitor; multiscanning monitor; video adapter.*

anchor: In desktop publishing, to fix a graphical object so that its position relative to some other object remains the same during repagination. Frequently, for example, you may want to *anchor* a picture next to a piece of text so that they always appear together.

AND operator: A Boolean operator that returns a value of TRUE if both its operands are TRUE, and FALSE otherwise.

➠ See also *Boolean operator; operand; operator.*

animation: A simulation of movement created by displaying a series of pictures, or frames. Cartoons on television, for example, is one example of animation. Animation on computers is one of the chief ingredients of multimedia presentations. There are many software applications that enable you to create animations that you can display on a computer monitor.

Note the difference between animation and video. Whereas video takes continuous motion and breaks it up into discrete frames, animation starts with independent pictures and puts them together to form the illusion of continuous motion.

➠ See also *multimedia.*

annotation: A comment attached to a particular section of a document. Many computer applications enable you to enter annotations on text documents, spreadsheets, presentations, and other objects. This is a particularly effective way to use computers in a workgroup environment to edit and review work. The creator of a document sends it to reviewers who then mark it up electronically with annotations and return it. The document's creator then reads the annotations and adjusts the document appropriately.

Many modern applications support voice annotations. If the computer is equipped with a microphone, the reviewer can voice his comments orally instead of writing them. These voice annotations are digitized and stored with the document. When a reader of the document selects the annotation icon, the spoken message is played back through the computer's speakers.

➠ See also *workgroup computing.*

ANSI: Acronym for the *American National Standards Institute.* Founded in 1918, ANSI is a voluntary organization composed of over 1,300 members (including all the large computer companies) that creates standards for the computer industry. For example, ANSI C is a version of the C language that has been approved by the ANSI committee. To a large degree, all ANSI C compilers, regardless of which company produces them, should behave similarly.

In addition to programming languages, ANSI sets standards for a wide range of technical areas, from electrical specifications to communications protocols. For example, FDDI, the main set of protocols for sending data over fiber optic cables, is an ANSI standard.

➠ See also *FDDI; portable; standard.*

ANSI Character Set: A collection of special characters and associated codes adopted by the ANSI standards organization (Table 3). The ANSI character set includes many foreign characters, special punctuation, and business symbols.

PC In Windows environments, you can enter ANSI characters by holding down the Alt key and typing the ANSI code with the numeric keypad.

Table 3
ANSI CHARACTERS

CHARACTER	NAME	ANSI CODE	MACINTOSH KEYSTROKES
…	ellipsis	0133	Option ;
'	opening single quote	0145	Option]
'	closing single quote	0146	Option Shift]
"	opening double quote	0147	Option [
"	closing double quote	0148	Option Shift [
•	bullet	0149	Option 8
–	en dash	0150	Option Hyphen
—	em dash	0151	Option Shift Hyphen
™	trademark symbol	0153	Option 2
©	copyright symbol	0169	Option g
®	registered trademark	0174	Option r
¼	one quarter	0188	font-dependent
½	one half	0189	font-dependent
¾	three quarters	0190	font-dependent

MAC On Macintoshes, you can enter ANSI characters by holding down the Option key and typing a character, as shown in Table 3.

➟ See also *ASCII*.

ANSI.SYS: PC Pronounced *ann-see-dot-siss*, the name of a DOS device driver that makes a monitor conform to the ANSI standard. The ANSI standard specifies a series of *escape sequences* that cause the monitor to behave in various ways. For example, one escape sequence clears the screen while another causes all subsequent characters to be inverted.

In general, DOS programs do not use the ANSI codes because these codes are slower than the built-in BIOS codes. DOS programs that do use ANSI codes for compatibility with other devices require that you load the ANSI.SYS device driver in the configuration file, CONFIG.SYS.

➟ See also *ANSI; BIOS; CONFIG.SYS; device driver; escape sequence.*

answer-only modem: A modem that can receive messages but cannot send them. Only the most inexpensive modems are answer-only.

➟ See also *modem.*

Bit Map   Smoothing   Antialiasing

Figure 4: *Antialiasing*

antialiasing: In computer graphics, *antialiasing* is a software technique for diminishing *jaggies*—stairstep-like lines that should be smooth (Figure 4). Jaggies occur because the output device, the monitor or printer, doesn't have a high enough resolution to represent a smooth line. Antialiasing reduces the prominence of jaggies by surrounding the stairsteps with intermediate shades of gray (for gray-scaling devices) or color (for color devices). Although this reduces the jagged appearance of the lines, it also makes them fuzzier.

Another method for reducing jaggies is called *smoothing,* in which the printer changes the size and horizontal alignment of dots to make curves smoother.

➡ See also *jaggies; resolution; smoothing.*

antistatic mat: A mat on which you can stand while repairing a computer or adding expansion cards. The mat absorbs static electricity which might otherwise damage electronic components. Another way to eliminate damage caused by static electricity is to wear an antistatic wristband.

antivirus program: A utility that searches a hard disk for viruses and removes any that are found.

➡ See also *virus.*

AOL: See *America Online.*

API: Abbreviation of *application program interface*, a set of routines, protocols, and tools for building software applications. A good API makes it easier to develop a program by providing all the building blocks. A programmer puts the blocks together.

Most operating environments, such as MS-Windows, provide an API so that programmers can write applications consistent with the operating environment. Although APIs are designed for programmers, they are ultimately good for users because they guarantee that all programs using a common API will have similar interfaces. This makes it easier for users to learn new programs.

➡ See also *application; interface; operating environment; routine.*

app: Short for *application.* A *killer app,* for example, is an application that surpasses (i.e., kills) its competitors.

append: To add something at the end. For example, you can append one file to another or you can append a field to a record. Do not confuse *append* with *insert*. *Append* always means to add at the end. *Insert* means to add in between.

➠ See also *insert*.

Apple Computer: A personal computer company founded in 1976 by Steven Jobs and Steve Wozniak. Throughout the history of personal computing, Apple has been one of the most innovative influences. In fact, some analysts say that the entire evolution of the PC can be viewed as an effort to catch up with the Apple Macintosh.

In addition to inventing new technologies, Apple also has often been the first to bring sophisticated technologies to the personal computer. Apple's innovations include:

Graphical user interface (GUI): First introduced in 1983 on its Lisa computer. Many components of the Macintosh GUI have become de facto standards and can be found in other operating systems, such as Microsoft Windows.

Color. The Apple II, introduced in 1977, was the first personal computer to offer color monitors.

Built-in networking. In 1985, Apple released a new version of the Macintosh with built-in support for networking (LocalTalk).

Plug & play expansion. In 1987, the Mac II introduced a new expansion bus called *NuBus* that made it possible to add devices and configure them entirely with software.

QuickTime. In 1991, Apple introduced QuickTime, a multi-platform standard for video, sound, and other multimedia applications.

Integrated television. In 1993, Apple released the Macintosh TV, the first personal computer with built-in television and stereo CD.

RISC. In 1994, Apple introduced the Power Mac, based on the PowerPC RISC microprocessor.

➠ See also *graphical user interface; LocalTalk; Macintosh; plug-and-play; PowerPC; QuickTime; RISC.*

Apple Desktop bus: See *ADB*.

Apple key: MAC A special key on Macintosh computers labeled with the Apple logo. On all but the oldest Apple computers, the Apple key serves as the Command key.

➠ See also *Command key*.

Apple Macintosh computer: See *Macintosh computer*.

AppleTalk: MAC An inexpensive local-area network (LAN) architecture built into all Apple Macintosh computers and laser printers. AppleTalk is based on a bus topology. The original version can connect up to 32 devices within a distance of about 1,000 feet. An updated version, known as *Phase 2*, can support 16 million devices.

Although AppleTalk is relatively slow (230 thousand bits per second) compared with other networks such as Ethernet (10 million bits per second) and the IBM Token Ring (4 million bits per second), it is popular because it is inexpensive and simple. It can connect Macintosh computers and printers, and even PCs if they are equipped with special AppleTalk hardware and software.

The standard cabling scheme for AppleTalk networks is known as *LocalTalk*. However, AppleTalk can be used with other cabling schemes as well.

➠ See also *local-area network; LocalTalk; Macintosh computer; topology*.

applet: A program designed to be executed from within another application. Unlike an application, applets cannot be executed directly from the operating system. With the growing popularity of OLE (object linking and embedding), applets are becoming more prevalent. A well-designed applet can be invoked from many different applications.

➠ See also *application; OLE*.

application: A program or group of programs designed for end users. Software can be divided into two general classes: *systems software* and *applications software* (Figure 5). Systems software consists of low-level programs that interact with the computer at a very basic level. This includes operating systems, compilers, and utilities for managing computer resources.

In contrast, applications software (also called *end-user programs*) includes database programs, word processors, and spreadsheets. Figuratively speaking, applications software sits on top of systems software because it is unable to run without the operating system and system utilities.

➥ See also *end user; operating system; software; systems software.*

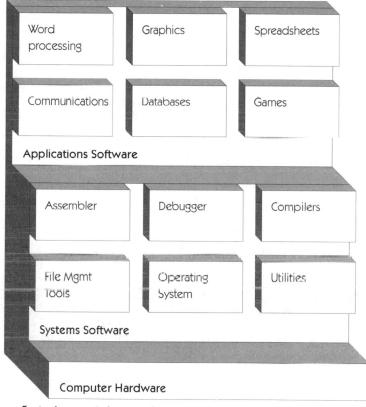

Figure 5: *Applications Software and Systems Software*

Application Program Interface: See *API.*

ARC: To compress a file using the ARC format. The ARC data compression format, created by Systems Enhancement Associates, is particularly popular among bulletin board systems (BBSs). Another common format is *ZIP*.

Files that have been compressed with an ARC utility end with a .ARC extension. To decompress them, you need a utility called *ARC-E* (stands for *arc-extract*).

➠ See also *data compression; ZIP.*

Archie: A program that enables you to search for files anywhere on the Internet by filename.

➠ See also *filename; Internet.*

architecture: A design. The term *architecture* can refer to either hardware or software, or to a combination of hardware and software. The architecture of a system always defines its broad outlines, and may define precise mechanisms as well.

An open architecture allows the system to be connected easily to devices and programs made by other manufacturers. Open architectures use off-the-shelf components and conform to approved standards. A system with a *closed architecture*, on the other hand, is one whose design is *proprietary*, making it difficult to connect the system to other systems.

➠ See also *open architecture; proprietary; standard.*

archival backup: A type of backup in which only files modified since the last backup are copied. Archival backups are much faster than full backups because fewer files are copied. Typically, users make a full backup of all data once a week and an archival backup each day between the full backups.

Archival backups are also called *incremental backups.*

➠ See also *archive; backup.*

archive: (v) (1) To copy files to a long-term storage medium for backup. Large computer systems often have two layers of backup, the first of which is a disk drive. Periodically, the computer operator will archive files on the disk to a second storage device, usually a tape drive. On smaller systems, archiving is synonymous with *backing up*.

➠ See also *archival backup; backup.*

(2) To compress a file.

➠ See also *ARC; zip.*

(n) (1) A disk, tape, or directory that contains files that have been backed up.

(2) A file that contains one or more files in a compressed format.

(adj) PC In DOS systems, the *archive attribute* marks files that have been modified since the last backup.

➠ See also *attribute.*

ARCnet: Short for *Attached Resource Computer network*, ARCnet is one of the oldest, simplest, and least expensive types of local-area network. ARCnet was introduced by Datapoint Corporation in 1968. It uses a token-ring architecture, supports data rates of 2.5 megabits per second, and connects up to 255 computers. A special advantage of ARCnet is that it permits various types of transmission media— twisted-pair wire, coaxial cable, and fiber optic cable—to be mixed on the same network.

Although it has less capacity than other networks such as Ethernet and IBM Token Ring, it is nevertheless extremely popular because of its simplicity. A new specification, called *ARCnet Plus*, will support data rates of 20 megabits per second.

➠ See also *Ethernet; local-area network; token-ring network.*

area chart: A type of presentation graphic that emphasizes a change in values by filling in the portion of the graph beneath the line connecting various data points.

➠ See also *presentation graphics.*

argument: In programming, a value that you pass to a *routine*. For example, if SQRT is a routine that returns the square root of a value, then SQRT(25) would return the value 5. The value 25 is the argument.

Argument is often used synonymously with *parameter*, although *parameter* can also mean any value that can be changed. In addition, some programming languages make a distinction between arguments, which are passed in only one direction, and parameters, which can be passed back and forth, but this distinction is by no means universal.

An argument can also be an option to a command, in which case it is often called a *command-line argument*.

➠ See also *option; parameter; routine*.

arithmetic expression: An expression that represents a numeric value. Other types of expressions can represent character or *Boolean* values.

➠ See also *expression*.

arithmetic operator: See under *operator*.

ARPANET: The precursor to the Internet, ARPANET was a large wide-area network created by the United States Defense Advanced Research Project Agency (ARPA). Established in 1969, ARPANET served as a testbed for new networking technologies, linking many universities and research centers.

➠ See also *Internet; NSFnet*.

array: A series of objects all of which are the same size and type. Each object in an array is called an *array element*. For example, you could have an array of integers or an array of characters or an array of anything that has a defined data type. The important characteristics of an array are:

■ Each element has the same data type (although they may have different values).

■ The entire array is stored contiguously in memory (that is, there are no gaps between elements).

Arrays can have more than one dimension. A one-dimensional array is called a *vector*; a two-dimensional array is called a *matrix*. To access a particular element in an array, you need to specify the array's name with one or more *subscripts*. For example:

A[5]

specifies the fifth element in a one-dimensional array named A.

➠ See also *data structure; data type; matrix; subscript; vector.*

arrow keys: Most computer keyboards contain four arrow keys for moving the cursor or insertion point right, left, up, or down. When combined with the Shift, Function, Control, or Alt keys (on PCs), the arrow keys can have different meanings. For example, pressing Shift + Up-arrow might move the cursor or pointer up an entire page. On Macintoshes, the arrow keys can be combined with the Shift, Option, and Command keys.

The exact manner in which the arrow keys function depends on which program is running. Some programs ignore them.

The arrow keys are also called *cursor control keys*.

➠ See also *keyboard.*

artificial intelligence: The branch of computer science concerned with making computers behave like humans. The term was coined in 1956 by John McCarthy at the Massachusetts Institute of Technology. Artificial intelligence includes:

games playing: programming computers to play games such as chess and checkers

expert systems: programming computers to make decisions in real-life situations (for example, some expert systems help doctors diagnose diseases based on symptoms)

natural language: programming computers to understand natural human languages

neural networks: Systems that simulate intelligence by attempting to reproduce the types of physical connections that occur in animal brains

robotics: programming computers to see and hear and react to other sensory stimuli

Currently, no computers exhibit full artificial intelligence (that is, are able to simulate human behavior). The greatest advances have occurred in the field of games playing. The best computer chess programs are now capable of beating most humans, although they still lose to grand masters.

In the area of robotics, computers are now widely used in assembly plants, but they are capable only of very limited tasks. Robots have great difficulty identifying objects based on appearance or feel, and they still move and handle objects clumsily.

Natural-language processing offers the greatest potential rewards because it would allow people to interact with computers without needing any specialized knowledge. You could simply walk up to a computer and talk to it. Unfortunately, programming computers to understand natural languages has proved to be more difficult than originally thought. Some rudimentary translation systems that translate from one human language to another are in existence, but they are not nearly as good as human translators. There are also voice recognition systems that can convert spoken sounds into written words, but they do not *understand* what they are writing; they simply take dictation. Even these systems are quite limited—you must speak slowly and distinctly.

In the early 1980s, expert systems were believed to represent the future of artificial intelligence and of computers in general. To date, however, they have not lived up to expectations. Many expert systems help human experts in such fields as medicine and engineering, but they are very expensive to produce and are helpful only in special situations.

Today, the hottest area of artificial intelligence is neural networks, which are proving successful in a number of disciplines such as voice recognition and natural-language processing.

There are several programming languages that are known as AI languages because they are used almost exclusively for AI applications. The two most common are *LISP* and *PROLOG.*

➠ See also *expert system; LISP; natural language; neural network; robotics; voice recognition.*

ascender: In typography, the portion of a lowercase letter that rises above the main body of the letter (that is, above the height of a lowercase *x*).

➠ See also *baseline; descender; x-height.*

ASCII: Acronym for the *American Standard Code for Information Interchange.* Pronounced *ask-ee,* ASCII is a code for representing English characters as numbers, with each letter assigned a number from 0 to 127 (Table 4 and Table 5). For example, the ASCII code for uppercase M is 77. Most computers use ASCII codes to represent text, which makes it possible to transfer data from one computer to another.

Text files stored in ASCII format are sometimes called *ASCII files.* Text editors and word processors are usually capable of storing data in ASCII format, although ASCII format is not always the default storage format. Most data files, particularly if they contain numeric data, are not stored in ASCII format. Executable programs are never stored in ASCII format.

The standard ASCII character set uses just 7 bits for each character. A larger character set, known as *extended ASCII* or *high ASCII,* uses 8 bits, which gives it 128 additional characters (Table 6). The extra characters are used to represent non-English characters, graphics symbols, and mathematical symbols. The extended characters and their ASCII codes have been defined by IBM, but they have not been officially standardized.

The ANSI standards organization has defined a character set that overlaps the extended character set, but uses different codes (see under *ANSI character set*).

Another set of codes that is used on large IBM computers is EBCDIC.

➠ See also *EBCDIC; extended ASCII; text file; Unicode.*

ASCII file: A text file in which each byte represents one character according to the ASCII code. Contrast with a binary file, in which there is no one-to-one mapping between bytes and characters. Files that have been formatted with a word processor must be stored and transmitted as binary files to preserve the formatting. ASCII files are sometimes called *plain text files.*

➠ See also *ASCII; binary file.*

Table 4
STANDARD ASCII (CONTROL CODES AND SPACE CHARACTERS)

DECIMAL VALUE	ABBREVIATION	DESCRIPTION
0	NUL	Null
1	SOH	Start of Heading
2	STX	Start of text
3	ETX	End of text
4	EOT	End of transmit
5	ENQ	Enquiry
6	ACK	Acknowledge
7	BEL	Audible bell
8	BS	Backspace
9	HT	Horizontal tab
10	LF	Line feed
11	VT	Vertical tab
12	FF	Form feed
13	CR	Carriage return
14	SO	Shift out
15	SI	Shift in
16	DLE	Data link escape
17	DC1	Device control 1
18	DC2	Device control 2
19	DC3	Device control 3
20	DC4	Device control 4
21	NAK	Negative acknowledge
22	SYN	Synchronous idle
23	ETB	End transmit block
24	CAN	Cancel
25	EM	End of Medium
26	SUB	Substitution
27	ESC	Escape
28	FS	Figures shift
29	GS	Group separator
30	RS	Record separator
31	US	Unit separator
32	SP	Blank space character (Space Bar)

Table 5
STANDARD ASCII (ALPHANUMERIC CHARACTERS)

DECIMAL VALUE	CHARACTER	DECIMAL VALUE	CHARACTER	DECIMAL VALUE	CHARACTER
33	!	65	A	97	a
34	"	66	B	98	b
35	#	67	C	99	c
36	$	68	D	100	d
37	%	69	E	101	e
38	&	70	F	102	f
39	'	71	G	103	g
40	(	72	H	104	h
41	)	73	I	105	i
42	*	74	J	106	j
43	+	75	K	107	k
44	,	76	L	108	l
45	–	77	M	109	m
46	.	78	N	110	n
47	/	79	O	111	o
48	0	80	P	112	p
49	1	81	Q	113	q
50	2	82	R	114	r
51	3	83	S	115	s
52	4	84	T	116	t
53	5	85	U	117	u
54	6	86	V	118	v
55	7	87	W	119	w
56	8	88	X	120	x
57	9	89	Y	121	y
58	:	90	Z	122	z
59	;	91	[	123	{
60	<	92	\	124		
61	=	93	]	125	}
62	>	94	^	126	~
63	?	95	_	127	_
64	@	96	`		

Table 6
EXTENDED ASCII (DE FACTO STANDARD FOR PCS)

Decimal Value	Character	Decimal Value	Character	Decimal Value	Character	Decimal Value	Character
128	Ç	160	á	192	L	224	α
129	ü	161	í	193	⊥	225	β
130	é	162	ó	194	⊤	226	Γ
131	â	163	ú	195	├	227	π
132	ä	164	ñ	196	─	228	Σ
133	à	165	Ñ	197	┼	229	σ
134	å	166	a	198	╞	230	μ
135	ç	167	o	199	╟	231	τ
136	ê	168	¿	200	╚	232	Φ
137	ë	169	⌐	201	╔	233	Θ
138	è	170	¬	202	╩	234	Ω
139	ï	171	½	203	╦	235	δ
140	î	172	¼	204	╠	236	∞
141	ì	173	¡	205	=	237	φ
142	Ä	174	«	206	╬	238	ε
143	Å	175	»	207	╧	239	∩
144	É	176	░	208	╨	240	≡
145	æ	177	▒	209	╤	241	±
146	Æ	178	▓	210	╥	242	≥
147	ô	179	│	211	╙	243	≤
148	ö	180	┤	212	╘	244	⌠
149	ò	181	╡	213	'	245	⌡
150	û	182	╢	214	╓	246	÷
151	ù	183	╖	215	╫	247	≈
152	ÿ	184	╕	216	╪	248	°
153	Ö	185	╣	217	┘	249	·
154	Ü	186	║	218	┌	250	·
155	¢	187	╗	219	█	251	√
156	£	188	╝	220	▄	252	ⁿ
157	¥	189	╜	221	▌	253	²
158	₧	190	╛	222	▐	254	■
159	ƒ	191	┐	223	▀	255	

aspect ratio: In computer graphics, the relative horizontal and vertical sizes. For example, if a graphic has an aspect ratio of 2:1, it means that the width is twice as large as the height. When resizing graphics, it is important to maintain the aspect ratio to avoid stretching the graphic out of proportion.

➠ See also *graphics.*

assembler: A program that translates programs from assembly language to machine language.

➠ See also *assembly language; machine language.*

assembly language: A programming language that is once removed from a computer's machine language (see Figure 68 at *programming language*). Machine languages consist entirely of numbers and are almost impossible to read and write. Assembly languages have the same structure and set of commands as machine languages, but they enable a programmer to use names instead of numbers.

Each type of CPU has its own machine language and assembly language, so an assembly language program written for one type of CPU won't run on another. In the early days of programming, all programs were written in assembly language. Now, most programs are written in a high-level language such as FORTRAN or C. Programmers still use assembly language when speed is essential or when they needs to perform an operation that isn't possible in a high-level language.

➠ See also *compile; machine language; programming language.*

assign: To give a value to a variable. In programming, you assign a value to a variable with a special symbol called an *assignment operator.* In many languages, the assignment operator is the equal sign (=). For example, the following C language statement assigns the value 5 to the variable x:

    x = 5

Such a statement is called an *assignment statement.*

➠ See also *operator; statement; variable.*

associate: To *link* a certain type of file to a specific application. In DOS and Windows environments, the file's type is specified by its three-character extension. For example, the .DOC extension identifies Microsoft Word documents. Once a file type has been associated with an application, selecting any file of that type automatically starts its associated application and loads the selected file.

➠ See also *extension; filename.*

Association for Computing Machinery: See under ACM.

asterisk: Also called a *star,* a punctuation mark denoted by a 6-pointed snowflake shape (*). In many operating systems and applications, the asterisk is used as a *wild card* symbol to represent any string of characters; a question mark (?) represents a single character.

➠ See also *wild card.*

async: Short for *asynchronous.*

asynchronous: Not synchronized; that is, not occurring at predetermined or regular intervals. The term *asynchronous* is usually used to describe communications in which data can be transmitted intermittently rather than in a steady stream. For example, a telephone conversation is asynchronous because both parties can talk whenever they like. If the communication were synchronous, each party would be required to wait a specified interval before speaking.

The difficulty with asynchronous communications is that the receiver must have a way to distinguish between valid data and noise. In computer communications, this is usually accomplished through a special *start bit* and *stop bit* at the beginning and end of each piece of data. For this reason, asynchronous communication is sometimes called *start-stop transmission* (Figure 6).

Most communications between computers and devices are asynchronous.

➠ See also *communications; start bit; stop bit.*

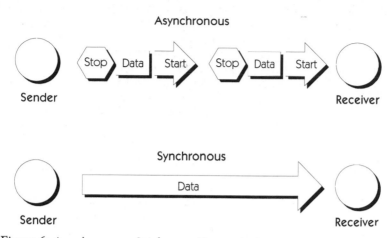

Figure 6: *Asynchronous vs. Synchronous Communication*

AT: [PC] Short for *advanced technology*, the AT is an IBM PC model introduced in 1984. It includes an Intel 80286 microprocessor, a 1.2MB floppy drive, and an 84-key AT keyboard.

Today, the term is used more generally to refer to any PC with an 80286 processor.

➠ See also *Intel microprocessors; PC.*

AT bus: [PC] The expansion bus on the IBM PC/AT and compatible computers. The bus is the collection of wires and electronic components that connect all device controllers and add-in cards. The controllers are the components that attach to peripheral devices. The bus, therefore, is the main highway for all data moving in and out of the computer.

The AT bus, which runs at 8 megahertz and has a 16-bit data path, is the de facto standard for PCs. Because all IBM PCs (until the high-end PS/2 models) had an AT bus, it has been possible for manufacturers to produce expansion boards that will work with any PC.

As processors have become more powerful, and applications more demanding, the AT bus has turned out to be the chief bottleneck in PCs. In response, IBM introduced the Micro Channel Architecture (MCA) in 1987. However, MCA was not accepted by the computer industry because it was not backward compatible with the AT bus, so IBM has been forced to drop it.

A more successful alternative to the AT bus is the *Extended Industry Standard Architecture (EISA)*, a high-speed 32-bit bus architecture developed by a group of IBM's competitors. Unlike MCA, EISA is backward compatible with the AT bus, so a computer equipped with an EISA bus can accept AT or EISA expansion boards.

While EISA has had limited success, its speeds are still insufficient for modern graphical applications. The most common solution to bypassing the AT-bus bottleneck is to include a local bus on the motherboard. A local bus communicates directly with the processor rather than using the standard computer bus. Currently, there are two competing standards for local buses: VESA local bus (VL-bus), promoted by the VESA standards group, and Peripheral Component Interconnect (PCI), designed and promoted by Intel.

The AT bus is sometimes referred to as the ISA bus, which stands for *Industry Standard Architecture*. However, ISA also includes the XT bus, which is an 8-bit version of the AT bus.

➠ See also *backward compatible; bus; EISA; expansion board; IBM PC; ISA bus; local bus; MCA; PCI; VL-bus.*

AT command set: Pronounced *ay-tee command set*, the de facto standard language for controlling modems. The AT command set was developed by Hayes and is recognized by virtually all personal computer modems.

➠ See also *Hayes-compatible; modem.*

AT keyboard: PC An 84-key keyboard introduced with the PC/AT. It was later replaced with the 101-key *Enhanced Keyboard*.

➠ See also *keyboard.*

Attached Resource Computer Network: See *ARCnet.*

attribute: (1) A characteristic. In a word processing application, an underlined word would be said to have the *underline attribute*. In database systems, a field can have various attributes. For example, if it contains numeric data, it has the *numeric attribute*.

(2) In database management systems, the term *attribute* is sometimes used as a synonym for *field*.

➠ See also *field*.

(3) PC In DOS systems, every file has a *file attribute* that indicates several properties of the file. For example, the file attribute indicates whether the file is read-only, whether it needs to be backed up, and whether it is visible or hidden.

➠ See also *DOS*; *file*; *hidden file*.

audio card: Same as *sound card*.

audit trail: A record showing who has accessed a computer system and what operations he or she has performed during a given period of time. Audit trails are useful both for maintaining security and for recovering lost transactions. Most accounting systems and database management systems include an audit trail component. In addition, there are separate audit trail software products that enable network administrators to monitor use of network resources.

➠ See also *security*.

authoring tool: A program that helps you write *hypertext* or *multimedia* applications. Authoring tools usually enable you to create a final application merely by linking together objects, such as a paragraph of text, an illustration, or a song. By defining the objects' relationships to each other, and by sequencing them in an appropriate order, authors (those who use authoring tools) can produce attractive and useful graphics applications. Most authoring systems also support a scripting language for more sophisticated applications.

The distinction between authoring tools and programming tools is not clear-cut. Typically, though, authoring tools require less technical knowledge to master and are used exclusively for applications that present a mixture of textual, graphical, and audio data.

➠ See also *Hypertext*; *multimedia*; *programming language*; *script*.

auto-answer: A feature supported by many modems that enables your computer to accept incoming calls even if you are not present. In *auto-answer mode,* a modem attempts to establish a connection whenever the telephone rings. This is an important feature if you are offering a service to which others can subscribe.

Auto-answer is also a critical feature for fax modems because it enables you to receive fax documents while you are away. All fax machines are auto-answer.

➤ See also *fax machine; fax modem; modem.*

autoexec.bat: PC Stands for *automatically executed batch file,* the file that DOS automatically executes when a computer boots up. This is a convenient place to put commands you always want to execute at the beginning of a computing session. For example, you can set system parameters such as the date and time, and install *memory-resident* programs.

➤ See also *batch file; boot.*

auto-redial: A feature supported by many modems that causes the modem to continue redialing a number until it makes a connection. This is a useful feature if you subscribe to an online service that is frequently busy.

➤ See also *modem.*

auto-repeat: A feature of some keys on computer keyboards that causes them to repeat as long as they are held down. Most keys are auto-repeat.

➤ See also *keyboard.*

automatic acceleration: See under *dynamic acceleration.*

automatic recalculation: In spreadsheets, a mode in which all cells are recalculated whenever a value changes. Automatic recalculation ensures that the spreadsheet data is always up-to-date, but it may make working on the spreadsheet slower. Alternatively, you can specify *manual recalculation*, where you must explicitly instruct the application to recalculate.

➠ See also *recalculate; spreadsheet application.*

autosave: A feature supported by many applications in which the program automatically saves data files at predetermined intervals. This is an important feature because it reduces the amount of work you would lose if your system crashed. Usually, you can specify how often you want the application to save data.

➠ See also *crash; save; word processing.*

autosizing: Refers to a monitor's ability to accept signals at one resolution and display the image at a different resolution. For example, a VGA video card outputs images at a resolution of 640 by 480. An SVGA monitor, however, can display images at a resolution of only 800 by 600, or even 1,024 by 768. If the monitor supports autosizing, it automatically adjusts the size of the image so that the proportions are correct. Without autosizing, you need to adjust an image manually so that it fills the screen properly.

➠ See also *monitor; resolution; SVGA; VGA; video adapter.*

autosync monitor: Same as *multiscanning monitor.*

autotracing: The process of converting a bit-mapped image (or *raster* image) into a *vector* image (Figure 7). In a bit-mapped image, each object is represented by a pattern of dots, while in a vector image every object is defined geometrically.

Most autotracing packages read files in a variety of bit-mapped formats (PCX and TIFF are the most common) and produce a file in a vector format such as *Encapsulated PostScript (EPS)*. The conversion techniques used, and the accuracy of the conversion process, differ from one package to another.

Autotracing is particularly useful for manipulating images produced by an optical scanner. Scanners produce bit-mapped images that cannot be manipulated by sophisticated tools until they have been converted into a vector format through autotracing.

➠ See also *bit map; bit-mapped graphics; EPS; optical scanner; PCX; Post-Script; TIFF; vector graphics.*

Bit Map Image   **Vector Image**

Figure 7: *Autotracing*

A/UX: [MAC] Pronounced *ox*, Apple's version of UNIX, which runs on Macintoshes and PowerPCs.

➠ See also *UNIX.*

AUX: [PC] Stands for *Auxiliary port*, the logical name in DOS systems for the standard communications port. This is usually the same as COM1.

➠ See also *COM; port.*

AVI: [PC] Short for *Audio Video Interleave*, the file format for Microsoft's Video for Windows standard. See under *Video for Windows.*

B

back end: See under *front end*.

backbone: Another term for bus, the main wire that connects nodes.

➠ See also *bus; network; node*.

background: (1) Multitasking computers are capable of executing several tasks, or programs, at the same time. In some multitasking systems, one of the processes is called the *foreground process*, and the others are called *background processes.*

The foreground process is the one that accepts input from the keyboard, mouse, or other input device. Background processes cannot accept interactive input from a user, but they can access data stored on a disk and write data to the video display. For example, some word processors print files in the background, enabling you to continue editing while files are being printed. This is called *print spooling*. In addition, many communications programs are designed to run in the background. Background processes generally have a lower priority than foreground processes so that they do not interfere with interactive applications.

Even though DOS is not a multitasking operating system, it can perform some specialized tasks, such as printing, in the background. Operating environments, such as Microsoft Windows and the Macintosh operating system, provide a more general multitasking environment.

➠ See also *Microsoft Windows; multitasking; spooling*.

(2) The area of a display screen not covered by characters and graphics. The background is like a canvas on top of which characters and

graphics are placed. Some monitors allow you to control the color or shading of the background. The background is also called the *matrix*.

➧ See also *display screen; monitor.*

backlighting: A technique used to make flat-panel displays easier to read. A backlit display is illuminated so that the foreground appears sharper in contrast with the background.

➧ See also *background; flat-panel display; notebook computer; supertwist.*

backslash: The backslash character is \; a simple slash or *forward slash* is /. In DOS and Windows systems, the backslash represents the root directory and is also used to separate directory names and filenames in a *pathname.*

➧ See also *pathname; root directory.*

backspace: A character that causes the cursor to move backward one character space, possibly deleting the preceding character. The backspace character has an ASCII value of 8. Most keyboards have a Backspace key that invokes this character. When inserted in a file, the character causes a printer or other device to move backward one space.

➧ See also *ASCII; Backspace key; cursor; keyboard; pointer.*

Backspace key: A key that moves the cursor or insertion point backward one character space. In addition to moving the cursor backward, the Backspace key usually deletes the character to the left of the cursor or insertion point. It is particularly useful, therefore, for correcting typos. Note that PCs also have a Delete key, which deletes the character under the cursor (or to the right of the insertion point). To move the cursor or insertion point backward without deleting characters, use the arrow keys.

➧ See also *arrow keys; backspace; Delete key; keyboard.*

backup: (v) To copy files to a second medium (a disk or tape) as a precaution in case the first medium fails. One of the cardinal rules in using computers is:

Backup your files regularly.

Even the most reliable computer is apt to break down eventually. Many professionals recommend that you make two, or even three, backups of all your files. To be especially safe, you should keep one backup in a different location from the others.

You can back up files using operating system commands, or you can buy a special-purpose backup utility. In general, backup programs are much faster than operating system shell commands because they use a DMA channel. In addition, the backup programs often compress the data so that backups require fewer disks.

➠ See also *archive; data compression; DMA.*

(n) (1) The act of backing up.

(2) A substitute or alternative. The term *backup* usually refers to a disk or tape that contains a copy of data.

backward compatible: Compatible with earlier models or versions of the same product. A new version of a program is said to be backward compatible if you can create a file with the new version and then use the file with an older version of the program. A computer is said to be backward compatible if it can run the same software as the previous model of the computer.

Backward compatibility is important because it eliminates the need to start over when you upgrade to a newer product. A backward-compatible word processor, for instance, allows you to edit documents created with a previous version of the program. In general, manufacturers try to keep all their products backward compatible. Sometimes, however, it is necessary to sacrifice backward compatibility to take advantage of a new technology.

The flip side of backward compatibility is *upward compatibility.* Upward compatible is the same as backward compatible, except that it is from the point of view of the older model.

Another term for *backward compatible* is *downward compatible.*

➠ See also *compatible; upward compatible.*

41

bad sector: A portion of a disk that cannot be used because it is flawed. When you format a disk, the operating system identifies any bad sectors on the disk and marks them so they will not be used. If a sector that already contains data becomes damaged, you will need special software to recover the data.

Almost all hard disks come with bad sectors (sectors damaged during the manufacturing process), so do not be alarmed if a utility reports that your hard disk has bad sectors. However, additional bad sectors should occur only infrequently if your drive is functioning properly. Floppy disks should not have any bad sectors.

➠ See also *disk; format; sector.*

ballistic tracking: See under *dynamic acceleration.*

BAK file: ⌷PC⌷ In DOS systems, a file with a .BAK extension, indicating that the file is a backup. Many applications produce BAK files as part of their autosave procedure. Periodically, you may want to search for BAK files and delete old ones.

➠ See also *autosave; extension.*

bandwidth: The amount of data that can be transmitted in a fixed amount of time. For digital devices, the bandwidth is usually expressed in bits or bytes per second (bps). For analog devices, the bandwidth is expressed in cycles per second, or Hertz (Hz).

The bandwidth is particularly important for I/O devices. For example, a fast disk drive can be hampered by a bus with a low bandwidth. This is the main reason that new buses, such as EISA and PCI, have been developed for the IBM PC.

➠ See also *bus; EISA; I/O; PCI.*

bar chart: In presentation graphics, a type of graph in which different values are represented by rectangular bars (Figure 8).

➠ See also *presentation graphics.*

base address: An address that serves as a reference point for other addresses (see Figure 1 at *address*). For example, a base address could

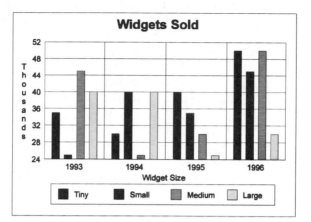

Figure 8: *Bar Chart*

indicate the beginning of a program. The address of every instruction in the program could then be specified by adding an offset to the base address. For example, the address of the fifth instruction would be the base address plus 5.

➠ See also *address; offset; relative address.*

baseband transmission: A type of digital data transmission in which each medium (wire) carries only one signal, or channel, at a time. In contrast, broadband transmission enables a single wire to carry multiple signals simultaneously.

Most communications involving computers uses baseband transmission. This includes communications from the computer to devices (printers, monitors, and so on), communications via modems, and the majority of networks. An exception is B-ISDN networks, which use broadband transmission.

➠ See also *broadband ISDN; broadband transmission; channel; communications; ISDN; local-area network; network.*

baseline: In typography, the imaginary line on which characters sit. The *x-height* of a font is measured from the baseline to the top of a lowercase x. The descender, for those characters that have one, is defined as the portion of the character that falls below the baseline.

➠ See also *descender; font; typeface; x-height.*

base memory: Same as *conventional memory.*

BASIC: Acronym for *Beginner's All-purpose Symbolic Instruction Code.* Developed by John Kemeney and Thomas Kurtz in the mid 1960s at Dartmouth College, BASIC is one of the earliest and simplest high-level programming languages. During the 1970s, it was the principal programming language taught to students, and continues to be a popular choice among educators.

Despite its simplicity, BASIC is used for a wide variety of business applications. There is an ANSI standard for the BASIC language, but most versions of BASIC include many proprietary extensions. Microsoft's popular Visual Basic, for example, adds many object-oriented features to the standard BASIC.

Recently, many variations of BASIC have appeared as programming, or macro, languages within applications. For example, Microsoft Word and Excel both come with a version of BASIC with which users can write programs to customize and automate these applications.

➠ See also *programming language.*

basic input/output system: See *BIOS.*

batch file: A file that contains a sequence, or batch, of commands. Batch files are useful for storing sets of commands that are always executed together because you can simply enter the name of the batch file instead of entering each command individually.

In DOS systems, batch files end with a .BAT extension. For example, the following DOS batch file prints the date and time and sets the prompt to GO>:

```
date
time
prompt [GO>]
```

Whenever you boot a DOS-based computer, the system automatically executes the batch file named AUTOEXEC.BAT, if it exists.

Many operating systems use the terms *command file* or *shell script* in place of *batch file.*

➠ See also *AUTOEXEC.BAT; batch processing; DOS.*

batch processing: Executing a series of noninteractive jobs all at one time. The term originated in the days when users entered programs on punch cards. They would give a batch of these programmed cards to the system operator, who would feed them into the computer.

Usually, batch jobs are stored up during working hours and then executed during the evening or whenever the computer is idle. Batch processing is particularly useful for operations that require the computer or a peripheral device for an extended period of time. Once a batch job begins, it continues until it is done or until an error occurs. Note that batch processing implies that there is no interaction with the user while the program is being executed.

The opposite of batch processing is *transaction processing* or *interactive processing.* In interactive processing, the application responds to commands as soon as you enter them.

➠ See also *interactive; transaction processing.*

BAT file: PC In DOS systems, batch files are often called *BAT files* because their filenames end with a *.BAT* extension.

➠ See also *batch file; extension; filename.*

battery pack: A rechargeable battery used in portable computer devices, such as notebook computers. The most common substances used in computer battery packs are nickel cadmium (Nicad) and nickel metal hydride (NiMH). Another substance, being used in some newer batteries, is lithium.

A new type of battery, called a *smart battery,* provides the computer with information about its power status so that the computer can conserve power intelligently. With a normal battery, the computer makes estimates about the battery's condition that are not always correct.

➠ See also *NiCad battery pack; NiMH battery pack.*

baud: Pronounced *bawd*, the number of electrical oscillations that occur each second. The term is named after J.M.E. Baudot, the inventor of the Baudot telegraph code.

At slow speeds, only one bit of information is encoded in each electrical change. The *baud rate*, therefore, indicates the number of bits per second that are transmitted. For example, a baud rate of 300 means that 300 bits are transmitted each second (abbreviated *300 bps*). Assuming asynchronous communication, which requires 10 bits per character, this translates to 30 characters per second (cps). For slow rates (below 1,200 baud), you can divide the baud rate by 10 to see how many characters per second are sent.

At higher baud rates, it is possible to encode more than one bit in each electrical change. A baud rate of 4,800 may allow 9,600 bits to be sent each second. At high baud levels, therefore, data transmission rates are usually expressed in bits per second (bps) rather than in baud rates. For example, a 9,600 bps modem may operate at only 2,400 baud.

➠ See also *bps; modem.*

bay: Short for *drive bay*, this refers to a site in a personal computer where a hard or floppy disk drive, CD-ROM drive or tape drive can be installed. Thus, the number of drive bays in a computer determines how many mass storage devices can be internally installed.

For PCs, bays come in a variety of sizes, the most common being 3.5 inch, which represents the bay's height. In addition, bays are described as either *internal* or *exposed.* An internal bay cannot be used for removable media, such as floppy drives. Some manufacturers use the terms *hidden* and *accessible* in place of *internal* and *exposed.*

Do not confuse bays with *slots,* which are openings in the computer where *expansion boards* can be installed.

➠ See also *disk drive; expansion board; mass storage; slot.*

BBS: See *bulletin board system.*

Bell 103: The de facto standard protocol in the United States for transmitting data over telephone lines at transmission rates of 300 baud.

The Bell 103A standard defines asynchronous, full-duplex communication. Europe and Japan use the CCITT V.21 protocol.

➠ See also *asynchronous; baud; CCITT; communications protocol; full duplex; protocol.*

Bell 212A: The de facto standard protocol in the United States for transmitting data over telephone lines at transmission rates of 1,200 bps. The Bell 212A standard defines asynchronous, full-duplex communications. Europe and Japan use the CCITT V.22 protocol.

➠ See also *asynchronous; baud; CCITT; communications protocol; full duplex; protocol.*

bells and whistles: Fancy features provided by an application. Typically, the term refers to small features that are needed only in special cases or to features that make the program more visibly attractive (i.e., like real bells and whistles, are aimed at attracting your attention). Depending on the author, the term can be used either favorably or negatively. Many users and critics, for example, lament the increasing addition of bells and whistles that, they feel, make an application harder to learn and use without providing commensurate new functionality.

➠ See also *feature.*

benchmark: A test used to compare performance of hardware and/or software. Many trade magazines have developed their own benchmark tests, which they use when reviewing a class of products. When comparing benchmark results, it is important to know exactly what the benchmarks are designed to test. A benchmark that tests graphics speed, for example, may be irrelevant to you if the type of graphical applications you use are different from those used in the test.

Bernoulli disk drive: Named after a Swiss scientist who discovered the principle of aerodynamic lift, the Bernoulli disk drive is a special type of floppy disk drive from Iomega Corporation that is faster and has greater storage capacity than traditional floppy drives.

A Bernoulli drive is really a cross between a hard disk drive and floppy drive. Like the platters in hard disk drives, Bernoulli disks float between the read/write heads, so there is no actual contact between the disk and the heads. But the disk itself is flexible and removable like a floppy disk. Because the disk is flexible, it is less susceptible than a hard disk to head crashes. Bernoulli disk drives, however, are not as fast as hard disk drives.

A Bernoulli disk drive is sometimes called a *Bernoulli box*.

➠ See also *disk; hard disk drive; mass storage.*

beta test: A test for a computer product prior to commercial release. Beta testing is the last stage of testing, and normally involves sending the product to *beta test sites* outside the company for real-world exposure.

Bézier curves: Pronounced "bez-ee-ay," curved lines defined by mathematical formulas. Nearly all draw programs support Bézier curves.

Named after the French mathematician Pierre Bézier, Bézier curves employ at least three points to define a curve (Figure 9). The two endpoints of the curve are called *anchor points*. The other points, which define the shape of the curve, are called *handles, tangent points,* or *nodes*. Attached to each handle are two *control points*. By moving the handles themselves, or the control points, you can modify the shape of the curve.

➠ See also *draw program; graphics; vector graphics.*

BFT: See *Binary File Transfer.*

Big Blue: A slang name for International Business Machines Corporation (IBM). Blue is IBM's corporate color.

➠ See also *IBM PC.*

binary: Pertaining to a number system that has just two unique digits. For most purposes, we use the decimal number system, which has ten unique digits, 0 through 9. All other numbers are then formed by combining these ten digits. Computers are based on the binary numbering system, which consists of just two unique numbers, 0 and 1. All operations that are possible in the decimal system (addition, subtraction, multiplication, division) are equally possible in the binary system.

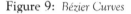

Figure 9: *Bézier Curves*

We use the decimal system in everyday life because it seems more natural (we have ten fingers and ten toes). For the computer, the binary system is more natural because of its electrical nature (charged versus uncharged).

In the decimal system, each digit position represents a value of 10 to the position's power. For example, the number 345 means:

3   three 100s (10^2)
+
4   four 10s (10^1)
+
5   five 1s (10^0)

In the binary system, each digit position represents a power of 2. For example, the binary number 1011 equals:

1   one 8 (2^3)
+
0   zero 4s (2^2)
+
1   one 2 (2^1)
+
1   one 1 (2^0)

So a binary 1011 equals a decimal 11. (See Table 7 for binary and decimal equivalents.)

Because computers use the binary number system, powers of 2 play an important role. This is why everything in computers seems to come in 8s (2^3), 64s (2^6), 128s (2^7), and 256s (2^8).

Programmers also use the octal (8 numbers) and hexadecimal (16 numbers) number systems because they map nicely onto the binary system. Each octal digit represents exactly three binary digits, and each hexadecimal digit represents four binary digits.

➠ See also *decimal; hexadecimal; octal.*

Table 7
DECIMAL AND BINARY EQUIVALENTS

DECIMAL	BINARY
1	1
2	10
3	11
4	100
5	101
6	110
7	111
8	1000
9	1001
10	1010
16	10000
32	100000
64	1000000
100	1100100
256	10000000
512	100000000
1000	111111010
1024	1000000000

---

binary compatible: Having the exact same data format, down to the binary level. That is, two files that are binary compatible will have the same pattern of zeroes and ones in the data portion of the file. The file header, however, may be different.

The term is used most commonly to state that data files produced by one application are exactly the same as data files produced by another application. For example, many software companies now produce applications for Windows and the Macintosh that are binary compatible, which means that a file produced in a Windows environment is interchangeable with a file produced on a Macintosh. This avoids many of the conversion problems caused by importing and exporting data.

➡ See also *binary file; compatible; cross-platform; export; heterogeneous network; import.*

binary file: A file stored in binary format. A binary file is computer-readable but not human-readable. All executable programs are stored in binary files, as are most numeric data files. In contrast, text files are stored in a form (usually ASCII) that is human-readable.

➡ See also *ASCII; binary format; executable file; text file.*

Binary File Transfer (BFT): A standard for transmitting data files using fax modems. There are actually two standards, both of which are referred to as BFT: *CCITT T.434* and *Microsoft At Work (MAW)*.

➡ See also *CCITT; fax modem; standard.*

binary format: A format for representing data used by some applications. The other main formats for storing data are *text formats* (such as ASCII and EBCDIC), in which each character of data is assigned a specific code number.

Binary formats are used for executable programs and numeric data, whereas text formats are used for textual data. Many files contain a combination of binary and text formats. Such files are usually considered to be binary files even though they contain some data in a text format.

➡ See also *ASCII; binary; binary file; EBCDIC; executable file; text file.*

bind: To assign a value to a symbolic placeholder. During compilation, for example, the compiler assigns symbolic addresses to some variables and instructions. When the program is bound, or *linked*, the binder replaces the symbolic addresses with real machine addresses. The moment at which binding occurs is called *bind time* or *link time*.

➡ See also *address; compile; link.*

binder: Same as *linker*.

BIOS: Pronounced "bye-ose," an acronym for *basic input/output system*. The BIOS is built-in software that determines what a computer can do without accessing programs from a disk. On PCs, the BIOS contains all the code required to control the keyboard, display screen, disk drives, serial communications, and a number of miscellaneous functions.

The BIOS is typically placed on a ROM chip that comes with the computer (it is often called a *ROM BIOS*). This ensures that the BIOS will always be available and will not be damaged by disk failures. It also makes it possible for a computer to boot itself. Because RAM is faster than ROM, though, many computer manufacturers design systems so that the BIOS is copied from ROM to RAM each time the computer is booted. This is known as *shadowing*.

Many modern PCs have a *flash BIOS*, which means that the BIOS has been recorded on a flash memory chip, which can be updated if necessary.

The PC BIOS is standardized, so all PCs are alike at this level (although there are different BIOS versions). Additional DOS functions are usually added through software modules. This means you can upgrade to a newer version of DOS without changing the BIOS.

PC BIOSes that can handle Plug-and-Play (PnP) devices are known as *PnP BIOSes*, or *PnP-aware BIOSes*. These BIOSes are always implemented with flash memory rather than ROM.

➠ See also *boot; flash memory; I/O; Phoenix BIOS; PnP; shadowing.*

B-ISDN: See *broadband ISDN*.

bit: Short for *binary digit*, the smallest unit of information on a machine. The term was first used in 1946 by John Tukey, a leading statistician and adviser to five presidents. A single bit can hold only one of two values: 0 or 1. More meaningful information is obtained by combining consecutive bits into larger units. For example, a byte is composed of 8 consecutive bits.

Computers are sometimes classified by the number of bits they can process at one time or by the number of bits they use to represent addresses. These two values are not always the same, which leads to confusion. For example, classifying a computer as a *32-bit machine* might mean that its data registers are 32 bits wide or that it uses 32 bits to identify each address in memory. Whereas larger registers make a computer faster, using more bits for addresses enables a machine to support larger programs.

Graphics are also often described by the number of bits used to represent each dot. A 1-bit image is monochrome; an 8-bit image supports 256 colors or grayscales; and a 24- or 32-bit graphic supports true color.

➠ See also *address space; register.*

bitblt: Pronounced *bit-blit,* short for *bit block transfer.*

bit block transfer: A transformation of a rectangular block of pixels. Typical transformations include changing the color or shade of all pixels or rotating the entire rectangle. Many modern graphics adapters include hardwired bit block transformations, which execute much faster than they do when executed by software routines.

➠ See also *graphics, pixel, video adapter.*

bit map: A representation, consisting of rows and columns of dots, of a graphics image in computer memory (Figure 10). The value of each dot (whether it is filled in or not) is stored in one or more bits of data. For simple monochrome images, one bit is sufficient to represent each dot, but for colors and shades of gray, each dot requires more than one bit of data. The more bits used to represent a dot, the more colors and shades of gray that can be represented.

The density of the dots, known as the *resolution,* determines how sharply the image is represented. This is often expressed in *dots per inch (dpi)* or simply by the number of rows and columns, such as 640 by 480.

To display a bit-mapped image on a monitor or to print it on a printer, the computer translates the bit map into pixels (for display screens) or ink dots (for printers). Optical scanners and fax machines work by transforming text or pictures on paper into bit maps.

Bit-mapped graphics are often referred to as *raster graphics.* The other method for representing images is known as *vector graphics* or *object-oriented graphics.* With vector graphics, images are represented as mathematical formulas that define all the shapes in the image. Vector graphics are more flexible than bit-mapped graphics because they look the same even when you scale them to different sizes. In contrast, bit-mapped graphics become ragged when you shrink or enlarge them.

Fonts represented with vector graphics are called *scalable fonts, outline fonts,* or *vector fonts.* The best-known example of a vector font system is PostScript. Bit-mapped fonts, also called *raster fonts,* must be designed for a specific device and a specific size and resolution.

➠ See also *bit-mapped graphics; digitize; graphics; optical scanner; pixel; resolution.*

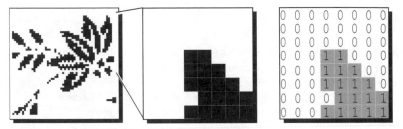

Figure 10: *Bit Map*

bit-mapped graphics: Refers to hardware and software that represent graphics images as bit maps (see Figure 10). The other method for representing images is known as *vector graphics.*

➠ See also *bit map; graphics; vector graphics.*

bit-mapped font: See under *font.*

BITNET: Short for *Because It's Time Network,* BITNET is one of the oldest and largest wide-area networks, used extensively by universities. A new version of BITNET, called *BITNET-II,* relies on the Internet network to transfer messages and files.

➠ See also *Internet; network; wide area network (WAN).*

bits per second: See *bps.*

blank character: Also called a *space character*. A blank character is produced when you press the space bar.

bleed: (n) Text or graphics that extends all the way to the edge of the paper. Bleeds are used for graphical effect and for printed tabs. Most printers cannot print all the way to the edge of the paper, so the only way to produce a bleed is to print on paper larger than the final page size and then trim the paper.

(v) To run to the edge of the paper, thereby producing a bleed.

block: (n) (1) In word processing, a block is a group of characters that you have marked to perform some action on them. For example, to move a section of text, you must first block it. This is sometimes called a *block move*.

To specify a block of text, you press special function keys (or click with a mouse) at the beginning and end of the block. The function keys differ from one word processor to another. Word processors usually display blocks by highlighting them on the screen.

➠ See also *word processing*.

(2) In data management, a block is a group of records on a storage device. Blocks are manipulated as units. For example, disk drives often read and write data in 512-byte blocks.

(3) In communications, a block is a fixed-size chunk of data that is transferred together. For example, the Xmodem protocol transfers blocks of 128 bytes. In general, the larger the block size, the faster the data transfer rate.

➠ See also *communications; Xmodem*.

(v) In word processing, to specify a section of text. See definition (1) above. Some applications call this *selecting*.

➠ See also *select*.

block graphics: Graphical images created in character mode.

➠ See also *character mode*.

55

BMP: PC The standard bit-mapped graphics format used in the Windows environment. By convention, graphics files in the BMP format end with a *.BMP* extension.

➡ See also *bit map; extension; graphics file formats.*

board: Short for *printed circuit board* or *expansion board.*

boilerplate: Text or graphics elements designed to be used over and over. For example, you could create a boilerplate for a fax message that contains all the standard fax information that doesn't change, such as your name, address, and phone number. Then whenever you want to create a new fax, you need only insert the boilerplate rather than retyping the information.

A boilerplate is similar to a template, but whereas a template holds layout and style information, a boilerplate contains actual text or graphics. Many applications, however, combine the two concepts.

➡ See also *template.*

boldface: A font that is darker than the regular face. For example

normal font   **boldface font**

Most word processors allow you to mark text as boldface.

➡ See also *font; word processing.*

bomb: To fail. The term *bomb* usually refers to a program hanging or ending prematurely. Note that bombing is usually less serious than crashing, because bombing refers to a single program, whereas crashing refers to the entire system. The two terms, however, are not always used consistently.

MAC The Apple Macintosh computer actually has a bomb message that sometimes appears just before the system crashes.

➡ See also *crash; hang; Macintosh computer.*

Boolean expression: An expression that results in a value of either TRUE or FALSE. For example, the expression

2 < 5 (2 is less than 5)

is a Boolean expression because the result is TRUE. All expressions that contain *relational operators*, such as the *less than* sign (<), are Boolean. The operators—AND, OR, XOR, NOR, and NOT—are Boolean operators.

Boolean expressions are also called *comparison expressions, conditional expressions*, and *relational expressions*.

➠ See also *Boolean operator; expression; relational operator.*

Boolean logic: Named after the nineteenth-century mathematician George Boole, Boolean logic is a form of algebra in which all values are reduced to either TRUE or FALSE. Boolean logic is especially important for computer science because it fits nicely with the binary numbering system, in which each bit has a value of either 1 or 0. Another way of looking at it is that each bit has a value of either TRUE or FALSE.

➠ See also *binary; Boolean expression.*

Boolean operator: There are five Boolean operators that can be used to manipulate TRUE/FALSE values. These operators have the following meanings (Table 8), where x and y represent values of TRUE or FALSE.

The OR operator is often called an *inclusive OR*, whereas XOR is an *exclusive OR*.

Boolean operators are used widely in programming and also in forming database queries. For example, the query

SELECT ALL WHERE LAST_NAME = "Smith" AND
FIRST_NAME = "John"

finds all records with the name John Smith. But the query

SELECT ALL WHERE LAST_NAME = "Smith" OR
FIRST_NAME = "John"

finds all records with the last name "Smith" *or* the first name "John."

▪➤ See also *Boolean expression; Boolean logic; operator; query.*

Table 8 BOOLEAN OPERATORS	
x AND y	Result is *TRUE* if both x and y are *TRUE*. Otherwise the result is *FALSE*.
x OR y	Result is *TRUE* if either x or y is *TRUE*. Otherwise the result is FALSE.
x XOR y	Result is *TRUE* only if x and y have different values. Otherwise the result is *FALSE*.
NOT x	Result is *TRUE* if x is *FALSE*. Result is *FALSE* if x is *TRUE*.

boot: (v) To load the first piece of software that starts a computer. Because the operating system is essential for running all other programs, it is usually the first piece of software loaded during the boot process.

Boot is short for *bootstrap,* which in olden days was a strap attached to the top of your boot that you could pull to help get your boot on. Hence, the expression "pull oneself up by the bootstraps." Similarly, *bootstrap utilities* help the computer get started.

(n) Short for *bootstrap,* the starting-up of a computer, which involves loading the operating system and other basic software. A cold boot is when you turn the computer on from an off position. A warm boot is when you reset a computer that is already on.

▪➤ See also *cold boot; load; operating system; warm boot.*

box: (1) In graphical user interfaces, a box is an enclosed area, resembling a window, on the screen. Unlike windows, however, you generally cannot move or resize boxes.

There are many different types of boxes. For example, *dialog boxes* are boxes that request some type of information from you. *Alert boxes* are boxes that suddenly appear on the screen to give you information.

Boxes can also be small rectangular icons that control windows. *Zoom boxes*, for example, enable you to make a window larger or smaller.

➠ See also *alert box; button; dialog box; graphical user interface; icon; window; zoom*.

(2) Slang for *personal computer* or *workstation*.

bps: Abbreviation of *bits per second*, the standard measure of data transmission speeds. Standard telephone lines are capable of transmitting data at a maximum speed of about 14,400 bps. However, the old metal telephone wires are steadily being replaced by fiber optic cables, which are capable of transmitting data at much faster rates. Specialized cables for transmitting data between devices support rates of over 500,000 bps.

A number of standards define the format for sending data at various rates.

➠ See also *CCITT; communications; modem*.

branch: In tree structures, a branch is a single line of the tree that ends with a *leaf*. The Windows File Manager, for example, has an *Expand Branch* command that shows all sub-directories of a specified directory.

➠ See also *directory; tree structure*.

Break key: A special key on computer keyboards that temporarily interrupts the computer's communications line. This usually terminates an established modem connection. Not all keyboards have a Break key, and not all programs respond to it. In DOS and Windows, you can abort the current application and reboot the program by pressing the Break key in combination with the Control and Alt keys.

➠ See also *keyboard*.

broadband ISDN (B-ISDN): A standard for transmitting voice, video and data at the same time over fiber optic telephone lines. Broadband

ISDN can support data rates of 1.5 million bits per second (bps), but it has not been widely implemented.

➠ See also *bps; fiber optics; ISDN.*

broadband transmission: A type of data transmission in which a single medium (wire) can carry several channels at once. Cable TV, for example, uses broadband transmission. In contrast, baseband transmission allows only one signal at a time.

Most communications between computers, including the majority of local-area networks, use baseband communications. An exception is *B-ISDN* networks, which employ broadband transmission.

➠ See also *broadband ISDN; channel; communications; local-area network; network.*

broadcast: To simultaneously send the same message to more than one receiver. Broadcasting is a useful feature in e-mail systems. It is also supported by some fax systems.

➠ See also *e-mail; fax.*

browse: (1) In database systems, *browse* means to view data. Many database systems support a special *browse mode,* in which you can flip through fields and records quickly. Usually, you cannot modify data while you are in browse mode.

➠ See also *database management system; field; record.*

(2) In object-oriented programming languages, *browse* means to examine data structures.

➠ See also *data structure; object oriented.*

buffer: (n) A temporary storage area, usually in RAM. The purpose of most buffers is to act as a holding area, enabling the CPU to manipulate data before transferring it to a device.

Because the processes of reading and writing data to a disk are relatively slow, many programs keep track of data changes in a buffer and then copy the buffer to a disk. For example, word processors employ a buffer to keep track of changes to files. Then when you *save* the file, the word processor updates the disk file with the contents of the buffer. This is much more efficient than accessing the file on the disk each time you make a change to the file.

Note that because your changes are initially stored in a buffer, not on the disk, all of them will be lost if the computer fails during an editing session. For this reason, it is a good idea to save your file periodically. Most word processors automatically save files at regular intervals.

Another common use of buffers is for printing documents. When you enter a PRINT command, the operating system copies your document to a print buffer (a free area in memory or on a disk) from which the printer can draw characters at its own pace. This frees the computer to perform other tasks while the printer is running in the background. Print buffering is called *spooling.*

Most keyboard drivers also contain a buffer so that you can edit typing mistakes before sending your command to a program. Many operating systems, including DOS, also use a *disk buffer* to temporarily hold data that they have read from a disk. The disk buffer is really a cache.

➠ See also *cache; save; spooling.*

(v) To move data into a temporary storage area.

bug: An error or defect in software or hardware that causes a program to malfunction. According to the folklore, the term originated when a moth trapped in the electrical workings of the first digital computer, the ENIAC, was discovered by Lieutenant Grace Hopper.

➠ See also *bomb; crash; hang.*

built-in font: Same as *resident font.*

built-in function: A function that is built into an application and can be accessed by end-users. For example, most spreadsheet applications support a built-in SUM function that adds up all cells in a row or column.

➠ See also *function.*

bullet: A small graphical element used to highlight or itemize a list:

- ● A round bullet.
- ■ A square bullet.
- ◆ A diamond bullet.
- ☞ A pointing-finger bullet.

bulletin board system (BBS): An electronic message center. Most bulletin boards serve specific interest groups. They allow you to dial in with a modem, review messages left by others, and leave your own message if you want. Bulletin boards are a particularly good place to find free or inexpensive software products. In the United States alone, there are tens of thousands of BBSs.

➠ See also *e-mail; modem; network; online service.*

bundled software: Software that is sold with a computer or other hardware component as part of a package. As competition between computer manufacturers has intensified, bundling software has become a key strategy for attracting consumers. In some cases, the bundled software is even more valuable than the hardware.

➠ See also *hardware; software.*

bus: (1) A collection of wires through which data is transmitted from one part of a computer to another. You can think of a bus as a highway on which data travels within a computer. When used in reference to personal computers, the term *bus* usually refers to the *expansion bus.* This is a bus that connects all the various computer components— expansion boards and external devices such as disk drives and printers—to the CPU. Personal computers also have an *address bus* and *data bus* that connect the CPU with RAM.

The size of a bus, known as its *width,* is important because it determines how much data can be transmitted at one time. For example, a 16-bit bus can transmit 16 bits of data, whereas a 32-bit bus can transmit 32 bits of data.

Every bus has a clock speed measured in MHz. A fast bus allows data to be transferred faster, which makes applications run faster. On PCs, the old ISA bus is being replaced by faster buses such as PCI and EISA.

Many PCs made today include a local bus for data that requires especially fast transfer speeds, such as video data. The local bus is a high-speed pathway that connects directly to the processor.

|MAC| Several different types of buses are used on Apple Macintosh computers. The fastest and most sophisticated is called the *NuBus* *expansion bus*.

➠ See also *ADB; clock speed; EISA; Industry Standard Architecture (ISA) bus; local bus; PCI*.

(2) In networking, a bus is a central cable that connects all devices on a local-area network (LAN). It is also called the *backbone*.

➠ See also *Ethernet; network; topology*.

business graphics: See under *presentation graphics*.

bus mouse: A mouse that connects to a computer via an expansion board. Another type of mouse is a *serial mouse*, which connects to a serial port. Serial mice are easier to install, but the advantage of bus mice is that they do not use up the serial port, so you can use the port for a different device (a modem, for example).

➠ See also *bus; mouse; serial port*.

bus topology: See under *topology*.

button: (1) In graphical user interfaces, a button is a small outlined area in a dialog box that you can click to select an option or command.

➠ See also *dialog box; graphical user interface; radio buttons*.

(2) A *mouse button* is a button on a mouse that you click to perform various functions, such as selecting an object. Examples of mouse buttons are illustrated in Figure 56.

➠ See also *click; mouse*.

byte: Abbreviation for binary *term*, a unit of storage capable of holding a single character. On almost all modern computers, a byte is equal to 8 bits. Large amounts of memory are indicated in terms of kilobytes (1,024 bytes), megabytes (1,048,576 bytes), and gigabytes (approximately 1 billion bytes). A disk that can hold 1.44 megabytes, for example, is capable of storing approximately 1.4 million characters, or about 3,000 pages of information.

➠ See also *gigabyte; kilobyte; megabyte.*

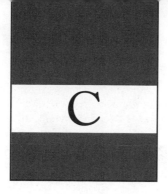

C: A high-level programming language developed by Dennis Ritchie and Brian Kernighan at Bell Labs in the mid 1970s. Although originally designed as a systems programming language, C has proved to be a powerful and flexible language that can be used for a variety of applications, from business programs to engineering. C is a particularly popular language for personal computer programmers because it is relatively small—it requires less memory than other languages.

The first major program written in C was the UNIX operating system, and for many years C was considered to be inextricably linked with UNIX. Now, however, C is an important language independent of UNIX.

Although it is a high-level language, C is much closer to assembly language than are most other high-level languages. This closeness to the underlying machine language allows C programmers to write very efficient code. The low-level nature of C, however, can make the language difficult to use for some types of applications.

➥ See also *assembly language; high-level language; machine language; programming language; UNIX.*

C++: A high-level programming language developed by Bjarne Stroustrup at Bell Labs. C++ adds object-oriented features to its predecessor, C. C++ is rapidly becoming the programming language of choice for graphical applications, such as those that run in Windows and Macintosh environments.

➥ See also *C; object oriented; programming language.*

cache: Pronounced *cash*, a special high-speed storage mechanism. It can be either a reserved section of main memory or an independent high-

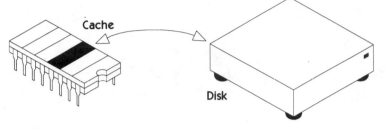

Figure 11: *Disk Cache*

speed storage device. Two types of caching are commonly used in personal computers: *memory caching* and *disk caching* (Figure 11).

A memory cache, sometimes called a *cache store* or *RAM cache,* is a portion of memory made of high-speed static RAM (SRAM) instead of the slower and cheaper dynamic RAM (DRAM) used for main memory. Memory caching is effective because most programs access the same data or instructions over and over. By keeping as much of this information as possible in SRAM, the computer avoids accessing the slower DRAM.

Some memory caches are built into the architecture of microprocessors. The Intel 80486 microprocessor, for example, contains an 8K memory cache, and the Pentium has a 16K cache. Such internal caches are often called *primary caches* or *Level 1 (L1) caches.* You can also add additional external cache memory, sometimes called *secondary* or *Level 2 (L2) caches.*

Disk caching works under the same principle as memory caching, but instead of using high-speed SRAM, a disk cache uses conventional main memory. The most recently accessed data from the disk (as well as adjacent sectors) is stored in a memory buffer. When a program needs to access data from the disk, it first checks the disk cache to see if the data is there. Disk caching can dramatically improve the performance of applications, because accessing a byte of data in RAM can be thousands of times faster than accessing a byte on a hard disk.

When data is found in the cache, it is called a *cache hit,* and the effectiveness of a cache is judged by its *hit rate.* Many cache systems use a technique known as *smart caching,* in which the system can recognize certain types of frequently used data. The strategies for determining which information should be kept in the cache constitute some of the more interesting problems in computer science.

➠ See also *buffer; disk cache; RAM disk.*

cache memory: See under *cache.*

CAD: Acronym for *computer-aided design.* A CAD system is a combination of hardware and software that enables engineers and architects to design everything from furniture to airplanes (Figure 12). In addition to the software, CAD systems require a high-quality graphics monitor; a mouse, light pen, or digitizing tablet for drawing; and a special printer or plotter for printing design specifications.

CAD systems allow an engineer to view a design from any angle with the push of a button and to zoom in or out for close-ups and long-distance views. In addition, the computer keeps track of design dependencies so that when the engineer changes one value, all other values that depend on it are automatically changed accordingly.

Until the mid 1980s, all CAD systems were specially constructed computers. Now, you can buy CAD software that runs on general-purpose workstations and powerful personal computers.

➡ See also CAD/CAM; CAE; *digitizing tablet; graphics; light pen; monitor; mouse; plotter; workstation.*

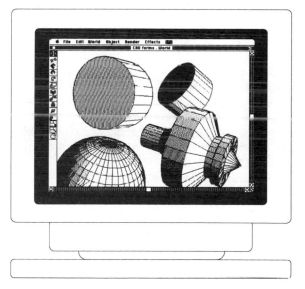

Figure 12: *CAD Application*

CAD/CAM: Acronym for *computer-aided design/computer-aided manufacturing*, computer systems used to design and manufacture products. The term CAD/CAM implies that an engineer can use the system both for designing a product and for controlling manufacturing processes. For example, once a design has been produced with the CAD component, the design itself can control the machines that construct the part.

➠ See also CAD; CAM.

CADD: Acronym for *computer-aided design and drafting*. CADD systems are CAD systems with additional drafting features. For example, CADD systems enable an engineer or architect to insert size annotations and other notes into a design.

➠ See also CAD; CAD/CAM.

CAE: Abbreviation of *computer-aided engineering*, computer systems that analyze engineering designs. Most CAD systems have a CAE component, but there are also independent CAE systems that can analyze designs produced by various CAD systems. CAE systems are able to simulate a design under a variety of conditions to see if it actually works.

➠ See also CAD.

calculator: (1) A small hand-held computer that performs mathematical calculations. Some calculators even permit simple text editing and programming.

(2) A program on a computer that simulates a hand-held calculator. Calculator programs let you perform simple math calculations without leaving the computer. The Apple Macintosh comes with a calculator desk accessory. Likewise, Microsoft Windows includes a calculator accessory.

➠ See also *desk accessory; Microsoft Windows; program.*

calendar: A program that enables you to record events and appointments on an electronic calendar. Computer calendars act like datebooks, but they have several advantages over traditional datebooks:

automatic entries for regular events: You can specify, for example, that the first Thursday of every month is bridge night, and the calendar program will automatically fill in the appropriate days.

signaling of upcoming events: Most calendars will let you know that an event is approaching by issuing beeps.

clean deletion: With an electronic calendar, you can erase an appointment without leaving a trace.

Calendar software is part of a more general category of software known as *PIMs* (personal information managers). A special type of calendar, called a *scheduler*, enables groups of users connected to a network to coordinate their schedules.

➡ See also *PIM; scheduler; utility.*

call: (v) To invoke a routine in a programming language. Calling a routine consists of specifying the routine name and, optionally, parameters. For example, the following is a *function call* in the C programming language:

    printf("Hello")

The name of the function is *printf* and the parameter is "Hello." This function call causes the computer to display the word *Hello* on the display screen.
    A routine that invokes another routine is sometimes referred to as the *calling routine*. The routine that is invoked is referred to as the *called routine*.

(n) An invocation of a routine.

➡ See also *function; routine.*

CAM: Acronym for *computer-aided manufacturing*, a type of computer application that helps automate a factory. For example, the following are types of CAM systems:

■ real-time control
■ robotics
■ materials requirements

All these systems are concerned with automatically directing the manufacture and inventory of parts.

➠ See also *CAD*; *CAD/CAM*; *robotics*.

camera-ready: In desktop publishing, camera-ready refers to the final state of a publication before it is printed. Historically, the term has meant that the copy is ready to be photographed and turned into plates for offset printing. Increasingly, however, it is possible to print directly from the electronic version, either by sending it to a high-resolution laser printer or to a special device that can generate plates directly from electronic elements rather than from photographs. In these cases, therefore, camera-ready means merely that the document is ready to be printed.

➠ See also *desktop publishing*; *imagesetter*; *offset printing*; *service bureau*.

caps: Short for *capital letters*. For example, "all caps" means all letters capitalized.

Caps Lock key: A *toggle key* on computer keyboards that, when activated, causes all subsequent alphabetic characters to be uppercase, but has no effect on other keys.

➠ See also *keyboard*; *toggle*; *uppercase*.

capture: To save a particular state of a program. The term *capture* often refers to saving the information currently displayed on a display screen. You can capture the screen to a printer or to a file. The act of saving a display screen is called a *screen capture.*

The term *capture* is also used to describe the recording of keystrokes during the definition of a *macro*.

➠ See also *learn mode*; *screen capture*.

card: (1) Same as *printed circuit board.*

(2) In hypertext systems such as HyperCard, a card is a single page of information.

➠ See also *HyperCard software; hypertext.*

caret: A wedge-shaped symbol (^) generally found above the 6 on computer keyboards. In older technical documentation, the caret is often used to indicate the Control key. For example, " ^ C" would mean press the "C" key while holding down the Control key. Most modern documentation, however, would specify this key sequence as Ctrl+C.

The caret symbol is also called a *hat.*

➠ See also *Control key.*

carpal tunnel syndrome: A common form of Repetitive Strain Injury (RSI) produced by repeating the same small movements many times. As more and more people use computers, carpal tunnel syndrome and other forms of RSI have become more prevalent. Typical symptoms are numbness or burning in the fingers or wrist. If not addressed early on, the injury can cause permanent damage.

There are a number of ways to avoid carpal tunnel syndrome, including adjusting the height and angle of your chair and keyboard, and taking frequent breaks from typing. Modern office furniture, designed especially for computer use, can help considerably.

➠ See also *ergonomics.*

carriage: The mechanism on a printer that feeds paper. A *wide carriage printer* is a printer that can accept very wide paper. A *narrow-carriage printer* is a printer that accepts only standard-sized paper.

➠ See also *paper feed; printer.*

carriage return: Often abbreviated *CR,* a carriage return is a special code that moves the cursor (or print head) to the beginning of the current line. In the ASCII character set, a carriage return has a decimal value of 13.

➠ See also *line feed; return.*

cartridge: (1) A removable storage medium (tape, disk, or memory chip). Some printers have slots in which you can insert cartridges to load different fonts. A font loaded from a cartridge is called a *font cartridge* or *cartridge font*.

The term *removable cartridge* usually refers to a type of hard disk that you can remove. Removable cartridges offer the speed of hard disks along with the portability of floppy disks.

➠ See also *font cartridge; removable hard disk; slot.*

(2) For laser printers, a *toner cartridge* is a metal container that holds the *toner.*

➠ See also *laser printer; toner.*

cartridge font: Same as *font cartridge.*

cascading windows: An arrangement of windows such that they overlap one another. Typically, the title bar remains visible so that you can always see which windows are open. Cascading windows are also called *overlaid windows.* An alternative arrangement of windows, in which every window is completely visible, is called *tiled windows.*

➠ See also *overlaid windows; tiled windows; window.*

case sensitive: A program's ability to distinguish between uppercase (capital) and lowercase (small) letters. Programs that distinguish between uppercase and lowercase are said to be *case sensitive.*

A case-sensitive program that expects you to enter all commands in uppercase will not respond correctly if you enter one or more characters in lowercase. It will treat the command *RUN* differently from *run.* Programs that do not distinguish between uppercase and lowercase are said to be *case insensitive.*

➠ See also *lowercase; uppercase.*

cathode ray tube: See *CRT.*

CBT: Acronym for *computer-based training*, a type of education in which the student learns by executing special training programs on a computer. CBT is especially effective for training people to use computer applications because the CBT program can be integrated with the applications so that students can practice using the application as they learn.

Historically, CBT's growth has been hampered by the enormous resources required: human resources to create a CBT program and hardware resources needed to run it. However, the increase in PC computing power, and especially the growing prevalence of computers equipped with CD-ROMs, is making CBT a more viable option for corporations and individuals alike. Many PC applications now come with some modest form of CBT, often called a *tutorial.*

➥ See also *tutorial.*

CCD: Short for *charge-coupled device*, an instrument whose semiconductors are connected so that the output of one serves as the input of the next. Digital cameras, video cameras, and optical scanners all use CCD arrays.

➥ See also *digital camera; optical scanner.*

CCITT: Abbreviation of *Comité Consultatif International Téléphonique et Télégraphique*, an organization that sets international communications standards. CCITT has defined many important standards for data communications, including the following:

Group 3: The universal protocol for sending fax documents across telephone lines. The Group 3 protocol specifies CCITT T.4 data compression and a maximum transmission rate of 9,600 baud. There are two levels of resolution: 203 by 98 and 203 by 196.

Group 4: A protocol for sending fax documents over ISDN networks. The Group 400 protocol supports images of up to 400 dpi resolution.

V.21: The standard for full-duplex communication at 300 baud in Japan and Europe. In the United States, Bell 103 is used in place of V.21.

V.22: The standard for half-duplex communication at 1,200 bps in Japan and Europe. In the United States, the protocol defined by Bell 212A is more common.

V.22bis: The worldwide standard for full-duplex modems sending and receiving data across telephone lines at 1,200 or 2,400 bps.

V.29: The standard for half-duplex modems sending and receiving data across telephone lines at 1,200, 2,400, 4,800, or 9,600 bps. This is the protocol used by fax modems.

V.32: The standard for full-duplex modems sending and receiving data across phone lines at 4,800 or 9,600 bps. V.32 modems automatically adjust their transmission speeds based on the quality of the lines.

V.32bis: The V.32 protocol extended to speeds of 7,200, 12,000, and 14,400 bps.

V.34: The standard for full-duplex modems sending and receiving data across phone lines at up to 28,800 bps. V.34 modems automatically adjust their transmission speeds based on the quality of the lines.

V.42: An error-detection standard for high-speed modems. V.42 can be used with digital telephone networks. See *MNP* for a competing standard.

V.42bis: A data compression protocol that can enable modems to achieve a data transfer rate of 34,000 bps.

X.25: The most popular packet-switching protocol for LANs. Ethernet, for example, is based on the X.25 standard.

X.400: The universal protocol for e-mail. X.400 defines the envelope for e-mail messages so all messages conform to a standard format.

X.500: An extension to X.400 that defines addressing formats so all e-mail systems can be linked together.

➠ See also *baud rate; bps; communications protocol; data compression; e-mail; fax machine; fax modem; full duplex; half duplex; ISDN; MNP; modem; protocol; standard.*

cdev: MAC Short for *control panel device*, and pronounced *see-dev*, a cdev is a special type of Macintosh utility that enables you to adjust basic system parameters. On newer Macs (System 7 and later) *cdevs* are called *control panels*.

➠ See also *control panel*.

CD-I (Compact Disc-Interactive): A software and hardware standard developed by Philips International for storing video, audio, and binary data on compact optical disks. It supports 552MB (megabytes) of binary data and specifies several different types of video and audio encoding formats. Unlike conventional CD-ROM drives, CD-I drives have a built-in microprocessor to handle many of the computing functions. It is sometimes referred to as the *Green Book* standard.

A competing standard, developed by Intel Corporation, is known as *DVI (Digital Video Interactive)*.

➠ See also *CD-ROM; DVI; optical disk.*

CD-R drive: Short for *Compact Disk-Recordable drive*, a type of disk drive that can create CD-ROMs. This allows users to "master" a CD-ROM for publishing. Until recently, CD-R drives were quite expensive, but prices have dropped dramatically.

CD-R drives can also read CD-ROMs.

➠ See also *CD-ROM; CD-ROM player.*

CD-recordable drive: See *CD-R drive.*

CD-ROM: Pronounced *see-dee-rom*, abbreviation of *Compact Disc-Read-Only Memory*. A type of optical disk capable of storing large amounts of data—up to 1GB, although the most common size is 630MB (megabytes). A single CD-ROM has the storage capacity of 700 floppy disks, enough memory to store about 300,000 text pages.

CD-ROMs require a special machine to record the data, and once recorded, they cannot be erased and filled with new data. To read a CD, you need a CD-ROM player. Almost all CD-ROMs conform to a standard size and format, so it is usually possible to load any type of CD into any ROM player. In addition, most CD-ROM players are capable of playing audio CDs, which share the same technology.

CD-ROMs are particularly well-suited to information that requires large storage capacity. This includes color graphics, sound, and especially video. In recent years, as the prices of CD-ROM players have decreased, and the tools for creating new CD-ROM titles have improved, the CD-ROM industry has been expanding rapidly. To date, the most popular CD-ROM titles have been computer games and multimedia reference works.

➠ See also *CD-ROM player; disk; erasable optical disk; mass storage; multimedia; optical disk*.

CD-ROM drive: Same as *CD-ROM player*.

CD-ROM player: Also called a *CD-ROM drive*, a CD-ROM player is a device that can read information from a CD-ROM. CD-ROM players can be either internal, in which case they fit in a bay, or external, in which case they generally connect to the computer's parallel port. Parallel CD-ROM players are easier to install, but they have several disadvantages: They're somewhat more expensive than internal players, they use up the parallel port which means that you can't use that port for another device such as a printer, and the parallel port itself may not be fast enough to handle all the data pouring through it.

There are a number of features that distinguish CD-ROM players, the most important of which is probably their speed. CD-ROM players are generally classified as single-speed, double-speed (2X), triple-speed (3X), quadruple-speed (4X), or six-times speed (6X). Within these groups, however, there is some variation. Two more precise measurements are the drive's *seek time* and *data transfer rate*. The seek time, also called the *access time*, measures how long, on average, it takes the drive to access a particular piece of information. The data transfer rate measures how much data can be read and sent to the computer in a second. Table 9 shows the range of values for the different categories of CD-ROM drives.

Aside from its speed, another important feature of a CD-ROM player is its compatibility with existing standards. If you plan to run CD-ROMs in a windows environment, you need a player that conforms to the MPC II standard. If you want to be able to view photographs stored on CD-ROM, make sure your player conforms to Kodak's PhotoCD format.

Finally, you should consider how the player connects to your computer. Most CD-ROMs connect via a SCSI bus. If your computer doesn't already contain such an interface, you will need to install one. Other CD-ROMs connect to an *IDE* or *Enhanced IDE interface,* which is the one used by the hard disk drive; still others use a proprietary interface.

➠ See also *access time; bay; CD-ROM; IDE interface; MPC; multimedia kit; parallel port; PhotoCD; SCSI.*

Table 9
CD-ROM DRIVES

GENERAL SPEED	SEEK TIME (MILLISECONDS)	DATA TRANSFER RATE
Single-Speed	600	150K per second
2X	320	300K per second
3X	250	450K per second
4X	125-220	600K per second
6X	135-145	900K per second

cell: In spreadsheet applications, a cell is a box in which you can enter a single piece of data. The data is usually text, a numeric value, or a formula. The entire spreadsheet is composed of rows and columns of cells. A spreadsheet cell is analogous to a *field* in database management systems.

Individual cells are usually identified by a column letter and a row number. For example, *D12* specifies the cell in column D and row 12.

➠ See also *field, formula, spreadsheet.*

central processing unit: See *CPU.*

Centronics interface: A standard interface for connecting printers and other parallel devices (see Figure 19 at *connector*). Although Centronics Corporation designed the original standard, the Centronics interface used by modern computers was designed by Epson Corporation. For PCs, almost all parallel ports conform to the Centronics standard. Two new parallel port standards that are backward compatible with

Centronics, but offer faster transmission rates, are *ECP (Extend Capabilities Port)* and *EPP (Enhanced Parallel Port)*.

➠ See also *ECP; EPP; interface; parallel interface; standard.*

CGA: PC Abbreviation of *color/graphics adapter*, an old graphics system for PCs. Introduced in 1981 by IBM, CGA was the first color graphics system for IBM PCs. Designed primarily for computer games, CGA does not produce sharp enough characters for extended editing sessions. CGA's highest resolution mode is 2 colors at a resolution of 640 by 200.

CGA has been superseded by VGA systems, which are backward compatible with CGA.

➠ See also *backward compatible; EGA; graphics mode; IBM PC; palette; resolution; SVGA; text mode; VGA; video adapter; XGA.*

CGM: Abbreviation of *Computer Graphics Metafile*, a file format designed by several standards organizations and formally ratified by ANSI. It is designed to be the standard vector graphics file format and is supported by a wide variety of software and hardware products.

➠ See also *ANSI; graphics file formats; vector graphics.*

channel: (1) In communications, the term *channel* refers to a communications path between two computers or devices. It can refer to the physical medium (the wires) or to a set of properties that distinguishes one channel from another. For example, *TV channels* refer to particular frequencies at which radio waves are transmitted.

➠ See also *bus; communications.*

(2) For IBM PS/2 computers, a channel is the same thing as an expansion bus.

➠ See also *bus.*

character: In computer software, any symbol that requires one byte of storage. This includes all the ASCII and extended ASCII characters, including the space character. In character-based software, everything that appears on the screen, including graphics symbols, is considered to be a character. In graphics-based applications, the term *character* is generally reserved for letters, numbers, and punctuation.

➠ See also *alphanumeric; ASCII; character based; extended ASCII; graphics based.*

character based: Describes programs capable of displaying only ASCII (and extended ASCII) characters. Character-based programs treat a display screen as an array of boxes, each of which can hold one character. When in text mode, for example, PC screens are typically divided into 25 rows and 80 columns. In contrast, *graphics-based* programs treat the display screen as an array of millions of pixels. Characters and other objects are formed by illuminating patterns of pixels.

Because the IBM *extended ASCII* character set includes shapes for drawing pictures, character-based programs are capable of simulating some graphics objects. For example, character-based programs can display windows and menus, bar charts, and other shapes that consist primarily of straight lines. However, they cannot represent more complicated objects that contain curves.

Unlike PCs, the Macintosh computer is a graphics-based machine. All programs that run on a Macintosh computer are graphics based.

➠ See also *character mode; extended ASCII; graphical user interface; text mode.*

character mode: Many video adapters support several different modes of resolution. All such modes are divided into two general categories: *character mode* (also called *text mode*) and *graphics mode*. In character mode, the display screen is treated as an array of blocks, each of which can hold one ASCII character. In graphics mode, the display screen is treated as an array of pixels, with characters and other shapes formed by turning on combinations of pixels.

Of the two modes, character mode is much simpler. Programs that run in character mode generally run much faster than those that run in graphics mode, but they are limited in the variety of fonts and shapes they can display. Programs that run entirely in character mode are called *character-based* programs.

➠ See also *ASCII; character based; pixel; video adapter.*

---

character recognition: See *optical character recognition.*

character set: A defined list of characters recognized by the computer hardware and software. Each character is represented by a number. The ASCII character set, for example, uses the numbers 0 through 127 to represent all English characters as well as special control characters. European ISO character sets are similar to ASCII, but they contain additional characters for European languages.

➠ See also *ASCII; character; control character; Unicode.*

characters per second: See under *cps.*

character string: A series of characters manipulated as a group. A character string differs from a name in that it does not represent anything—a name stands for some other object.

A character string is often specified by enclosing the characters in single or double quotes. For example, WASHINGTON would be a name, but 'WASHINGTON' and "WASHINGTON" would be character strings.

The length of a character string is usually the number of characters in it. For example, the character string "WASHINGTON" has a length of 10 (the quote marks are not included). Some programs, however, mark the beginning or end of a character string with an invisible character, so the length might actually be one greater than the number of characters.

charge-coupled device: See under *CCD.*

chassis: A metal frame that serves as the structural support for electronic components. Every computer system requires at least one chassis to house the circuit boards and wiring. The chassis also contains slots for expansion boards. If you want to insert more boards than there are slots, you will need an *expansion chassis,* which provides additional slots.

There are two basic flavors of chassis designs—desktop models and tower models—but there are many variations on these two basic types.

➠ See also *desktop model computer; expansion board; slot; tower model.*

chat: Real-time communication between two users via computer. Once a chat has been initiated, either user can enter text by typing on the keyboard and the entered text will appear on the other user's monitor. Most networks and online services offer a chat feature, but it is not widely used because it is easier to communicate by telephone, and messages that aren't urgent can be sent by e-mail.

➠ See also *e-mail; online service.*

check box: In graphical user interfaces, a box that you can click to turn an option on or off. When the option is on, an X appears in the box.

➠ See also *box; dialog box; graphical user interface; option.*

checksum: A simple error-detection scheme in which each transmitted message is accompanied by a numerical value based on the number of set bits in the message. The receiving station then applies the same formula to the message and checks to make sure the accompanying numerical value is the same. If not, the receiver knows that the message has been garbled.

➠ See also *communications; CRC; error detection.*

Chicago: See under *Windows 95.*

chip: A small piece of semiconducting material (usually silicon) on which an integrated circuit is embedded (Figure 13). A typical chip is less than $\frac{1}{4}$-square inches and can contain millions of electronic components (transistors). Computers consist of many chips placed on electronic boards called *printed circuit boards.*

There are different types of chips. For example, CPU chips (also called *microprocessors*) contain an entire processing unit, whereas memory chips contain blank memory.

Chips come in a variety of packages. The three most common are:

DIPs: Dual in-line packages are the traditional buglike chips that have anywhere from 8 to 40 legs, evenly divided in two rows.

PGAs: Pin-grid arrays are square chips in which the pins are arranged in concentric squares.

SIPs: Single in-line packages are chips that have just one row of legs in a straight line like a comb.

In addition to these types of chips, there are also single in-line memory modules (SIMMs), which consist of up to nine chips packaged as a single unit.

➠ See also *CPU; integrated circuit; microprocessor; PGA; printed circuit board; semiconductor; SIMM.*

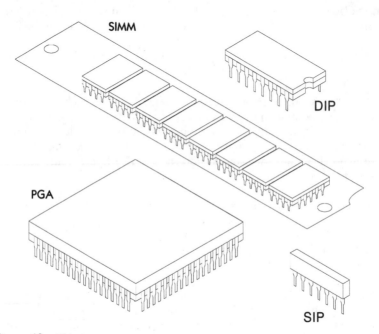

Figure 13: *Chips*

choose: To pick a command or option. To choose a menu command or command button in a graphical user interface, you click on it. The terms *choose* and *select* are often used interchangeably, but some authors make a distinction between choosing, which actually activates a command, and selecting, which merely highlights a command or other object.

➠ See also *click; command; command button; graphical user interface; menu command; option; select.*

Chooser: MAC A Macintosh desk accessory (DA) that enables you to select and configure printers and network devices, such as file servers.

➠ See also *desk accessory*.

CIE color model: A color model based on human perception developed by the CIE (Commission Internationale de l'Eclairage) committee. While widely regarded as the most accurate color model, CIE is unsuitable for many technologies, including color printing and color monitors. Consequently, these systems need to use other color models, such as CMYK and RGB. There is a growing trend, however, to make all color models relative to the CIE model. This would make it easier to translate from one model to another.

➠ See also *CMYK; color matching; RGB monitor*.

Cinepak: A popular codec (compression/decompression technology) for computer video developed by SuperMac Inc.

➠ See also *codec*.

circuit board: Short for *printed circuit board*.

CIS: Short for *CompuServe Information Service*. See under *CompuServe*.

CISC: Pronounced *sisk*, and stands for *complex instruction set computer*. Most personal computers use a CISC architecture, in which the CPU supports as many as two hundred instructions. An alternative architecture, used by many workstations and also some personal computers, is *RISC (reduced instruction set computer)*, which supports fewer instructions.

➠ See also *architecture; CPU; machine language; RISC*.

class: In object-oriented programming, a category of objects. For example, there might be a class called *shape* that contains objects which are circles, rectangles, and triangles. The class defines all the common properties of the different objects that belong to it.

➠ See also *object-oriented programming*.

clear: To erase. *Clear the screen*, for example, means to erase everything on the display screen. *Clear a variable* means to remove whatever data is currently stored in the variable. *Clear memory* means to erase all data currently stored in memory.

➠ See also *display screen; memory; variable*.

click: (v) To tap on a mouse button, pressing it down and then immediately releasing it. Note that *clicking* a mouse button is different from *pressing* (or *dragging*) a mouse button, which implies that you hold the button down without releasing it. The phrase *click on* means to select (a screen object) by moving the mouse pointer to the object's position and clicking a mouse button.

Some operations require a double click, meaning that you must click a mouse button twice in rapid succession. *Shift clicking* refers to clicking the mouse button while holding the Shift key down.

➠ See also *double click; drag; graphical user interface; mouse; shift clicking*.

(n) The pressing down and rapid release of a mouse button.

client/server architecture: A network architecture in which each computer or process on the network is either a *client* or a *server*. Servers are powerful computers or processes dedicated to managing disk drives (*file servers*), printers (*print servers*), or network traffic (*network servers*). Clients are less powerful PCs or workstations on which users run applications. Clients rely on servers for resources, such as files, devices, and even processing power.

Another type of network architecture is known as a *peer-to-peer architecture* because each *node* has equivalent responsibilities. Both client/server and peer-to-peer architectures are widely used, and each has unique advantages and disadvantages.

➠ See also *architecture; local-area network; network; node; peer-to-peer architecture; process; server*.

clip: In computer graphics, to cut off a portion of a graphic at a defined boundary. Most bit-mapped graphics utilities provide a clip feature than enables you to draw a window around an object and clip everything outside of the window.

➠ See also *graphics; window.*

clip art: Electronic illustrations that can be inserted into a document (Figure 14). Many clip-art packages are available, some general and others specialized for a particular field. Most clip-art packages provide the illustrations in several file formats so that you can insert them into various word-processing systems.

➠ See also *desktop publishing.*

Figure 14: *Clip Art*

clipboard: A special file or memory area (*buffer*) where data is stored temporarily before being copied to another location. Many word processors, for example, use a clipboard for cutting and pasting. When you cut a block of text, the word processor copies the block to the clipboard; when you paste the block, the word processor copies it from the clipboard to its final destination. In Microsoft Windows and the Apple Macintosh operating system, the *Clipboard* (with a capital C) can be used to copy data from one application to another.

▨MAC The Macintosh uses two types of clipboards. The one it calls the *Clipboard* can hold only one item at a time and is flushed when you turn the computer off. The other, called the *Scrapbook,* can hold several items at once and retains its contents from one working session to another.

➠ See also *cut; paste.*

clock rate: Same as *clock speed.*

clock speed: Also called *clock rate,* the speed at which a microprocessor executes instructions. Every computer contains an internal clock that regulates the rate at which instructions are executed and synchronizes all the various computer components. The CPU requires a fixed number of clock ticks (or *clock cycles*) to execute each instruction. For example, an Intel 80286 microprocessor needs about 20 clock cycles to multiply two numbers together. The faster the clock, the more instructions the CPU can execute per second.

Clock speeds are expressed in megahertz (MHz), 1MHz being equal to 1 million cycles per second. Personal computers have clock speeds of anywhere from 4MHz to over 100MHz. Usually, the clock rate is a fixed characteristic of the microprocessor. Some computers, however, have a switch that lets you choose between two or more different clock speeds. This is useful because programs written to run on a machine with a high clock rate may not work properly on a machine with a slower clock rate, and vice versa. In addition, some add-on components may not be able to run at high clock speeds.

The internal architecture of a CPU has as much to do with a CPU's performance as the clock speed, so two CPUs with the same clock speed will not necessarily perform equally. Whereas an Intel 80286 microprocessor requires 20 cycles to multiply two numbers, an Intel 80486 or later processor can perform the same calculation in a single clock tick. These newer processors, therefore, would be 20 times faster than the older processors even if their clock speeds were the same.

Like CPUs, expansion buses also have clock speeds. Ideally, the CPU clock speed and the bus clock speed should be the same so that neither component slows down the other. In practice, the bus clock speed is often slower than the CPU clock speed.

➠ See also *bus; CPU; instruction; microprocessor; wait state.*

clone: A computer, software product, or device that functions exactly like another, better-known product. For example, IBM PC clones are personal computers that offer the same functionality as an IBM PC but are produced by other companies. If the clone is good, you should be unable to tell the difference between it and the real product.

The term *clone* implies that the product is an exact duplicate. Note that the term *clone* is a bit stronger than the term compatible. For example, an IBM PC clone is a computer that has most, if not all, the same components as a real IBM PC. The term IBM-compatible, on the other hand, implies only that the computer is capable of running any program that an IBM PC can run. This does not mean that it is the same internally.

➠ See also *compatible; IBM PC; PC.*

close: (1) To finish work on a data file and save it.

➠ See also *open; save.*

(2) In graphical user interfaces, to close a window means to exit an application or file, thereby removing the window from the screen.

➠ See also *graphical user interface; window*

cluster: A group of disk sectors. The operating system assigns a unique number to each cluster and then keeps track of files according to which clusters they use. Occasionally, the operating system marks a cluster as being used even though the file that is supposedly using it no longer exists. This is called a *lost cluster.* You can free up disk space by deleting lost clusters, but you should first make sure that the clusters do not, in fact, contain valuable data.

➠ See also *fragmentation; sector.*

CMOS: Abbreviation of *complementary metal oxide semiconductor.* Pronounced *see-moss,* CMOS is a widely used type of semiconductor. CMOS semiconductors require less power than NMOS transistors, making them particularly attractive for use in battery-powered devices, such as portable computers. Many personal computers contain a small amount of battery-powered CMOS memory to hold the date, time, and system setup parameters.

➠ See also *semiconductor.*

CMS: See *color management system.*

CMYK: Short for *Cyan-Magenta-Yellow-Black,* and pronounced as sepa-rate letters. CMYK is a color model in which all colors are described as a mixture of these four *process colors.* CMYK is the standard color model used in offset printing for full-color documents. Because such printing uses inks of these four basic colors, it is often called *four-color printing.*

In contrast, display devices generally use a different color model called *RGB,* which stands for *Red-Green-Blue.* One of the most diffi-cult aspects of desktop publishing in color is color matching—prop-erly converting the RGB colors into CMYK colors so that what gets printed looks the same as what appears on the monitor.

➠ See also *color matching; color separation; desktop publishing; offset printing; RGB monitor; spot color; WYSIWYP.*

coaxial cable: A type of wire that consists of a center wire surrounded by insulation and then a grounded shield of braided wire. The shield minimizes electrical and radio frequency interference.

Coaxial cabling is the primary type of cabling used by the cable tele-vision industry and is also widely used for computer networks. Although more expensive than standard telephone wire, it is much less susceptible to interference and can carry much more data. Because the cable television industry has already connected millions of homes with coaxial cable, many analysts believe that they are the best positioned to capitalize on the much-heralded information high-way.

➠ See also *information highway; network.*

COBOL: Acronym for *common business oriented language.* Developed in the late 1950s and early 1960s, COBOL is the second-oldest high-level programming language (FORTRAN is the oldest). It is particu-larly popular for business applications that run on large computers.

COBOL is a wordy language; programs written in COBOL tend to be much longer than the same programs written in other languages. This can be annoying when you program in COBOL, but the wordi-ness makes it easy to understand programs because everything is spelled out. Although disparaged by many programmers for being outdated, COBOL is still the most widely used programming language in the world.

➠ See also *programming language.*

code: (n) (1) A set of symbols for representing something. For example, most computers use ASCII codes to represent characters.

➠ See also *ASCII.*

(2) Written computer instructions. The term *code* is somewhat colloquial. For example, a programmer might say: "I wrote a lot of code this morning" or "There's one piece of code that doesn't work."
   Code can appear in a variety of forms. The code that a programmer writes is called *source code*. After it has been compiled, it is called *object code*. Code that is ready to run is called *executable code* or *machine code.*

➠ See also *executable file; machine language; object code; source code.*

(v) Colloquial for *to program* (that is, to write source code).

➠ See also *compile; program.*

codec: Short for *compressor/decompressor*, a codec is any technology for compressing and decompressing data. Codecs can be implemented in software, hardware, or a combination of both. Some popular codecs for computer video include MPEG, Indeo, Cinepak, QuickTime, and Video for Windows.

➠ See also *Cinepak; data compression; Indeo; MPEG; QuickTime; Video for Windows.*

cold boot: The start-up of a computer from a powered-down state.

➠ See also *boot.*

collapse: To compress a view of a hierarchy so that only the roots of each branch are visible (Figure 15). The opposite of collapse is *expand*, which makes the entire branch visible.

➠ See also *branch; hierarchical; root directory.*

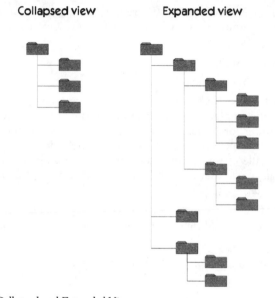

Figure 15: *Collapsed and Expanded Views*

color depth: The number of distinct colors that can be represented by a piece of hardware or software. Color depth is sometimes referred to as *bit depth* because it is directly related to the number of bits used for each pixel. A 16-bit video adapter, for example, has a color depth of 2^{16} (about 16.7 million) colors.

➠ See also *optical scanner; video adapter.*

color/graphics adapter: See CGA.

color management system (CMS): A system for ensuring that colors remain the same regardless of the device or medium used to display the colors. This is extremely difficult because different devices use different technologies and models to produce colors. In addition, color is highly subjective. The same colors look different to different people.

➠ See also *CIE color model; CMYK; color matching; Pantone Matching System; process colors; RGB monitor; WYSIWYP.*

color matching: The process of assuring that a color on one medium remains the same when converted to another medium. This is extremely difficult because different media use different color models. Color monitors, for example, use the RGB model, whereas process printing uses the CMYK model. As color desktop publishing matures, color matching is gaining more and more attention. The most recent Windows and Macintosh operating systems include a color management system (CMS) to assist in color matching.

➠ See also *CIE color model; CMYK; color management system; RGB monitor.*

color monitor: A display monitor capable of displaying many colors. In contrast, a monochrome monitor can display only two colors—one for the background and one for the foreground. Color monitors implement the RGB color model by using three different phosphors that appear red, green, and blue when activated. By placing the phosphors directly next to each other, and activating them with different intensities, color monitors can create an unlimited number of colors. In practice, however, the real number of colors that any monitor can display is controlled by the video adapter.

➠ See also *monitor; RGB monitor; video adapter.*

color printer: A printer capable of printing more than one color. Most color printers are based on the CMYK color model, which prints in four basic colors: cyan, magenta, yellow, and black. By printing combinations of different colors close to each other (or, in the case of thermal dye transfer printers, on top of each other), the CMYK model can simulate most other colors (except for special colors such as fluorescent yellow). This is the same technique used in process color offset printing, which is the technology used to print most color books, magazines, and other paper materials. Some lower-price printers use only three colors—cyan, magenta, and yellow—but these printers cannot print true black and their colors tend to be a bit faded.

Color printers use a variety of techniques to lay down the different colors:

Thermal dye transfer printers, also called *dye sublimation printers,* heat ribbons containing dye and then diffuse the dyes onto specially coated paper or transparencies. These printers are the most expensive and slowest, but they produce continuous-tone images that mimic actual photographs. Note that these printers require special paper, which is quite expensive.

Thermal wax transfer printers use wax-based inks that are melted and then laid down on regular paper or transparencies. Unlike thermal dye transfer printers, these printers print images as dots, which means that images must be dithered first. As a result images are not quite photo-realistic, although they are very good. The big advantages of these printers over thermal dye transfer printers are that they don't require special paper and they are faster.

Solid ink-jet printers, also called *wax jet* or *phase change printers,* work by melting dyed wax and then spraying it on paper. This produces bright colors on virtually any type of paper. The downside to solid ink-jet printers is that they are slow and relatively expensive.

Color laser printers use the same principle as monochrome laser printers, but they include four toners rather than one. Although laser printers produce better quality output than ink-jet printers, they are also three to four times more expensive.

Color ink-jet printers are the least expensive color printers. They contain three or four separate nozzles, each of which sprays a different color of ink.

➠ See also CMYK; *ink-jet printer; laser printer; printer; process colors.*

color separation: The act of decomposing a color graphic or photo into single-color layers. For example, to print full-color photos with an offset printing press, one must first separate the photo into the four basic ink colors: cyan, magenta, yellow, and black (CMYK). Each single-color layer is then printed separately, one on top of the other, to give the impression of infinite colors.

This type of color separation, mixing three or four colors to produce an infinite variety of colors, is called *process color separation.* Another type of color separation, called *spot color separation,* is used to separate colors that are not to be mixed. In this case, each spot color is represented by its own ink, which is specially mixed. Spot colors are effective for highlighting text, but they cannot be used to reproduce full-color images.

Traditionally, *process color separation* has been performed photographically with different colored filters. However, many modern desktop publishing systems are now capable of producing color separations for graphics stored electronically. This capability is essential if you want to create full-color documents on your computer and then print them using an offset printer. You don't need to perform color separation if you are printing directly to a color printer because in this case the printer itself performs the color separation internally.

➡ See also CMYK; *color management system; color printer; desktop publishing; process colors.*

column: (1) On a display screen in character mode, a column is a vertical line of characters extending from the top to the bottom of the screen. The size of a text display is usually measured in rows and columns.

➡ See also *character mode; display screen.*

(2) In spreadsheets, a column is a vertical row of cells. Spreadsheet columns are usually identified by letters.

➡ See also *cell; spreadsheet.*

(3) In database management systems, *column* is another name for *field.*

➡ See also *database management system; field.*

(4) In documents, a column is a vertical area reserved for text. Most newspapers, for example, contain four or more columns per page. Modern word processors and desktop publishing systems enable you to automatically divide a page into columns.

➡ See also *desktop publishing; word processing.*

column graph: A type of presentation graphic in which numerical values are illustrated with horizontal columns. Column graphs are particularly effective for showing values that are categorized by two separate characteristics, such as year and sector (Figure 16).

➠ See also *presentation graphics.*

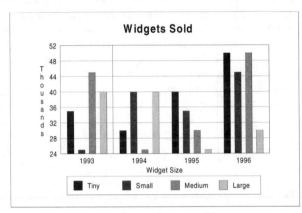

Figure 16: *Column Graph*

COM: PC In DOS systems, the name of a serial communications port. DOS supports four serial port names: COM1, COM2, COM3, and COM4, but most PCs have only two physical serial ports. This means that the names overlap. Typically, COM1 and COM3 refer to one port, while COM2 and COM4 refer to the other. So if you have two devices, one of which is attached to COM1 and the other to COM3, you cannot use them simultaneously.

➠ See also *port; serial communications.*

COM file: PC In DOS environments, a COM *file* is an executable command file with a .COM filename extension. COM files can be directly executed and are usually slightly smaller than equivalent *EXE files.* However, COM files cannot exceed 64K, so large programs are usually stored in EXE files.

➠ See also *DOS; executable file; EXE file; extension; file.*

Comité Consultatif International Téléphonique et Télégraphique:
See *CCITT*.

command: An instruction to a computer or device to perform a specific task. Commands come in different forms. They can be:

- special words (*keywords*) that a program understands.
- function keys
- choices in a menu
- buttons or other graphical objects on your screen

Every program that interacts with people responds to a specific set of commands. The set of commands and the syntax for entering them is called the *user interface* and varies from one program to another.

The DOS operating system makes a distinction between *internal* and *external* commands. Internal commands are commands, such as COPY and DIR, that can be handled by the COMMAND.COM program. External commands include the names of all other COM files, as well as EXE and BAT files.

Another word for *command* is *directive*.

➥ See also *BAT file; COM file; EXE file; external command; function keys; internal command; keyword; menu; DOS; user interface.*

command buffer: A temporary storage area where commands are kept. (In DOS environments, the command buffer is called a *template*.) DOS and UNIX support several operations for manipulating the command buffer. For example, you can use the F3 function key in DOS to copy the template's contents to the display screen. This is useful for repeating a command or for correcting a mistake.

Command buffers also make it possible for programs to *undo* commands.

➥ See also *buffer; command; undo.*

comma-delimited: A data format in which each piece of data is separated by a comma.

➥ See also *export; import.*

COMMAND.COM: [PC] The DOS file that contains all of the DOS *command processor.*

➠ See also *command processor; internal command.*

command driven: Refers to programs that accept commands in the form of special words or letters. In contrast, programs that allow you to choose from a list of options in a menu are said to be *menu driven.* Command-driven software is often more flexible than menu-driven software, but it is more difficult to learn.

➠ See also *command; menu driven; user interface.*

Command key: [MAC] Macintosh computers have a special command key marked by a four-leaf clover or an apple. The Command key is similar to a PC's Alt key—you hold it down while pressing another key to execute some operation. Typically, command-key combinations are shorthands for menu choices. For example, on the desktop, pressing the command key and O is equivalent to selecting the *open* option from the *file* menu.

The Command key is sometimes called the *Apple key* or *Open Apple.*

➠ See also *control key; keyboard.*

command language: The programming language through which a user communicates with the operating system or an application. For example, the DOS command language includes the commands DIR, COPY, and DEL, to name a few. The part of an operating system that responds to operating system commands is called the *command processor.*

With graphical user interfaces, the command language consists of operations you perform with a mouse or similar input device.

➠ See also *command; command processor; graphical user interface; operating system; shell.*

command line: The line on the display screen where a command is expected. Generally, the command line is the line that contains the most recently displayed command prompt.

➠ See also *command; prompt.*

command line interpreter: Same as *command processor.*

command processor: The part of the operating system that receives and executes operating system commands. Every operating system has a command processor. When the command prompt is displayed, the command processor is waiting for a command. After you enter a command, the command processor analyzes the syntax to make sure the command is valid, and then either executes the command or issues an error warning. For operating systems with a graphical user interface, the command processor interprets mouse operations and executes the appropriate command.
   Another term for command processor is *command line interpreter.*

➠ See also *command language; operating system.*

Commodore Amiga: See *Amiga.*

common carrier: Same as *public carrier.*

communications: The transmission of data from one computer to another, or from one device to another. A communications device, therefore, is any machine that assists data transmission. For example, modems, cables, and ports are all communications devices. Communications software refers to programs that make it possible to transmit data.

➠ See also *communications protocol; communications software; modem; network; port.*

communications protocol: All communications between devices require that the devices agree on the format of the data. The set of rules defining a format is called a *protocol*. At the very least, a communications protocol must define the following:

- rate of transmission (in baud or bps)
- whether transmission is to be *synchronous* or *asynchronous*
- whether data is to be transmitted in *half-duplex* or *full-duplex* mode

In addition, protocols can include sophisticated techniques for detecting and recovering from transmission errors and for encoding and decoding data.

Table 10 lists the most commonly used protocols for communications via modems. These protocols are almost always implemented in the hardware; that is, they are built into modems.

Table 10
COMMUNICATIONS PROTOCOLS

PROTOCOL	MAXIMUM TRANSMISSION RATE	DUPLEX MODE
Bell 103	300 bps	Full
CCITT V.21	300 bps	Full
Bell 212A	1,200 bps	Full
CCITT V.22	1,200 bps	Half
CCITT V.22bis	2,400 bps	Full
CCITT V.29	9,600 bps	Half
CCITT V.32	9,600 bps	Full
CCITT V.32bis	14,400 bps	Full
CCITT V.34	28,800 bps	Full

In addition to the standard protocols listed in the table, there are a number of protocols that complement these standards by adding additional functions such as file-transfer capability, error detection and recovery, and data compression. The best-known are *Xmodem, Kermit, MNP*, and *CCITT V.42*. These protocols can be implemented either in hardware or software.

➠ See also *asynchronous; Bell 103; Bell 212A; bps; CCITT; full duplex; half duplex; protocol.*

communications software: Software that makes it possible to send and receive data over telephone lines through modems. The following features differentiate various communications software packages:

maximum bps rate: The software package should be able to transmit data as fast as your modem. Maximum bps rates for communications packages vary between 9,600 and 57,600 bps.

automatic queue and redial: This is a useful feature if you use your modem to access a service that is frequently busy, such as a *bulletin board system (BBS)*. When you enter the telephone number in a queue, the communications software will keep redialing the number until it gets through. This feature can also be implemented by the modem itself rather than by the software.

macros: The ability to create macros is very important because you often go through the same steps every time you make a connection. By storing the connection sequence in a macro, you can perform the entire process with a single keystroke.

file transfer protocols: File transfer protocols enable you to transmit ASCII or binary files over a telephone line. The more protocols the package supports, the better. At the very least, it should support Xmodem and Kermit. For high-speed communication, you may require additional protocols, such as Zmodem.

script language: A script is like a program or batch file. It is a file of commands that can be executed without your interaction. The ability to write scripts is useful if you need to log on to services and transfer files while away from your computer.

remote: Packages that support a remote option enable your computer to accept calls while you are not there. This feature is also called *auto-answer*.

spooling: Packages that support spooling enable you to run another program while files are being transferred in the background. This is sometimes called *background processing*.

terminal emulation drivers: This is important if you plan to log on to a mainframe from your PC. Most mainframes require that the PC emulate a particular type of terminal. The more terminal emulation drivers a package has, the more mainframes you can log on to. Most packages support TTY emulation and emulate one or more DEC terminals (such as the VT52, VT100/102, or VT220).

In addition to these features, some communications packages offer more advanced programming capabilities that enable you to customize the interface using windows.

➡ See also *auto answer; batch file; bulletin board system; communications protocol; editor; emulation; Kermit; log on; macro; mainframe; modem; multitasking; queue; script; spooling; terminal; window; word wrap; Xmodem; Ymodem; Zmodem.*

compact disc: Known by its abbreviation, CD, a compact disk is a polished metal platter capable of storing digital information. The most prevalent types of compact disks or those used by the music industry to store digital recordings and CD-ROMs used to store computer data. Both of these types of compact disk are *read-only,* which means that once the data has been recorded onto them, they can only be read, or played.

Another type of compact disk, generally called an *erasable optical disk,* can have its data erased and overwritten by new data. Currently, erasable optical storage is too slow to be used as a computer's main storage facility, but as the speed improves and the cost comes down, optical storage devices are becoming a popular alternative to tape systems as a backup method.

➡ See also CD-ROM; *erasable optical disk; mass storage; optical disk;* WORM.

comparison operator: Same as *relational operator.*

compatible: (n) Indicates that a product can work with or is equivalent to another, better-known product. The term is often used as a shorthand for *IBM-compatible PC,* a computer that is compatible with an IBM PC. Another term for a compatible is *clone.*

➡ See also *clone; compatibility; PC.*

(adj) The ability of one device or program to work with another device or program. The term *compatible* implies different degrees of partnership. For example, a printer and a computer are said to be compatible if they can be connected to each other. An *IBM compatible PC,* on the other hand, is a computer that can run the same software as an IBM PC. (Note, however, that many manufacturers claim IBM compatibility even though their computers cannot run 100 percent of the software made for IBM PCs.)

Compatibility of two devices, such as printers, usually means that they react to software commands in the same way. Some printers achieve compatibility by tricking the software into believing that the printer is a different machine. This is called *emulation.*

Be aware, however, that hardware compatibility does not always extend to expansion slots. For example, two compatible printers may not accept the same font cartridges. Complete hardware compatibility is denoted by the term *plug compatible.*

Software products are compatible if they use the same data formats. For example, many programs are compatible with dBASE. This means that the files they produce can easily be transformed into a dBASE database or that they can *import* dBASE files.

➡ See also *backward compatible; clone; dBASE; emulation; font cartridge; IBM PC; plug compatible; standard; upward compatible.*

compile: To transform a program written in a high-level programming language from *source code* into *object code.* Programmers write programs in a form called *source code.* Source code must go through several steps before it becomes an executable program (Figure 17). The first step is to pass the source code through a *compiler,* which translates the high-level language instructions into object code.

The final step in producing an executable program—after the compiler has produced object code—is to pass the object code through a *linker.* The linker combines modules and gives real values to all symbolic addresses.

➡ See also *assembly language; compiler; interpreter; link; object code; programming language; source code.*

compiler: A program that translates *source code* into *object code.* The compiler derives its name from the way it works, looking at the entire piece of source code and collecting and reorganizing the instructions. Thus, a compiler differs from an *interpreter,* which analyzes and executes each line of source code in succession, without looking at the entire program. The advantage of interpreters is that they can execute a program immediately. Compilers require some time before an executable program emerges. However, programs produced by compilers run much faster than the same programs executed by an interpreter.

Every high-level programming language (except strictly interpretive languages) comes with a compiler. In effect, the compiler is the language, because it defines which instructions are acceptable.

Because compilers translate source code into object code, which is unique for each type of computer, many compilers are available for the same language. For example, there is a FORTRAN compiler for PCs and another for Apple Macintosh computers. In addition, the compiler industry is quite competitive, so there are actually many compilers for each language on each type of computer. More than a dozen companies develop and sell C compilers for the PC.

➠ See also *assembly language; interpreter; link; object code; programming language; source code.*

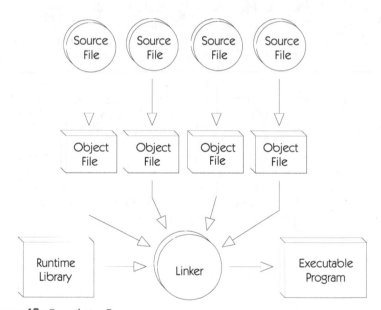

Figure 17: *Compilation Process*

complementary metal oxide semiconductor: See CMOS.

complex instruction set computer: See CISC.

component software: Sometimes called *componentware,* software designed to work as a component of a larger application. A good analogy is the way personal computers are built up from a collection of standard components: memory chips, CPUs, buses, keyboards, mice, disk drives, monitors, etc. Because all of the interfaces between components are standardized, it is possible to mix components from different manufacturers in a single system.

Similarly, the goal of component software is to standardize the interfaces between software components so that they too can work together seamlessly. Two new standards—OLE and OpenDoc—are designed to help programmers develop components that can work together. Many analysts believe that component software is the natural extension of object-oriented programming and that it will become the standard programming paradigm for years to come.

➡ See also *object-oriented programming; OLE; OpenDoc.*

componentware: See under *component software.*

composite video: A type of video signal in which all information—the red, blue, and green signals (and sometimes audio signals as well)—are mixed together. This is the type of signal used by televisions in the United States (see *NTSC*).

In contrast, most computers use *RGB video,* which consists of three separate signals for red, green, and blue. In general, RGB video produces sharper images than composite video.

➡ See also *NTSC; RGB monitor.*

compound document: A document that contains elements from a variety of computer applications. For example, a single compound document might include text from a word processor, graphics from a draw program, and a chart from a spreadsheet application. Most importantly, each element in the compound document is stored in such a way that it can be manipulated by the application that created it.

Many computer experts believe that compound documents represent the most useful metaphor for utilizing computers because they allow people to mix different forms of expression rather than artificially separating them. With the emergence of OLE as an important standard, compound documents are likely to become more and more a part of everyday computing.

➠ See also *document; OLE; OpenDoc.*

compression: See *data compression.*

CompuServe: Short for *CompuServe Information Service,* one of the first and largest online services. CompuServe supports a wide array of *forums* and provides many types of electronic-mail services. In addition, it is connected to hundreds of different database systems.

➠ See also *online service.*

computer: A programmable machine. The two principal characteristics of a computer are:

■ It responds to a specific set of instructions in a well-defined manner.
■ It can execute a prerecorded list of instructions (a program).

Modern computers (Figure 18) are electronic and digital. The actual machinery—wires, transistors, and circuits—is called *hardware;* the instructions and data are called *software.*

All general-purpose computers require the following hardware components:

memory: Enables a computer to store, at least temporarily, data and programs.

mass storage device: Allows a computer to permanently retain large amounts of data. Common mass storage devices include disk drives and tape drives.

input device: Usually a keyboard or mouse, the input device is the conduit through which data and instructions enter a computer.

output device: A display screen, printer, or other device that lets you see what the computer has accomplished.

central processing unit (CPU): The heart of the computer, this is the component that actually executes instructions.

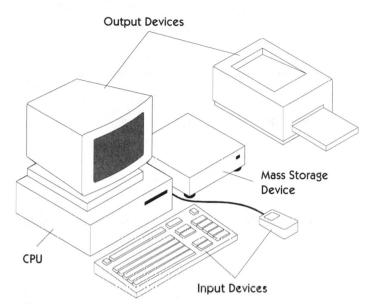

Figure 18: *Computers*

In addition to these components, many others make it possible for the basic components to work together efficiently. For example, every computer requires a bus that transmits data from one part of the computer to another.

Computers can be classified by size and power as follows:

personal computer: A small, single-user computer based on a microprocessor. In addition to the microprocessor, a personal computer has a keyboard for entering data, a monitor for displaying information, and a storage device for saving data.

workstation: A powerful, single-user computer. A workstation is like a personal computer, but it has a more powerful microprocessor and a higher-quality monitor.

minicomputer: A multi-user computer capable of supporting from 10 to hundreds of users simultaneously.

mainframe: A powerful multi-user computer capable of supporting many hundreds of users simultaneously.

supercomputer: An extremely fast computer that can perform hundreds of millions of instructions per second.

➡ See also *CPU; hardware; mainframe; microprocessor; minicomputer; personal computer; software; supercomputer; workstation.*

computer-aided design: See *CAD.*

computer-aided engineering: See *CAE.*

computer-aided instruction: Same as *computer-based training.* See under *CBT.*

computer-aided manufacturing: See *CAM.*

computer-based training: See *CBT.*

Computer Graphics Metafile: See *CGM.*

computer literacy: The level of expertise and familiarity someone has with computers. Computer literacy generally refers to the ability to use applications rather than to program. Individuals who are very computer literate are sometimes called *power users.*

➡ See also *power user.*

computer science: The study of computers, including both hardware and software design. Computer science is composed of many broad disciplines, including artificial intelligence and software engineering. Most universities now offer bachelor, master, and doctorate degrees in computer science.

➡ See also *artificial intelligence; program.*

computer system: A complete, working computer. The computer system includes not only the computer, but also any software and peripheral devices that are necessary to make the computer function. Every computer system, for example, requires an operating system.

➠ See also *computer; operating system.*

concatenate: To link together or join. For example, concatenating the three words *in, as,* and *much* yields the single word *inasmuch.* Computer manuals often refer to the process of *concatenating strings,* a string being any series of characters. You can also concatenate files by appending one to another.

➠ See also *append; character string.*

concatenation: The act of linking together two or more objects.

➠ See also *concatenate.*

conditional: Referring to an action that takes place only if a specific condition is met. Conditional expressions are one of the most important components of programming languages because they enable a program to act differently each time it is executed, depending on the input. Most programming languages use the word *if* for conditional expressions. For example, the conditional statement:

    if x equals 1 exit

directs the program to exit if the variable x is equal to 1.

➠ See also *expression; programming language*

conference: Same as forum, an area in a bulletin board or online service in which participants can meet to discuss a topic of common interest.

➠ See also *bulletin board service; forum; online service.*

CONFIG.SYS: PC The configuration file for DOS systems. Whenever a DOS computer boots up, it reads the CONFIG.SYS file (if it exists) and executes any commands in it. The most common commands are *BUFFERS=* and *FILES=*, which enable you to specify the buffer size and the number of files that can be open simultaneously. In addition, you can enter commands that install drivers for devices.

➥ See also *boot; configuration; driver.*

configuration: The way a system is set up, or the assortment of components that make up the system. Configuration can refer to either hardware or software, or the combination of both. For instance, a typical configuration for a PC consists of 4MB (megabytes) main memory, a floppy drive, a hard disk, a VGA monitor, and the DOS and/or Windows operating system.

Many software products require that the computer have a certain *minimum configuration.* For example, the software might require a graphics display monitor and a video adapter, a particular microprocessor, and a minimum amount of main memory.

When you install a new device or program, you often need to configure it, which means to set various switches and jumpers (for hardware) and to define values of parameters (for software). For example, the device or program may need to know what type of video adapter you have and what type of printer is connected to the computer.

In DOS systems, you can configure the operating environment by placing commands in a file called *CONFIG.SYS.* These commands can install drivers for various devices. In the Macintosh operating systems, you configure the system through *control panels.* In the Windows operating system, you configure the system through the *Control Panel.*

➥ See also *CONFIG.SYS; control panel; DIP switch; jumper; parameter.*

configuration file: A file that contains configuration information for a particular program. When the program is executed, it consults the configuration file to see what parameters are in effect. The configuration file for DOS is called *CONFIG.SYS.* The Windows operating system stores configuration information in files with a *.INI* extension. The two most important configuration files are *WIN.INI* and *SYS.INI.*

➥ See also *CONFIG.SYS; configuration; .INI file.*

configure: To set up a program or computer system for a particular application.

➠ See also *configuration.*

connectivity: A computer buzzword that refers to a program or device's ability to link with other programs and devices. For example, a program that can *import* data from a wide variety of other programs and can *export* data in many different formats is said to have *good connectivity*. On the other hand, computers that have difficulty linking into a network (many laptop computers, for example) have *poor connectivity*.

➠ See also *export; import.*

connector: The part of a cable that plugs into a port or interface to connect one device to another. There are many types of connectors, some of the more common of which are shown in Figure 19. Most connectors are either *male* (containing one or more exposed pins) or *female* (containing holes in which the male connector can be inserted).

➠ See also *interface; port.*

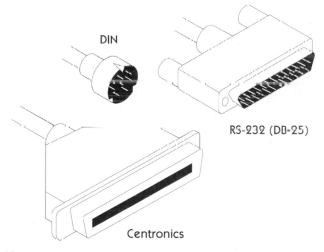

DIN

RS-232 (DB-25)

Centronics

Figure 19: *Connectors*

connect time: The amount of time a computer is logged in to a remote computer. Many online services charge users per connect time. Other services offer unlimited connect time for a flat monthly fee.

➠ See *online service.*

console: (1) The combination of display monitor and keyboard (or other device that allows input). Another term for console is *terminal.*

➠ See also *display screen; keyboard; terminal.*

(2) Another term for *monitor* or *display screen.*

(3) A bank of meters and lights indicating a computer's status, and switches that allow an operator to control the computer in some way.

constant: In programming, a constant is a value that never changes. The other type of values that programs use is *variables,* symbols that can represent different values throughout the course of a program.
A constant can be:

- a number, like 25 or 3.6
- a character, like *a* or $
- a character string, like "this is a string"

Constants are also used in spreadsheet applications to place non-changing values in cells. In contrast, a spreadsheet formula can produce a different value each time the spreadsheet is opened or changed.

➠ See also *character string; formula; variable.*

context sensitive: Refers to a program feature that changes depending on what you are doing in the program. For example, *context-sensitive help* provides documentation for the particular feature that you are in the process of using.

➠ See also *help.*

context switching: Same as *task switching.*

contiguous: Being immediately adjacent. For example, contiguous sectors on a disk are sectors that come one after the other. Frequently, a file stored on disk can become fragmented, which means that it is stored on non-contiguous sectors.

➠ See also *fragmentation.*

continuous-form paper: A type of printing paper which consists of a single sheet or roll of paper, normally perforated at regular intervals so that sheets can be easily separated. Most continuous-form paper has holes punched along each side so that the paper can be pulled through the printer by a tractor-feed mechanism.

➠ See also *paper feed; tractor feed.*

continuous tone: Refers to images that have a virtually unlimited range of color or shades of grays. Photographs and television images, for example, are continuous-tone images. In contrast, computer hardware and software is digital, which means that they can represent only a limited number of colors and gray levels. Converting a black-and-white continuous-tone image into a computer image is known as *gray scaling.*

➠ See also *digital; gray scaling; halftone.*

control character: A special, non-printing character. The ASCII character set defines 32 control characters, as shown in Table 11. Originally, these codes were designed to control teletype machines. Now, however, they are often used to control display monitors, printers, and other modern devices.

➠ See also *ASCII; Break key; Control key; keyboard.*

Control key: A key on PC keyboards labeled *Ctrl.* You use the Control key in the same way that you use the Shift key—keeping it pressed down while pressing another character. The result is a *control key combination,* which can have different meanings depending on which program is running.

Table 11
ASCII CONTROL CHARACTERS

OCT	DEC	HEX	CHAR	SYMBOL	MEANING
0	0	0	^@	NUL	Null
1	1	1	^A	SOH	Start of Heading
2	2	2	^B	STX	Start of Text
3	3	3	^C	ETX	End of Text
4	4	4	^D	EQT	End of Transmit
5	5	5	^E	ENQ	Enquiry
6	6	6	^F	ACK	Acknowledge
7	7	7	^G	BEL	Bell
10	8	8	^H	BS	Backspace
11	9	9	^I	HT	Horizontal Tab
12	10	A	^J	LF	Line Feed
13	11	B	^K	VT	Vertical Tab
14	12	C	^L	FF	Form Feed
15	13	D	^M	CR	Carriage Return
16	14	E	^N	SO	Shift Out
17	15	F	^O	SI	Shift In
20	16	10	^P	DLE	Data Link Escape
21	17	11	^Q	DC1	Device Control 1
22	18	12	^R	DC2	Device Control 2
23	19	13	^S	DC3	Device Control 3
24	20	14	^T	DC4	Device Control 4
25	21	15	^U	NAK	Negative Acknowledge
26	22	16	^V	SYN	Synchronous Idle
27	23	17	^W	ETB	End Transmit Block
30	24	18	^X	CAN	Cancel
31	25	19	^Y	EM	End of Medium
32	26	1A	^Z	SUB	Substitution
33	27	1B	^[	ESC	Escape
34	28	1C	^|	FS	Figures Shift
35	29	1D	^]	GS	Group Separator
36	30	1E	^^	RS	Record Separator
37	31	1F	^	US	Unit Separator

$\boxed{\text{MAC}}$ On Macintoshes, the Control key is called an *Apple key* or *Command key.*

➠ See also *Apple key; Command key; control key combination.*

Control key combination: A command issued by pressing a keyboard character in conjunction with the Control key. Manuals usually represent control key commands with the prefix *CTRL-* or *CNTL-*. For example, CTRL-N means the Control key and *N* pressed at the same time. Sometimes a control character is represented by a caret (for example, ^N is the same as CTRL-N).

What happens after you enter a Control key combination depends on what application is active. Certain Control key combinations are semi-standardized. For example, CTRL-C often has the same effect as the Break key—it interrupts a program. And Ctrl-X often exits the current application.

➠ See also *command; Control key.*

controller: A device that controls the transfer of data from a computer to a peripheral device and vice versa. For example, disk drives, display screens, keyboards, and printers all require controllers.

In personal computers, the controllers are often single chips. When you purchase a computer, it comes with all the necessary controllers for standard components, such as the display screen, keyboard, and disk drives. If you attach additional devices, however, you may need to insert new controllers that come on expansion boards.

Controllers must be designed to communicate with the computer's expansion bus. There are three standard bus architectures for PCs—the AT bus, the *Extended Industry Standard Architecture (EISA)*, and the SCSI bus. When you purchase a controller, therefore, you must ensure that it conforms to the bus architecture that your computer uses.

➠ See also *AT bus; bus; chip; CPU; driver; EISA; expansion board; peripheral device; printed circuit board; SCSI.*

control panel: $\boxed{\text{MAC}}$ A Macintosh utility that permits you to set many of the system parameters. For example, you can control the type of beeps the Mac makes and the sensitivity of the mouse. On older Macs (System 6 and earlier), control panels are called *cdevs.*

PC The Windows operating system has a Control Panel program that offers many of the same features as the Macintosh control panels.

➟ See also *cdev*.

control panel device: See *cdev*.

control program: (1) A program that enhances an operating system by creating an environment in which you can run other programs. Control programs generally provide a graphical interface and enable you to run several programs at once in different windows.
Control programs are also called *operating environments*.

➟ See also *graphical interface; Microsoft Windows; operating environment; operating system*.

(2) Another term for *operating system*.

conventional memory: PC On DOS systems, conventional memory refers to the portion of memory that is available to normal programs. DOS systems have an *address space* of 1MB (megabyte), but the top 384K (called *high memory*) is reserved for system use. This leaves 640K of conventional memory. Everything above 1MB is either *extended* or *expanded memory*.

➟ See also *expanded memory; extended memory; main memory*.

convergence: (1) The coming together of two or more disparate disciplines or technologies. For example, the so-called fax revolution was produced by a convergence of telecommunications technology, optical scanning technology, and printing technology.

(2) In graphics, convergence refers to how sharply an individual color pixel on a monitor appears. Each pixel is composed of three dots—a red, blue, and green one. If the dots are badly misconverged, the pixel will appear blurry. All monitors have some convergence errors, but they differ in degree.

➟ See also *graphics; monitor; pixel; RGB monitor*.

convert: To change data from one format to another.

➠ See also *export; import.*

cooperative multitasking: A type of multitasking in which the process currently controlling the CPU must offer control to other processes. It is called *cooperative* because all programs must cooperate for it to work. If one program does not cooperate, it can hog the CPU. In contrast, *preemptive multitasking* forces applications to share the CPU whether they want to or not. Both the Macintosh and Windows operating systems are based on cooperative multitasking, whereas UNIX is based on preemptive multitasking.

➠ See also *Microsoft Windows; multitasking; UNIX.*

coprocessor: A special-purpose processing unit that assists the CPU in performing certain types of operations. For example, a *math coprocessor* performs mathematical computations, particularly floating-point operations. Math coprocessors are also called *numeric* and *floating-point* coprocessors.

Some computers come with coprocessors built in. For others, you can add a coprocessor. A math coprocessor can increase a computer's speed and power dramatically, particularly if you are running programs that perform a lot of floating-point arithmetic (engineering and scientific applications, statistical analysis, and graphics). Note, however, that the program itself must be written to take advantage of the coprocessor. If the program contains no coprocessor instructions, the coprocessor will never be utilized.

In addition to math coprocessors, there are also *graphics coprocessors* for manipulating graphic images. These are often called *accelerator boards.*

➠ See also *accelerator board; CPU; floating-point number.*

copy: (v) (1) To copy a piece of data to a temporary location. In word processing, for example, *copying* refers to duplicating a section of a document and placing it in a *buffer* (sometimes called a *clipboard*). The term *copy* differs from *cut*, which refers to actually removing a section of a document and placing it in a buffer. After cutting or copying, you can move the contents of the buffer by *pasting* it somewhere else.

➠ See also *buffer; clipboard; cut; paste.*

(2) In file management, the term *copy* refers to making a duplicate of a file.

➠ See also *file management.*

(n) A duplicate of a piece of data, such as a file or a directory.

copy protection: Refers to techniques used to prevent the unauthorized copying of software. The idea of copy-protected software was created by software manufacturers who wanted to prevent *software piracy*—users copying programs and giving them to friends and colleagues free of charge.

As enticing an idea as it may be, copy protection has not proved to be a viable strategy. For one, it is practically impossible to create software that cannot be copied by a knowledgeable programmer. Second, many consumers shy away from copy-protected software because backup copies are difficult to make. Thus, if their original copy of the software is damaged, the user must contact the manufacturer for a new copy. Finally, some copy-protection techniques can actually damage other software on the system. For these reasons, copy-protected software is becoming less common.

Most software producers now protect their programs by issuing registration numbers with each package. When you install the software, you must enter the registration number. This does not prevent all piracy, but it limits it. In addition, users cannot get updates to a product unless they own the original diskettes and documentation.

An alternative strategy for dealing with the problem of software piracy is *shareware,* where users are actually encouraged to copy and disseminate programs. Shareware publishers rely on people's honesty to pay for the products used.

➠ See also *shareware; software piracy.*

corrupted: Refers to data that has been damaged in some way.

Courier font: A common monospaced (*fixed-pitch*) font. `This sentence is in Courier font.` Most printers support the Courier font.

➠ See also *fixed-pitch; font; monospacing.*

courseware: Software designed to be used in an educational program.

➠ See also *CBT.*

CP/M: Abbreviation of *Control Program for Microprocessors.* Created by Digital Research Corporation, CP/M was one of the first operating systems for personal computers. However, Digital Research Corporation made a critical strategic error by not agreeing to produce an operating system for the first IBM PC. According to the folklore, the president of Digital Research was flying his airplane when IBM came to call. IBM marched out and never looked back.

Instead, IBM turned to Microsoft Corporation, which developed MS-DOS. By the mid 1980s, MS-DOS had become the standard operating system for IBM-compatible personal computers. Although still used on some old models, CP/M is practically obsolete.

➠ See also *DOS; operating system.*

cps: Abbreviation of *characters per second,* a unit of measure used to describe the speed of dot-matrix and daisy-wheel printers. The speed of laser and ink-jet printers is described in terms of pages per minute (ppm)

➠ See also *printer.*

CPU: Abbreviation of *central processing unit,* and pronounced as separate letters. The CPU is the brains of the computer. Sometimes referred to simply as the *processor* or *central processor,* the CPU is where most calculations take place. In terms of computing power, the CPU is the most important element of a computer system.

On large machines, CPUs require one or more printed circuit boards. On personal computers and small workstations, the CPU is housed in a single chip called a *microprocessor.*

Two typical components of a CPU are:

- The *arithmetic logic unit (ALU)*, which performs arithmetic and logical operations.
- The *control unit*, which extracts instructions from memory and decodes and executes them, calling on the ALU when necessary.

➧ See also *chip*; *CISC*; *clock speed*; *coprocessor*; *Intel microprocessors*; *microprocessor*; *PowerPC*; *RISC*.

CPU time: The amount of time the CPU is actually executing instructions. During the execution of most programs, the CPU sits idle much of the time while the computer fetches data from the keyboard or disk, or sends data to an output device. The CPU time of an executing program, therefore, is generally much less than the total execution time of the program. Multitasking operating systems take advantage of this by sharing the CPU among several programs.

CPU times are used for a variety of purposes: to compare the speed of two different processors, to gauge how CPU-intensive a program is, and to measure the amount of processing time being allocated to different programs in a multitasking environment.

➧ See also *CPU*; *multitasking*.

crash: (n) A serious computer failure. A *computer crash* means that the computer itself stops working or that a program *aborts* unexpectedly. A crash signifies either a hardware malfunction or a very serious software bug.

If your computer crashes, it is not your fault. If the program is good and your hardware is functioning properly, there is nothing you can do to make your system crash.

(v) To fail or break. Other terms for *crash* include *hang* and *bomb*.

➧ See also *bomb*; *bug*; *hang*; *head crash*.

CRC: Abbreviation of *cyclic redundancy check*, a common technique for detecting data transmission errors. A number of file transfer protocols, including Zmodem, use CRC in addition to *checksum*.

➧ See also *checksum*; *communications protocol*; *error detection*; *Zmodem*.

crippled version: A demonstration version of a piece of software that has one or more critical features disabled. Many software companies distribute crippled versions of their applications free with the hope that users will get hooked and buy the full version.

crop: In computer graphics, to cut off the sides of an image to make it the proper size or to remove unwanted parts. Most graphics applications allow you to crop images with a *clip* feature.

➠ See also *clip.*

crop marks: Printed or drawn lines indicating where the paper should be cut to produce the correct page size. Crop marks are necessary for offset printing because the original paper that goes through the printing press is usually larger than the final page size. Many desktop publishing systems are capable of automatically printing crop marks for camera-ready copy.

➠ See also *camera-ready; desktop publishing; offset printing.*

cross-platform: Refers to the capability of software or hardware to run identically on different platforms. Many applications for Windows and the Macintosh, for example, now produce binary-compatible files, which means that users can switch from one platform to the other without converting their data to a new format.

Cross-platform computing is becoming increasingly important as local-area networks become better at linking machines of different types.

➠ See also *binary compatible; local-area network; platform.*

CRT: Abbreviation of *cathode-ray tube,* the technology used in most televisions and computer display screens. A CRT works by moving an electron beam back and forth across the back of the screen. Each time the beam makes a pass across the screen, it lights up phosphor dots on the inside of the glass tube, thereby illuminating the active portions of the screen (Figure 20). By drawing many such lines from the top to the bottom of the screen, it creates an entire screenful of images.

➠ See also *display screen; monitor; refresh.*

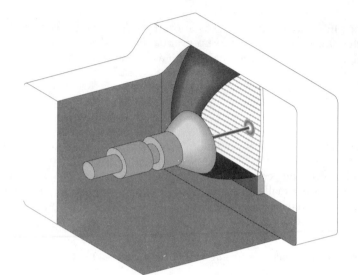

Figure 20: CRT

Ctrl: See under *Control key combination.*

current: Refers to an object that is acting as a reference point. For example, the *current directory* is the same as the *working directory* or *default directory.* The *current drive* is the *default mass storage device.* In a spreadsheet application, the *current cell* is the *active cell,* the cell that you are manipulating at the moment.

➠ See also *active; default; working directory.*

cursor: (1) A special symbol, usually a solid rectangle or a blinking underline character, that signifies where the next character will be displayed on the screen. To type in different areas of the screen, you need to move the cursor. You can do this with the arrow keys, or with a mouse if your program supports it.

If you are running a graphics-based program, the cursor may appear as a small arrow, called a *pointer*. (The terms *cursor* and *pointer* are often used interchangeably.) In text processing, a cursor sometimes appears as an *I-beam pointer*, a special type of pointer that always appears between two characters. Note also that programs that support a mouse may use two cursors: a *text cursor*, which indicates where characters from the keyboard will be entered, and a *mouse cursor* for selecting items with the mouse.

➠ See also *arrow keys; pointer.*

(2) A device, similar in appearance to a mouse, that is used to sketch lines on a digitizing tablet. Cursors for digitizing tablets are sometimes called *pucks*.

➠ See also *digitizing tablet; mouse.*

cursor control keys: Special keys on computer keyboards that move the cursor. The arrow keys, for example, move the cursor up, down, right, and left. In addition, most keyboards have *End, Home, Page Up, Page Down,* and *Backspace* keys.

➠ See also *arrow keys; cursor; keyboard.*

cursor position: The position of the cursor on the display screen. While in text mode, a display screen is capable of displaying a certain number of lines and a certain number of characters on each line. The cursor position is represented by the *line number* and the *character number* and signifies where the next character will be displayed. For example, cursor position 1,1 always indicates the upper-leftmost corner position on the terminal. Cursor position 10,30 indicates the 30th character position on the 10th line.

➠ See also *cursor; display screen; text mode.*

customer support: Service that computer and software manufacturers, and third-party service companies, offer to customers. For personal computer products, the following are common customer-support options:

mail-in service: The manufacturer will repair your equipment if you mail it in. Typical turnaround time is about four days. In some service plans, the manufacturer charges you for shipping expenses.

carry-in service: The manufacturer will repair your equipment, but you must deliver it to a local service site. This is sometimes called *depot service.*

on-site contract: For a monthly or annual fee, a repair person will come to your site to fix problems. (The fee is included in the purchase price of some machines.) Most on-site contracts guarantee that the service will be rendered within a fixed number of hours from when you report a problem.

hot lines: Many software manufacturers provide a phone number that you can call for advice and trouble-shooting. Often the number is toll-free. The quality of this type of support varies considerably from one company to another. Some hot lines are so good that they enable you to solve most problems yourself. Others are so bad that you are unable even to get through.

bulletin board system: Some companies maintain electronic bulletin boards (or forums within online services) staffed by service engineers. If you have a modem, you can report a problem to the bulletin board and a technician will respond. This can be convenient because bulletin boards are usually open 24 hours a day. Also, bulletin boards enable you to download software updates that correct known bugs.

➠ See also *bulletin board system; download.*

cut: To remove an object from a document and place it in a *buffer.* In word processing, for example, *cut* means to move a section of text from a document to a temporary buffer. This is one way to delete text. However, because the text is transferred to a buffer, it is not lost forever. You can copy the buffer somewhere else in the document or in another document, which is called *pasting.* To move a section of text from one place to another, therefore, you need to first cut it and then paste it. This is often called *cut-and-paste.*

Most applications have only one buffer, sometimes called a *clipboard.* If you make two cuts in succession, the text from the original cut will be replaced by the text from the second cut.

Graphical user interfaces, such as MS-Windows and the Macintosh interface, allow you to cut and paste graphics as well as text.

➠ See also *buffer; clipboard; paste.*

cut-sheet feeder: See under *sheet feeder.*

cyber: A prefix used in a growing number of terms to describe new things that are being made possible by the spread of computers. Cyberphobia, for example, is an irrational fear of computers. Cyberpunk is a genre of science fiction that draws heavily on computer science ideas. Cyberspace is the non-physical terrain created by computer systems.

➠ See also *cyberspace; virtual reality.*

cyberspace: A metaphor for describing the non-physical terrain created by computer systems. Online systems, for example, create a cyberspace within which people can communicate with one another (via e-mail), do research, or simply window shop. Like physical space, cyberspace contains *objects* (files, mail messages, graphics, etc.) and different modes of transportation and delivery. Unlike real space, though, exploring cyberspace does not require any physical movement other than pressing keys on a keyboard or moving a mouse.

Some programs, particularly computer games, are designed to create a special cyberspace, one that resembles physical reality in some ways but defies it in others. In its extreme form, called *virtual reality,* users are presented with visual, auditory, and even tactile feedback that makes cyberspace feel real.

➠ See also *information highway; online service; virtual reality.*

cycle time: A measurement of how quickly two back-to-back accesses of a memory chip can be made. Note that a DRAM chip's cycle time is usually much longer than its access time, which measures only a single access. This is because DRAM chips require a pause between accesses.

➠ See also *access time; DRAM; SRAM.*

cyclic redundancy check: See under CRC.

cylinder: A single track location on all the *platters* making up a hard disk. For example, if a hard disk has four platters, each with 600 tracks, then there will be 600 cylinders, and each cylinder will consist of 8 tracks (2 for each platter).

➠ See also *hard disk; platter; track.*

DA: MAC Pronounced as separate letters, *DA* stands for *desk accessory.* See under *desk accessory.*

daisy chain: (n) A hardware configuration in which devices are connected one to another in a series. The *SCSI interface,* for example, supports a daisy chain of up to 7 devices.

➡ See also *SCSI.*

(v) To connect devices in a daisy chain pattern.

daisy-wheel printer: A type of printer that produces letter-quality type. A daisy-wheel printer works on the same principle as a ball-head typewriter. The daisy wheel is a disk made of plastic or metal on which characters stand out in relief along the outer edge. To print a character, the printer rotates the disk until the desired letter is facing the paper. Then a hammer strikes the disk, forcing the character to hit an ink ribbon, leaving an impression of the character on the paper. You can change the daisy wheel to print different fonts.

Daisy-wheel printers cannot print graphics, and in general they are noisy and slow, printing from 10 to about 75 characters per second. As the price of laser ink-jet printers has declined, and the quality of dot-matrix printers has improved, daisy-wheel printers have become almost obsolete.

➡ See also *printer.*

DAT: Acronym for *digital audio tape,* a type of magnetic tape that uses an ingenious scheme called *helical scan* to record data. A DAT cartridge is slightly larger than a credit card and contains a magnetic tape that can hold from 2 to 5 gigabytes of data. It can support data transfer rates of about 10 megabytes per minute. Like other types of tapes, DATs are *sequential-access* media.

The most common format for DAT cartridges is *DDS (digital data storage)*.

➤ See also *gigabyte; mass storage; megabyte; sequential access; tape.*

data: (1) Information, usually formatted in a special way. All software is divided into two general categories: *data* and *programs*. Programs are collections of instructions for manipulating data.

Data can exist in a variety of forms—as numbers or text on pieces of paper, as bits and bytes stored in electronic memory, or as facts stored in a person's mind.

Strictly speaking, data is the plural of *datum*, a single piece of information. In practice, however, people use *data* as both the singular and plural form of the word.

➤ See also *program; software.*

(2) The term *data* is often used to distinguish binary machine-readable information from textual human-readable information. For example, some applications make a distinction between *data files* (files that contain binary data) and *text files* (files that contain ASCII data).

➤ See also *binary; ASCII.*

(3) In database management systems, data files are the files that store the database information, whereas other files, such as index files and data dictionaries, store administrative information.

➤ See also *database management system; data dictionary.*

database: (1) A collection of information organized in such a way that a computer program can quickly select desired pieces of data. You can think of a database as an electronic filing system.

Traditional databases are organized by *fields, records,* and *files.* A field is a single piece of information; a record is one complete set of fields; and a file is a collection of records. For example, a telephone book is analogous to a file. It contains a list of records, each of which consists of three fields: name, address, and telephone number (Figure 21).

An alternative concept in database design is known as *Hypertext*. In a Hypertext database, any object, whether it be a piece of text, a picture, or a film, can be linked to any other object. Hypertext databases are particularly useful for organizing large amounts of disparate information, but they are not designed for numerical analysis.

To access information from a database, you need a *database management system (DBMS)*. This is a collection of programs that enables you to enter, organize, and select data in a database.

➠ See also *database management system; field; file; Hypertext; record; relational database.*

(2) Increasingly, the term *database* is used as shorthand for *database management system.*

➠ See also *database management system..*

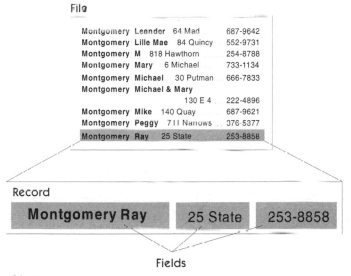

File

Montgomery	Leander	64 Mad	687-9642
Montgomery	Lille Mae	84 Quincy	552-9731
Montgomery	M	818 Hawthorn	254-8788
Montgomery	Mary	6 Michael	733-1134
Montgomery	Michael	30 Putman	666-7833
Montgomery	Michael & Mary		
		130 E 4	222-4896
Montgomery	Mike	140 Quay	687-9621
Montgomery	Peggy	711 Narrows	376-5377
Montgomery	Ray	25 State	253-8858

Record

Montgomery Ray   25 State   253-8858

Fields

Figure 21: *Database*

database management system (DBMS): A collection of programs that enables you to store, modify, and extract information from a database. There are many different types of DBMSs, ranging from small systems that run on personal computers to huge systems that run on mainframes. The following are examples of database applications:

- computerized library systems
- automated teller machines
- flight reservation systems
- computerized parts inventory systems

From a technical standpoint, DBMSs can differ widely. The terms *relational*, *network*, *flat*, and *hierarchical* all refer to the way a DBMS organizes information internally. The internal organization can affect how quickly and flexibly you can extract information.

Requests for information from a database are made in the form of a *query*, which is a stylized question. For example, the query

SELECT ALL WHERE NAME = "SMITH" AND AGE > 35

requests all records in which the NAME field is SMITH and the AGE field is greater than 35. The set of rules for constructing queries is known as a *query language*. Different DBMSs support different query languages, although there is a semi-standardized query language called *SQL* (*structured query language*). Sophisticated languages for managing database systems are called *fourth-generation languages*, or *4GLs* for short.

The information from a database can be presented in a variety of formats. Most DBMSs include a *report writer program* that enables you to output data in the form of a report. Many DBMSs also include a graphics component that enables you to output information in the form of graphs and charts.

➧ See also *database; flat-file database; fourth-generation language; Hypertext; query; relational database; report writer; SQL*

data bus: See under *bus.*

data communications: See *communications.*

data compression: Storing data in a format that requires less space than usual. *Compressing* data is the same as *packing* data.

Data compression is particularly useful in communications because it enables devices to transmit the same amount of data in fewer bits. There are a variety of data compression techniques, but only a few have been standardized. The CCITT has defined a standard data compression technique for transmitting faxes (Group 3 standard) and a compression standard for data communications through modems (CCITT V.42*bis*). In addition, there are file compression formats, such as ARC and ZIP.

Data compression is also widely used in backup utilities, spreadsheet applications, and database management systems. Certain types of data, such as bit-mapped graphics, can be compressed to a small fraction of their normal size.

In recent years, *compression boards* have appeared in the marketplace. These are expansion boards that automatically compress data as it is written to a disk and then decompress the data when it is fetched. The data compression is invisible to the user, but can effectively double or triple the capacity of a disk drive.

➠ See also *ARC; CCITT; JPEG; MNP; ZIP.*

data dictionary: In database management systems, a file that defines the basic organization of a database. A data dictionary contains a list of all files in the database, the number of records in each file, and the names and types of each field. Most database management systems keep the data dictionary hidden from users to prevent them from accidentally destroying its contents.

Data dictionaries do not contain any actual data from the database, only bookkeeping information for managing it. Without a data dictionary, however, a database management system cannot access data from the database.

➠ See also *database management system.*

data encryption: See under *encryption.*

data entry: The process of entering data into a computerized database or spreadsheet. Data entry can be performed by an individual typing at a keyboard or by a machine entering data electronically.

➠ See also *database; spreadsheet.*

data processing: Refers to a class of programs that organize and manipulate data, usually large amounts of numeric data. Accounting programs are the prototypical examples of data processing applications. In contrast, word processors, which manipulate text rather than numbers, are not usually referred to as data processing applications.

➠ See also *accounting software; application.*

data rate: Short for *data transfer rate.*

data structure: In programming, the term *data structure* refers to a scheme for organizing related pieces of information. The basic types of data structures include:

- files
- lists
- arrays
- records
- trees
- tables

Each of these basic structures has many variations and allows different operations to be performed on the data.

➠ See also *array; file; record; tree structure.*

data transfer rate: The speed with which data can be transmitted from one device to another. Data rates are often measured in *megabits* (million bits) or *megabytes* (million bytes) *per second.*
Another term for data transfer rate is *throughput.*

➠ See also *access time.*

data type: In programming, classification of a particular type of information. It is easy for humans to distinguish between different types of data. We can usually tell at a glance whether a number is a percentage, a time, or an amount of money. We do this through special symbols—%, :, and $—that indicate the data's *type.* Similarly, a computer uses special symbols to keep track of the different types of data it processes.
Most programming languages require the programmer to declare the data type of every data object, and most database systems require the user to specify the type of each data field. The available data types

vary from one programming language to another, and from one database application to another, but the following usually exist in one form or another:

integer: In more common parlance, whole number; a number that has no fractional part.

floating-point: A number with a decimal point. For example, 3 is an integer, but 3.5 is a floating-point number.

character (text): Readable text.

➥ See also *character; database; declare; field; floating-point number; integer; variable.*

dBASE: A popular database management system produced by Ashton Tate Corporation. The original version, called *Vulcan*, was created by Wayne Ratliff. In 1981, Ashton-Tate bought Vulcan and marketed it as dBASE II. Subsequent versions with additional features are known as dBASE III, dBASE III+, and dBASE IV, all of which are currently owned and developed by Borland Corporation.

The dBASE format for storing data has become a de facto standard, and is supported by nearly all database management and spreadsheet systems. Even systems that do not use the dBASE format internally are able to import and export data in dBASE format.

➥ See also *database management system; export; import.*

DBMS: See *database management system.*

DDE: Acronym for *Dynamic Data Exchange,* an *interprocess communication (IPC)* system built into the Macintosh, Windows, and OS/2 operating systems. DDE enables two running applications to share the same data. For example, DDE makes it possible to insert a spreadsheet chart into a document created with a word processor. Whenever the spreadsheet data changes, the chart in the document changes accordingly.

Although the DDE mechanism is still used by many applications, it is being supplanted by OLE, which provides greater control over shared data.

➠ See also *interprocess communication; OLE.*

debug: To find and remove errors (*bugs*) from a program or design.

➠ See also *bug.*

debugger: A special program used to find errors (*bugs*) in other programs. A debugger allows a programmer to stop a program at any point and examine and change the values of variables.

➠ See also *bug.*

decimal: Refers to numbers in base 10 (the numbers we use in everyday life). For example, the following are decimal numbers:

```
9
100345000
-256
```

Note that a decimal number is not necessarily a number with a decimal point in it. Numbers with decimal points (that is, numbers with a fractional part) are called *fixed-point* or *floating-point numbers.*
  In addition to the decimal format, computer data is often represented in binary, octal, and hexadecimal formats.

➠ See also *binary; floating-point number; hexadecimal; integer; octal.*

declare: In programming, *to declare* is to define the name and data type of a variable or other programming construct. Many programming languages, including C and Pascal, require you to declare variables before using them.

➠ See also *data type; programming language; variable.*

decrement: To subtract. For example, if you count down consecutively from 10 to 0, you decrement by 1. If you count down by twos, you decrement by 2. The opposite of decrementing is *incrementing*.

➠ See also *increment*.

decryption: The process of decoding data that has been *encrypted* into a secret format. Decryption requires a secret *key* or *password*.

➠ See also *encryption; security*.

dedicated: Reserved for just one use. In communications, a *dedicated channel* is a line reserved exclusively for one type of communication. This is the same as a *leased line* or *private line*.

A *dedicated server* is a single computer in a network reserved for serving the needs of the network. For example, some networks require that one computer be set aside to manage communications between all the other computers. A dedicated server could also be a computer that manages printer resources. Note, however, that not all servers are dedicated. In some networks, it is possible for a computer to act as a server and perform other functions as well.

The opposite of dedicated is *general purpose*.

➠ See also *channel; expansion slot; network; server*.

de facto standard: A format, language, or protocol that has become a standard not because it has been approved by a standards organization but because it is widely used and recognized by the industry as being standard. Some examples of de facto standards include:

- Hayes command set for controlling modems
- Kermit Communications Protocol
- Xmodem Communications Protocol
- Hewlett-Packard Printer Control Language (PCL) for laser printers.
- PostScript page description language for laser printers

➠ See also *Hayes compatible; Kermit; PCL; PostScript; standard; Xmodem*.

default: A value or setting that a device or program automatically selects if you do not specify a substitute. For example, word processors have default margins and default page lengths that you can override or reset.

The *default drive* is the disk drive the computer accesses unless you specify a different disk drive. Likewise, the *default directory* is the directory the operating system searches unless you specify a different directory.

The default can also be an action that a device or program will take. For example, some word processors generate backup files *by default.*

defragment: To optimize a disk by unfragmenting files. See also *fragmentation.*

delete: To remove or erase. For example, deleting a character means removing it from a file or erasing it from the display screen. Deleting a file means erasing it from a disk. Unlike cutting, deleting does not necessarily place the removed object in a buffer from where it can be recovered.

➠ See also *cut.*

Delete key: Often abbreviated as *Del,* the Delete key is used to remove characters and other objects.

PC On PCs, the Delete key generally removes the character immediately under the cursor (or to the right of the insertion point), or the highlighted text or object. Note the difference between the Delete key, which deletes the character under the cursor, and the Backspace key, which deletes the character to the left of the cursor or insertion point.

MAC On Macintoshes, the Delete key generally acts like a PC's Backspace key, deleting the character immediately in front of the insertion point.

➠ See also *backspace; insertion point; keyboard.*

delimiter: A punctuation character or group of characters that separates two names or two pieces of data, or marks the beginning or end of a programming construct. Delimiters are used in almost every computer application. For example, in specifying DOS *pathnames,* the backslash (\) is the delimiter that separates directories and filenames. Other common delimiters include the comma (‚), semicolon (;), quotes ("), and braces ({}).

➠ See also *pathname*.

demand paging: In virtual memory systems, demand paging is a type of *swapping* in which pages of data are not copied from disk to RAM until they are needed. In contrast, some virtual memory systems use *anticipatory paging*, in which the operating system attempts to anticipate which data will be needed next and copies it to RAM before it is actually required.

➠ See also *paging; RAM; swap; virtual memory*.

Table 12
FLOPPY DISK DENSITIES

	5¼ INCHES		
	SINGLE	DOUBLE	HIGH
IBM	360K	720K	1.2MB
MAC	NA	NA	NA

	3½ INCHES		
	SINGLE	DOUBLE	HIGH
IBM	NA	720K	1.44MB
MAC	400K	800K	1.2MB

density: How tightly information is packed together on a storage medium (tape or disk). A higher density means that data are closer together, so the medium can hold more information. Floppy disks can be *single-density, double-density, high-density,* or *extra-high-density.* To use a double-density, high-density, or extra-high-density disk, you must have a disk drive that supports the density level. *Density,* therefore, can refer both to the media and the device.

Table 12 shows the storage capacities of double- and high-density floppies on the PC and the Apple Macintosh. Note that the only difference between double-density and high-density disks is that the high-density disks were found to be higher quality during the testing process. High-quality disks are sold as high-density, and lower-quality disks are sold as double-density. It is often possible, therefore, to format a double-density disk as a high-density disk, but this practice is not encouraged.

➦ See also *disk; disk drive; double-density disk; FDHD; floppy disk; high-density disk.*

descender: In typography, the portion of a lowercase letter that falls below the baseline. In the English alphabet, 5 letters have descenders: *g, j, p, q,* and *y.*

➦ See also *ascender; baseline; x-height.*

desk accessory (DA): MAC On Apple Macintoshes, a utility—that is, a small, stand-alone program designed to perform one small task. For example, Apple's Calculator is a desk accessory.

➦ See also *utility.*

desktop: In graphical user interfaces, a *desktop* is the metaphor used to portray file systems. Such a desktop consists of pictures, called *icons*, that show cabinets, files, folders, and various types of documents (that is, letters, reports, pictures). You can arrange the icons on the electronic desktop just as you can arrange real objects on a real desktop—moving them around, putting one on top of another, reshuffling them, and throwing them away (Figure 22).

➦ See also *graphical user interface.*

desktop model computer: A computer designed to fit comfortably on top of a desk, typically with the monitor sitting on top of the computer. Desktop model computers are broad and low, whereas *tower model* computers are narrow and tall. Because of their shape, desktop model computers are generally limited to three internal mass storage

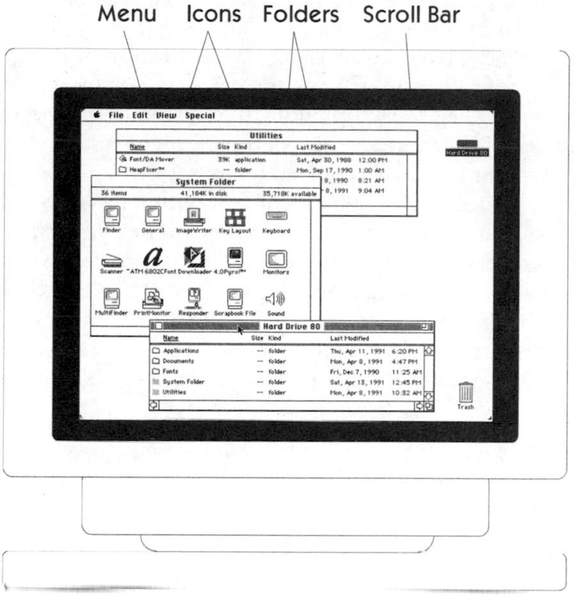
Menu
Icons
Folders
Scroll Bar
File Edit View Special
Utilities
System Folder
Hard Drive 80
Trash

Figure 22: *Macintosh Desktop*

devices. Desktop models designed to be very small are sometimes referred to as *slimline models*.

➡ See also *tower model.*

desktop publishing: Using a personal computer or workstation to produce high-quality printed documents. A desktop publishing system allows you to use different typefaces, specify various margins and justifications, and embed illustrations and graphs directly into the text. The most powerful desktop publishing systems enable you to create illustrations, while less powerful systems let you insert illustrations created by other programs.

As word-processing programs become more and more powerful, the line separating such programs from desktop publishing systems is becoming blurred. In general, though, desktop publishing applications give you more control over typographical characteristics, such as kerning, and provide more support for full-color output.

A particularly important feature of desktop publishing systems is that they enable you to see on the display screen exactly how the document will appear when printed. Systems that support this feature are called *WYSIWYGs* (*what you see is what you get*).

Until recently, hardware costs made desktop publishing systems impractical for most uses. But as the prices of personal computers and printers have fallen, desktop publishing systems have become increasingly popular for producing newsletters, brochures, books, and other documents that formerly required a typesetter.

Once you have produced a document with a desktop publishing system, you can output it directly to a printer or you can produce a PostScript file which you can then take to a service bureau. The service bureau has special machines that convert the PostScript file to film, which can then be used to make plates for offset printing. Offset printing produces higher-quality documents, especially if color is used, but is generally more expensive than laser printing.

➠ See *offset printing; page layout program; service bureau.*

destination: Many computer commands move data from one file to another or from one storage device to another. This is referred to as moving the data from the *source* to the *destination* (or *target*). The term is also used as an adjective, as in *destination file* or *destination device.*

device: Any machine or component that attaches to a computer. Examples of devices include disk drives, printers, mice, and modems. These particular devices fall into the category of peripheral devices because they are separate from the main computer. Display monitors and keyboards are also devices, but because they are integral parts of the computer, they are not considered peripheral.

Every device, whether peripheral or not, requires a program called a *device driver* that acts as a translator, converting general commands from an application into specific commands that the device understands.

➠ See also *computer; CONFIG.SYS; driver.*

device dependent: Like *machine dependent, device dependent* refers to programs that can run only on a certain type of hardware.

➠ See also *machine dependent.*

device driver: See *driver*.

dialog box: A box that appears on a display screen to present information or request input (Figure 23). Typically, dialog boxes are temporary—they disappear once you have entered the requested information.

In the Macintosh and Microsoft Windows interfaces, there is a convention that any menu option followed by ellipsis points (...) will, when selected, bring up a dialog box. Options without ellipsis points are executed directly.

➮ See also *box; graphical user interface; pop-up window; window.*

Dialog Box

Figure 23: *Dialog Box*

digital: Describes any system based on discontinuous data or events. Computers are digital machines because at their most basic level they can distinguish between just two values, 0 and 1, or off and on. There is no simple way to represent all the values in between, such as 0.25.

All data that a computer processes must be encoded digitally, as a series of zeroes and ones.

The opposite of digital is *analog*. A typical analog device is a clock in which the hands move continuously around the face. Such a clock is capable of indicating every possible time of day. In contrast, a digital clock is capable of representing only a finite number of times (every tenth of a second, for example). (See Figure 3 at *analog*.)

In general, humans experience the world analogically. Vision, for example, is an analog experience because we perceive infinitely smooth gradations of shapes and colors. Most analog events, however, can be simulated digitally. Photographs in newspapers, for instance, consist of an array of dots that are either black or white. From afar, the viewer does not see the dots (the digital form), but only lines and shading, which appear to be continuous. Although digital representations are approximations of analog events, they are useful because they are relatively easy to store and manipulate electronically. The trick is in converting from analog to digital, and back again.

This is the principle behind *compact discs (CDs)*. The music itself exists in an analog form, as waves in the air, but these sounds are then translated into a digital form that is encoded onto the disk. When you play a compact disc, the CD player reads the digital data, translates it back into its original analog form, and sends it to the amplifier and eventually the speakers.

Internally, computers are digital because they consist of discrete units called *bits* that are either on or off. But by combining many bits in complex ways, computers simulate analog events. In one sense, this is what computer science is all about.

➠ See also *analog; modem.*

digital audio tape: See *DAT.*

digital camera: A camera that stores images digitally rather than recording them on film. Once a picture has been taken, it can be downloaded to a computer system, and then manipulated with a graphics program and printed. Unlike film photographs, which have an almost infinite resolution, digital photos are limited by the amount of memory in the camera, the optical resolution of the digitizing mechanism, and, finally, the resolution of the final output device. Even the best digital cameras connected to the best printers cannot produce film-quality photos. However, if the final output device is a laser printer, it doesn't really matter whether you take a real photo and then scan it, or take a digital photo. In both cases, the image must eventually be reduced to the resolution of the printer.

The big advantage of digital cameras is that making photos is both inexpensive and fast because there is no film processing. Interestingly, one of the biggest boosters of digital photography is Kodak, the largest producer of film. Kodak developed the Kodak PhotoCD format, which has become the de facto standard for storing digital photographs.

➠ See also *digital; PhotoCD.*

digital monitor: A monitor that accepts digital rather than analog signals. All monitors (except flat-panel displays) use CRT technology, which is essentially analog. The term *digital,* therefore, refers only to the type of input received from the video adapter. A digital monitor then translates the digital signals into analog signals that control the actual display.

Although digital monitors are fast and produce clear images, they cannot display continuously variable colors. Consequently, only low-quality video standards, such as *MDA, CGA,* and *EGA,* specify digital signals. *VGA* and *SVGA,* on the other hand, require an analog monitor. Some monitors are capable of accepting either analog or digital signals.

➠ See also *analog; analog monitor; digital; monitor; video adapter.*

digital signal processing: See *DSP.*

Digital Video Interactive: See *DVI.*

digitize: To translate into a digital form. For example, optical scanners digitize images by translating them into bit maps. It is also possible to digitize sound, video, and any type of movement. In all these cases, digitization is performed by sampling at discrete intervals. To digitize sound, for example, a device measures pitch and volume many times per second. These numeric values can then be recorded digitally.

➠ See also *bit map; digital; optical scanner; sampling.*

digitizing tablet: An input device that enables you to enter drawings and sketches into a computer. A digitizing tablet consists of an *electronic tablet* and a *cursor* or *pen*. A cursor (also called a *puck*) is similar to a mouse, except that it has a window with cross hairs for pinpoint placement, and it can have as many as 16 buttons. A pen (also called a *stylus*) looks like a simple ballpoint pen but uses an electronic head instead of ink. The tablet contains electronics that enable it to detect movement of the cursor or pen and translate the movements into digital signals that it sends to the computer.

For digitizing tablets, each point on the tablet represents a point on the display screen in a fixed manner. This differs from mice, in which all movement is relative to the current cursor position. The static nature of digitizing tablets makes them particularly effective for tracing drawings. Most modern digitizing tablets also support a *mouse emulation mode*, in which the pen or cursor acts like a mouse.

Digitizing tablets are also called *digitizers, graphics tablets, touch tablets*, or simply *tablets*.

➠ See also *cursor; input device; mouse.*

DIN connector: *DIN* is an acronym for *Deutsche Industrinorm*, the standards-setting organization for Germany. A DIN connector is a connector that conforms to one of the many standards defined by DIN. DIN connectors are used widely in personal computers. For example, the keyboard connector for PCs is a DIN connector (see Figure 19 at *connector*).

➠ See also *connector.*

dingbat: A small picture, such as a star or a pointing finger, that can be inserted into a document (Figure 24). Many sets of dingbats are available as a special font. One of the most popular is *Zapf dingbats*, named after its creator, Hermann Zapf.

➠ See also *font.*

DIP: Acronym for *dual in-line package*, a type of *chip* housed in a rectangular casing with two rows of connecting pins on either side.

➠ See also *chip.*

Figure 24: *Dingbats*

DIP switch: A DIP (dual in-line package) switch is a series of tiny switches built into circuit boards (Figure 25). The housing for the switches, which has the same shape as a chip, is the DIP.

DIP switches enable you to configure a circuit board for a particular type of computer or application. The installation instructions should tell you how to set the switches. DIP switches are always toggle switches, which means they have two possible positions—on or off. (Instead of on and off, you may see the numbers 1 and 0.)

One of the historic advantages of the Macintosh over the PC was that it allowed you to configure circuit boards by entering software commands instead of setting DIP switches. However, the new Plug & Play standard developed by Microsoft makes DIP switches obsolete for PC expansion cards too.

➡ See also *chip; configuration; expansion board; printed circuit board; toggle.*

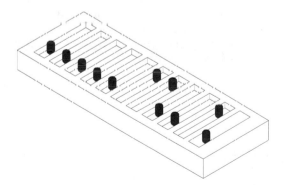

Figure 25: *DIP Switches*

direct access: Same as *random access.*

direct-connect modem: A modem that connects directly to a tele-phone line via modular connectors rather than requiring an acoustic coupler. Almost all modern modems are direct-connect.

➠ See also *acoustic coupler; modem.*

directive: ➠Same as *command.*

direct memory access: See *DMA.*

directory: A special kind of file used to organize other files into a hier-archical structure. Directories contain bookkeeping information about files that are, figuratively speaking, beneath them. You can think of a directory as a folder or cabinet that contains files and per-haps other folders. In fact, many graphical user interfaces, such as the Macintosh interface, use the term *folder* instead of *directory.*

Computer manuals often describe directories and file structures in terms of an *inverted tree,* as shown in Figure 26. The files and directo-ries at any level are contained in the directory above them. To access a file, you may need to specify the names of all the directories above it. You do this by specifying a *path.*

The topmost directory in any file is called the *root directory.* A direc-tory that is below another directory is called a *subdirectory.* A direc-tory above a subdirectory is called the *parent directory.*

To read information from, or write information into, a directory, you must use an operating system command. You cannot directly edit directory files. For example, the DIR command in DOS reads a direc-tory file and displays its contents.

➠ See also *file; file management system; folder; hierarchical; path; root directory; tree structure.*

disc: Alternative spelling of *disk. Disc* is often used for optical discs, while *disk* generally refers to magnetic discs, but there is no real rule.

➠ See also *disk; optical disk.*

144

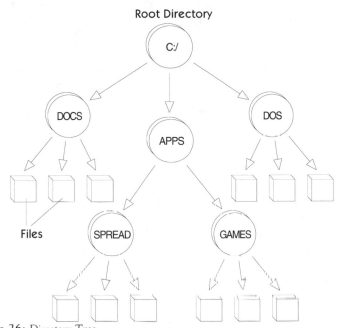

Figure 26: *Directory Tree*

discretionary hyphen: See under *hyphenation.*

disk: A round plate on which data can be encoded. There are two basic types of disks: *magnetic disks* and *optical disks*

A magnetic disk is like a phonograph record, except that the data is encoded as microscopic magnetized *needles* on the disk's surface rather than as grooves in the vinyl. Also, you can record and erase data on a magnetic disk any number of times, just as you can with a cassette tape. Magnetic disks come in a number of different forms:

floppy disk: A typical 5¼-inch floppy can hold 1.2MB. A 3½-inch floppy can hold 1.44MB. New floppy disks can hold up to 100MB, but the industry has not yet chosen a standard format for these new disks.

hard disk: Hard disks can store anywhere from 20MB to more than 3GB. Hard disks are also from 2 to 20 times faster than floppy disks.

145

removable cartridge: Removable cartridges are hard disks encased in a metal or plastic cartridge, so you can remove them just like a floppy disk. Removable cartridges are very fast, often faster than fixed hard disks. A typical cartridge has a capacity of about 80MB.

Optical disks record data by burning microscopic holes in the surface of the disk with a laser. To read the disk, another laser beam shines on the disk and detects the holes by changes in the reflection pattern.
  Optical disks have a much larger data capacity than magnetic disks, but they are slower.
  Optical disks come in three forms:

CD-ROM: Most optical disks are read-only. When you purchase them, they are already filled with data. You can read the data from a CD-ROM, but you cannot modify, delete, or write new data.

WORM: Stands for *write-once, read-many*. WORM disks can be written on once and then read any number of times; however, you need a special WORM disk drive to write data onto a WORM disk.

erasable optical (EO): EO disks can be read to, written to, and erased just like magnetic disks. The machine that spins a disk is called a *disk drive*. Within each disk drive is one or more *heads* (often called *read/write heads*) that actually read and write data.
  Accessing data from a disk is not as fast as accessing data from main memory, but disks are cheaper and more stable. Unlike RAM, disks hold on to data even when the computer is turned off. Consequently, disks are the storage medium of choice for most types of data.
  Another storage medium is the magnetic tape. But tapes are used only for backup and archiving because they are *sequential-access* devices (to access data in the middle of a tape, the tape drive must pass through all the preceding data).
  A new disk, called a *blank disk*, has no data on it. Before you can store data on a blank disk, however, you must *format* it. In DOS systems, disks are formatted with the FORMAT command. When you execute the FORMAT command, the operating system allocates space for directories and other bookkeeping information. Every operating system formats disks somewhat differently, so a disk formatted by one operating system usually cannot be read by another operating system.

➡ See also CD-ROM; *disk drive; erasable optical disk; floppy disk; format; hard disk; head; mass storage; optical disk; removable hard disk.*

disk cache: A portion of RAM used to speed up access to data on a disk. The RAM can be part of the disk drive itself (sometimes called a *hard disk cache*) or it can be general-purpose RAM in the computer that is reserved for use by the disk drive (sometimes called a *soft disk cache*). Hard disk caches are more effective, but they are also much more expensive (see Figure 11 at *cache*).

In both cases, a disk cache works by storing the most recently accessed data in the RAM cache. When a program needs to access new data, the operating system first checks to see if the data is in the cache before reading it from the disk. Because computers can access data from RAM much faster than from a disk, disk caching can significantly increase performance. Many cache systems also attempt to predict what data will be requested next so they can place that data in the cache ahead of time.

Although caching improves performance, there is some risk involved. If the computer crashes (due to a power failure, for example), the system may not have time to copy the cache back to the disk. In this case, whatever changes you made to the data will be lost. Usually, however, the cache system updates the disk frequently so that even if you lose some data, it will not be much. A special type of disk cache, called a *write-thru cache*, removes the risk of losing data because it only caches data for *read operations, write operations* are always sent directly to the disk.

➡ See also *buffer; cache; disk drive; RAM.*

disk controller: A chip and associated circuitry that is responsible for controlling a disk drive. There are different controllers for different interfaces. For example, an IDE interface requires an IDE controller and a SCSI interface requires a SCSI controller. On Macintosh computer systems, the disk controller is built into the motherboard. On PCs, the disk controller is sometimes housed on a separate card.

➡ See also *controller; disk drive; EISA; IDE; SCSI.*

disk crash: See under *head crash.*

disk drive: A machine that reads data from and writes data onto a disk. A disk drive resembles a stereo turntable in that it rotates the disk very fast. It has one or more heads that read and write data.

There are different types of disk drives for different types of disks. For example, a *hard disk drive* reads and writes hard disks, and a *floppy drive* accesses floppy disks. A *magnetic disk drive* reads magnetic disks, and an *optical drive* reads optical disks.

Disk drives can be either *internal* (housed within the computer) or *external* (housed in a separate box that connects to the computer).

➠ See also *disk; floppy disk; hard disk; mass storage; optical disk.*

diskette: Same as *floppy disk.*

diskless workstation: A workstation or PC on a *local-area network (LAN)* that does not have its own disk. Instead, it stores files on a network file server. Diskless workstations can reduce the overall cost of a LAN because one large-capacity disk drive is usually less expensive than several low-capacity drives. In addition, diskless workstations can simplify backups and security because all files are in one place—on the file server. Also, accessing data from a large remote file server is often faster than accessing data from a small local storage device.

One disadvantage of diskless workstations, however, is that they are useless if the network fails.

When the workstation is a PC, it is often called a *diskless PC.*

➠ See also *disk drive; local-area network; server; workstation.*

disk operating system: See *DOS.*

disk optimizer: A program that makes a disk more efficient by defragmenting the disk. Fragmentation occurs naturally when a disk is used often.

➠ See also *fragmentation.*

disk pack: A stack of removable hard disks encased in a metal or plastic container.

➠ See also *hard disk; removable hard disk.*

display: (v) To make data or images appear on a monitor.

(n) Short for *display screen*.

display adapter: Same as *video adapter*.

display screen: The display part of a monitor. Most display screens work under the same principle as a television, using a *cathode ray tube (CRT)*. Consequently, the term CRT is often used in place of display screen.

➡ See also *CAD/CAM; desktop publishing; flat-panel display; graphics; monitor; notebook computer; resolution.*

distributed database: A database that consists of two or more data files located at different sites on a computer network. Because the database is distributed, different users can access it without interfering with one another. However, the database management system (DBMS) must periodically synchronize the scattered databases to make sure that they all have consistent data.

➡ See also *database; database management system; distributed processing; network.*

distributed processing: Refers to any of a variety of computer systems that use more than one computer, or processor, to run an application. This includes *parallel processing*, in which a single computer uses more than one *CPU* to execute programs. More often, however, distributed processing refers to *local-area networks (LANs)* designed so that a single program can run simultaneously at various sites. Most distributed processing systems contain sophisticated software that detects idle CPUs on the network and parcels out programs to utilize them.

Another form of distributed processing involves *distributed databases*, databases in which the data is stored across two or more computer systems. The database system keeps track of where the data is so that the distributed nature of the database is not apparent to users.

➡ See also *database management system; distributed database; local-area network; parallel processing.*

dithering: Creating the illusion of new colors and shades by varying the pattern of dots. Newspaper photographs, for example, are dithered. If you look closely, you can see that different shades of gray are produced by varying the patterns of black and white dots (Figure 27). There are no gray dots at all. The more dither patterns a device or program supports, the more shades of gray it can represent. In printing, dithering is usually called *halftoning,* and shades of gray are called *halftones.*

Note that *dithering* differs from *gray scaling.* In gray scaling, each individual dot can have a different shade of gray.

➡ See also *halftone; gray scaling.*

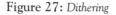

Line Art   Gray Scaled

Dithered

Figure 27: *Dithering*

DMA: Abbreviation of *direct memory access,* a technique for transferring data from main memory to a device without passing it through the CPU. Computers that have DMA channels can transfer data to and from devices much more quickly than computers without a DMA channel can. This is useful for making quick backups and for *real-time* applications.

Some expansion boards, such as CD-ROM cards, are capable of accessing the computer's DMA channel. When you install the board, you must specify which DMA channel is to be used, which sometimes involves setting a jumper or DIP switch.

➡ See also *backup; channel; CPU; DIP switch; expansion board; jumper; main memory; real time.*

docking station: A platform into which you can install a portable computer. The docking station typically contains slots for expansion cards, bays for storage devices, and connectors for peripheral devices, such as printers and monitors. Once inserted in a docking station, the portable computer essentially becomes a desktop model computer. When it is taken out, it becomes a portable computer again. Most importantly, the same data is accessible in both modes because it resides on the portable computer's drives. The idea behind docking stations is to let you simultaneously enjoy the expansion possibilities of desktop model computers with the portability of notebook computers. In addition, the docking station enables you to use a full-size keyboard and monitor when you're not traveling.

There is no standard for docking stations, so you must purchase one that is made specifically for your type of portable computer.

➡ See also *bay; desktop model computer; expansion board; notebook computer; portable computer; slot.*

document: (1) In the PC world, a file created with a word processor. In addition to text, documents can contain graphics, charts, and other objects.

Increasingly, the line separating word processing files from files produced by other applications is becoming blurred. A word processing application can produce graphics and a graphics application can produce words. This trend is accelerating with new technologies such as OLE and OpenDoc that allow an application to combine many components. Consequently, the term *document* is used more and more to describe any file produced by an application. Interestingly, this is the way the term has always been used in Macintosh environments.

➡ See also *file.*

(2) To enter written explanations. For example, programmers are always exhorted to document their code by inserting comments.

➡ See also *documentation.*

documentation: Instructions for using a computer device or program. Documentation can appear in a variety of forms, the most common being manuals. When you buy a computer product (hardware or software), it almost always comes with one or more manuals that describe how to install and operate the product. In addition, many software products include an online version of the documentation that you can display on your screen or print out on a printer. A special type of online documentation is a *help system,* which has the documentation embedded into the program. Help systems are often called *context-sensitive* because they display different information depending on the user's position (context) in the application.

Documentation is often divided into the following categories:

installation: Describes how to install a program or device but not how to use it.

reference: Detailed descriptions of particular items presented in alphabetical order. Reference documentation is designed for people who are already somewhat familiar with the product but need reminders or very specific information about a particular topic.

tutorial: Teaches a user how to use the product. Tutorials move at a slower pace than reference manuals and generally contain less detail. A frequent lament from computer users is that their documentation is inscrutable. Fortunately, this situation is improving, thanks largely to advances in help systems and online tutorials. These forms of documentation make it much easier to deliver the specific information a user needs when he or she needs it.

➠ See also *help.*

DOS: [PC] Acronym for *disk operating system.* The term *DOS* can refer to any operating system, but it is most often used as a shorthand for MS-DOS *(Microsoft disk operating system).* Originally developed by Microsoft for IBM, MS-DOS is the standard operating system for IBM-compatible personal computers.

The initial versions of DOS were very simple and resembled another operating system called *CP/M.* Subsequent versions have become increasingly sophisticated as they have incorporated features of minicomputer operating systems. However, DOS is still a 16-bit operating system, does not support multiple users or multitasking, and has a built-in limitation of 1MB of memory. To exceed this limit, you need a special memory system called *EMS (Expanded Memory Specification).*

For some time, it has been widely acknowledged that DOS is insufficient for modern computer applications. Microsoft Windows helped alleviate some problems, but until Windows 95, it sat on top of DOS and relied on DOS for many services. New operating systems, including Windows 95 and OS/2 Warp, do not rely on DOS to the same extent, although they can execute DOS-based programs. It is expected that as these operating systems gain market share, DOS will eventually disappear. In the meantime, both IBM and Novell are competing with Microsoft with their own versions of DOS, called *PC-DOS* and *Novell DOS*, respectively.

➡ See also *Microsoft Windows; operating system; OS/2; PC.*

dot: (1) Same as the period character ( ). In DOS, Windows, and OS/2 systems, the dot is used to separate a filename from its extension. For example, the filename CONFIG.SYS is pronounced *config-dot-sys*.

➡ See also *extension; filename.*

(2) In bit-mapped representations, a dot is a single point, the smallest identifiable part of an image. Laser printers, for example, create characters and images by printing patterns of dots. Likewise, monitors display images as arrays of dots. The resolutions of devices are often measured in *dots per inch (dpi)*.

➡ See also *bit map; dpi; resolution.*

dot-matrix printer: A type of printer that produces characters and illustrations by striking pins against an ink ribbon to print closely spaced dots in the appropriate shape. Dot-matrix printers are inexpensive and relatively fast, but they do not produce high-quality output.
    Dot-matrix printers vary in two important characteristics:

speed: Given in *characters per second (cps)*, the speed can vary from about 50 to over 500 cps. Most dot-matrix printers offer different speeds, depending on the quality of print desired.

print quality: Determined by the number of pins (the mechanisms that print the dots), it can vary from 9 to 24. The best dot-matrix printers (24 pins) can produce near letter-quality type, although you can still see a difference if you look closely.

In addition to these characteristics, you should also consider the noise factor. Compared to laser and ink-jet printers, dot-matrix printers are notorious for making a racket. Although the prices of laser and ink-jet printers are dropping rapidly, dot-matrix printers are still cheaper to operate. A page printed by a dot-matrix printer costs about a penny, whereas a laser-printed page costs two to three cents. In addition, most dot-matrix printers can print to multi-page forms (that is, carbon copies), something laser and ink-jet printers cannot do.

➡ See also *printer*.

dot pitch: A measurement that indicates the vertical distance between each pixel on a display screen. Measured in millimeters, the dot pitch is one of the principal characteristics that determines the quality of display monitors. The lower the number, the crisper the image. The dot pitch of color monitors for personal computers ranges from about 0.22 mm to 0.42 mm.

➡ See also *monitor; pixel*.

dots per inch: See *dpi*.

double click: Tapping a mouse button twice in rapid succession. Note that the second click must immediately follow the first, otherwise the program will interpret them as two separate clicks rather than one double click.

In Microsoft Windows and the Macintosh interface, you can use a double click to open files and applications. Both systems let you set the double-click speed (the longest acceptable interval between each click).

➡ See also *click; mouse*.

double-density disk: A floppy disk that has twice the storage capacity of a single-density floppy. Single-density disks are now practically obsolete. Double-density 5¼-inch disks for PCs can hold 360K of data. Double-density 3½-inch disks can hold 720K.

Although high-density disk drives can format both high-density and double-density disks, double-density disks formatted by a high-density drive may not be readable by a double-density drive. Similarly, high-density drives may not be able to read disks that have been formatted by a double-density disk drive.

➡ See also *density; floppy disk*.

double precision: Refers to a type of floating-point number that has more precision (that is, more digits to the right of the decimal point) than a *single-precision* number. The term *double precision* is something of a misnomer because the precision is not really double. The word *double* derives from the fact that a double-precision number uses twice as many bits as a regular floating-point number. For example, if a single-precision number requires 32 bits, its double-precision counterpart will be 64 bits long.

The extra bits increase not only the precision but also the range of magnitudes that can be represented. The exact amount by which the precision and range of magnitudes are increased depends on what format the program is using to represent floating-point values. Most computers use a standard format known as the *IEEE floating-point format.*

➠ See also *floating-point number; IEEE.*

double-scan display: Same as *dual-scan display.*

double-sided disk: A floppy disk with both sides prepared for recording data. You can store twice as much data on a double-sided disk, but you need to use a double-sided disk drive. Nearly all modern disks and disk drives are double-sided.

➠ See also *disk drive; floppy disk.*

double-speed CD-ROM: See under *CD-ROM.*

double supertwist: See under *supertwist.*

down: Not working. A computer system is said to be down when it is not available to users. This can occur because it is broken (that is, it has crashed), or because it has been made temporarily unavailable to users so that routine servicing can be performed.

➠ See also *crash.*

download: To copy data (usually an entire file) from a main source to a peripheral device. The term is often used to describe the process of copying a file from an online service or *bulletin board service (BBS)* to one's own computer. Downloading also refers to copying a file from a network file server to a computer on the network.

In addition, the term is used to describe the process of loading a font into a laser printer. The font is first copied from a disk to the printer's local memory. A font that has been downloaded like this is called a *soft font* to distinguish it from the *hard fonts* that are permanently in the printer's memory.

The opposite of download is *upload*, which means to copy a file from your own computer to another computer.

➠ See also *bulletin board service; font; online service; upload.*

downloadable font: Same as *soft font.*

downward compatible: Same as *backward compatible.*

DP: See *data processing.*

dpi: Abbreviation of *dots per inch,* which indicates the resolution of images. The more dots per inch, the higher the resolution. A common resolution for laser printers is 300 dots per inch. This means 300 dots across and 300 dots down, so there are 90,000 dots per square inch.

➠ See also *laser printer; resolution.*

draft mode: A printing mode in which the printer prints text as fast as possible without regard to the print quality. Most dot-matrix printers support two modes: draft mode and either *letter-quality (LQ)* or *near letter quality (NLQ)* mode. In addition, many word processors support a draft mode in which they display and print pages without all the formatting detail specified for the document.

➠ See also *dot-matrix printer; letter quality; near letter quality.*

draft quality: Describes print whose quality is less than *near letter quality* (see Figure 46 at *letter quality*). Most 9-pin dot-matrix printers produce draft-quality print.

➠ See also *dot-matrix printer; draft mode; letter quality; near letter quality.*

drag: (1) In graphical user interfaces, *drag* refers to moving an icon or other image on a display screen. To drag an object across a display screen, you usually select the object with a mouse button ("grab" it) and then move the mouse while keeping the mouse button pressed down.

The term *drag* is also used more generally to refer to any operation in which the mouse button is held down while the mouse is moved. For example, you would drag the mouse to select a block of text.

➠ See also *drag-and-drop; graphical user interface; mouse; select.*

drag-and-drop: Describes applications that allow you to drag objects to specific locations on the screen to perform actions on them. For example, in the Macintosh environment, you can drag a document to the trashcan icon to delete it. This is a classic case of drag-and-drop functionality.

When implemented well, drag-and-drop functionality is both faster and more intuitive than alternatives, such as selecting options from a menu or typing in commands.

Modern operating systems, including Windows and the Macintosh operating system, even allow you to drag and drop *between* applications. You can, for example, create a picture with a draw program, select it, and then drag it into a document that you are editing with a word processor.

➠ See also *drag; graphical user interface.*

DRAM: Pronounced *dee-ram,* DRAM stands for *dynamic random access memory,* a type of memory used in most personal computers.

➠ See also *dynamic RAM.*

draw program: A graphics program that enables you to draw pictures, then store the images in files, merge them into documents, and print them. Unlike paint programs, which represent images as bit maps, draw programs use *vector graphics*, which makes it easy to scale images to different sizes. In addition, graphics produced with a draw program have no inherent resolution. Rather, they can be represented at any resolution, which makes them ideal for high-resolution output.

➠ See also *graphics; paint program; vector graphics.*

drawing tablet: Same as *digitizing tablet.*

drive: Short for *disk drive.*

drive bay: An area of reserved space in a personal computer where hard or floppy disk drives (or tape drives) can be installed. The number of drive bays in a computer determines the total number of internal mass storage devices it can handle.

➠ See also *bay; disk drive; mass storage.*

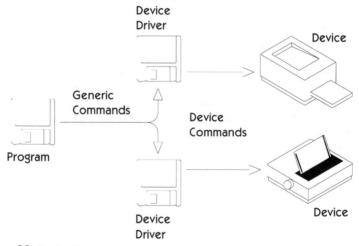

Figure 28: *Device Driver*

driver: A program that controls a device. Every device, whether it be a printer, disk drive, or keyboard, must have a driver program. Many drivers, such as the keyboard driver, come with the operating system. For other devices, you may need to load a new driver when you connect the device to your computer. In DOS systems, drivers are files with a .SYS extension. In Windows environments, drivers have a .DRV extension.

A driver acts like a translator between the device and programs that use the device. Each device has its own set of specialized commands that only its driver knows. In contrast, most programs access devices by using generic commands. The driver, therefore, accepts generic commands from a program and then translates them into specialized commands for the device (Figure 28).

➠ See also *CONFIG.SYS; controller; device.*

drop cap: In desktop publishing, the first letter of a paragraph that is enlarged to "drop" down two or more lines, as in the next paragraph.

D rop caps are used to make a page more visually interesting and to draw the reader's eyes to the beginning of a section.

➠ See also *desktop publishing.*

drop-down menu: Same as *pull-down menu.*

DSP: Short for *digital signal processing,* which refers to manipulating analog information, such as sound or photographs, that has been converted into a digital form. DSP also implies the use of a data compression technique.

When used as a noun, DSP stands for *digital signal processor,* a special type of coprocessor designed for performing the mathematics involved in DSP. Most DSPs are programmable, which means that they can be used for manipulating different types of information, including sound, images, and video.

➠ See also *coprocessor; data compression; digitize; graphics accelerator; sound card.*

DTP: See *desktop publishing.*

dual in-line package: See *DIP*.

dual-scan display: A type of passive-matrix LCD display that provides faster refresh rates that conventional passive-matrix displays by refreshing the screen twice as fast. Dual-scan displays are not as sharp or bright as active-matrix displays, but they consume less power.

➠ See also *active-matrix display; flat-panel display; LCD; passive-matrix display.*

dual supertwist: See under *supertwist*.

dumb terminal: A display monitor that has no processing capabilities. A dumb terminal is simply an output device that accepts data from the CPU. In contrast, a *smart terminal* is a monitor that has its own processor for special features, such as bold and blinking characters. Dumb terminals are not as fast as smart terminals, and they do not support as many display features, but they are adequate for most applications.

➠ See also *display screen; intelligent terminal; smart terminal; terminal.*

dummy: A placeholder. A dummy variable, for example, is a *dummy variable* that doesn't contain any useful data, but it does reserve space that a real variable will use later.

➠ See also *variable.*

dump: (n) The act of copying raw data from one place to another with little or no formatting for readability. Usually, *dump* refers to copying data from main memory to a display screen or a printer. Dumps are useful for diagnosing bugs. After a program fails, you can study the dump and analyze the contents of memory at the time of the failure. Dumps are usually output in a difficult-to-read form (that is, binary, octal, or hexadecimal), so a dump will not help you unless you know exactly what to look for.

(v) To output an image of computer memory.

duplex: Same as *full duplex.*

DVI: Abbreviation of *Digital Video Interactive,* a technology developed by General Electric that enables a computer to store and display moving video images like those on television. The most difficult aspect of displaying TV-like images on a computer is overcoming the fact that each frame requires an immense amount of storage. A single frame can require up to 2MB (megabytes) of storage. Televisions display 30 frames per second, which can quickly exhaust a computer's mass storage resources. It is also difficult to transfer so much data to a display screen at a rate of 30 frames per second.

DVI overcomes these problems by using specialized processors to compress and decompress the data. DVI is a hardware-only *codec (compression/decompression)* technology. A competing hardware codec is MPEG. Intel has developed a software version of the DVI algorithms, which it markets under the name *Indeo.*

See also *codec; Indeo; MPEG.*

Figure 29: *Dvorak Keyboard*

Dvorak keyboard: A keyboard designed for speed typing. The Dvorak keyboard was designed in the 1930s by August Dvorak, a professor of education, and his brother-in-law, William Dealy. Unlike the traditional QWERTY keyboard, the Dvorak keyboard is designed so that most words fall in the middle row of keys. In addition, common letter combinations are positioned in such a way that they can be typed quickly (Figure 29).

It has been estimated that in an average eight-hour day, a typist's hands travel 16 miles on a QWERTY keyboard, but only 1 mile on a Dvorak keyboard.

In addition to the standard Dvorak keyboard, there are two additional Dvorak keyboards, a left-handed and right-handed keyboard. These keyboards are designed for people who have only one hand for typing.

➡ See also *keyboard; macro; QWERTY keyboard.*

DXF: Abbreviation of *Data Exchange File*, a two-dimensional graphics file format supported by virtually all PC-based CAD products. It was created by AutoDesk for the AutoCAD system.

➡ See also *CAD; graphics; graphics file formats.*

dynamic: Refers to actions that take place at the moment they are needed rather than in advance. For example, many programs perform *dynamic memory allocation,* which means that they do not reserve memory ahead of time, but seize sections of memory when needed. In general, such programs require less memory, although they may run a little more slowly.

The opposite of dynamic is *static.*

➡ See also *dynamic variable; static variable.*

dynamic acceleration: A feature supported by some mice that causes the mouse resolution to depend on how fast the mouse is moved. When you move the mouse fast, the cursor moves proportionally further (the resolution is low). This is useful for jumping across the screen. Without this feature, you might need to sweep the mouse several times to move the cursor from one side of the display screen to the other. When you move the mouse slowly, the resolution increases to enable you to pinpoint specific pixels.

Dynamic resolution is also called *ballistic tracking, automatic acceleration, variable acceleration,* and *dynamic acceleration.*

➠ See also *mouse; resolution.*

Dynamic Data Exchange: See *DDE.*

dynamic RAM: A type of physical memory used in most personal computers. The term *dynamic* indicates that the memory must be constantly *refreshed* (reenergized) or it will lose its contents. RAM *(random-access memory)* is sometimes referred to as *DRAM* (pronounced *dee-ram*) to distinguish it from *static RAM (SRAM).* Static RAM is faster and more stable than dynamic RAM, but it requires more power and is more expensive.

➠ See also *main memory; RAM; refresh; static RAM.*

dynamic variable: In programming, a dynamic variable is a variable whose address is determined when the program is run. In contrast, a *static variable* has memory reserved for it at compilation time.

➠ See also *static variable; variable.*

E

EBCDIC: Abbreviation of *Extended Binary-Coded Decimal Interchange Code.* Pronounced *eb-see-dik,* EBCDIC is an IBM code for representing characters as numbers (Table 13). Although it is widely used on large IBM computers, most other computers, including PCs and Macintoshes, use ASCII codes.

➠ See also *ASCII.*

ECP: 〔PC〕 Short for *Extended Capabilities Port,* a parallel-port standard for PCs that supports bi-directional communication between the PC and attached devices (such as a printer). ECP is about 10 times faster than the older Centronics standard.

Another modern parallel port for PCs that offers similar performance is the *EPP (Enhanced Parallel Port).*

➠ See also *Centronics interface; parallel port.*

edge connector: The part of a printed circuit board that plugs into a computer or device. The edge connector generally has a row of broad metallic tracks that provide the electrical connection (see Figure 67 at *printed circuit board*).

➠ See also *printed circuit board.*

editor: Sometimes called *text editor,* a program that enables you to create and edit text files. There are many different types of editors, but they all fall into two general categories:

line editors: A primitive form of editor that requires you to specify a specific line of text before you can make changes to it.

Table 13
EBCDIC CODES

DECIMAL	HEXADECIMAL	CHARACTER
129	81	a
130	82	b
131	83	c
132	84	d
133	85	e
134	86	f
135	87	g
136	88	h
137	89	i
145	91	j
146	92	k
147	93	l
148	94	m
149	95	n
150	96	o
151	97	p
152	98	q
153	99	r
162	A2	s
163	A3	t
164	A4	u
165	A5	v
166	A6	w
167	A7	x
168	A8	y
169	A9	z
240	F0	0
241	F1	1
242	F2	2
243	F3	3
244	F4	4
245	F5	5
246	F6	6
247	F7	7
248	F8	8
249	F9	9
122	7A	:
123	7B	#
124	7C	@
125	7D	'
126	7E	=
127	7F	"
193	C1	A

Table 13 (Continued)
EBCDIC CODES

DECIMAL	HEXADECIMAL	CHARACTER
194	C2	B
195	C3	C
196	C4	D
197	C5	E
198	C6	F
199	C7	G
200	C8	H
201	C9	I
209	D1	J
210	D2	K
211	D3	L
212	D4	M
213	D5	N
214	D6	O
215	D7	P
216	D8	Q
217	D9	R
226	E2	S
227	E3	T
228	E4	U
229	E5	V
230	E6	W
231	E7	X
232	E8	Y
233	E9	Z
64	40	blank
76	4C	<
77	4D	(
78	4E	+
79	4F		
80	50	&
90	5A	!
91	5B	$
92	5C	*
93	5D	)
94	5E	;
96	60	-
97	61	/
107	6B	,
108	6C	%
109	6D	_
110	6E	>
111	6F	?

screen-oriented editors: Also called *full-screen editors,* these editors enable you to modify any text that appears on the display screen by moving the cursor to the desired location.

The distinction between editors and word processors is not clear-cut, but in general, word processors provide many more formatting features.

➧ See also *word processing.*

EDO DRAM: Short for *Enhanced Data Output Dynamic Access Random Memory,* a type of DRAM that is 30 to 50 percent faster than conventional DRAM. Unlike conventional DRAM, EDO DRAM does not need to be refreshed between each access, so its cycle time is much shorter.

➧ See also *access time; cycle time; DRAM.*

EEMS: PC Abbreviation of *Enhanced Expanded Memory Specification,* an enhanced version of the original EMS, which enables DOS applications to use more than 1MB (megabyte) of memory. EEMS was developed by AST, Quadram, and Ashton-Tate to improve the performance of the original version of EMS. Subsequently, Lotus, Intel, and Microsoft developed the LIM 4.0 version of EMS, which supports both the original EMS and EEMS.

➧ See also *expanded memory; LIM memory.*

EEPROM: Acronym for *electrically erasable programmable read-only memory.* Pronounced *double-ee-prom,* an EEPROM is a special type of PROM that can be erased by exposing it to an electrical charge. Like other types of PROM, EEPROM retains its contents even when the power is turned off. Also like other types of ROM, EEPROM is not as fast as RAM.

A special type of EEPROM, referred to as *flash memory* or *flash EEPROM,* can be rewritten while it is in the computer rather than requiring a special device called a *PROM reader.*

➧ See also *EPROM; flash memory; memory; PROM; RAM; ROM.*

EGA: PC Abbreviation of *enhanced graphics adapter*, a graphics display system for PCs introduced by IBM in 1984. EGA supports 16 colors from a palette of 64 and provides a resolution of 640 by 350. This is better than CGA but not as good as VGA.

➠ See also *video adapter*.

EIA (Electronics Industry Association) interface: Same as *RS-232C*.

EIDE: Short for *Enhanced IDE*, a new version of the IDE mass storage device interface standard developed by Western Digital Corporation. It supports data rates of between 11.1 and 13.3MB (megabytes) per second, about three to four times faster than the old IDE standard. In addition, it can support mass storage devices of up to 8.4 gigabytes, whereas the old standard was limited to 528MB. Because of its lower cost, enhanced IDE is expected to replace SCSI in many areas.

EIDE is sometimes referred to as *Fast ATA*, or *Fast IDE*, which is essentially the same standard, developed and promoted by Seagate Technologies.

➠ See also *IDE; SCSI*.

8086: Short for the *Intel 8086 microprocessor*.

➠ See also *Intel microprocessors*.

8514/A: PC A high-resolution video standard for PCs developed by IBM in 1987. It is designed to extend the capabilities of VGA. The 8514/A standard provides a resolution of 1,024 by 768 pixels, which gives it about 2.5 times the pixels of VGA (640 by 480). Like VGA, 8514/A provides a palette of 262,000 colors, of which 256 can be displayed at one time. On monochrome displays, 8514/A provides 64 shades of gray.

In its original version, 8514/A relies on *interlacing*, a technique that makes it possible to provide resolution at low cost. Interlacing, however, carries a performance penalty, so many manufacturers produce *noninterlaced* 8514/A clones.

In 1990, IBM released the *Extended Graphics Array (XGA)* standard, which supersedes 8514/A.

➠ See also *interlacing; monochrome; palette; resolution; SVGA; video adapter; XGA.*

EISA: PC Acronym for *Extended Industry Standard Architecture,* a bus architecture designed for PCs using an Intel 80386, 80486, or Pentium microprocessor. EISA buses are 32 bits wide and support multiprocessing.

The EISA bus was designed by nine IBM competitors (sometimes called the *Gang of Nine*): AST Research, Compaq Computer, Epson, Hewlett-Packard, NEC Information Systems, Olivetti, Tandy, WYSE, and Zenith Data Systems. They designed the architecture to compete with IBM's own high-speed bus architecture, called the *Micro Channel architecture (MCA).*

The principal difference between EISA and MCA is that EISA is backward compatible with the ISA bus (also called the *AT bus*), while MCA is not. This means that computers with an EISA bus can use new EISA expansion cards as well as old AT expansion cards. Computers with an MCA bus can use only MCA expansion cards.

EISA and MCA are not compatible with each other. This means that the type of bus in your computer determines which expansion cards you can install.

Neither EISA nor MCA has been very successful. Instead, a new technology called *local bus* is being used in combination with the old ISA bus. There are two competing local bus standards—*PCI* and *VL-bus*—but it now seems that PCI will become the de facto standard for PCs, and possibly for Macintoshes as well.

➠ See also *bus; expansion board; ISA bus; local bus; Micro Channel architecture; multiprocessing; PCI; VL-bus.*

ELD: See *electroluminescent display.*

electrically erasable programmable read-only memory: See *EEPROM.*

electroluminescent display (ELD): A technology used to produce a very thin display screen, called a *flat-panel display,* used in some portable computers. An ELD works by sandwiching a thin film of phosphorescent substance between two plates. One plate is coated with vertical wires and the other with horizontal wires, forming a grid. When an electrical current is passed through a horizontal and vertical wire, the phosphorescent film at the intersection glows, creating a point of light, or *pixel*.

Other types of flat-panel displays include *LCD displays* and *gas-plasma displays*, both of which are more common than ELDs.

➠ See also *active-matrix display; flat-panel display; gas-plasma display; LCD; notebook computer.*

electronic mail: See under *e-mail*.

electronic publishing: Publishing information in an electronic form. This includes publishing CD-ROMs as well as making information available through online services.

➠ See also CD-ROM; *multimedia; online service.*

elevator: Same as *scroll box.* See under *scroll bar.*

ELF emission: ELF stands for *extremely low frequency,* and ELF emissions are magnetic fields generated by common electrical appliances. There is considerable debate about whether ELF emissions from computer monitors pose a threat. Some European countries have adopted regulations controlling the amount of allowable emission. The most well-know regulation is Sweden's *MPR II standard.* You can play it safe by buying MPR II-compliant monitors.

e-mail: Short for *electronic mail,* the transmission of messages over communications networks. The messages can be notes entered from the keyboard or electronic files stored on disk. Most mainframes, minicomputers, and computer networks have an e-mail system. Some electronic-mail systems are confined to a single computer system or network, but others have gateways to other computer systems, enabling users to send electronic mail anywhere in the world. Companies that are fully computerized make extensive use of e-mail because it is fast, flexible, and reliable. In 1995, approximately 25 billion e-mail messages were sent.

Most e-mail systems include a rudimentary text editor for composing messages, but many allow you to edit your messages using any editor you want. You then send the message to the recipient by specifying the recipient's address. You can also send the same message to several users at once. This is called *broadcasting*.

Sent messages are stored in electronic mailboxes until the recipient fetches them. To see if you have any mail, you may have to check your electronic mailbox periodically, although many systems alert you when mail is received. After reading your mail, you can store it in a text file, forward it to other users, or delete it. Copies of memos can be printed out on a printer if you want a paper copy.

All online services offer e-mail, and most also support gateways so that you can exchange mail with users of other systems. Usually, it takes only a few seconds or minutes for mail to arrive at its destination. This is a particularly effective way to communicate with a group because you can broadcast a message or document to everyone in the group at once.

Although different e-mail systems use different formats, there are some emerging standards that are making it possible for users on all systems to exchange messages. In the PC world, an important e-mail standard is MAPI. The CCITT standards organization has developed the X.400 standard, which attempts to provide a universal way of addressing messages. To date, though, the de facto addressing standard is the one used by the Internet system because almost all e-mail systems have an Internet gateway.

In recent years, the use of e-mail has exploded. By some estimates, there are now 25 million e-mail users sending 15 billion messages per year.

➡ *See also* CCITT; *gateway; mailbox;* MAPI; *network; online service; username; workgroup computing.*

embedded command: In word processing, an embedded command is a sequence of special characters inserted into a document that affects the formatting of the document when it is printed. For example, when you change fonts in a word processor (by specifying bold type), the word processor inserts an embedded command that causes the printer to change fonts. Embedded commands can also control the display screen, causing it to display blinking characters or produce other special effects.

Embedded commands are usually invisible when you edit a file, but many word processors support a special mode that lets you see these commands.

➠ See also *command; font; word processing.*

embedded object: An object created with one application and embedded into a document created by another application. *Embedding* the object, rather than simply inserting or pasting it, ensures that the object retains its original format. In fact, you can modify the embedded object with the original program. In Windows environments, embedding objects is made possible by a technology called OLE.

➠ See also *document; OLE.*

emoticon: Short for *emotion icon*, a small icon composed of punctuation characters that indicates how an e-mail message should be interpreted (that is, the writer's mood). For example, a :-) *smiley* indicates that the message is meant as a joke and shouldn't be taken seriously. Table 14 lists some of the most common emoticons and their meanings.

➠ See also *e-mail.*

Table 14
EMOTICONS

EMOTICON	MEANING
:-)	Joking
: 0	Bored
;-)	Winking
:-(	Sad
:-<	Frowning

EMS: Abbreviation of *Expanded Memory Specification.*

➠ See also *expanded memory.*

emulation: Refers to the ability of a program or device to imitate another program or device. Many printers, for example, are designed to emulate Hewlett-Packard LaserJet printers because so much software is written for the HP printers. By emulating an HP printer, a printer can work with any software written for a real HP printer. Emulation tricks the software into believing that a device is really some other device.

Communications software packages often include *terminal emulation drivers*. This enables your PC to emulate a particular type of terminal so that you can log on to a mainframe.

It is also possible for a computer to emulate another type of computer. For example, there are programs that enable an Apple Macintosh to emulate a PC.

➠ See also *communications software; log on; mainframe; terminal.*

Encapsulated PostScript: See *EPS.*

encryption: The translation of data into a secret code. Encryption is the most effective way to achieve data security. To read an encrypted file, you must have access to a secret key or password that enables you to *decrypt* it.

➠ See also *password; security.*

End key: A special cursor control key on PC keyboards and Macintosh extended keyboards. The End key has different meanings depending on which program is running. For example, it might move the cursor to the end of the line, the end of the page, or the end of the file.

➠ See also *keyboard.*

end of file: See *EOF.*

end of line: See *EOL mark.*

end user: The final or ultimate user of a computer system. The end user is the individual who uses the product after it has been fully developed and marketed. The term is useful because it distinguishes two classes of users, users who require a bug-free and finished product (end users), and users who may use the same product for development purposes. The term *end user* usually implies an individual with a relatively low level of computer expertise. Unless you are a programmer or engineer, you are almost certainly an end user.

➠ See also *user*.

Energy Star: A set of guidelines issued by the U.S. Environmental Protection Agency to minimize energy consumption. Energy Star devices can detect when they are idle and switch to a low-energy mode in which they consume 30 watts or less.

Enhanced Data Output DRAM: See *EDO DRAM*.

Enhanced Expanded Memory Specification: See *EEMS*.

enhanced graphics adapter: See *EGA*.

Enhanced IDE: See under *EIDE*.

Enhanced Keyboard: PC (1) A 101- or 102-key keyboard from IBM that supersedes the keyboard for the PC/AT computer. The most significant difference between the enhanced keyboard and previous models is that the enhanced keyboard has a row of 12 function keys at the top instead of 10 function keys grouped on the left side of the keyboard. Nearly all PCs made today come with an Enhanced Keyboard.

➠ See also *function keys; keyboard*.

(2) MAC For Macintoshes, see under *extended keyboard*.

Enhanced Parallel Port: See *EPP*.

Enhanced Small Device Interface: See *ESDI*.

Enter key: A key that moves the cursor (or insertion point) to the beginning of the next line, or returns control to whatever program is currently running. After a program requests information from you (by displaying a prompt), it will usually not respond to your input until you have pressed the Enter or Return key. This allows you to correct typing mistakes or to reconsider your entry before it is too late. In many applications, pressing the Enter key moves the cursor to the next field. In graphical user interfaces, pressing Enter activates the currently selected button or option.

➠ See also *Return key.*

environment: (1) The state of a computer, usually determined by which programs are running and basic hardware and software characteristics. For example, when one speaks of running a program in a UNIX environment, it means running a program on a computer that has the UNIX operating system.

One ingredient of an environment, therefore, is the operating system. But operating systems include a number of different parameters. For example, many operating systems allow you to choose your command prompt or a default command path. All these parameters taken together constitute the environment.

Another term for environment in this sense is *platform.*

➠ See also *operating system; parameter; platform.*

(2) PC In DOS systems, the environment is an area in memory that the operating system and other programs use to store various types of miscellaneous information. For example, your word processor may use the environment area to store the location of backup files. You can view or modify the environment with the SET command.

➠ See also *DOS.*

EO: See *erasable optical disk.*

EOF mark: Short for *end-of-file mark,* a special character or sequence of characters that marks the end of a file. Operating systems need to keep track of where every file ends. There are two techniques for doing this: One is to put a special end-of-file mark at the end of each file. The other is to keep track of how many characters are in the file.

In many operating systems, including DOS and OS/2, the end-of-file mark is CTRL-Z. In UNIX, the end-of-file mark is CTRL-D.

EOL mark: Short for *end-of-line mark*, a special character or sequence of characters that marks the end of a line. For many programs, the EOL character is CTRL-M (carriage return) or CTRL-J (newline). End-of-line can also be abbreviated *EOLN*.

EPP: PC Short for *Enhanced Parallel Port*, a parallel port standard for PCs that supports bi-directional communication between the PC and attached devices (such as a printer). EPP is about 10 times faster than the older Centronics standard.

Another modern parallel port for PCs that offers similar performance is the *ECP (Extended Capabilities Port)*.

➥ See also *Centronics interface; parallel port.*

EPROM: Acronym for *erasable programmable read-only memory*, and pronounced *ee-prom*, EPROM is a special type of memory that retains its contents until it is exposed to ultraviolet light. The ultraviolet light clears its contents, making it possible to reprogram the memory. To write to and erase an EPROM, you need a special device called a *PROM programmer* or *PROM burner*.

An EPROM differs from a PROM in that a PROM can be written to only once and cannot be erased. EPROMs are used widely in personal computers because they enable the manufacturer to change the contents of the PROM before the computer is actually shipped. This means that bugs can be removed and new versions installed shortly before delivery.

➥ See also *memory; PROM.*

EPS: Abbreviation of *Encapsulated PostScript*. Pronounced as separate letters, EPS is the graphics file format used by the PostScript language.

EPS files can be either binary or ASCII. The term *EPS* usually implies that the file contains a bit-mapped representation of the graphics for display purposes. In contrast, *PostScript files* include only the PostScript commands for printing the graphic.

➠ See also *graphics; graphics file formats; PostScript.*

erasable optical disk: A type of optical disk that can be erased and loaded with new data, just like magnetic disks. In contrast, most optical disks, called CD-ROMs, are read-only.

Although the technology is still young, erasable optical disks seem destined to become the future medium of choice. A single optical disk can hold 5 gigabytes of data, about 1,000 times more than a typical floppy disk. And unlike hard disks, optical disks are portable.

The data-access speed of optical disks varies considerably, from about 20 to 200 milliseconds. Though comparable to floppy disks, they are not yet as fast as magnetic hard disk drives.

➠ See also *access time; CD-ROM; disk; floppy disk; mass storage; optical disk.*

erasable programmable read only memory: See *EPROM.*

ergonomics: The science concerned with designing safe and comfortable machines for humans. For example, one branch of ergonomics deals with designing furniture that avoids causing backaches and muscle cramps. In the computer field, ergonomics plays an important role in the design of monitors and keyboards.

Another term for ergonomics is *human engineering.*

error detection: In communications, *error detection* refers to a class of techniques for detecting garbled messages. Two of the simplest and most common techniques are called *checksum* and CRC. More sophisticated strategies include *MNP* and *CCITT V.42.*

➠ See also *CCITT; checksum; CRC; Kermit; MNP; Xmodem.*

ESC: Short for *Escape key.* For example, *ESC-Q* means *press the Escape key and then the Q key.*

➠ See also *escape character; Escape key.*

escape character: A special character that can have many different functions. It is often used to abort the current command and return to a previous place in the program. It is also used to send special instructions to printers and other devices. An escape character is generated with the *Escape key*, a special key that exists on most computer keyboards.

When the escape character is combined with other characters, it is called an *escape sequence*.

➡ See also *escape sequence; keyboard.*

Escape key: A key on computer keyboards, usually labeled *Esc.* In DOS and Windows environments, pressing the Escape key usually cancels or aborts the current operation.

➡ See also *abort; keyboard.*

escape sequence: A sequence of special characters that sends a command to a device or program. Typically, an escape sequence begins with an *escape character*, but this is not universally true.

➡ See also *escape character.*

ESDI: ⟦PC⟧ Abbreviation of *Enhanced Small Device Interface,* an interface standard developed by a consortium of the leading personal computer manufacturers for connecting disk drives to PCs. ESDI is two to three times faster than the older ST-506 standard. To use an ESDI drive, your computer must have an ESDI controller.

Introduced in the early 80s, ESDI is already obsolete. Instead, modern computers use a SCSI, IDE, or EIDE interface.

➡ See also *disk drive; EIDE; IDE interface; SCSI; ST-506 interface.*

Ethernet: A local-area network (LAN) protocol developed by Xerox Corporation in cooperation with DEC and Intel in 1976. Ethernet uses a bus topology and supports data transfer rates of 10 megabits (10 million bits) per second. The Ethernet specification served as the basis for the IEEE 802.3 standard, which specifies the physical and lower software layers. It is one of the most widely implemented LAN standards.

A new version of Ethernet, called *100BaseX* (or *Fast Ethernet*), supports data transfer rates of 100 megabits per second.

➠ See also *IEEE*; *local-area network*; *network*; *protocol*; *topology*.

even header: In word processing, a header that appears only on even-numbered pages.

➠ See also *header*.

even parity: Refers to the parity-checking mode in which each set of transmitted bits must have an even number of set bits. The parity checking system ensures even parity by setting the extra *parity bit* if necessary.

➠ See also *parity checking*.

event: An action or occurrence detected by a program. Events can be user actions, such as clicking a mouse button or pressing a key, or system occurrences, such as running out of memory. Most modern applications, particularly those that run in Macintosh and Windows environments, are said to be *event-driven*, because they are designed to respond to events.

exclusive OR: A Boolean operator that returns a value of TRUE only if both its operands have different values. Contrast with the *inclusive OR operator*, which returns a value of TRUE if *either* of its operands is TRUE.

➠ See also *Boolean operator*.

executable file: A file in a format that the computer can directly execute. Unlike source files, executable files cannot be read by humans. To transform a source file into an executable file, you need to pass it through a compiler or assembler.

[PC] In DOS systems, executable files have either a .COM or .EXE extension and are called *COM files* and *EXE files*, respectively.

➠ See also *assembler*; *COM file*; *compiler*; *EXE file*; *file*; *source code*.

execute: Same as *run. Execute* means to perform an action, as in executing a program or a command.

EXE file: [PC] Pronounced *ee-ex-ee file*, in DOS and Windows systems, an EXE file is an executable file with a .EXE extension.

➠ See also COM *file; executable file; extension; program.*

expanded memory: [PC] Also known as EMS *(Expanded Memory Specification)*, expanded memory is a technique for utilizing more than 1MB (megabyte) of main memory in DOS-based computers. The limit of 1MB is built into the DOS operating system. The upper 384K is reserved for special purposes, leaving just 640K of conventional memory for programs.

There are several versions of EMS. The original versions, called *EMS 3.0* and *3.2,* enable programs to use an additional 8MB of memory, but for data only. An improved version developed by AST, Quadram and Ashton-Tate is known as *EEMS (Extended EMS).* EEMS enables programs to use extra memory for code as well as for data. The most recent version of EMS (created in 1987) is known as *EMS 4.0* or *LIM 4.0,* LIM being the initials of the three companies that developed the specification: Lotus, Intel, and Microsoft. EMS 4.0 raises the available amount of memory to 32MB.

Until the release of Microsoft Windows 3.0 in 1990, expanded memory was the preferred way to add memory to a PC. The alternative method, called *extended memory,* was less flexible and could be used only by special programs such as RAM disks. Windows 3.0 and all later versions of Windows, however, contain an *extended memory manager* that enables programs to use extended memory without interfering with one another. In addition, Windows can simulate expanded memory for those programs that need it.

➠ See also *conventional memory; EEMS; extended memory; main memory; RAM disk.*

expansion board: A printed circuit board that you can insert into a computer to give it added capabilities. For example, all of the following are expansion boards:

- video adapters
- graphics accelerators

- sound cards
- accelerator boards
- internal modems

Expansion boards for PCs can be *half-size* (also *half-length*) or *full-size* (also *full-length*). Most PCs have slots for each type of board. A half-size board is sometimes called an *8-bit board* because it can transmit only 8 bits at a time. A full-size board is called a *16-bit board*. In addition, some expansion boards are designed to operate with a local bus, such as PCI.

Expansion boards are also called *adapters*; *cards*; *add-ins*; and *add-ons*.

➠ See also *accelerator board*; *add-in*; *add-on*; *CPU*; *expansion slot*; *graphics accelerator*; *PCI*; *printed circuit board*; *sound card*; *video adapter*.

expansion card: Same as *expansion board*.

expansion bus: A collection of wires and protocols that allows the expansion of a computer by inserting printed circuit boards (*expansion boards*). Traditionally, PCs have utilized an expansion bus called the *ISA bus*. In recent years, however, the ISA bus has become a bottleneck, and there are now several competing standards for a new PC expansion bus. These include *EISA*, *PCI*, and *VL-Bus*.

➠ See also *bus*; *EISA*; *expansion board*; *local bus*; *PCI*; *protocol*; *VL-Bus*.

expansion slot: An opening in a computer where a circuit board can be inserted to add new capabilities to the computer. Nearly all personal computers except portables contain expansion slots for adding more memory, graphics capabilities, and support for special devices. The boards inserted into the expansion slots are called *expansion boards, expansion cards, cards, add-ins,* and *add-ons.*

[PC] Expansion slots for PCs come in two basic sizes: *half-* and *full-size.* Half-size slots are also called *8-bit slots* because they can transfer 8 bits at a time. Full-size slots are sometimes called *16-bit slots*. In addition, many modern computers include *local-bus slots* for expansion boards that connect directly to the machine's local bus.

➠ See also *expansion board*; *local bus*; *printed circuit board*.

expert system: A computer application that performs a task that would otherwise be performed by a human expert. For example, there are expert systems that can diagnose human illnesses, make financial forecasts, and schedule routes for delivery vehicles. Some expert systems are designed to take the place of human experts, while others are designed to aid them.

Expert systems are part of a general category of computer applications known as *artificial intelligence.* To design an expert system, one needs a *knowledge engineer,* an individual who studies how human experts make decisions and translates the rules into terms that a computer can understand.

➠ See also *artificial intelligence.*

exploded view: A picture or diagram that shows the components of an object slightly separated, as if there had been a neat explosion in the middle of the object. Many spreadsheet applications can automatically create exploded diagrams, such as exploded pie charts.

➠ See also *spreadsheet.*

export: To format data in such a way that it can be used by another application. An application that can export data can create a file in a format that another application understands, enabling the two programs to share the same data. The two programs might be different types of word processors, or one could be a word processor while the other could be a database management system.

The flip side of exporting is *importing.* Importing refers to the ability of an application to read and use data produced by a different application. Exporting implies that the sending application reformats the data for the receiving application, whereas importing implies that the receiving application does the reformatting.

➠ See also *import.*

expression: In programming, an expression is any legal combination of symbols that represents a value. Each programming language and application has its own rules for what is legal and illegal. For example, in the C language $x+5$ is an expression, as is the character string "MONKEYS."

Every expression consists of at least one *operand* and can have one or more *operators*. Operands are values, whereas operators are symbols that represent particular actions. In the expression

$$x + 5$$

x and 5 are operands, and + is an operator.

Expressions are used in programming languages, database systems, and spreadsheet applications. For example, in database systems, you use expressions to specify which information you want to see. These types of expressions are called *queries.*

Expressions are often classified by the type of value that they represent. For example:

Boolean expressions: Evaluate to either TRUE or FALSE

integer expressions: Evaluate to whole numbers, like 3 or 100

Floating-point expressions: Evaluate to real numbers, like 3.141 or - 0.005

String expressions: Evaluate to character strings

➡ See also *Boolean expression; character string; data type; floating-point number; integer; operand; operator; query.*

extended ASCII: A set of codes that extends the basic ASCII set. The basic ASCII set uses 7 bits for each character, giving it a total of 128 unique symbols. The extended ASCII character set uses 8 bits, which gives it an additional 128 characters. The extra characters represent characters from foreign languages and special symbols for drawing pictures. See *ASCII* for a table of ASCII and extended ASCII character codes.

➡ See also *ASCII.*

Extended Binary-Coded Decimal Interchange Code: See *EBCDIC.*

Extended Capabilities Port: See *ECP.*

extended graphics array: See XGA.

Extended Industry Standard Architecture: See EISA.

extended keyboard: MAC A keyboard for Macintosh computers that contains up to 15 function keys above the alphanumeric keys, and a numeric keypad. It is sometimes called an *enhanced keyboard* because of its similarity to the PC enhanced keyboard.

➠ See *enhanced keyboard; keyboard.*

extended memory: PC Memory above and beyond the standard 1MB (megabyte) of main memory that DOS supports. Extended memory is only available in PCs with an Intel 80286 or later microprocessor.

Two types of memory can be added to a PC to increase memory beyond 1MB: *expanded memory* and *extended memory*. Expanded memory conforms to a published standard called *EMS* that enables DOS programs to take advantage of it. Extended memory, on the other hand, is not configured in any special manner and is therefore unavailable to most DOS programs. However, MS-Windows and OS/2 can use extended memory.

➠ See also *expanded memory; protected mode; RAM disk; XMS.*

Extended Memory Specification: See XMS.

extended VGA: See SVGA.

extension: (1) An extra feature added to a standard programming language or system.

(2) In DOS and some other operating systems, one or several letters at the end of a filename. Filename extensions usually follow a period (dot) and indicate the type of information stored in the file. For example, in the filename *EDIT.COM*, the extension is *COM*, which indicates that the file is a command file. (Depending on the operating system, the punctuation separating the extension from the rest of the filename may or may not be considered part of the extension itself.)

184

(3) ⬛MAC⬛ In Macintosh environments, a program that extends the system's capabilities. When they reside in the Extensions folder, extensions are loaded into memory when the system starts. On older Macs (System 6 and earlier), extensions were called *inits.*

➠ See also *init; memory resident.*

external cache: Same as *secondary cache.*

external command: ⬛PC⬛ In DOS systems, any command that does not reside in the COMMAND.COM file. This includes all other COM files, as well as EXE and BAT files. Commands in the COM-MAND.COM file are called *internal commands.*

➠ See also COMMAND.COM; *internal command.*

external modem: A modem that resides in a self-contained box outside the computer system. Contrast with an *internal modem,* which resides on a printed circuit board inserted into the computer (see Figure 55 at *modem*).

External modems tend to be slightly more expensive than internal modems. Many experts consider them superior because they contain lights that indicate how the modem is functioning. In addition, they can easily be moved from one computer to another.

➠ See also *modem; printed circuit board.*

extremely low-frequency (ELF) emission: See *ELF emission.*

F

F1, F2...F15: The names of the function keys. See under *function key*.

facsimile machine: See *fax machine*.

FAQ: Pronounced *fak*, and short for *frequently asked questions*, a FAQ is a document that answers questions about some technical topic. Frequently, FAQs are formatted as help files or hypertext documents.

➠ See also *hypertext; help*.

Fast AT Attachment (ATA): See under *EIDE*.

Fast Ethernet: See under *Ethernet*.

fast IDE: Short for *Fast AT Attachment (ATA)*. See under *EIDE*.

FAT: See *file allocation table*.

fatal error: An error that causes a program to abort. Sometimes a fatal error returns you to the operating system. When a fatal error occurs, you may lose whatever data the program was currently processing.

➠ See also *abort; crash*.

fault tolerance: The ability of a system to respond gracefully to an unexpected hardware or software failure. There are many levels of fault tolerance, the lowest being the ability to continue operation in the event of a power failure. Many fault-tolerant computer systems *mirror* all operations—that is, every operation is performed on two or more duplicate systems, so if one fails the other can take over.

fax: (v) To send a document via a fax machine.

(n) (1) A document that has been sent, or is about to be sent, via a fax machine.

(2) Short for *Facsimile machine.*

➡ See also *fax machine.*

fax board: See under *fax modem.*

fax machine: Abbreviation of *facsimile machine,* a fax machine is a device that can send or receive pictures and text over a telephone line. Fax machines work by digitizing an image—dividing it into a grid of dots. Each dot is either on or off, depending on whether it is black or white. Electronically, each dot is represented by a bit that has a value of either 0 (off) or 1 (on). In this way, the fax machine translates a picture into a series of zeros and ones (called a *bit map*) that can be transmitted like normal computer data. On the receiving side, a fax machine reads the incoming data, translates the zeros and ones back into dots, and reprints the picture.

The idea of fax machines has been around since 1842, when Alexander Bain invented a machine capable of receiving signals from a telegraph wire and translating them into images on paper. In 1850, a London inventor named F. C. Blakewell received a patent for a similar machine, which he called a *copying telegraph.*

But while the idea of fax machines has existed since the 1800s, fax machines did not become popular until the mid 1980s. The spark igniting the fax revolution was the adoption in 1983 of a standard protocol for sending faxes at rates of 9,600 bps. The standard was created by the CCITT standards organization and is known as the *Group 3* standard. Now, faxes are commonplace in offices of all sizes. They provide an inexpensive, fast, and reliable method for transmitting correspondence, contracts, résumés, handwritten notes, and illustrations.

A fax machine consists of an optical scanner for digitizing images on paper, a printer for printing incoming fax messages, and a telephone for making the connection. The optical scanner generally does not offer the same quality of resolution as stand-alone scanners. Most printers on fax machines are *thermal*, which means they require a special kind of paper.

All fax machines conform to the CCITT Group 3 protocol. (There is a new protocol called *Group 4*, but it requires ISDN lines.) The Group 3 protocol supports two classes of resolution: 203 by 98 dpi and 203 by 196 dpi. The protocol also specifies a data-compression technique and a maximum transmission speed of 9,600 bps.

Some of the features that differentiate one fax machine from another include the following:

speed: fax machines transmit data at different rates, from 4,800 bps to 28,800 bps. A 9,600-bps fax machine typically requires 10 to 20 seconds to transmit one page.

printer type: Most fax machines use a thermal printer that requires special paper that tends to turn yellow or brown after a period. More expensive fax machines have printers that can print on regular bond paper.

paper size: The thermal paper used in most fax machines comes in two basic sizes: 8.5-inches wide and 10.1-inches wide. Some machines accept only the narrow-sized paper.

paper cutter: Most fax machines include a paper cutter because the thermal paper that most fax machines use comes in rolls. The least expensive models and portable faxes, however, may not include a paper cutter.

paper feed: Most fax machines have paper feeds so that you can send multiple-page documents without manually feeding each page into the machine.

autodialing: fax machines come with a variety of dialing features. Some enable you to program the fax to send a document at a future time so that you can take advantage of the lowest telephone rates.

As an alternative to stand-alone fax machines, you can also put together a fax system by purchasing separately a fax modem and an optical scanner. You may not even need the optical scanner if the documents you want to send are already in electronic form.

➠ See also *bps; digitize; fax modem; optical scanner; thermal printer.*

fax modem: A device you can attach to a personal computer that enables you to transmit (and sometimes receive) electronic documents as faxes. A fax modem is like a regular modem except that it is designed to transmit documents to a fax machine or another fax modem. Some, but not all, fax modems do double duty as regular modems. As with regular modems, fax modems can be either *internal* or *external.* Internal fax modems are often called *fax boards.*

Documents sent through a fax modem must already be in an electronic form (that is, in a disk file), and the documents you receive are likewise stored in files on your disk. To create fax documents from images on paper, you need an optical scanner.

Fax modems come with communications software similar to communications software for regular modems. This software can give the fax modem many capabilities that are not available with stand-alone fax machines. For example, you can broadcast a fax document to several sites at once. In addition, fax modems offer the following advantages over fax machines:

price: fax modems are less expensive. In addition, they require less maintenance because there are no moving parts. However, if you need to purchase an optical scanner in addition to the fax modem, there is no price advantage.

convenience: fax modems are more convenient if the documents you want to send are already in electronic form. With a fax machine, you would first need to print the document. A fax modem lets you send it directly.

speed: fax modems can almost always transmit documents at the maximum speed of 9,600 bps, whereas not all fax machines support such high data-transmission rates.

image quality: The image quality of documents transmitted by fax modems is usually superior because the documents remain in electronic form.

The principal disadvantage of fax modems is that you cannot fax paper documents unless you buy a separate optical scanner, which eliminates any cost and convenience advantages of fax modems. Another problem with fax modems is that each document you receive requires an enormous amount of disk storage (about 100K per page). Not only does this eat up disk storage, but it takes a long time to print such files.

➠ See also *broadcast; fax machine; modem; optical scanner.*

FCC: Abbreviation of *Federal Communications Commission.* Among other duties, the FCC is responsible for rating personal computers and other equipment as either Class A or Class B. The ratings indicate how much radiation a personal computer emits. Almost all personal computers satisfy Class A requirements, which means they are suitable for office use. Class B machines, which are suitable for use anywhere (including the home), must pass more stringent tests. Class B indicates that the machine's radio frequency (RF) emissions are so low that they do not interfere with other devices such as radios and TVs.

FDDI: Abbreviation of *Fiber-Optic Digital Device Interface*, a set of ANSI protocols for sending digital data over fiber optic cable. FDDI supports data rates of up to 100 megabits (100 million bits) per second. An extension to FDDI, called *FDDI-2*, supports the transmission of voice and video information as well as data.

➠ See also *fiber optics; network; protocol.*

FDHD: ⬚MAC Short for *floppy drive, high density*, and pronounced *fud-hud*. FDHD refers to a disk drive that can read double-density and high-density 3½-inch floppy disks formatted for a PC. This enables Macintosh computers and PCs to share data. FDHD drives are often called *SuperDrives*.

➠ See also *density; floppy disk; Macintosh computer; SuperDrive disk drive.*

feathering: In desktop publishing, feathering is the process of adding space between all lines on a page or in a column to force vertical justification.

➠ See also *vertical justification.*

feature: A notable property of a device or software application. Many analysts bemoan the advent of *featurism*—the seemingly endless addition of more and more features onto what was once a simple application. One of the principal challenges of modern applications is to offer a multitude of features without making the application complex.

➠ See also *bells and whistles.*

Federal Communications Commission: See *FCC.*

female connector: See under *connector.*

FF: See *form feed.*

Fiber Optic Digital Device Interface: See *FDDI.*

fiber optics: A technology that uses glass (or plastic) threads (fibers) to transmit data. A fiber optic cable consists of a bundle of glass threads, each of which is capable of transmitting messages at close to the speed of light (Figure 30).

Fiber optics has several advantages over traditional metal communications lines:

- Fiber optic cables have a much greater bandwidth than metal cables. This means that they can carry more data.
- Fiber optic cables are less susceptible than metal cables to interference.
- Fiber optic cables are much thinner and lighter than metal wires.
- Data can be transmitted digitally (the natural form for computer data) rather than analogically.

The main disadvantage of fiber optics is that the cables are expensive to install. In addition, they are more fragile than wire and are difficult to split.

Fiber optics is a particularly popular technology for local-area networks. In addition, telephone companies are steadily replacing traditional telephone lines with fiber optic cables. In the future, almost all communications will employ fiber optics.

➡ See also *FDDI*; *ISDN*; *local-area network*.

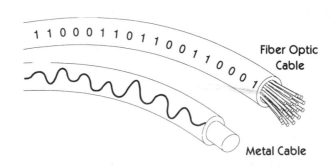

Figure 30: *Fiber Optics*

field: (1) A space allocated for a particular item of information. A tax form, for example, contains a number of fields: one for your name, one for your Social Security number, one for your income, and so on. In database systems, fields are the smallest units of information you can access. In spreadsheets, fields are called *cells*.

Most fields have certain attributes associated with them. For example, some fields are numeric whereas others are textual, some are long while others are short. In addition, every field has a name, called the *field name*.

In database management systems, a field can be *required, optional*, or *calculated*. A *required field* is one in which you must enter data, while an *optional field* is one you may leave blank. A calculated field is one whose value is derived from some formula involving other fields. You do not enter data into a calculated field; the system automatically determines the correct value.

A collection of fields is called a *record*.

➡ See also *attribute*; *cell*; *database management system*; *data type*; *record.*

(2) The phrase *in the field* refers to any geographical location other than the factory or office where a product was created. Similarly, a *field representative* is an employee who represents a company in distant locations.

file: A collection of data or information that has a name, called the *file-name*. Almost all information stored in a computer must be in a file. There are many different types of files: *data files, text files, program files, directory files,* and so on. Different types of files store different types of information. For example, program files store programs, whereas text files store text.

Table 15 lists some common types of files.

➠ See also *directory; document; executable file; library.*

Table 15
FILE TYPES

FILE TYPE	DESCRIPTION
Batch file	Same as command file—contains operating system commands
Binary file	Contains data or instructions in binary format
Command file	Contains operating system commands
Data file	Contains data
Directory file	Contains bookkeeping information about files that are below it
Executable file	Contains a program or commands in an executable format
Library file	Contains functions in object format
Map file	Contains a map of a program
Object file	Contains code that has been compiled
Text file	Contains textual data (that is, data that can be read by humans), including files you create with a text editor and any file in ASCII format

file allocation table (FAT): A table that the operating system uses to locate files on a disk. Due to fragmentation, a file may be divided into many sections that are scattered around the disk. The FAT keeps track of all these pieces.

In DOS systems, FATs are stored in *hidden files,* called *FAT files.*

➠ See also *cluster; disk; file; fragmentation.*

file attribute: See under *attribute.*

file compression: See under *data compression* and *packed file.*

file defragmentation: See under *fragmentation.*

file extension: See *extension.*

file format: A format for encoding information in a file. Each different type of file has a different file format. The file format specifies first whether the file is a binary or ASCII file, and second, how the information is organized. Table 16 and Table 17 at *graphics file formats*, for example, list a number of types of file formats for storing graphics.

➠ See also *file; format; graphics file formats.*

file fragmentation: See *fragmentation.*

file locking: See under *lock.*

file management system: The system that an operating system or program uses to organize and keep track of files. For example, a *hierarchical file system* is one that uses directories to organize files into a tree structure (see Figure 26 at *directory*).

Although the operating system provides its own file management system, you can buy separate file management systems. These systems interact smoothly with the operating system but provide more features, such as improved backup procedures and stricter file protection.

➠ See also *directory; hierarchical.*

filename: The name of a file. All files have names. Different operating systems impose different restrictions on filenames. Most operating systems, for example, prohibit the use of certain characters in a filename and impose a limit on the length of a filename. In addition, many systems, including DOS and UNIX, allow a *filename extension* that consists of one or more characters following the proper filename. The filename extension usually indicates what type of file it is.

Within a single directory, filenames must be unique. However, two files in different directories may have the same name. Some operating systems, such as UNIX and the Macintosh operating system, allow a file to have more than one name, called an *alias*.

➠ See also *alias; directory; extension; file*.

filename extension: See *extension*.

file server: See under *server*.

file system: Same as *file management system*.

File Transfer Program: See *FTP*.

fill: (1) In graphics applications, to paint the inside of an enclosed object (Figure 31). Typically, you can choose a color and pattern, and then paint the object with a *fill tool*. The area that is painted is called the *fill area*.

➠ See also *graphics*.

(2) In spreadsheet applications, to copy the contents of one cell to an entire range of cells—that is, to *fill* the range with a formula or value.

➠ See also *spreadsheet*.

Figure 31: *Fills*

filter: (1) A program that accepts a certain type of data as input, transforms it in some manner, and then outputs the transformed data. For example, a program that sorts names is a filter because it accepts the names in unsorted order, sorts them, and then outputs the sorted names.

Utilities that allow you to import or export data are also sometimes called *filters*.

➠ See also *export; import.*

(2) A pattern through which data is passed. Only data that matches the pattern is allowed to pass through the filter.

(3) In paint programs and image editors, a filter is an effect that can be applied to a bit map. Some filters mimic conventional photographic filters, but many transform images in unusual ways. A *pointillism filter*, for example, can make a digitized photograph look like a pointillistic painting (Figure 32).

➠ See also *image editor; image enhancement; photo illustration.*

Original photo   Photo with pointillism filter applied

Figure 32: *Pointillism Filter*

Finder: MAC The desktop management and file management system for Apple Macintosh computers. In addition to managing files and disks, the Finder is responsible for managing the Clipboard and Scrapbook and all desktop icons and windows.

➠ See also *clipboard; desktop; file management; Multifinder; multitasking.*

firmware: Software (programs or data) that has been permanently written onto read-only memory (ROM). Firmware is a combination of software and hardware. ROMs and PROMs that have data or programs recorded on them are firmware.

➠ See also *hardware*; *PROM*; *ROM*; *software*.

fixed disk: Same as *hard disk*.

fixed-frequency monitor: A monitor that can only accept signals in one frequency range. In contrast, *multiscanning monitors* automatically adjust themselves to the frequency at which data is being sent.

➠ See also *monitor*; *multiscanning monitor*.

fixed length: Having a set length that never varies. In database systems, a field can have a *fixed* or a *variable length*. A variable-length field is one whose length can be different in each record, depending on what data is stored in the field.

The terms *fixed length* and *variable length* can also refer to the entire record. A fixed-length record is one in which every field has a fixed length. A variable-length record has at least one variable-length field.

➠ See also *database management system*; *field*; *record*; *variable length*.

fixed pitch: Refers to fonts in which every character has the same width. Most typewriters and inexpensive printers use fixed-pitch fonts. Newspapers, magazines, and books, however, usually use *proportional fonts*, in which different characters have different widths (see Figure 69 at *proportional spacing*).

The use of a fixed-pitch font is called *monospacing*.

➠ See also *font*; *monospacing*; *pitch*; *proportional spacing*.

fixed width: Same as *fixed pitch*.

➠ See also *fixed pitch*; *font*.

flag: (n) (1) A software or hardware mark that signals a particular condition or status. A flag is like a switch that can be either on or off. The flag is said to be *set* when it is turned on.

(2) A special mark indicating that a piece of data is unusual. For example, a record might contain an *error flag* to indicate that the record consists of unusual, probably incorrect, data.

(v) To mark an object to indicate that a particular event has occurred or that the object marked is unusual is some way.

flame: (n) A searing e-mail message in which the writer attacks another e-mail participant in overly harsh, and often personal, terms. Flames are an unfortunate, but inevitable, element of unmoderated conferences.

(v) To post a flame.

➠ See also *conference; forum; e-mail; online service.*

flash BIOS: See under *BIOS.*

flash memory: A special type of *EEPROM* that can be erased and reprogrammed inside a computer. Unlike conventional EEPROM, which requires a special device called a *PROM reader* that exposes the memory to higher-than-normal voltages, flash memory can be erased using the normal voltages inside a PC.
　　Many modern PCs have their BIOS stored on a flash memory chip so that it can easily be updated if necessary. Such a BIOS is sometimes called a *flash BIOS.*

➠ See also *BIOS; EEPROM.*

flash ROM: Same as *flash memory.*

flatbed scanner: A type of *optical scanner* that consists of a flat surface on which you lay documents to be scanned. Flatbed scanners are particularly effective for bound documents.

➠ See also *optical scanner.*

flat-file database: A relatively simple database system in which each database is contained in a single table. In contrast, *relational database* systems can use multiple tables to store information, and each table can have a different record format. Relational systems are more suitable for large applications, but flat databases are adequate for many small applications.

➠ See also *database management system; relational database.*

flat-panel display: A very thin display screen used in portable computers. Nearly all modern flat-panel displays use LCD technologies. Most LCD screens are backlit to make them easier to read in bright environments.

➠ See also *active-matrix display; backlighting; display screen; dual-scan display; electroluminescent display; gas-plasma display; LCD; notebook computer; TFT.*

flat screen: Same as *flat-panel display.*

flat technology monitor: Often abbreviated as FTM, flat technology monitors are monitors that have a flat display screen to reduce glare. Conventional display screens are curved, which makes them more susceptible to reflections from external light sources.

Do not confuse flat technology monitors with *flat-panel displays.* Flat-panel displays are the display screens used in laptops and other portable computers.

➠ See also CRT; *flat-panel display; monitor.*

flicker: See *screen flicker.*

floating: In graphical user interfaces, floating refers to application elements that you can move to different places. Many applications support *floating toolbars*, which are collections of icons that represent tools. By moving them wherever you want on the screen, you can create your own customized working environment. In addition to toolbars, many graphics programs support *floating palettes*.

➠ See also *palette*.

floating-point number: A real number (that is, a number that can contain a fractional part). The following are floating-point numbers:

```
3.0
-111.5
3E-5
```

The last example is a computer shorthand for scientific notation. It means $3*10^{-5}$ (or 10 to the negative 5th power multiplied by 3).

In essence, computers are integer machines and are capable of representing real numbers only by using complex codes. The most popular code for representing real numbers is called the *IEEE Floating-Point Standard.*

The term *floating point* is derived from the fact that there is no fixed number of digits before and after the decimal point; that is, the decimal point can float. There are also representations in which the number of digits before and after the decimal point is set, called *fixed-point* representations. In general, floating-point representations are slower and less accurate than fixed-point representations, but they can handle a larger range of numbers.

Note that most floating-point numbers a computer can represent are just approximations. One of the challenges in programming with floating-point values is ensuring that the approximations lead to reasonable results. If the programmer is not careful, small discrepancies in the approximations can snowball to the point where the final results become meaningless.

Because mathematics with floating-point numbers requires a great deal of computing power, many microprocessors come with a chip, called a *floating point unit (FPU)*, specialized for performing floating-point arithmetic. FPUs are also called *math coprocessors* and *numeric coprocessors.*

➠ See also *FPU; precision; scientific notation.*

floating-point unit: See *FPU*.

floppy disk: A soft magnetic disk (Figure 33). It is called *floppy* because it flops if you wave it (at least, the 5st hard disks, floppy disks (often called *floppies* or *diskettes*) are portable, because you can remove them from a disk drive. Disk drives for floppy disks are called *floppy drives.* Floppy disks are slower to access than hard disks and have less storage capacity, but they are much less expensive. And most importantly, they are portable.

Floppies come in two basic sizes:

5¼-inch: The common size for PCs made before 1987. This type of floppy is generally capable of storing between 100K and 1.2MB (megabytes) of data. The most common sizes are 360K and 1.2MB.

3½-inch: *Floppy* is something of a misnomer for these disks, as they are encased in a rigid envelope. Despite their small size, microfloppies have a larger storage capacity than their cousins—from 400K to 1.4MB of data. The most common sizes for PCs are 720K (double-density) and 1.44MB (high-density). Macintoshes support disks of 400K, 800K, and 1.2MB.

➠ See also *density; disk; FDHD.*

Write Protect Switch   Write Protect Notch

3½-inch   5¼-inch

Figure 33: *Floppy Disk*

floppy drive: Short for floppy disk drive, a disk drive that can read and write to floppy disks.

➠ See also *disk drive; floppy disk.*

floptical: A type of disk drive technology that uses a combination of magnetic and optical techniques to achieve greater storage capacity than normal floppy disks without sacrificing access speeds.

flow: In desktop publishing, to insert a body of text into a document such that it wraps (or *flows*) around any objects on the page.

➠ See also *desktop publishing.*

flush: (adj) Aligned along a margin. For example, text that is *flush left* is aligned along the left margin. *Flush-right* text is aligned along the right margin. For example:

This text	This text
is flush	is flush
left.	right.

The opposite of flush is *ragged*. For example, the first example has a ragged right margin and second example has a ragged left margin. Text that is both flush left and flush right is said to be *justified*.

➠ See also *justify; margins; ragged.*

(v) To copy data from a temporary storage area such as RAM to a more permanent storage medium such as a disk.

folder: In graphical user interfaces such as Windows and the Macintosh environment, a folder is an object that can contain multiple documents. Folders are used to organize information. In the DOS and UNIX worlds, folders are called *directories.*

➠ See also *desktop; directory; file; graphical user interface.*

font: A design for a set of characters (Figure 34). A font is the combination of typeface and other qualities, such as size, pitch, and spacing. For example, Times Roman is a typeface that defines the shape of each character. Within Times Roman, however, there are many fonts to choose from—different sizes, italic, bold, and so on. (The term *font* is often used incorrectly as a synonym for *typeface*.)

The height of characters in a font is measured in *points*, each point being approximately 1/72 inch. For example, the text in this book is printed with 10-point type. The width is measured by *pitch*, which refers to how many characters can fit in an inch. Common pitch values are 10 and 12. A font is said to be *fixed pitch* if every character has the same width. If the widths vary depending on the shape of the character, it is called a *proportional font.*

Helvetica

ABCDEFGHIJKLMNOPQRSTUVWXYZ
Fonts are designed for a set of characters. A font is the combination of

Courier

```
ABCDEFGHIJKLMNOPQRSTUVWXYZ
Fonts are designed for a set
of characters. A font is the
```

Times Roman

ABCDEFGHIJKLMNOPQRSTUVWXYZ
Fonts are designed for a set of characters. A font is the combination of typeface and other

Optima

ABCDEFGHIJKLMNOPQRSTUVWXYZ
Fonts are designed for a set of characters. A font is the combination of typeface and

Figure 34: *Popular Fonts*

Most applications that support text enable you to choose from among many fonts. Laser, ink-jet, and dot-matrix printers offer the widest selection of fonts. These printers support a certain set of built-in fonts, but you can expand this set by loading different fonts from software (*soft fonts*) or from font cartridges.

Computers and devices use two methods to represent fonts. In a *bit-mapped font*, every character is represented by an arrangement of dots. To print a bit-mapped character, a printer simply locates the character's bit-mapped representation stored in memory and prints the corresponding dots. Each different font, even when the typeface is the same, requires a different set of bit maps.

The other method utilizes a *vector graphics system* to define fonts. In vector graphics systems, the shape or outline of each character is defined geometrically. The typeface can be displayed in any size, so a single font description really represents innumerable fonts. For this reason, vector fonts are called *scalable fonts*—they can be any size (scale). Other terms for vector fonts are *object-oriented fonts* or *outline fonts*. The most widely used scalable-font systems are PostScript and TrueType.

Aside from the scalability of vector fonts, their other main advantage over bit-mapped fonts is that they make the most of high-resolution devices. Bit-mapped fonts look almost the same whether printed on a 300-dpi printer or a 1,200-dpi printer. Vector fonts look better, the higher the resolution.

Despite the advantages of vector fonts, bit-mapped fonts are still widely used. One reason for this is that small vector fonts do not look very good on low-resolution devices, such as display monitors (which are low-resolution when compared with laser printers). Many computer systems, therefore, use bit-mapped fonts for screen displays. These are sometimes called *screen fonts*. In addition, some professionals prefer to use bit-mapped fonts on high-resolution printers because characters can be individually tailored to the printing device.

An additional drawback of vector fonts is that every character must be generated as it is needed. This is a computation-intensive process that requires a powerful microprocessor to make it acceptably fast.

➠ See also *bit-mapped graphics; fixed pitch; font cartridge; page description language; pitch; point; PostScript; proportional pitch; scalable font; soft font; TrueType; typeface; vector graphics*

font card: Same as *font cartridge.*

font cartridge: A ROM cartridge that contains one or more fonts. By inserting the cartridge into a laser printer, you give the printer the ability to print different fonts. Another way to load fonts into a printer is to download them from the computer's storage device.

➟ See also *cartridge; download; font; laser printer; soft font.*

font family: A set of fonts all with the same typeface, but with different sizes, weights and slants.

➟ See also *font; typeface.*

footer: One or more lines of text that appear at the bottom of every page of a document. Once you specify what text should appear in the footer, the application automatically inserts it.

Most applications allow you to use special symbols in the footer that represent changing values. For example, you can enter a symbol for the page number, and the application will replace the symbol with the correct number on each page. If you enter the date symbol, the application will insert the current date, which will change if necessary each time you print the document.

You can usually specify at least two different footers, one for odd-numbered pages (*odd footer*) and one for even-numbered pages (*even footer*).

A footer is sometimes called a *running foot.*

➟ See also *header.*

footprint: The amount of floor or desk space required by a device. For example, a *small-footprint* computer is a computer whose dimensions (width and depth) are relatively small.

➟ See also *desktop model computer; tower model.*

forced page break: A page break that you explicitly insert. The application cannot override a forced page break. Forced page breaks are sometimes called *hard page breaks.*

➟ See also *hard; page break; soft.*

foreground: (1) In multiprocessing systems, the process that is currently accepting input from the keyboard or other input device is sometimes called the *foreground process.*

➠ See also *background; multiprocessing.*

(2) On display screens, the foreground consists of the characters and pictures that appear on the screen. The background is the uniform canvas behind the characters and pictures.

➠ See also *background.*

format: (v) (1) To prepare a storage medium, usually a disk, for reading and writing. When you format a disk, the operating system erases all bookkeeping information on the disk, tests the disk to make sure all sectors are reliable, marks bad sectors (that is, those that are scratched), and creates internal address tables that it later uses to locate information. You must format a disk before you can use it.

Note that reformatting a disk does not erase the data on the disk, only the address tables. Do not panic, therefore, if you accidentally reformat a disk that has useful data. A computer specialist should be able to recover most, if not all, of the information on the disk. You can also buy programs that enable you to recover a disk yourself.

The previous discussion, however, applies only to *high-level* formats, the type of formats that most users execute. In addition, hard disks have a *low-level format,* which sets certain properties of the disk such as the interleave factor. The low-level format also determines what type of disk controller can access the disk (e.g., *RLL* or *MFM*).

Almost all hard disks that you purchase have already had a low-level format. It is not necessary, therefore, to perform a low-level format yourself unless you want to change the interleave factor or make the disk accessible by a different type of disk controller. Performing a low-level format erases all data on the disk.

➠ See also *controller; disk; hard disk; initialize; interleaving; low-level format; MFM; RLL; sector.*

(2) To specify the properties, particularly visible properties, of an object. For example, word processing applications allow you to format text, which involves specifying the font, alignment, margins, and other properties.

(n) A particular arrangement. Almost everything associated with computers has a format.

form feed: (1) Printers that use continuous paper normally have a form feed button or command that advances the paper to the beginning of the next page.

(2) A special character that causes the printer to advance one page length or to the top of the next page. In systems that use the ASCII character set, a form feed has a decimal value of 12. *Form feed* is some-times abbreviated *FF*.

➠ See also *ASCII*.

forms software: A type of program that enables you to design and fill in forms on a computer. Most forms packages contain a number of sample forms that you can modify for your own purposes.

formula: (1) An equation or expression.

➠ See also *expression*.

(2) In spreadsheet applications, a formula is an expression that defines how one cell relates to other cells. For example, you might define cell C5 (column C, row 5) with the formula

    +A4*D7

which means to multiply the value in cell A4 by the value in cell D7.

➠ See also *cell; expression; spreadsheet*.

FORTRAN: Acronym for *formula translator*, FORTRAN is the oldest high-level programming language. Designed by Jim Backus for IBM in the late 1950s, it is still popular today, particularly for scientific appli-cations that require extensive mathematical computations.

The two most common versions of FORTRAN are FORTRAN IV and FORTRAN 77. FORTRAN IV was approved as a USASI stan-dard in 1966. FORTRAN 77 is a version of FORTRAN that was approved by ANSI in 1978 (they had expected to approve it in 1977, hence the name). FORTRAN 77 includes a number of features not available in older versions of FORTRAN. A new ISO and ANSI standard for FORTRAN, called *FORTRAN-90*, was recently developed.

➠ See also *ANSI; ISO; programming language.*

forum: An online discussion group. Online services and bulletin board services (BBSs) provide a variety of forums, in which participants with common interests can exchange open messages. Forums are sometimes called *newsgroups* (in the Internet world) or conferences.

➠ See also *bulletin board service; online service; USENET.*

486: Short for the *Intel 80486 microprocessor.*

➠ See also *Intel microprocessors.*

4GL: See *fourth-generation language.*

fourth-generation language: Often abbreviated *4GL,* fourth-generation languages are programming languages closer to human languages than typical high-level programming languages (see Figure 68 at *programming language*). Most 4GLs are used to access databases. For example, a typical 4GL command is

FIND ALL RECORDS WHERE NAME IS "SMITH"

The other three generations of computer languages are

first generation: machine language

second generation: assembly language

third generation: high-level programming languages

➠ See also *database management system; programming language; query; query language.*

fps: Stands for *frames per second,* a measure of how much information is used to store and display motion video. The term applies equally to film video and digital video. Each frame is a still image; displaying frames in quick succession creates the illusion of motion. The more frames per second (fps), the smoother the motion appears. Television in the U.S., for example, is based on the NTSC format, which displays 60 frames per second. In general, the minimum fps need to avoid jerky motion is about 30. Some computer video formats, such as AVI, provide only 15 frames per second.

➠ See also *AVI; NTSC.*

FPU: Short for *floating-point unit,* a specially designed chip that performs *floating-point* calculations. Computers equipped with an FPU perform certain types of applications much faster than computers that lack one. In particular, graphics applications are faster with an FPU. Some microprocessors, such as the Intel 80486 and Pentium, have a built-in FPU. With other microprocessors, you can usually add an FPU by inserting the FPU chip on the *motherboard.*

Floating-point units are also called *numeric coprocessors, math coprocessors,* and *floating-point processors.*

➠ See also *coprocessor; Intel microprocessors; floating-point number.*

fractal: A word coined by Benoit Mandelbrot in 1975 to describe shapes that are "self-similar"—that is, shapes that look the same at different magnifications. To create a fractal, you start with a simple shape and duplicate it successively according to a set of fixed rules. Oddly enough, such a simple formula for creating shapes can produce very complex structures, some of which have a striking resemblance to objects that appear in the real world (Figure 35). For example, graphics designers use fractals to generate images of mountainous landscapes, coastlines, and flowers. In fact, many of the computer-generated images that appear in science fiction films utilize fractals.

fragmentation: (1) Refers to the condition of a disk in which files are divided into pieces scattered around the disk. Fragmentation occurs naturally when you use a disk frequently, creating, deleting, and modifying files. At some point, a file becomes too large for the space originally allotted for it, so the operating system splits the file into two or more chunks. This is entirely invisible to users, but it can slow down

Figure 35: *Fractal image of moon, mountains and lake.*

the speed at which data is accessed because the disk drive must search through different parts of the disk to put together a single file.

In DOS 6.0 and later systems, you can defragment a disk with the DEFRAG command. You can also buy software utilities, called *disk optimizers* or *defragmenters,* that defragment a disk.

➠ See also *cluster; disk optimizer; file allocation table.*

(2) Fragmentation can also refer to RAM that has small, unused holes scattered throughout it.

frame: (1) In graphics and desktop publishing applications, a rectangular area in which text or graphics can appear.

(2) In communications, a packet of transmitted information.

(3) In video and animation, a single image. See under *fps.*

frames per second: See *fps*.

freeware: Copyrighted software given away for free by the author. Although it is available for free, the author retains the copyright, which means that you cannot do anything with it that is not expressly allowed by the author. Usually, the author allows people to use the software, but not sell it.

➠ See also *public domain software; shareware.*

friction feed: A method of feeding paper through a printer. Friction-feed printers use plastic or rubber rollers to squeeze a sheet of paper and pull it through the printer.

The other principal form of feeding paper into a dot-matrix or daisy-wheel printer is through a *tractor feed,* in which sprocketed wheels on either side of the printer fit into holes in the paper. As the wheels revolve, the paper is pulled through the printer.

Tractor-feed printers require special paper, whereas friction-feed printers can handle most types of cut-sheet paper, including envelopes. Many printers support both types of feeding mechanisms (see Figure 83 at *tractor feed*).

➠ See also *printer; sheet feeder; tractor feed.*

front end: (1) For software applications, *front end* is the same as *user interface.*

➠ See also *user interface.*

(2) In client/server applications, the client part of the program is often called the *front end* and the server part is called the *back end.*

➠ See also *client/server architecture; distributed processing.*

(3) Compilers, the programs that translate source code into object code, are often composed of two parts: a *front end* and a *back end.* The front end is responsible for checking syntax and detecting errors, whereas the back end performs the actual translation into object code.

➠ See also *compiler.*

frozen: Unresponsive. The term is used to describe a monitor, keyboard, or the entire computer when it no longer reacts to input due to a malfunction.

➦ See also *crash.*

FTM: See *flat technology monitor.*

FTP: Abbreviation of *File Transfer Protocol,* the protocol used on the Internet for sending files.

➦ See also *communications; Internet.*

full duplex: Refers to the transmission of data in two directions simultaneously. For example, a telephone is a full-duplex device because both parties can talk at once. In contrast, a walkie-talkie is a *half-duplex* device because only one party can transmit at a time.

Most modems have a switch that lets you choose between full-duplex and half-duplex modes. The choice depends on which communications program you are running.

In full-duplex mode, data you transmit does not appear on your screen until it has been received and sent back by the other party. This enables you to validate that the data has been accurately transmitted. If your display screen shows two of each character, it probably means that your modem is set to half-duplex mode when it should be in full-duplex mode.

➦ See also *communications; half duplex; modem.*

full-length: See under *expansion board* and *expansion slot.*

function: (1) In programming, a named section of a program that performs a specific task. In this sense, a function is a type of procedure or routine. Some programming languages make a distinction between a *function,* which returns a value, and a *procedure,* which performs some operation but does not return a value.

Most programming languages come with a prewritten set of functions that are kept in a library. You can also write your own functions to perform specialized tasks.

➡ See also *library; procedure; program; routine.*

(2) The term *function* is also used synonymously with *operation* and command. For example, you execute the delete *function* to erase a word.

➡ See also *command.*

function keys: Special keys on the keyboard that have different meanings depending on which program is running. Function keys are normally labeled F1 to F10 or F12 (or F15 on Macintoshes). On older PCs, for example, ten function keys are grouped on the left side of the keyboard; new PCs have the enhanced keyboard, with twelve function keys aligned along the top of the keyboard.

➡ See also *Alt key; enhanced keyboard; keyboard.*

fuzzy logic: A type of logic that recognizes more than simple true and false values. With fuzzy logic, propositions can be represented with probabilities of truthfulness and falsehood. Fuzzy logic has proved to be particularly useful in expert system and other artificial intelligence applications.

➡ See also *artificial intelligence.*

G: The symbol used for *giga* or gigabyte.

➠ See also *giga.*

garbage in, garbage out: Often abbreviated as GIGO, this is a famous computer axiom meaning that if invalid data is entered into a system, the resulting output will also be invalid. Although originally applied to computer software, the axiom holds true for all systems, including, for example, decision-making systems.

gas-plasma display: A type of thin display screen, called a *flat-panel display,* used in some portable computers. A gas-plasma display works by sandwiching neon gas between two plates. One plate is coated with vertical wires and the other with horizontal wires, forming a grid. When electric current is passed through a horizontal and vertical wire, the gas at the intersection glows, creating a point of light, or *pixel.* You can think of a gas-plasma display as a collection of very small neon bulbs. Images on gas-plasma displays generally appear as orange objects on top of a black background.

Although gas-plasma displays produce very sharp monochrome images, they require much more power than the more common LCD displays.

➠ See also *flat-panel display; LCD; notebook computer.*

gateway: In networking, a combination of hardware and software that links two different types of networks. Gateways between e-mail systems, for example, allow users on different e-mail systems to exchange messages. Contrast with Bridge, which connects to networks of the same type.

➠ See also *bridge; network.*

GB: Short for *gigabyte.*

GDI printer: PC A printer that has built-in support for Windows Graphical Device Interface (GDI). GDI is used by most Windows applications to display images on a monitor, so when printing from a Windows application to a GDI printer, there is no need to convert the output to another format such as PostScript or PCL.

➠ See also *PCL; PostScript; printer; Windows.*

GEM: A graphical user interface developed by Digital Research that is built into personal computers made by Atari, and is also used as an interface for some DOS programs. Like the Macintosh interface and Microsoft Windows, GEM provides a windowed environment for running programs.

GEM also refers to a special graphics file format used in GEM-based applications.

➠ See also *graphical user interface; Macintosh computer; Microsoft Windows.*

genlock: Short for *generator locking device,* a genlock is a device that enables a composite video machine, such as a TV, to accept two signals simultaneously. A genlock locks one set of signals while it processes the second set. This enables you to combine graphics from a computer with video signals from a second source such as a video camera.

➠ See also *composite video.*

GIF: Pronounced *jiff,* stands for *graphics interchange format,* a bit-mapped graphics file format used by CompuServe and many BBSs. GIF supports color and various resolutions. It also includes data compression, making it especially effective for scanned photos.

➦ See also *data compression; graphics file format.*

giga (G): (1) When decimal notation is used, giga stands for one billion. For example, a *gigavolt* is 1 billion volts.

(2) When applied to computers, which use the binary notation system, giga represents 2 to the 30th power, which is 1,073,741,824, a little more than 1 billion. A gigabyte, therefore, is about 1.073 billion bytes.

➦ See also *binary; mass storage; megabyte.*

gigabyte: 2 to the 30th power (1,073,741,824) bytes. One gigabyte is equal to 1,024 megabytes. Gigabyte is often abbreviated as G or GB.

➦ See also *byte; giga; megabyte.*

GIGO: See *garbage in, garbage out.*

glitch: A malfunction. *Glitch* is sometimes used as a synonym for bug, but more often it refers to a hardware problem.

➦ See also *bug.*

gopher: A menu-based program that helps Internet users find files and other resources. It was developed at the University of Minnesota and named after the school's mascot. It is a particularly apt name, because the program excels at digging out otherwise difficult-to-find information.

➦ See also *Archie; Internet; World Wide Web.*

gppm: Abbreviation for *graphics pages per minute*, the speed with which laser printers can print nontext pages. Typically, laser printers are rated in terms of *pages per minute (ppm)*, but this refers only to the speed with which they print text pages. The gppm is always much less and may be the more important figure if you are using the printer to print graphics-intensive documents.

➠ See also *laser printer; ppm.*

grabber: (1) A device that captures data. The term is used most often to describe devices that can capture full-motion video from a television or video camera and convert it to digital form for storage on a computer's disk.

(2) In some applications, a special tool or cursor that enables you to grab objects on the screen and move them or manipulate them in some other way. A grabber cursor is often represented by a hand icon.

➠ See also *cursor.*

graphical user interface (GUI): Λ program interface that takes advantage of the computer's graphics capabilities to make the program easier to use (Figure 36). Well-designed graphical user interfaces can free the user from learning complex command languages. On the other hand, many users find that they work more effectively with a command-driven interface, especially if they already know the command language.

Graphical user interfaces, such as Microsoft Windows and the one used by the Apple Macintosh, feature the following basic components:

pointer: A symbol that appears on the display screen and that you move to select objects and commands. Usually, the pointer appears as a small angled arrow. Text-processing applications, however, use an I-beam pointer that is shaped like a capital I.

pointing device: A device, such as a mouse or trackball, that enables you to select objects on the display screen.

icons: Small pictures that represent commands, files, or windows. By moving the pointer to the icon and pressing a mouse button, you can execute a command or convert the icon into a window. You can also move the icons around the display screen as if they were real objects on your desk.

desktop: The area on the display screen where icons are grouped is often referred to as the desktop because the icons are intended to represent real objects on a real desktop.

windows: You can divide the screen into different areas. In each window, you can run a different program or display a different file. You can move windows around the display screen, and change their shape and size at will.

menus: Most graphical user interfaces let you execute commands by selecting a choice from a menu.

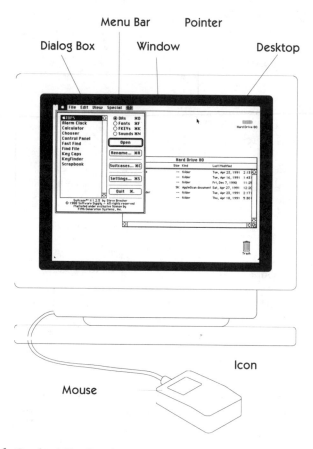

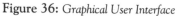

Figure 36: *Graphical User Interface*

The first graphical user interface was designed by Xerox Corporation's Palo Alto Research Center in the 1970s, but it was not until the 1980s and the emergence of the Apple Macintosh that graphical user interfaces became popular. One reason for their slow acceptance was the fact that they require considerable CPU power and a high-quality monitor, which until recently were prohibitively expensive.

In addition to their visual components, graphical user interfaces also make it easier to move data from one application to another. A true GUI includes standard formats for representing text and graphics. Because the formats are well-defined, different programs that run under a common GUI can share data. This makes it possible, for example, to copy a graph created by a spreadsheet program into a document created by a word processor.

Many DOS programs include some features of GUIs, such as menus, but are not *graphics based*. Such interfaces are sometimes called *graphical character-based user interfaces* to distinguish them from true GUIs.

➠ See also *character based; desktop; icon; Macintosh computer; Microsoft Windows; pointer; pointing device; user interface.*

graphics: Pertains to any computer device or program that makes a computer capable of displaying and manipulating pictures. For example, laser printers and plotters are *graphics devices* because they permit the computer to output pictures. A *graphics monitor* is a display monitor that can display pictures. A *graphics board* (or *graphics card*) is a printed circuit board that, when installed in a computer, permits the computer to display pictures.

Many software applications include graphics components. Such programs are said to *support* graphics. For example, certain word processors support graphics because they let you draw or import pictures. All CAD/CAM systems support graphics. Some database management systems and spreadsheet programs support graphics because they let you display data in the form of graphs and charts. Such applications are often referred to as *business graphics.*

The following are also considered *graphics applications:*

paint programs: Allow you to create rough freehand drawings. The images are stored as bit maps and can easily be edited.

illustration/design programs: Supports more advanced features than paint programs, particularly for drawing curved lines. The images are usually stored in vector-based formats. Illustration/design programs are often called *draw programs.*

presentation graphics software: Lets you create bar charts, pie charts, graphics, and other types of images for slide shows and reports. The charts can be based on data imported from spreadsheet applications.

animation software: Enables you to chain and sequence a series of images to simulate movement. Each image is like a frame in a movie.

CAD software: Enables architects and engineers to draft designs.

desktop publishing: Provides a full set of word-processing features as well as fine control over placement of text and graphics, so that you can create newsletters, advertisements, books, and other types of documents.

In general, applications that support graphics require a powerful CPU and a large amount of memory. Many graphics applications—for example, computer animation systems—require more computing power than is available on personal computers and will run only on powerful workstations or specially designed graphics computers. This is true of all three-dimensional computer graphics applications.

In addition to the CPU and memory, graphics software requires a graphics monitor and support for one of the many graphics standards. Most PC programs, for instance, require VGA graphics. If your computer does not have built-in support for a specific graphics system, you can insert a video adapter card.

The quality of most graphics devices is determined by their *resolution*—how many points per square inch they can represent—and their color capabilities.

➡ See also *bit map; bit-mapped graphics; CAD; CAD/CAM; character based; clip art; CPU; desktop publishing; display screen; laser printer; monitor; Microsoft Windows; personal computer; plotter; presentation graphics; resolution; spreadsheet; vector graphics; video adapter; workstation.*

graphics accelerator: A special type of video adapter that contains its own processor to boost performance levels. These processors are specialized for computing graphical transformations, so they achieve better results than the general-purpose CPU used by the computer. In addition, they free up the computer's CPU to execute other commands while the graphics accelerator is handling graphics computations.

The popularity of graphical applications, and especially multimedia applications, has made graphics accelerators not only a common enhancement, but a necessity. Most computer manufacturers now bundle a graphics accelerator with their mid-range and high-end systems.

Aside from the graphics processor used, the other characteristics that differentiate graphics accelerators are:

memory: Graphics accelerators have their own memory, which is reserved for storing graphical representations. The amount of memory determines how much resolution and how many colors can be displayed. Some accelerators use conventional DRAM, but others use a special type of video RAM (VRAM), which enables both the video circuitry and the processor to simultaneously access the memory.

bus: Each graphics accelerator is designed for a particular type of video bus. As of 1995, most are designed for the PCI bus.

register width: The wider the register, the more data the processor can manipulate with each instruction. 64-bit accelerators are already becoming common, and we can expect 128-bit accelerators in the near future.

➠ See also *CPU; DRAM; graphics; multimedia; PCI; video adapter; VRAM.*

graphics adapter: Same as *video adapter.*

graphics based: Refers to software and hardware that treat objects on a display screen as bit maps or geometrical shapes rather than as characters. In contrast, character-based systems treat everything as ASCII or extended ASCII characters.

All graphics software is by definition graphics based. Systems that manipulate text can also be graphics based; for example, desktop publishing systems are essentially graphics-based word processors.

Traditionally, most DOS applications—word processors, spreadsheets, and database management systems—have been character based. This enables them to run on any PC, even those with limited CPU, memory, and graphics capabilities. Increasingly, however, software manufacturers are spurning backward compatibility to create fully graphics-based applications.

Because the Macintosh is a graphical computer, all programs that run on a Macintosh computer are graphics based.

➠ See also *character based.*

graphics character: A character that represents a shape. By combining graphics characters, even character-mode programs can display rudimentary graphics, known as block graphics. Many of the characters in the extended ASCII character set are graphics characters.

➠ See also *block graphics; character mode; extended ASCII.*

graphics coprocessor: A microprocessor specially designed for handling graphics computations. Most graphics accelerators include a graphics coprocessor.

➠ See also *coprocessor; graphics accelerator.*

graphics display system: The combination of monitor and video adapter that makes a computer capable of displaying graphics.

➠ See also *graphics; monitor; video adapter.*

Table 16
BIT-MAPPED GRAPHICS FILE FORMATS

FORMAT	DESCRIPTION
BMP	The bit-mapped file format used by Microsoft Windows.
GIF	The bit-mapped file format used by CompuServe and many other BBSs.
PCX	Originally developed by ZSOFT for its PC Paintbrush program, PCX is a common graphics file format supported by many graphics programs, as well as most optical scanners and fax modems.
TIFF (Tagged Image File Format)	A standard file format for storing images as bit maps. It is used especially for scanned images because it can support any size, resolution, and color depth.

---

graphics file formats: A file format designed specifically for representing graphical images. Graphics file formats can be broadly categorized into bit-mapped formats and vector formats. Table 16 and Table 17 list the most common of both file formats.

➡ See also *CGM; DXF; EPS; GEM; graphics; HPGL; IGES; PCX; PIC; PICT; TIFF; WMF.*

Table 17
VECTOR GRAPHICS FILE FORMATS

FORMAT	DESCRIPTION
CGM (Computer Graphics Metafile)	A format developed by several standards organizations, CGM is supported by many PC software products.
DXF (Data Exchange File)	A format created by AutoDesk. Almost all PC-based CAD systems support DXF.
EPS (Encapsulated PostScript)	The file format for the PostScript language. EPS uses a combination of PostScript commands and TIFF or PICT formats.
GEM	The graphics file format used by GEM-based applications. GEM is a graphical user interface (GUI) developed by Digital Research.
HPGL (Hewlett-Packard Graphics Language)	One of the oldest file formats. Although it is not very sophisticated, it is supported by many PC-based graphics products.
IGES (Initial Graphics Exchange Specification)	An ANSI standard for three-dimensional wire frame models. IGES is supported by most PC-based CAD systems.
PIC (Lotus Picture File)	A relatively simple file format developed by Lotus for representing graphs generated by Lotus 1-2-3. PIC is supported by a wide variety of PC applications.
PICT	Developed by Apple Computer in 1984 as the standard format for storing and exchanging graphics files. It is supported by all graphics programs that run on a Macintosh.
WMF (Windows Metafile Format)	A file format for exchanging graphics between Microsoft Windows applications. WMF files can also hold bit-mapped images.

graphics mode: Many video adapters support several different modes of resolution, all of which are divided into two general categories: character mode and *graphics mode*. In character mode, the display screen is treated as an array of blocks, each of which can hold one ASCII character. In graphics mode, the display screen is treated as an array of pixels. Characters and other shapes are formed by turning on combinations of pixels.

Of the two modes, graphics mode is the more sophisticated. Programs that run in graphics mode can display an unlimited variety of shapes and fonts, whereas programs running in character mode are severely limited. Programs that run entirely in graphics mode are called *graphics-based* programs.

➠ See also *character based; graphics based; pixel; video adapter.*

graphics monitor: A monitor capable of displaying graphics. That is, any monitor that supports a graphics mode in addition to text modes. Nearly all modern monitors are graphics monitors.

➠ See also *graphics; monitor.*

graphics pages per minute: See *gppm.*

graphics tablet: Same as digitizing tablet.

gray scaling: The use of many shades of gray to represent an image. *Continuous-tone* images, such as black-and-white photographs, use an almost unlimited number of shades of gray. Conventional computer hardware and software, however, can only represent a limited number of shades of gray (typically 16 or 256). Gray-scaling is the process of converting a continuous-tone image to an image that a computer can manipulate.

While gray scaling is an improvement over monochrome, it requires larger amounts of memory because each dot is represented by from 4 to 8 bits. At a resolution of 300 dpi, you would need about 6 megabytes to represent a single 8 page using 256 shades of gray. This can be reduced somewhat through data compression techniques, but gray scaling still requires a great deal of memory.

Many optical scanners are capable of gray scaling, using from 16 to 256 different shades of gray. However, gray scaling is only useful if you have an output device—monitor or printer—that is capable of displaying all the shades. Most color monitors are capable of gray scaling, but the images are generally not as good as on dedicated gray-scaling monitors.

Note that gray scaling is different from dithering. Dithering simulates shades of gray by altering the density and pattern of black and white dots. In gray scaling, each individual dot can have a different shade of gray (See Figure 27 at dithering).

➡ See also *continuous tone; data compression; dithering; monitor; optical scanner.*

greeking: (1) The approximation of text characters on a screen display (Figure 37). Greeking is often used by word processors that support a *preview* function. In preview mode, the word processor attempts to show what a document will look like when printed. Frequently, however, the graphics display capabilities of the monitor are not sufficient to show text at a small size. To give a general idea of what the text will look like and how page layout will appear, the word processor uses graphics symbols to approximate the text. These symbols suggest greek letters, hence the term *greeking.*

➡ See also *layout; preview.*

(2) The term greeking is also used to describe nonsense text inserted in a document to check a layout. This allows a layout artist to concentrate on the overall appearance of a page without worrying about the actual text that will be inserted later.

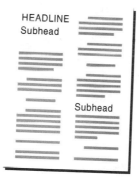

Figure 37: *Greeking*

green PC: PC A PC especially designed to minimize power consumption. Green PCs draw less power than normal PCs and support *sleep modes*, in which the computer powers down all unnecessary components when it is inactive.

➠ See also *sleep mode; energy star.*

Group 3 protocol: The universal protocol defined by the CCITT for sending faxes.

➠ See also *CCITT; fax machine.*

Group 4 protocol: A protocol defined by CCITT for sending faxes over ISDN networks.

➠ See also *CCITT; fax machine; ISDN.*

groupware: A class of software that helps groups of colleagues (*workgroups*) attached to a local-area network organize their activities. Typically, groupware supports the following operations:

- scheduling meetings and allocating resources
- e-mail
- password protection for documents
- telephone utilities
- electronic newsletters

Groupware is sometimes called *workgroup productivity software.*

➠ See also *e-mail; local-area network; scheduler; workgroup computing.*

GUI: Pronounced *goo-ee*, acronym for *graphical user interface.* See under *graphical user interface.*

gutter: In desktop publishing, the space between columns in a multiple-column document.

➠ See also *desktop publishing.*

GW-BASIC: PC A dialect of the BASIC programming language that comes with many versions of the DOS operating system.

➠ See also *BASIC.*

H

hack: (n) An inelegant and usually temporary solution to a problem.

(v) To modify a program, often in an unauthorized manner, by changing the code itself.

hacker: A slang term for a computer enthusiast. Among professional programmers, the term *hacker* implies an amateur or a programmer who lacks formal training. Depending on how it used, the term can be either complimentary or derogatory, although it is developing an increasingly derogatory connotation. The pejorative sense of *hacker* is becoming more prominent largely because the popular press has co-opted the term to refer to individuals who gain unauthorized access to computer systems for the purpose of stealing and corrupting data.

➠ See also *programmer.*

half duplex: Refers to the transmission of data in just one direction at a time. For example, a walkie-talkie is a half-duplex device because only one party can talk at a time. In contrast, a telephone is a *full-duplex* device because both parties can talk simultaneously.

Most modems contain a switch that lets you select between half-duplex and full-duplex modes. The correct choice depends on which program you are using to transmit data through the modem. In half-duplex mode, each character transmitted is immediately displayed on your screen. (For this reason, it is sometimes called *local echo*—characters are echoed by the local device). In full-duplex mode, transmitted data is not displayed on your monitor until it has been received and returned (remotely echoed) by the other device. If you are running a communications program and every character appears twice, it probably means that your modem is in half-duplex mode when it should be in full-duplex mode, and every character is being both locally and remotely echoed.

➠ See also *communications; full duplex; modem.*

half height: PC PCs support both full-height and half-height bays for disk drives and other mass storage devices. The half-height models take up less space but usually have less storage capacity.

➠ See also *bay.*

halftone: In printing, a continuous tone image, such as a photograph, that has been converted into a black-and-white image. Halftones are created through a process called *dithering,* in which the density and pattern of black and white dots are varied to simulate different shades of gray.

In conventional printing, halftones are created by photographing an image through a screen. The *screen frequency,* measured in lines per inch, determines how many dots are used to make each spot of gray. In theory, the higher the screen frequency (the more lines per inch), the more accurate the halftone will be. However, actual screen frequencies are limited by the technology because higher screen frequencies create smaller, more tightly packed dots. If you are printing on a low resolution device, therefore, you may get better results with a lower screen frequency.

Modern desktop publishing systems can create halftones by simulating the conventional photographic process. This is why some programs allow you to specify a screen frequency even when no actual screen is used.

➠ See also *desktop publishing; dithering.*

hand-held computer: A portable computer that is small enough to be held in one's hand. Although extremely convenient to carry, hand-held computers have not replaced notebook computers because of their small keyboards and screens. The most popular hand-held computers are those that are specifically designed to provide PIM (personal information manager) functions, such as a calendar and address book.

Some manufacturers are trying to solve the small keyboard problem by replacing the keyboard with an electronic pen. However, these pen-based devices rely on handwriting recognition technologies, which are still in their infancy.

➠ See also *handwriting recognition; notebook computer; palmtop; PDA; PIM.*

handle: (1) In many applications, when you select a graphical object, an outline of the object appears with small boxes. Each box is a handle. By dragging the handles, you can change the shape and size of the object. (See Figure 9 at *Bézier curves*).

➠ See also *graphics; pointer.*

(2) In programming, a handle is a token, typically a pointer, that enables the program to access a resource, such as a library function.

(3) When communicating via an online service, your handle is the name that you use to identify yourself. It could be your real name, a nickname, or a completely fictitious name.

➠ See also *chat; online service.*

handshaking: The process by which two devices initiate communications. Handshaking begins when one device sends a message to another device indicating that it wants to establish a communications channel. The two devices then send several messages back and forth that enable them to agree on a communications protocol.

➠ See also *communications; protocol.*

handwriting recognition: The technique by which a computer system can recognize characters and other symbols written by hand. In theory, handwriting recognition should free us from our keyboards, allowing us to write and draw in a more natural way. It is considered one of the key technologies that will determine the ultimate success or failure of PDAs and other hand-held devices. To date, however, the technology has had only limited success. This is partly because it is still a young technology and is not as fast or accurate as it needs to be. Another reason for its slow acceptance, however, is that the keyboard is in fact more convenient in many situations. Many people can write much faster with a keyboard than they can by hand.

➠ See also *hand-held computer; PDA; pen computer.*

hang: To crash in such a way that the computer does not respond to input from the keyboard or mouse. If your computer is hung, you usually need to reboot it, although sometimes hitting the correct sequence of control characters will free it up.

➠ See also *bomb; crash.*

hanging indent: In word processing, a paragraph that has all lines but the first indented. For example:

This is an example of a hanging indent.
A hanging indent is also known as a
hanging paragraph.

With many word processors, you can create hanging indents by specifying a negative indentation for the first line of each paragraph.

➠ See also *word processing.*

hanging paragraph: Same as *hanging indent.*

hard: The term *hard* is used to describe anything that is permanent or physically exists. In contrast, the term *soft* refers to concepts, symbols and other intangible and changeable objects.

➠ See also *hardware; software.*

hard card: A hard disk drive and controller on an expansion card. Unlike most disk drives that are either external to the computer or fit in one of the disk drive bays, a hard card slips into an expansion slot. Hard cards are often faster than conventional disk drives, and easier to install. Their storage capacities, however, are more limited.

➠ See also *bay; controller; expansion board; expansion slot; hard disk.*

hard coded: Unchangeable. Hard-coded features are built into the hardware or software in such a way that they cannot be modified.

hard copy: A printout of data stored in a computer. It is considered *hard* because it exists physically on paper, whereas a *soft* copy exists only electronically.

➠ See also *hard; soft.*

hard disk: A magnetic disk on which you can store computer data. The term *hard* is used to distinguish it from a soft, or *floppy*, disk. Hard disks hold more data and are faster than floppy disks. A hard disk, for example, can store anywhere from 10 megabytes to over one gigabyte, whereas most floppies have a maximum storage capacity of 1.4 megabytes.

A single hard disk usually consists of several *platters*. Each platter requires two read/write heads, one for each side. All the read/write heads are attached to a single access arm so that they cannot move independently. Each platter has the same number of *tracks*, and a track location that cuts across all platters is called a *cylinder*. For example, a typical 84 megabyte hard disk for a PC might have two platters (four sides) and 1,053 cylinders.

In general, hard disks are less portable than floppies, although it is possible to buy removable hard disks. There are two types of removable hard disks: disk packs and removable cartridges.

➠ See also *cache; cylinder; disk drive; disk pack; enhanced IDE; floppy disk; IDE interface; interleaving; mass storage; platter; removable disk drive; track.*

hard disk drive: The mechanism that reads and writes data on a hard disk. Hard disk drives for PCs generally have access times of about 15 milliseconds or less. Many disk drives improve their performance through a technique called *caching*.

The disk drives for hard disks are called *hard disk drives* or *Winchester drives*, Winchester being the name of one of the first popular hard disk drive technologies developed by IBM in 1973.

There are several interface standards for passing data between a hard disk and a computer. The most common are:

ST-506: The standard interface on all PC/XT and PC/AT computers. The ST-506 standard supports both MFM and RLL encoding formats.

SCSI (Small Computer System Interface): The standard interface for Apple Macintoshes, SCSI is also popular on UNIX systems and is available on many PC compatibles.

IDE (Integrated Drive Interface): Not as fast as SCSI, but faster than ST-506.

Enhanced IDE (EIDE): A new version of the IDE interface that supports data transfer rates comparable to SCSI.

➠ See also *disk drive; hard disk.*

hard disk type: A number that indicates important features of a hard disk, such as the number of platters and cylinders. Hard disk manufacturers have agreed on a numbering scheme so that it is possible to install and configure a new hard disk simply by entering the disk's type number into the BIOS setup.

➠ See also *BIOS; hard disk.*

hard drive: Same as *hard disk drive.*

hard hyphen: See under *hyphenation.*

hard return: A *return* is the process of jumping from the end of one line of text to the beginning of the next line. Word processors utilize two types of returns: *hard returns* and *soft returns.*
   A hard return is an actual symbol inserted into the text. The hard-return symbol is usually invisible, but most word processors support a mode that lets you see them. Whenever you press the Return or Enter key while editing a document, the word processor inserts a hard return.
   Hard returns cause the word processor to start a new line regardless of how margins are set. Therefore, if a document contains hard returns, the lines will end at the same place even if you change the

margins. In contrast, soft returns, inserted by the program rather than the user, depend on how the margins are set.

➠ See also *return; soft return.*

hardware: Refers to objects that you can actually touch, like disks, disk drives, display screens, keyboards, printers, boards, and chips. In contrast, software is untouchable. Software exists as ideas, concepts, and symbols, but it has no substance.

Books provide a useful analogy for describing the difference between software and hardware. The pages and the ink are the hardware, while the words, sentences, paragraphs, and the overall meaning are the software. A computer without software is like a book full of blank pages—you need software to make the computer useful just as you need words to make a book meaningful.

➠ See also *firmware; software.*

hardwired: Refers to elements of a program or device that cannot be changed. Originally, the term was used to describe functionality that was built into the circuitry (i.e., the wires) of a device. Nowadays, however, the term is also used to describe constants built into software.

➠ See also *constant; hard.*

Hayes compatible: Hayes Microcomputer Products is one of the leading manufacturers of modems and has developed a language for controlling modems that has become the de facto standard. Any modem that recognizes Hayes modem commands is said to be *Hayes-compatible.* This is very useful because many communications programs use Hayes modem commands.

➠ See also *communications; de facto standard; modem.*

head: The mechanism that reads data from or writes data to a magnetic disk or tape. If the head becomes dirty, it will not work properly. This is one of the first things to check if your disk drive or tape drive begins to malfunction.

The head is sometimes called a *read/write head*. Double-sided floppy disk drives have two heads, one for each side of the disk. Hard disk drives have many heads, two for each *platter*.

➡ See also *disk drive; head crash; platter.*

head crash: A serious disk drive malfunction. A head crash usually means that the head has scratched or burned the disk. In a hard disk drive, the head normally hovers a few microinches from the disk. If the head becomes misaligned or if dust particles come between it and the disk, it can touch the disk. When this happens, you usually lose much of the data on the hard disk and will need to replace both the head and the disk. For this reason, it is important to operate disk drives, particularly hard disk drives, in as clean an environment as possible. Even smoke particles can cause a head crash.

Head crashes are less common for floppy disks because the head touches the disk anyway under normal operation.

Another term for *head crash* is *disk crash*.

➡ See also *crash; disk; disk drive; head.*

header: (1) In word processing, a line of text that appears at the top of each page of a document. Once you specify the text that should appear in the header, the word processor automatically inserts it. Most word processors allow you to use special symbols in the header that represent changing values. For example, you can enter a symbol for the page number, and the word processor will automatically replace the symbol with the correct number on each page. If you enter the date symbol, the word processor will insert the current date, which will change if necessary each time you print the document.

Most word processors allow you to specify different headers, for example, one for odd-numbered pages (*odd headers*) and another for even-numbered pages (*even headers*). Headers are also called *running heads*.

➡ See also *footer; word processing.*

(2) In many disciplines of computer science, a header is a unit of information that precedes a data object. In file management, for example, a header is a region at the beginning of each file where bookkeeping information is kept. The file header may contain the date the file was created, the date it was last updated, and the file's

size. The header can be accessed only by the operating system or by specialized programs.

helical-scan cartridge: A type of magnetic tape that uses the same technology as VCR tapes. The term *helical scan* usually refers to 8 mm tapes, although 4 mm tapes (called DAT *tapes*) use the same technology. The 8 mm helical-scan tapes have data capacities from 2.5GB to 5GB.

➡ See also *DAT; mass storage; tape.*

Help: Online documentation. Many programs come with the instruction manual, or a portion of the manual, integrated into the program. If you encounter a problem or forget a command while running the program, you can summon the documentation by pressing a designated *Help key* or entering a *HELP command.* In Windows, the Help key is the function key labeled *F1.*

Once you summon the Help system, the program often displays a menu of Help topics. You can choose the appropriate topic for whatever problem you are currently encountering. The program will then display a *help screen* that contains the desired documentation.

Some programs are more sophisticated, displaying different Help messages depending on where you are in the program. Such systems are said to be context sensitive.

MAC The Macintosh Help system is often referred to as *Balloon Help* because the help messages appear in a cartoon-like balloon. Newer Macs (starting with System 7.5) also have something called *Interactive Help,* which contains tutorials that show you how to perform different operations.

➡ See also *context sensitive; documentation.*

Hercules graphics: PC A graphics display system for PCs developed by Van Suwannukul, founder of Hercules Computer Technology. Suwannukul developed the system so that he could produce his doctoral thesis on PC equipment using his native Thai alphabet.

First offered in 1982, the original Hercules system filled a void left by IBM's MDA (*monochrome display adapter*) system. MDA produces high-resolution monochrome text but cannot generate graphics. Hercules systems generate both high-resolution text and graphics for monochrome monitors. The resolution is 720 by 348.

➠ See also MDA; *video adapter.*

heterogeneous network: A network that includes computers and other devices from different manufacturers. For example, local-area networks (LANs) that connect PCs with Apple Macintosh computers are heterogeneous.

➠ See also *local-area network; network.*

Hewlett-Packard Graphics Language: See IIPGL.

hex: Short for *hexadecimal.*

hexadecimal: Refers to the base-16 number system, which consists of 16 unique symbols: the numbers 0 to 9 and the letters A to F (Table 18). For example, the decimal number 15 is represented as F in the hexadecimal numbering system. The hexadecimal system is useful because it can represent every byte (8 bits) as two consecutive hexadecimal digits. It is easier for humans to read hexadecimal numbers than binary numbers.

To convert a value from hexadecimal to binary, you merely translate each hexadecimal digit into its 4-bit binary equivalent. For example, the hexadecimal number

3F7A

translates to the following binary number:

0011 1111 1000 1010

➠ See also *binary; decimal; octal.*

hidden file: A file with a special *hidden attribute* turned on, so that the file is not normally visible to users. For example, hidden files are not listed when you execute the DOS DIR command. However, most file management utilities allow you to view hidden files.

Table 18
TABLE OF HEXADECIMAL VALUES

DECIMAL	HEXADECIMAL	BINARY
0	0	0000
1	1	0001
2	2	0010
3	3	0011
4	4	0100
5	5	0101
6	6	0110
7	7	0111
8	8	1000
9	9	1001
10	A	1010
11	B	1011
12	C	1100
13	D	1101
14	E	1110
15	F	1111

DOS hides some files, such as MSDOS.SYS and IO.SYS, so that you will not accidentally corrupt them. You can also turn on the hidden attribute for any normal file, thereby making it invisible to casual snoopers.

MAC On a Macintosh, you can hide files with the ResEdit utility.

➠ See also *attribute; file management.*

hierarchical: Refers to systems that are organized in the shape of a pyramid, with each row of objects linked to objects directly beneath it. Hierarchical systems pervade everyday life (Figure 38). The army, for example, which has generals at the top of the pyramid and privates at the bottom, is a hierarchical system. Similarly, the system for classifying plants and animals according to species, family, genus, and so on, is also hierarchical.

Hierarchical systems are as popular in computer systems as they are in other walks of life. The most obvious example of a hierarchical system in computers is a file system, in which directories have files and subdirectories beneath them. Such a file organization is, in fact, called a *hierarchical file system*.

In addition to file systems, many data structures for storing information are hierarchical in form. Menu-driven programs are also hierarchical, because they contain a *root menu* at the top of the pyramid and *submenus* below it.

➡ See also *directory; file management; tree structure.*

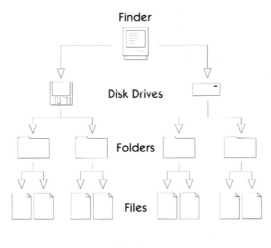

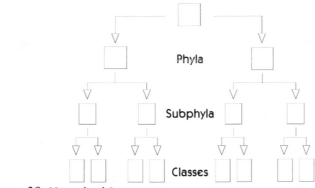

Figure 38: *Hierarchical Systems*

high ASCII: Same as *extended ASCII*.

high-density disk: A high-quality floppy disk capable of holding more data than a double-density disk. High-density 5¼-inch disks for PCs can hold 1.2MB of data. High-density 3½-inch disks can hold 1.44MB of data.

➠ See also *density; floppy disk*.

high-level language: A programming language such as C, FORTRAN, or Pascal that enables a programmer to write programs that are more or less independent of a particular type of computer. Such languages are considered high-level because they are closer to human languages and further from machine languages. In contrast, assembly languages are considered low-level because they are very close to machine languages (see Figure 68 at *programming language*).

The main advantage of high-level languages over low-level languages is that they are easier to read, write, and maintain. Ultimately, programs written in a high-level language must be translated into machine language by a compiler or interpreter.

The first high-level programming languages were designed in the 1950s. Now there are dozens of different languages, including Ada, Algol, BASIC, COBOL, C, C++, FORTRAN, LISP, Pascal, and PROLOG.

➠ See also *Ada; assembly language; BASIC; C; C++; COBOL; compile; FORTRAN; LISP; low-level language; machine language; Pascal; object-oriented programming language; programming language*.

highlight: To make an object on a display screen stand out by displaying it in a different mode from other objects. Typical highlighted objects include menu options, command buttons, and selected blocks of text.

➠ See also *select*.

high memory: PC In DOS-based systems, high memory refers to the memory area between the first 640K and 1 megabyte. It is also called the *upper memory area*.

➠ See also *conventional memory; DOS; expanded memory; extended memory; TSR*.

high memory area: PC In DOS-based systems, the high memory area refers to the first 64K of extended memory.

➠ See also *extended memory.*

high resolution: See under *resolution.*

home computer: A personal computer specially configured for use in a home rather than an office. Typically, home computers have only medium-power microprocessors, but are equipped with a full complement of multimedia devices. In addition, manufacturers often bundle recreational and educational software with home computers.

➠ See also *multimedia; personal computer.*

Home key: A key on PC and newer Macintosh keyboards that controls cursor movement. Usually, the Home key moves the cursor to the top left corner of the screen or to the beginning of the file, but it can have other meanings depending on which program is running.

➠ See also *keyboard.*

home page: The main page of a web site. Typically, the home page serves as an index or table of contents to other documents stored at the site.

➠ See also web site.

host: A computer system that is accessed by a user working at a remote location. Typically, the term is used when there are two computer systems connected by modems and telephone lines. The system that contains the data is called the host, while the computer at which the user sits is called the *remote terminal.*

➠ See also *remote control.*

hot key: A user-defined key sequence that executes a command or causes the operating system to switch to another program. In DOS systems, for example, you can use hot keys to open memory-resident programs (*TSRs*). In Windows environments, you can often press a hot key to execute common commands. For example, Ctrl+C usually copies the selected objects.

➠ See also *control character; function keys; memory resident; TSR.*

hot link: (n) A link between two applications such that changes in one affect the other. For example, some desktop publishing systems let you establish hot links between documents and databases or spreadsheets. When data in the spreadsheet changes, the corresponding charts and graphs in the document change accordingly.

(v) To establish a link between two applications.

➠ See also *database; link; OLE; spreadsheet.*

hot spot: An area of a graphics object, or a section of text, that activates a function when selected. Hot spots are particularly common in multimedia applications, where selecting a hot spot can make the application display a picture, run a video, or open a new window of information.

➠ See also *multimedia.*

HP-compatible printer: Hewlett-Packard was one of the first companies to produce a laser printer for PCs, and most software products include drivers for HP printers. The drivers control the printers through a language called *PCL (printer control language)*. Other manufacturers of laser printers design their printers so that they, too, understand PCL, making them able to emulate HP printers. In this way, their printers are HP-compatible and are thus automatically supported by many software products.

No non-HP printer, however, is 100 percent HP-compatible. Manufacturers claim HP compatibility even if their printers only recognize a subset of PCL commands. Note also that there are different versions of PCL. A printer may be able to emulate an HP LaserJet Plus but not a LaserJet II. Finally, HP laser printers support font car-

tridges, and not all HP-compatible printers can accept the same cartridges.

➠ See also *compatible; driver; emulation; font cartridge; laser printer;*
PCL; PostScript.

HPGL: Abbreviation of *Hewlett-Packard Graphics Language,* a set of commands for controlling plotters and printers. HPGL is part of Hewlett-
Packard's PCL Level 5 page description language.

➠ See also *PCL; plotter.*

HTML: Short for *Hypertext Markup Language,* the authoring language
used to create documents on the World Wide Web. HTML is similar
to SGML, although it is not a strict subset.

➠ See also *hypertext; SGML; World Wide Web.*

human engineering: Same as *ergonomics.*

HyperCard: ⬚MAC⬚ A hypertext programming environment for the Macintosh introduced by Apple in 1987. The HyperCard model consists
of cards, and collections of cards, called *stacks.* You can connect the
cards in various ways, and leaf through them the way you would with
a set of Rolodex cards. In addition to data, each card can contain
graphics and buttons that trigger other events, such as sound or
video.
   Each object in a HyperCard system—stack, card, text field, button,
or background—can have a *script* associated with it. A script is a set of
instructions that specify what actions should take place when a user
selects an object with the mouse or when some other event occurs.
   Writing HyperCard applications is known as *authoring.*

➠ See also *authoring tool; hypertext.*

hypertext: A special type of database system, invented by Ted Nelson
in the 1960s, in which objects (text, pictures, music, programs, and so
on) can be creatively linked to each other. When you select an object,
you can see all the other objects that are linked to it. You can move

from one object to another even though they might have very different forms. For example, while reading a document about Mozart, you might click on the phrase *Violin Concerto in A Major,* which could display the written score or perhaps even invoke a recording of the concerto. Clicking on the name *Mozart* might cause various illustrations of Mozart to appear on the screen. The icons that you select to view associated objects are called *Hypertext links* or buttons.

Hypertext systems are particularly useful for organizing and browsing through large databases that consist of disparate types of information. There are several Hypertext systems available for Apple Macintosh computers and PCs that enable you to develop your own databases. Such systems are often called *authoring systems.* HyperCard software from Apple Computer is the most famous.

➡ See also *authoring tool; HTML; HyperCard software; multimedia; online help; SGML.*

Hypertext Markup Language: See *HTML.*

hyphenation: In word processing, hyphenation refers to splitting a word that would otherwise extend beyond the right margin. Not all word processors support hyphenation, and of those that do support it, not all perform it correctly.

Word processors use two basic techniques to perform hyphenation. The first employs an internal dictionary of words that indicates where hyphens may be inserted. The second uses a set of logical formulas to make hyphenation decisions. The dictionary method is more accurate but is usually slower. The most sophisticated programs use a combination of both methods.

Most word processors allow you to override their own hyphenation rules and define yourself where a word should be divided.
Hyphens inserted automatically by a hyphenation utility are called *discretionary* or *soft hyphens.* Hyphens that you add explicitly by entering the dash character are called *hard hyphens.*

➡ See also *word processing; word wrap.*

I-beam pointer: A pointer shaped like a capital I used in graphics-based text processing applications. Many desktop publishing systems and word processors use an I-beam pointer to mark blocks of text and move the insertion point. Note that the I-beam pointer is not the same as the selection pointer, which is usually shaped like an arrow (see Figure 65 at *pointer*).

➠ See also *insertion point; pointer.*

IBM compatible: See under *IBM PC.*

IBM PC: Refers to a family of personal computers produced by IBM. The term can also refer to computers that conform to set of loosely controlled standards. These are also called *IBM clones, IBM compatibles,* or simply compatibles. These terms are actually misnomers because many of the PCs produced by IBM do not conform to industry standards. For example, IBM attempted to change the expansion bus to MCA in its PS/2 line of PCs, but the industry did not follow suit.

➠ See also *PC.*

icon: A small picture that represents an object or program. Icons are very useful in applications that use windows, because with the click of a mouse button you can shrink an entire window into a small icon. (This is sometimes called *minimizing.*) To redisplay the window, you merely move the pointer to the icon and click (or double click) a mouse button. (This is sometimes called *restoring* or *maximizing.*) Icons are a principal feature of graphical user interfaces (see Figure 22 at *desktop*).

➠ See also *graphical user interface.*

IDE interface: Abbreviation of either *Intelligent Drive Electronics* or *Integrated Drive Electronics*, depending on who you ask. An IDE interface is an interface for mass storage devices, in which the controller is integrated into the disk or CD-ROM drive. It is a low-cost alternative to SCSI interfaces.

The original IDE interface supports data transfer rates of about 3.3 megabytes per second and has a limit of 538 megabytes per device. However, a recent version of IDE, called *enhanced IDE (EIDE)* or *Fast IDE*, supports data transfer rates of about 12 megabytes per second and 18.4 gigabytes per second. These numbers are comparable to what SCSI offers. To take advantage of EIDE, you need both an EIDE mass storage device and an EIDE interface installed in your computer.

➠ See also *EIDE; hard disk drive; interface; SCSI; ST-506 interface.*

identifier: Same as *name.* The term *identifier* is usually used for variable names.

➠ See also *name; variable.*

IEEE: Abbreviation of *Institute of Electrical and Electronic Engineers*, pronounced *I-triple-E.* Founded in 1963, the IEEE is an organization composed of engineers, scientists, and students. The IEEE is best know for developing standards for the computer and electronics industry. In particular, the IEEE 802 standards for local-area networks are widely followed.

➠ See also *Ethernet; floating-point number; network; token-ring network.*

IGES: Acronym for *Initial Graphics Exchange Specification*, an ANSI graphics file format for three-dimensional wire frame models.

➠ See also *ANSI; graphics file formats.*

image editor: A graphics program that provides a variety of special features for altering bit-mapped images. The difference between image editors and paint programs is not always clear-cut, but in general image editors are specialized for *modifying* bit-mapped images, such as scanned photographs, whereas paint programs are specialized for *creating* images.

In addition to offering a host of filters and image transformation algorithms, image editors also enable you to create and superimpose layers.

➠ See also *image enhancement; paint program; photo illustration.*

image enhancement: In computer graphics, the process of improving the quality of a digitally stored image by manipulating the image with software. It is quite easy, for example, to make an image lighter or darker, or to increase or decrease contrast. Advanced image enhancement software also supports many filters for altering images in various ways. Programs specialized for image enhancement are sometimes called *image editors.*

➠ See also *image editor; photo illustration.*

imagesetter: A typesetting device that produces very high-resolution output on paper or film. Imagesetters are too expensive for homes or most offices, but you can obtain imagesetter output by bringing a PostScript file to a service bureau. One reason that PostScript has become the standard for desktop publishing is that nearly all image-setters support it. This means that you can produce drafts on an inexpensive PostScript laser printer with high assurance that the final output from an imagesetter will look the same, but with higher resolution (up to 3,540 dots per inch).

➠ See also *desktop publishing; PostScript; service bureau.*

ImageWriter: MAC Refers to any in a family of dot-matrix printers that Apple offers for the Macintosh computer. Laser printers for the Macintosh are called *LaserWriters.*

➠ See also *dot-matrix printer; LaserWriter; letter quality; Macintosh computer; printer.*

impact printer: Refers to a class of printers that work by banging a head or needle against an ink ribbon to make a mark on the paper. This includes dot-matrix printers, daisy-wheel printers, and line printers. In contrast, laser and ink-jet printers are *nonimpact printers.* The distinction is important because impact printers tend to be considerably noisier than nonimpact printers but are useful for multipart forms such as invoices.

➠ See also *daisy-wheel printer; dot-matrix printer; ink-jet printer; laser printer; line printer; printer.*

import: To use data produced by another application. The ability to import data is very important in software applications because it means that one application can complement another. Many programs, for example, are designed to be able to import graphics in a variety of formats.

The opposite of importing is *exporting*, which refers to the ability of one application to format data for another application.

➠ See also *export.*

inclusive OR operator: A Boolean operator that returns a value of TRUE if *either* of its operands is TRUE. Contrast with the *exclusive OR operator,* which returns a value of TRUE only if both operands have different values.

➠ See also *Boolean operator.*

increment: (v) To add a fixed amount. For example, if you count consecutively from 1 to 10, you increment by one. If you count by twos, you increment by two. A large proportion of computer software consists of loops of instructions in which one or more values are incremented each time the loop is executed.

➠ See also *decrement; loop.*

(n) An amount that is added. For example, if you count by threes, the increment is three.

incremental backup: A backup procedure that backs up only those files that have been modified since the previous backup. Contrast with an archival backup, in which all files are backed up regardless of whether they have been modified since the last backup.

➠ See also *archival backup; backup.*

Indeo: A codec (compression/decompression technology) for computer video developed by Intel Corporation. Although it is a software-only codec, Indeo is based on the DVI, which is a hardware-only codec. Competing video standards include Cinepak and MPEG.

➠ See also *DVI; Cinepak; codec; MPEG.*

Industry Standard Architecture (ISA) bus: PC The bus architecture used in the IBM PC/XT and PC/AT. The AT version of the bus is called the *AT bus* and has become a de facto industry standard. Since the late 80s, the industry has been searching for a successor to the ISA bus, which is not sufficient for modern devices and applications. It now appears that the successor will be the PCI local bus architecture. Most computers made today include both an AT bus for slower devices and a local bus for devices that need better bus performance.

In 1993, Intel and Microsoft introduced a new version of the ISA specification called *Plug and Play ISA.* Plug and Play ISA enables the operating system to configure expansion boards automatically so that users do not need to fiddle with DIP switches and jumpers.

➠ See also *AT bus; bus; local bus; PCI; plug-and-play.*

information highway: A popular buzzword to describe the system of bulletin board services, online services, and other services that enable people to obtain information from telecommunications networks. In the U.S., there is currently a national debate about how to shape and control these avenues of information. Many people believe that the information highway should be designed and regulated by government, just like conventional highway systems. Others argue that government should adopt a more *laissez faire* attitude. Nearly everyone agrees that accessing the information highway is going to be a normal part of everyday life in the near future.

➠ See also *online service; bulletin board service; telecommunications.*

Infrared Data Association: See *IrDA.*

.INI file: PC Pronounced *dot-in-ee file,* a file that has a .INI extension and contains configuration information for MS-Windows. Two .INI files, WIN.INI and SYSTEM.INI, are required by MS-Windows. In addition, many applications have their own .INI files.

➠ See also *extension.*

init: MAC On Macintoshes an old term (before System 7) for *System extensions.* See under *extension.*

Initial Graphics Exchange Specification: See *IGES.*

initialize: (1) MAC On Apple Macintosh computers, *initializing* a disk means *formatting* it.

➠ See also *format.*

(2) In programming, *initialize* means to assign a starting value to a variable.

➠ See also *assign; variable.*

(3) *Initialize* can refer to the process of starting up a program or system.

ink-jet printer: A type of printer that works by spraying ionized ink at a sheet of paper. Magnetized plates in the ink's path direct the ink onto the paper in the desired shapes. Ink-jet printers are capable of producing high quality print approaching that produced by laser printers. A typical ink-jet printer provides a resolution of 300 dots per inch, although some newer models offer higher resolutions.

In general, the price of ink-jet printers is lower than that of laser printers. However, they are also considerably slower. Another drawback of ink-jet printers is that they require a special type of ink that is apt to smudge on inexpensive copier paper.

Because ink-jet printers require smaller mechanical parts than laser printers, they are especially popular as portable printers. In addition, color ink-jet printers provide an inexpensive way to print full-color documents.

➠ See also *color printer; dots per inch; download; font; font cartridge; laser printer; printer; solid ink-jet printer.*

input: (n) Whatever goes into the computer. Input can take a variety of forms, from commands you enter from the keyboard to data from another computer or device. A device that feeds data into a computer, such as a keyboard or mouse, is called an *input device*.

(v) The act of entering data into a computer.

➡ See also *I/O; output*.

input device: Any machine that feeds data into a computer. For example, a keyboard is an input device, whereas a display monitor is an output device. Input devices other than the keyboard are sometimes called *alternate input devices*. Mice, trackballs, and light pens are all alternate input devices.

➡ See also *device; I/O; light pen; mouse; output; trackball*.

input/output: See *I/O*.

insert: To place an object between two other objects. Inserting characters, words, paragraphs and documents is common in word processing. Note that *insert* differs from append, which means to add at the end.
   Most computer keyboards have an *Insert key*, which turns *insert mode* on and off.

➡ See also *append; insert mode; Ins key*.

insertion point: In graphics-based programs, the insertion point is the point where the next characters typed from the keyboard will appear on the display screen. The insertion point is usually represented by a blinking vertical line. You can reposition the insertion point by pressing arrow keys or by moving the I-beam pointer.

➡ See also *I-beam pointer; insert mode; pointer*.

251

Insert key: A key on computer keyboards that turns the insert mode on and off. The Insert key does not work for all programs, but most word processors and text editors support it.

➠ See also *insert mode.*

insert mode: Most text editors and word processors have two text entry modes from which you can choose. In *insert mode,* the editor inserts all characters you type at the cursor position (or to the right of the insertion point). With each new insertion, the editor pushes over characters to the right of the cursor or pointer to make room for the new character.

If insert mode is turned off, the editor overwrites existing characters instead of inserting the new ones before the old ones. This is often called *overstrike* (or *overwrite*) *mode.* Most PC keyboards have an *Ins key* that lets you switch back and forth between insert and overwrite modes.

For most programs, the default text entry mode is insert mode.

➠ See also *Ins key; insertion point; overstrike; word processing.*

Ins key: MAC The Insert key on Macintosh keyboards.

➠ See also *Insert key.*

Institute of Electrical and Electronic Engineers: See *IEEE.*

instruction: A basic command. The term *instruction* is often used to describe the most rudimentary programming commands. For example, a computer's *instruction set* is the list of all the basic commands in the computer's machine language.

➠ See also *CISC; command; machine language; RISC.*

integer: A whole number. The following are integers:

    0
    1
    -125
    144457

In contrast, the following are *not* integers:

5
-1.0
1.3E4
"string"

The first three are *floating-point numbers*; the last is a character string. Integers, floating-point numbers, and character strings constitute the basic data types that most computers support. There are often different sizes of integers available; for example, PCs support short integers, which are 2 bytes, and long integers, which are 4 bytes.

➡ See also *character string; data type; floating-point number.*

integrated: (1) A popular computer buzzword that refers to two or more components merged together into a single system. For example, any software product that performs more than one task can be described as *integrated.*

(2) Increasingly, the term *integrated software* is reserved for applications that combine word processing, database management, spreadsheet functions, and communications into a single package.

integrated circuit (IC): Another name for a chip, an IC is a small electronic device made out of a semiconductor material. The first integrated circuit was developed in the 1950s by Jack Kilby of Texas Instruments and Robert Noyce of Fairchild Semiconductor.
  Integrated circuits are used for a variety of devices, including microprocessors, audio and video equipment, and automobiles. Integrated circuits are often classified by the number of transistors and other electronic components they contain:

SSI (small-scale integration): Up to 100 electronic components per chip

MSI (medium-scale integration): From 100 to 3,000 electronic components per chip

LSI (large-scale integration): From 3,000 to 100,000 electronic components per chip

VLSI (very large-scale integration): From 100,000 to 1,000,000 electronic components per chip

ULSI (ultra large-scale integration): More than 1 million electronic components per chip

➠ See also *chip; semiconductor.*

Integrated Drive Electronics: See *IDE.*

integrated services digital network: See *ISDN.*

Intellifont: A *scalable font* technology that is part of Hewlett-Packard's *PCL 5* page description language.

➠ See also *page description language; PCL; scalable font.*

intelligent terminal: A terminal (monitor and keyboard) that contains processing power. Intelligent terminals include memory and a processor to perform special display operations. In contrast, a *dumb terminal* has no processing capabilities; it must rely entirely on the central computer. A *smart terminal* has some processing capabilities, but not as much as an intelligent terminal.

➠ See also *dumb terminal; monitor; smart terminal; terminal.*

Intel microprocessors: Microprocessors made by Intel Corporation form the foundation of all PCs. See Table 19 for a partial list of Intel microprocessors.

Models after the 8086 are often referred to by the last three digits (for example, the 286, 386, and 486). Many of the microprocessors come in different varieties that run at various clock rates. The 80486 architecture, for example, supports clock rates of from 33 to 66 MHz.

All Intel microprocessors are backward compatible, which means that they can run programs written for a less powerful processor. The 80386, for example, can run programs written for the 8086, 8088, and 80286. The 80386 and later models, however, offer special programming features not available on previous models. Software written specifically for these processors, therefore, may not run on older microprocessors.

Until the late 80s, Intel was essentially the only producer of PC microprocessors. Increasingly, however, Intel is facing competition from other manufacturers who produce "Intel-compatible" chips. These chips support the Intel instruction set and are often less expensive than Intel chips. In some cases, they also offer better performance.

➠ See also *bus; clock speed; microprocessor; multitasking; Pentium; register; RISC; virtual memory.*

Table 19
INTEL MICROPROCESSORS

MICRO-PRO-CESSOR	DATE	ESTI-MATED POWER (IN MIPS)	REGISTER WIDTH (BITS)	BUS WIDTH (BITS)	CLOCK RATES (IN MHZ)	NOTES
8086	1978	0.5	16	16	5, 8, and 10	
8088	1979	0.5	16	8	5 and 8	Used in the original IBM PC and PC/XT.
80286	1982	1.5	16	16	8, 10, and 12	Supports virtual memory and an address space of 16MB (megabytes); 5 to 20 times faster than the 8086.
80386 DX	1985	10	32	32	16, 20, 25, and 33	Built-in multitasking and virtual memory, has an address space of 4GB; 2 to 4 times faster than the 80286
80386 SX	1988	2.5	32	16	16, 20, 25, and 33	Compatible with both the 80286 and the 80386.
80386 SL	1990	5	32	32	20 and 25	Same architecture as the 80386DX, but with added power management features; popular in portable computers that rely on battery power.

Table 19   (Continued)
INTEL MICROPROCESSORS

MICRO-PRO-CESSOR	DATE	ESTI-MATED POWER (IN MIPS)	REGISTER WIDTH (BITS)	BUS WIDTH (BITS)	CLOCK RATES (IN MHZ)	NOTES
80486 DX	1989	30	32	32	25, 33 and 50	Similar to the 386 but much faster; uses a built-in memory cache to avoid wait states and includes a numeric coprocessor; uses pipelining techniques.
80486 SX	1991	20	32	32	16, 20, 25, and 33	An inexpensive variety of the 80486DX that runs at low speeds and lacks a numeric coprocessor.
80486 SL	1992	20	32	32	20, 25, and 33	Based on 80486DX architecture, with power management features for battery-operated computers.
80486 DX2 and Over-Drive	1992	50	32	32	50 and 66	Same architecture as the 80486DX, but with the internal clock speed doubled.
486DX4	1994	70	32	32	75 and 100	Same architecture as the 80486DX, but with the internal clock rate tripled.
Pentium	1993	125	32	64	60, 66, 75, 100, 120, 133, 150 and 180	Although basically a CISC architecture, the Pentium chip includes many RISC features, such as pipelining and superscaling; contains more than 3 million transistors.
Pentium Over-Drive	1995		32	64	60, 66, and 100	A Pentium chip that can be installed in a 486-based computer that has an OverDrive socket.

Intelligent Drive Electronics: See *IDE.*

interactive: Accepting input from a human. Interactive computer systems are programs that allow users to enter data or commands. Most popular programs, such as word processors and spreadsheet applications, are interactive.

A noninteractive program is one that, when started, continues without requiring human contact. A compiler is a noninteractive program, as are all batch processing applications.

➠ See also *batch processing.*

interface: (n) Something that connects two separate entities. For example, a *user interface* is the part of a program that connects the computer with a human operator (user).

There are also interfaces to connect programs, to connect devices, and to connect programs to devices. An interface can be a program or a device, such as an electrical connector.

➠ See also *user interface.*

(v) To communicate. For example, two devices that can transmit data between each other are said to *interface with each other.* This use of the term is scorned by language purists because *interface* has historically been used as a noun.

interlacing: A display technique that enables a monitor to provide more resolution inexpensively. With interlacing monitors, the electron guns draw only half the horizontal lines with each pass (for example, all odd lines on one pass and all even lines on the next pass). Because an interlacing monitor refreshes only half the lines at one time, it can display twice as many lines per refresh cycle, giving it greater resolution. Another way of looking at it is that interlacing provides the same resolution as noninterlacing, but less expensively.

A shortcoming of interlacing is that the reaction time is slower, so programs that depend on quick refresh rates (animation and video, for example), may experience flickering or streaking. Given two monitors that offer the same resolution, the noninterlacing one will generally be better.

➠ See also CRT; *monitor; refresh; resolution.*

interleaved memory: Main memory divided into two or more sections. The CPU can access alternate sections immediately, without waiting for memory to catch up (through wait states). Interleaved memory is one technique for compensating for the relatively slow speed of dynamic RAM (DRAM). Other techniques include page-mode memory and memory caches.

➠ See also *access time; cache; clock speed; CPU; dynamic RAM; memory; page-mode memory; wait state.*

interleaving: Refers to the way *sectors* on a disk are organized. In one-to-one interleaving, the sectors are placed sequentially around each track. In two-to-one interleaving, sectors are staggered so that consecutively numbered sectors are separated by an intervening sector (Figure 39).

The purpose of interleaving is to make the disk drive more efficient. The disk drive can access only one sector at a time, and the disk is constantly spinning beneath the read/write head. This means that by the time the drive is ready to access the next sector, the disk may have already spun beyond it. If a data file spans more than one sector and if the sectors are arranged sequentially, the drive will need to wait a full rotation to access the next chunk of the file. If instead the sectors are staggered, the disk will be perfectly positioned to access sequential sectors.

The optimum interleaving factor depends on the speed of the disk drive, the operating system, and the application. The only way to find the best interleaving factor is to experiment with various factors and various applications.

➠ See also *disk; disk drive; sector; track.*

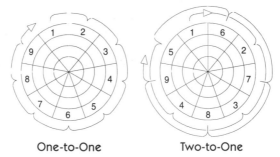

One-to-One   Two-to-One

Figure 39: *Interleaving*

internal cache: Same as *primary cache.*

internal command: ⌐PC⌐ In DOS systems, an internal command is any command that resides in the COMMAND.COM file. This includes the most common DOS commands, such as COPY and DIR. Commands that reside in other COM files, or in EXE or BAT files, are called *external commands*.

➠ See also *command; external command; DOS.*

internal font: Same as *resident font.*

internal modem: A modem that resides on an expansion board that plugs into a computer. In contrast, an *external modem* is a stand-alone box that attaches to a computer via cables (See Figure 55 at *modem*).

➠ See also *expansion board; external modem; modem.*

International Standards Organization: See *ISO.*

Internet: A global web connecting more than a million computers. Currently, the Internet has more than 30 million users worldwide, and that number is growing rapidly. More than 70 countries are linked into exchanges of data, news and opinions.

Unlike online services, which are centrally controlled, the Internet is decentralized by design. Each Internet computer, called a *host,* is independent. Its operators can choose which Internet services to provide to its local users and which local services to make available to the global Internet community. Remarkably, this anarchy by design works exceedingly well.

There are a variety of ways to access the Internet. Most online services, such as CompuServe and Prodigy, offer access to some Internet services. It is also possible to gain access through a commercial Internet provider.

➠ See also *Mosaic; online service; Usenet; World Wide Web.*

interpreter: A program that executes instructions written in a high-level language. There are two ways to run programs written in a high-level language. The most common is to compile the program; the other method is to pass the program through an interpreter.

An interpreter translates high-level instructions into an intermediate form, which it then executes. In contrast, a compiler translates high-level instructions directly into machine language. Compiled programs generally run faster than interpreted programs. The advantage of an interpreter, however, is that it does not need to go through the compilation stage during which machine instructions are generated.

This process can be time-consuming if the program is long. The interpreter, on the other hand, can immediately execute high-level programs. For this reason, interpreters are sometimes used during the development of a program, when a programmer wants to add small sections at a time and test them quickly. In addition, interpreters are often used in education because they allow students to program interactively.

Both interpreters and compilers are available for most high-level languages. However, BASIC and LISP are especially designed to be executed by an interpreter. In addition, page description languages, such as PostScript, use an interpreter. Every PostScript printer, for example, has a built-in interpreter that executes PostScript instructions.

➠ See also *BASIC; compile; LISP; page description language; PostScript; programming language.*

interprocess communication (IPC): A capability supported by some operating systems that allows one *process* to communicate with another process. The processes can be running on the same computer or on different computers connected through a network.

IPC enables one application to control another application, and for several applications to share the same data without interfering with one another. IPC is required in all multiprocessing systems, but it is not generally supported by single-process operating systems such as DOS. OS/2 and MS-Windows support an IPC mechanism called *DDE.*

➠ See also *DDE; multiprocessing; network; operating system; process.*

interrupt: (n) A signal informing a program that an event has occurred. When a program receives an interrupt signal, it takes a specified action (which can be to ignore the signal). Interrupt signals can cause a program to suspend itself temporarily to service the interrupt.

Interrupt signals can come from a variety of sources. For example, every keystroke generates an interrupt signal. Interrupts can also be generated by other devices, such as a printer, to indicate that some event has occurred. These are called *hardware interrupts.* Interrupt signals initiated by programs are called *software interrupts.*

(v) To send an interrupt signal.

interrupt request line: See *IRQ.*

inverse video: Same as *reverse video.*

inverted tree: See under *tree structure.*

invisible file: Same as *hidden file.*

invocation: The execution of a program or function.

➠ See also *invoke.*

invoke: To activate. One usually speaks of *invoking* a function or routine in a program. In this sense, the term *invoke* is synonymous with *call.*

➠ See also *call; function; routine.*

I/O: Short for *input/output,* and pronounced *eye oh.* I/O refers to any operation, program, or device whose purpose is to enter data into a computer or to extract data from a computer.

One usually uses the term *I/O* to distinguish noncomputational parts of a program from other parts that are strictly computational, or to distinguish certain devices from other devices. For example, a printer is an I/O device, whereas a CPU is a computational device.

All computer applications contain both I/O and computational parts. A word-processing system, for instance, contains I/O components (for entering, displaying, and printing text) as well as non-I/O components (for checking spelling, searching for words, and so on).

➠ See also *input; output.*

IPC: See *interprocess communication.*

IrDA: Short for *Infrared Data Association,* a group of device manufacturers that developed a standard for transmitting data via infrared light waves. Increasingly, computers and other devices (such as printers) come with IrDA ports. This enables you to transfer data from one device to another without any cables. For example, if both your laptop computer and printer have IrDA ports, you can simply put your computer in front of the printer and output a document, without needing to connect the two with a cable.

IrDA ports support roughly the same transmission rates as traditional parallel ports. The only restrictions on their use is that the two devices must be within a few feet of each other and there must be a clear line of sight between them.

➡ See also *parallel port.*

IRMA board: A popular expansion board for PCs and Macintoshes that enables these personal computers to emulate IBM 3278 and 3279 mainframe terminals. In other words, personal computers with IRMA boards can function as both stand-alone computers and as terminals connected to a mainframe computer. IRMA boards are made by a company called *DCA.*

➡ See also *emulation; expansion board; mainframe; stand-alone; terminal.*

IRQ: PC Abbreviation of *interrupt request line,* and pronounced *I-R-Q.* IRQs are hardware lines over which devices can send interrupt signals to the microprocessor. When you add a new device to a PC, you often need to set its IRQ number by setting a DIP switch. This specifies which interrupt line the device may use. IRQ conflicts are a common problem when adding expansion boards, but the new Plug and Play ISA specification may remove this headache.

➡ See also *DIP switch; expansion bus; plug-and-play.*

ISA: Abbreviation of *Industry Standard Architecture* and pronounced *eye-sa.* See under *Industry Standard Architecture (ISA) bus.*

ISA bus: See under *Industry Standard Architecture (ISA) bus.*

ISDN: Abbreviation of *integrated services digital network,* an international communications standard for sending voice, video, and data over digital telephone lines. ISDN requires special metal wires and supports data transfer rates of 64,000 bits per second.

The original version of ISDN employs baseband transmission. Another version, called *B-ISDN,* uses broadband transmission and is able to support transmission rates of 1.5 million bits per second. B-ISDN requires fiber optic cables.

➠ See also *broadband ISDN; FDDI; fiber optics.*

ISO: Acronym for *International Standards Organization.* Founded in 1946, ISO is an international organization composed of national standards bodies from over 75 countries. For example, ANSI (American National Standards Institute) is a member of ISO. ISO has defined a number of important computer standards, the most significant of which is perhaps OSI (Open Systems Interconnection), a standardized architecture for designing networks.

➠ See also *ANSI; network; standard.*

Roman
abcdefghijklmnopqrstuvwxyz

Slanted
abcdefghijklmnopqrstuvwxyz

Italic
abcdefghijklmnopqrstuvwxyz

Figure 40: *Roman, slanted, and italic versions of the Times Roman font.*

italic: In typography, *italic* refers to fonts with characters slanted to the right. An italic font, however, often includes one or more character shapes, such as the *a* and the *f,* that differ from those in the roman font of the same family (Figure 40).

➠ See also *font*

iteration: A single pass through a group of instructions. Most programs contain loops of instructions that are executed over and over again. The computer *iterates* through the loop, which means that it repeatedly executes the loop.

➠ See also *loop*.

jaggies: Stairlike lines that appear where there should be smooth straight lines or curves (See Figure 4 at antialiasing). Jaggies can occur for a variety of reasons, the most common being that the output device (display monitor or printer) does not have enough resolution to portray a smooth line. In addition, jaggies often occur when a bit-mapped image is converted to a different resolution. This is one of the advantages vector graphics has over bit-mapped graphics—the output looks the same regardless of the resolution of the output device.

The effect of jaggies can be reduced somewhat by a graphics technique known as antialiasing. Antialiasing smooths out jagged lines by surrounding the jaggies with shaded pixels. In addition, some printers can reduce jaggies with a technique known as *smoothing*.

➠ See also *antialiasing; smoothing.*

job: A task performed by a computer system. For example, printing a file is a job. Jobs can be performed by a single program or by a collection of programs.

➠ See also *program; task.*

join: In relational databases, a *join operation* is a query that retrieves data from two separate databases. The two databases must be *joined* by at least one common field. That is, the *join field* is a member of both databases.

➠ See also *database; field; query; relational database.*

Joint Photographic Experts Group: See *JPEG.*

joystick: A lever that moves in all directions and controls the movement of a pointer or some other display symbol (Figure 41). A joystick
is similar to a mouse, except that with a mouse the cursor stops moving as soon as you stop moving the mouse. With a joystick, the
pointer continues moving in the direction the joystick is pointing. To
stop the pointer, you must return the joystick to its upright position.
Most joysticks include two buttons called *triggers*.

Joysticks are used mostly for computer games, but they are also
used occasionally for CAD/CAM systems and other applications.

➠ See also *mouse; pointer.*

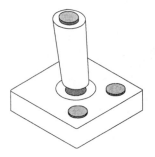

Figure 41: *Joystick*

JPEG: Short for *Joint Photographic Experts Group,* and pronounced *jay-
peg.* JPEG is a *lossy compression* technique for color images. Although it
can reduce files sizes to about 5% of their normal size, some detail is
lost in the compression.

➠ See also *data compression; motion-JPEG; MPEG.*

jumper: A metal bridge that closes an electrical circuit (Figure 42).
Typically, a jumper consists of a plastic plug that fits over a pair of
protruding pins. Jumpers are sometimes used to configure expansion
boards. By placing a jumper plug over a different set of pins, you can
change a board's parameters.

➠ See also *configure; expansion board.*

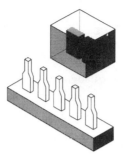

Figure 42: *Jumper*

justification: Alignment of text along a margin. For example, the following is both left- and right-justified:

```
This  text  is  left-  and
right justified  because
the  left  and  right  mar-
gins  are  aligned.  The
justification  does  not
look  very  good  because
the text is printed with
a fixed-pitch font.
```

The text above looks a bit funny because there are wide gaps between some letters but not between others. To produce good-looking justification, the word processor and printer must be capable of microspacing; that is, they must be able to separate letters by less than a full space. In addition, justified text always looks better when a *proportional font* is used. For example:

> This text is left- and right-justified, and microspacing is in effect. Compare this to the previous example, which did not use microspacing.

Vertical justification refers to adjusting the vertical space between lines so that columns and pages have an even bottom margin. One vertical justification technique, called *feathering*, inserts an even amount of space between each line so that the page or column has a specified vertical length.

➡ See also *alignment; feathering; microspacing; vertical justification.*

justify: In word processing, to align text along the left and right margins.

➡ See also *justification.*

KB: Short for kilobyte (1,024 bytes).

➠ See also *kilobyte.*

Kbps: Short for *kilobits per second,* a measure of data transfer speed. Modems, for example, are measured in Kbps.

➠ See also *data transfer rate; modem.*

Kermit: A file-transfer *protocol* developed at Columbia University. Kermit can be used by modems and communications software to send files over telephone lines. Although it is a relatively slow protocol, Kermit is noted for its transmission accuracy. Kermit is not in the public domain, but Columbia University allows people to use the protocol for free, so almost all communications products support it.

There are actually two versions of Kermit, the original version and a later version called *Super Kermit.* Unlike standard Kermit, Super Kermit supports *full-duplex* transmission, which makes it much faster.

Other file-transfer protocols used by slow- to medium-speed modems include Xmodem and Zmodem.

➠ See also CCITT; *communications; full duplex;* MNP; *modem; protocol; Xmodem; Zmodem.*

kerning: In typography, *kerning* refers to adjusting the space between characters, especially by placing two characters closer together than normal (Figure 43). Kerning makes certain combinations of letters, such as WA, MW, TA, and VA, look better.

Only the most sophisticated word processors and desktop publishing systems perform kerning. Normally, you can activate or deactivate kerning for particular fonts.

➠ See also *desktop publishing; font; word processing.*

OCTAVE
Before

OCTAVE
After

Figure 43: *Kerning*

key: (1) A button on a keyboard.

(2) In database management systems, a key is a field that you use to sort data. It can also be called a *key field, sort key, index,* or *key word.* For example, if you sort records by age, then the age field is a key. Most database management systems allow you to have more than one key so that you can sort records in different ways.

➠ See also *database management system; field.*

(3) A password or table needed to decipher encoded data.

➠ See also *encryption; password.*

keyboard: The set of typewriter-like keys that enables you to enter data into a computer. Computer keyboards are similar to electric-typewriter keyboards but contain additional keys. The keys on computer keyboards are often classified as follows:

alphanumeric keys: letters and numbers.

punctuation keys: comma, period, semicolon, and so on.

special keys: function keys, control keys, arrow keys, Caps Lock key, and so on.

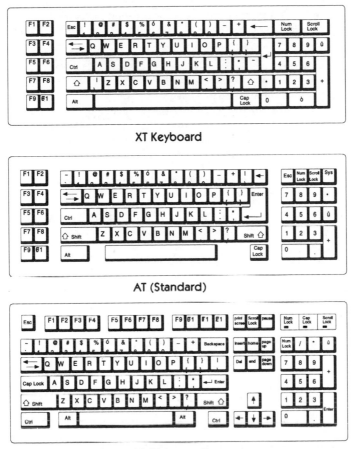

XT Keyboard

AT (Standard)

AT (Enhanced)

Figure 44: *Keyboards*

The standard layout of letters, numbers, and punctuation is known as a *QWERTY keyboard* because the first five keys on the top row of letters spell *QWERTY*. The QWERTY keyboard was designed in the 1800s for mechanical typewriters and was actually designed to slow typists down to avoid jamming the keys. Another keyboard design, which has letters positioned for speed typing, is the *Dvorak keyboard*.

PC There is no standard computer keyboard, although many manufacturers imitate the keyboards of PCs. There are actually three different PC keyboards: the original PC keyboard, with 84 keys; the AT

Table 20
SPECIAL KEYS ON PC KEYBOARDS

KEY	DESCRIPTION
Alt key	Short for Alternate, this key is like a second Control key.
Arrow keys	Most keyboards have four arrow keys that enable you to move the cursor (or insertion point) up, down, right, or left. Used in conjunction with the Shift or Alt keys, the arrow keys can move the cursor more than one position at a time, but this depends on which program is running.
Backspace key	Deletes the character just to the left of the cursor (or insertion point) and moves the cursor to that position.
Caps Lock Key	A toggle key that, when activated, causes all alphabetic characters to be uppercase.
Ctrl key	Short for Control, this key is used in conjunction with other keys to produce control characters. The meaning of each control character depends on which program is running.
Delete key	Sometimes labeled Del, deletes the character at the current cursor position, or the selected object, but does not move the cursor. For graphics-based applications, the Delete key deletes the character to the right of the insertion point.
Enter key	Used to enter commands or to move the cursor to the beginning of the next line. Sometimes labeled Return instead of Enter.
Esc key	Short for Escape, this key is used to send special codes to devices and to exit (or escape) from programs and tasks.
Fn key	Short for Function, this key is used in conjunction with other keys to produce special actions that vary depending on which program is running. This key is found most frequently on portable computers that do not have full-size keyboards.
Function Keys	Special keys labeled F1 to Fx, x being the number of function keys on the keyboard. These keys have different meanings depending on which program is running.
Return key	Another name for the Enter key.

keyboard, also with 84 keys; and the *enhanced keyboard*, with 101 keys. They are shown in Figure 44. The three differ somewhat in the placement of function keys, the Control key, the Return key, and the Shift keys. Despite the placement differences, almost all computer keyboards contain the special-purpose keys shown in Table 20.

In addition to these keys, PC keyboards contain the following keys: Page Up, Page Down, Home, End, Insert, Pause, Num Lock, Scroll Lock, Break, Caps Lock, Print Screen.

MAC There are several different types of keyboards for the Apple Macintosh. All of them are called *ADB keyboards* because they connect to the Apple Desktop bus (ADB). The two main varieties of Macintosh keyboards are the *standard* keyboard and the *extended keyboard*, which has 15 additional special-function keys.

➟ See also *ADB; alphanumeric; Alt key; arrow keys; Backspace key; Break key; Caps Lock key; Control key; cursor; Delete key; Dvorak keyboard; End key; enhanced keyboard; Enter key; Escape key; function keys; Home key; Ins key; Num Lock key; Pause key; Page Down key; Page Up key; Print Screen key; QWERTY keyboard.*

keyboard buffer: See under *buffer.*

keyboard template: See under *template.*

key field: See under *key.*

keypad: See under *numeric keypad.*

keystroke: The pressing of a key. The efficiency of software programs is sometimes measured by the number of keystrokes it requires to perform a specific function. The fewer the keystrokes, claim some software producers, the faster and more efficient the program. The number of keystrokes, however, is generally less important than other characteristics of the software.

keyword: (1) In text editing and database management systems, a *keyword* is an index entry that identifies a specific record or document.

(2) In programming, a keyword is a word that is reserved by a program because the word has a special meaning. Keywords can be commands or parameters. Every programming language has a set of keywords that cannot be used as variable names. Keywords are sometimes called *reserved names*.

➠ See also *command; parameter; variable.*

killer app: See under *app.*

kilobyte: In decimal systems, *kilo* stands for 1,000, but in binary systems, a *kilo* is 1,024 (2 to the 10th power). Technically, therefore, a kilobyte is 1,024 bytes, but it is often used loosely as a synonym for 1,000 bytes. For example, a computer that has 256K main memory can store approximately 256,000 bytes (or characters) in memory at one time.

A megabyte is 2^{20} (approximately 1 million) and a gigabyte is 2^{30} (approximately 1 billion).

In computer literature, kilobyte is usually abbreviated as K or Kb. To distinguish between a decimal K (1,000) and a binary K (1,024), the IEEE has suggested following the convention of using a small k for a decimal kilo and a capital K for a binary kilo, but this convention is by no means strictly followed.

➠ See also *binary; byte; giga; megabyte; memory.*

kludge: Pronounced *klooj*, a derogatory term that refers to a poor design. Like *hacks*, kludges use nonstandard techniques. But, whereas a hack can connote a clever solution to a problem, a kludge always implies that the solution is inelegant.

➠ See also *hack.*

L

L1 cache: Short for Level 1 cache, a memory cache built into the micro-processor. See under cache.

L2 cache: Short for Level 2 cache, an external cache. See under cache.

label: (1) A name.

➠ See also *name.*

(2) For mass storage devices, a label is the name of a storage volume. It is sometimes referred to as a *volume label.* Each operating system has its own set of rules for labeling volumes. The label provides a mne-monic name that indicates what type of information is stored on the media.

➠ See also *disk; mass storage; volume.*

(3) In spreadsheet programs, a label is any descriptive text placed in a cell.

➠ See also *cell; spreadsheet.*

(4) In programming languages, a label refers to a particular location in a program, usually a particular line of source code.

(5) The term *label* is also commonly used to mean a small, sticky piece of paper that you can place on an object to identify it. For example, you can paste labels on floppy disks to indicate what data is stored on them.

LAN: See *local-area network.*

landscape: In word processing and desktop publishing, the terms *portrait* and *landscape* refer to whether the document is oriented vertically or horizontally (Figure 45). A page with landscape orientation is wider than it is tall.

Not all printers are capable of generating text in landscape mode. Of those that are, some require special landscape versions of their fonts; others can rotate the standard portrait fonts 90 degrees.

Orientation is also a characteristic of monitors.

➠ See also *monitor; portrait; printer; word processing.*

Landscape   Portrait

Figure 45: *Landscape vs. Portrait*

language: A system for communicating. Written languages use symbols (that is, characters) to build words. The entire set of words is the language's *vocabulary.* The ways in which the words can be meaningfully combined are defined by the language's *syntax* and *grammar.* The actual meaning of words and combinations of words is defined by the language's *semantics.*

In computer science, human languages are known as *natural languages.* Unfortunately, computers are not sophisticated enough to understand natural languages. As a result, we must communicate with computers using special computer languages. There are many different classes of computer languages, including *machine languages, programming languages,* and *fourth-generation languages.*

➠ See also *artificial intelligence; fourth-generation language; machine language; natural language; programming language; syntax.*

laptop computer: A small, portable computer—small enough that it can sit on your lap. Nowadays, laptop computers are more frequently called *notebook computers*.

➠ See also *notebook computer; portable computer*

large-scale integration (LSI): Refers to the placement of thousands of electronic components on a single integrated circuit.

➠ See also *chip; integrated circuit; VLSI.*

laser printer: A type of printer that utilizes a laser beam to produce an image on a drum. The light of the laser alters the electrical charge on the drum wherever it hits. The drum is then rolled through a reservoir of toner, which is picked up by the charged portions of the drum. Finally, the toner is transferred to the paper through a combination of heat and pressure. This is also the way copy machines work.

Because an entire page is transmitted to a drum before the toner is applied, laser printers are sometimes called *page printers*. There are two other types of page printers that fall under the category of *laser printers* even though they do not use lasers at all. One uses an array of *LEDs* to expose the drum, and the other uses *LCDs*. Once the drum is charged, however, they both operate like a real laser printer.

One of the chief characteristics of laser printers is their resolution—how many dots per inch (dpi) they lay down. The available resolutions range from 300 dpi at the low end to 1,200 dpi at the high end. By comparison, offset printing usually prints at 1,200 or 2,400 dpi. Some laser printers achieve higher resolutions with special techniques known generally as *resolution enhancement.*

In addition to the standard monochrome laser printer, which uses a single toner, there also exist color laser printers that use four toners to print in full color. Color laser printers tend to be about five to ten times as expensive as their monochrome siblings.

Laser printers produce very high-quality print and are capable of printing an almost unlimited variety of fonts. Most laser printers come with a basic set of fonts, called *internal* or *resident fonts*, but you can add additional fonts in one of two ways:

font cartridges: Laser printers have slots in which you can insert font cartridges, ROM boards on which fonts have been recorded. The advantage of font cartridges is that they use none of the printer's memory.

soft fonts: All laser printers come with a certain amount of RAM memory, and you can usually increase the amount of memory by adding memory boards in the printer's expansion slots. You can then copy fonts from a disk to the printer's RAM. This is called *downloading* fonts. A font that has been downloaded is often referred to as a soft font, to distinguish it from the hard fonts available on font cartridges. The more RAM a printer has, the more fonts that can be downloaded at one time.

In addition to text, laser printers are very adept at printing graphics. However, you need significant amounts of memory in the printer to print high-resolution graphics. To print a full-page graphic at 300 dpi, for example, you need at least 1 MB (megabyte) of printer RAM. For a 600-dpi graphic, you need at least 4 MB RAM.

Because laser printers are *nonimpact* printers, they are much quieter than dot-matrix or daisy-wheel printers. They are also relatively fast, although not as fast as some dot-matrix printers. The speed of laser printers ranges from about 4 to 20 pages of text per minute (ppm). A typical rate of 6 ppm is equivalent to about 40 characters per second (cps).

Laser printers are controlled through *page description languages (PDLs)*. There are two de facto standards for PDLs:

PCL: Hewlett-Packard (HP) was one of the pioneers of laser printers and has developed a Printer Control Language (PCL) to control output. There are several versions of PCL, so a printer may be compatible with one but not another. In addition, many printers that claim compatibility cannot accept HP font cartridges.

PostScript: This is the de facto standard for Apple Macintosh printers and for all desktop publishing systems.

Most software can print using either of these PDLs. PostScript tends to be a bit more expensive, but it has some features that PCL lacks and it is the standard for desktop publishing. Some printers support both PCL and PostScript.

➠ See also *color printer; font cartridge; LCD printer; offset printing; page description language; PCL; PostScript; printer; resident font; resolution enhancement; smoothing; soft font; toner.*

LaserWriter: MAC A family of Apple laser printers designed to run off a Macintosh computer.

➥ See also *laser printer; Macintosh computer; PostScript; printer; Quick-Draw.*

launch: To start a program.

➥ See also *execute; load; run.*

LAWN: See *local-area wireless network.*

layout: (1) In word processing and desktop publishing, layout refers to the arrangement of text and graphics. The layout of a document can determine which points are emphasized, and whether the document is aesthetically pleasing.

While no computer program can substitute for a professional layout artist, a powerful desktop publishing system can make it easier to lay out professional-looking documents. A WYSIWYG aids layout considerably because it allows you to lay out a document on the display screen and see what it will look like when printed.

➥ See also *desktop publishing; word processing; WYSIWYG.*

(2) In database management systems, *layout* refers to the way information is displayed. You can change the layout by selecting different fields.

➥ See also *database management system; field; report writer.*

LCD: Abbreviation of *liquid crystal display*, a type of display used in digital watches and many portable computers. LCD displays utilize two sheets of polarizing material with a liquid crystal solution between them. An electric current passed through the liquid causes the crystals to align so that light cannot pass through them. Each crystal, therefore, is like a shutter, either allowing light to pass through or blocking the light.

Monochrome LCD images usually appear as blue or dark gray images on top of a grayish-white background. Color LCD displays use two basic techniques for producing color: *Passive matrix* is the less expensive of the two technologies, but its colors are not particularly sharp and it has slow reaction times. The other technology, called *thin film transistor* (TFT) or *active-matrix*, produces color images that are as sharp as traditional CRT displays, but the technology is expensive.

Most LCD screens used in notebook computers are backlit to make them easier to read in bright environments.

➡ See also *active-matrix display; backlighting; flat-panel display; gas-plasma display; LCD printer; notebook computer; supertwist; TFT.*

LCD printer: A type of printer similar to a laser printer. Instead of using a laser to create an image on the drum, however, it shines a light through a liquid crystal panel. Individual pixels in the panel either let the light pass or block the light, thereby creating an image composed of dots on the drum.

Liquid crystal shutter printers produce print quality equivalent to that of laser printers.

➡ See also *laser printer; LCD; pixel.*

leader: Rows of dots, dashes or other characters that lead your eye from one text element to another. Leaders are used commonly in tables of contents. For example:

Chapter 5 233

leading: Pronounce *ledd-ing,* a typographical term that refers to the vertical space between lines of text. The word derives from the fact that typographers once used thin strips of lead to separate lines. Now, the leading value also includes the size of the font. For example, 10-point text with 2 points of spacing between lines would mean a leading of 12 points.

Many word processors and all desktop publishing systems allow you to specify the leading. In addition, some systems automatically adjust leading so that columns and pages have even bottom margins. This feature is called *vertical justification.*

Leading is also called *line spacing.*

➡ See also *font; justification; point; vertical justification.*

leading zero: A zero that appears in the leftmost digit(s) of a number. Many programs that display numbers in columns allow you to specify whether the number should be preceded with spaces or leading zeros, as shown below.

LEADING ZEROS	SPACES
0003.45	3.45
0148.70	148.70
0002.01	2.01

leaf: Items at the very bottom of a hierarchical tree structure. In hierarchical file systems, files are leaves because they can have nothing below them. Directories, on the other hand, are *nodes*.

➠ See also *hierarchical; node; tree structure.*

learn mode: A mode in which a program learns. The term is usually used to describe a process of defining *macros*. Once you switch the program into learn mode, it will record all subsequent keystrokes you make. You can then assign these keystrokes to a function key to create a macro.

➠ See also *macro.*

LED: Abbreviation of *light emitting diode*, an electronic device that lights up when electricity is passed through it. LEDs are usually red. They are good for displaying images because they can be relatively small, and they do not burn out. However, they require more power than LCDs.

➠ See also *laser printer; LCD.*

LED printer: See under *laser printer.*

left justify: To align text along the left margin. *Left-justified* text is the same as *flush-left* text.

➠ See also *flush; justify.*

legend: In presentation graphics, text that describes the meaning of colors and patterns used in the chart.

➠ See also *presentation graphics.*

letter quality (LQ): Refers to print that has the same quality as that produced by a typewriter. Computer printers are sometimes divided into two classes: those that produce letter-quality type, such as laser, ink-jet, and daisy-wheel printers; and those that do not, including most dot-matrix printers (Figure 46).

The term *letter quality* is really something of a misnomer now, because laser printers produce print that is considerably better than that produced by a typewriter.

Many dot-matrix printers produce a high-quality print known as *near letter quality.* You have to look closely to see that the print is not really letter quality. A lower classification of print quality is called *draft quality.*

➠ See also *daisy-wheel printer; dot-matrix printer; draft quality; ink-jet printer; laser printer; near letter quality; printer.*

Draft Quality   Near Letter Quality   Letter Quality

Figure 46: *Letter Quality vs. Draft Quality*

Level 2 cache: Same as *external cache.* See under *cache.*

library: (1) A collection of files.

(2) In programming, a library is a collection of precompiled routines that a program can use. The routines, sometimes called *modules,* are stored in object format. Libraries are particularly useful for storing frequently used routines because you do not need to explicitly link them to every program that uses them. The linker automatically looks

in libraries for routines that it does not find elsewhere. In MS-Windows environments, library files have a .DLL extension.

➠ See also *linker; module; object code; routine.*

light bar: On a display screen, a highlighted region that indicates a selected component in a menu. The light bar can be produced by using a different color or by reversing the image so that black-on-white text becomes white-on-black.

➠ See also *highlight; menu; reverse video.*

light-emitting diode: See *LED.*

light pen: An input device that utilizes a light-sensitive detector to select objects on a display screen. A light pen is similar to a mouse, except that with a light pen you can move the pointer and select objects on the display screen by directly pointing to the objects with the pen (Figure 47).

➠ See also *CAD/CAM; display screen; input device; mouse; pixel; pointer.*

LIM memory: [PC] A technique for adding memory to DOS systems. LIM memory lets you exceed the 1MB (megabyte) memory limit imposed by DOS. The name derives from the initials of the three companies that designed the technique—Lotus, Intel, and Microsoft—and is sometimes referred to as *LIM 4.0,* which is its official name.

LIM memory has been largely superseded by extended memory.

➠ See also *expanded memory; extended memory.*

line: (1) A hardware circuit connecting two devices.

(2) In programming, a single program statement.

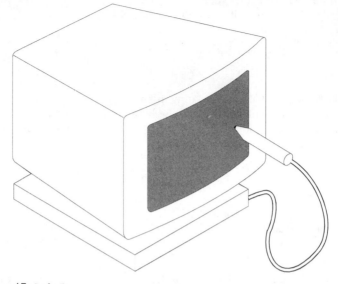

Figure 47: *Light Pen*

line art: A type of graphic consisting entirely of lines, without any shading. Most art produced on computers is *not* line art because the computer makes it so easy to add subtle shadings.

line editor: A primitive type of editor that allows you to edit only one line of a file at a time.

➠ See also *editor*.

line feed: Often abbreviated *LF*, a line feed is a code that moves the cursor on a display screen down one line. In the ASCII character set, a line feed has a decimal value of 10.

On printers, a line feed advances the paper one line. Some printers have a button labeled *LF* that executes a line feed when pressed. (Note, however, that the printer must be in *off-line mode* to execute a line feed.)

➠ See also *ASCII; carriage return; off-line*.

line graph: A type of graph that highlights trends by drawing connecting lines between data points (Figure 48). Compare with bar chart and *pie graph.*

➡ See also *bar chart; pie graph; presentation graphics*

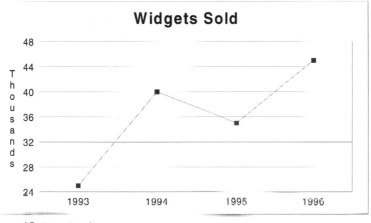

Figure 48: *Line Graph*

line printer: A high-speed printer capable of printing an entire line at one time. A fast line printer can print as many as 3,000 lines per minute. The disadvantages of line printers are that they can print only one font, they cannot print graphics, the print quality is low, and they are very noisy.

➡ See also *printer.*

line spacing: See under *leading.*

lines per inch: See under *halftone.*

link: (v) (1) To bind together.

(2) In programming, the term *link* refers to execution of a *linker.*

➡ See also *linker.*

(3) To paste a copy of an object into a document in such a way that it retains its connection with the original object. Updates to the original object can be reflected in the duplicate by *updating* the link.

➠ See also *OLE*.

(4) In spreadsheet programs, *linking* refers to the ability of a worksheet to take its data for particular cells from another worksheet. Two or more files are thus *linked* by common cells.

➠ See also *cell; spreadsheet*.

(n) (1) In communications, a link is a line or channel over which data is transmitted.

➠ See also *channel; communications*.

(2) In data management systems, a link is a pointer to another record. You can connect one or more records by inserting links into them.

➠ See also *database management system; record*.

(3) In some operating systems (UNIX, for example), a link is a pointer to a file. Links make it possible to reference a file by several different names and to access a file without specifying a full *path*.

➠ See also *filename; path; UNIX*.

link edit: To run a linker.

➠ See also *linker*.

linker: Also called *link editor* and *binder*, a linker is a program that combines object modules to form an executable program (see Figure 17 at compile). Many programming languages allow you to write different pieces of code, called *modules*, separately. This simplifies the programming task because you can break a large program into small, more manageable pieces. Eventually, though, you need to put all the modules together. This is the job of the linker.

In addition to combining modules, a linker also replaces symbolic addresses with real addresses. Therefore, you may need to link a program even if it contains only one module.

➠ See also *address; compile; executable file; module; object code.*

Lino: Short for *Linotronic,* a type of imagesetter. Although Linotronic is a brand name, the terms *Lino* and *Linotronic* are often used to refer to any imagesetter.

➠ See also *imagesetter; Linotronic.*

Linotronic: A common type of high-quality printer, called an *imagesetter,* capable of printing at resolutions of up to 2540 dots per inch. Linotronic printers are too expensive for homes or most offices, but you can obtain Linotronic output by taking a PostScript file to a Service Bureau.

➠ See also *imagesetter; PostScript; Service Bureau.*

liquid crystal display: See *LCD.*

liquid crystal shutter printer: See under *LCD printer.*

LISP: Acronym for *list processor,* a high-level programming language especially popular for artificial intelligence applications. LISP was developed in the early 1960s by John McCarthy at MIT.

➠ See also *artificial intelligence; programming language.*

list: (v) To display data in an ordered format. For example, the LIST command in BASIC displays lines of a program.

(n) Any ordered set of data.

listing: A printout of text, usually a source program.

➠ See also *printout; source code.*

load: (1) To install. For example, to load a disk means to mount it in a disk drive.

(2) To copy a program from a storage device into memory. Every program must be loaded into memory before it can be executed. Usually the loading process is performed invisibly by a part of the operating system called the *loader*. You simply enter the name of the program you want to run, and the operating system loads it and executes it for you.

➠ See also *loader; main memory; operating system; program.*

(3) In programming, *load* means to copy data from main memory into a data register.

➠ See also *main memory; register.*

(4) In networking, load refers to the amount of data (traffic) being carried by the network.

➠ See also *traffic.*

loader: An operating system utility that copies programs from a storage device to main memory, where they can be executed. In addition to copying a program into main memory, the loader can also replace virtual addresses with physical addresses.

Most loaders are invisible: that is, you cannot directly execute them, but the operating system uses them when necessary.

➠ See also *load; main memory; program; utility; virtual memory.*

local: In networks, *local* refers to files, devices, and other resources at your workstation. Resources located at other *nodes* on the networks are *remote*.

➠ See also *local-area network; network; node; remote; workstation.*

local-area network (LAN): A computer network that spans a relatively small area. Most LANs are confined to a single building or group of buildings. However, one LAN can be connected to other LANs over any distance via telephone lines and radio waves. A system of LANs connected in this way is called a *wide-area network (WAN)*.

Most LANs connect workstations and personal computers. Each *node* (individual computer) in a LAN has its own CPU with which it executes programs, but it is also able to access data and devices anywhere on the LAN. This means that many users can share expensive devices, such as laser printers, as well as data. Users can also use the LAN to communicate with each other, by sending e-mail or engaging in chat sessions.

There are many different types of LANs, token-ring networks, Ethernets, and ARCnets being the most common for PCs. Most Apple Macintosh networks are based on Apple's AppleTalk network system, which is built into Macintosh computers.

The following characteristics differentiate one LAN from another:

topology: The geometric arrangement of devices on the network. For example, devices can be arranged in a ring or in a straight line.

protocols: The rules and encoding specifications for sending data. The protocols also determine whether the network uses a peer-to-peer or client/server architecture.

media: Devices can be connected by twisted-pair wire, coaxial cables, or fiber optic cables. Some networks do without connecting media altogether, communicating instead via radio waves.

LANs are capable of transmitting data at very fast rates, much faster than data can be transmitted over a telephone line; but the distances are limited, and there is also a limit on the number of computers that can be attached to a single LAN.

➠ See also *AppleTalk*; *ARCnet*; *client/server architecture*; *e-mail*; *Ethernet*; *Netware*; *network*; *node*; *peer-to-peer architecture*; *personal computer*; *protocol*; *token-ring network*; *topology*; *TOPS*; *workstation*.

local-area wireless network (LAWN): A type of local-area network that uses high-frequency radio waves rather than wires to communicate between nodes.

➠ See also *local-area network*.

local bus: A data bus that connects directly, or almost directly, to the microprocessor. Although local buses can support only a few devices, they provide very fast throughput. Most modern PCs include both a local bus, for video data, as well as a more general expansion bus for other devices that do not require such fast data throughput.

➠ See also *bus; expansion bus; PCI; VL-Bus.*

local echo: Same as *half duplex.*

LocalTalk: MAC The cabling scheme supported by the AppleTalk network protocol for Macintosh computers. Most local-area networks that use AppleTalk, such as *TOPS,* also conform to the LocalTalk cable system. Such networks are sometimes called *LocalTalk networks.*
   Although LocalTalk networks are relatively slow, they are popular because they are easy and inexpensive to install and maintain. An alternative cabling scheme that is faster is Ethernet.

➠ See also *AppleTalk; Ethernet; local-area network; Macintosh computer; TOPS.*

lock: (1) To make a file or other piece of data inaccessible. *File locking* is a critical component of all multi-user computer systems, including local-area networks. When users share files, the operating system must ensure that two or more users do not attempt to modify the same file simultaneously. It does this by *locking* the file as soon as the first user opens it. All subsequent users may read the file, but they cannot write to it until the first user is finished.
   In addition to file locking, many database management systems support *record locking,* in which a single record, rather than an entire file, is locked. This enables different users to access different records within the same file without interfering with one another.

➠ See also *database management system; file; local-area network; multi-user; operating system; record.*

(2) MAC In Macintosh environments, locking a diskette means write-protecting it.

➠ See also *write-protect.*

logical: Refers to a user's view of the way data or systems are organized. The opposite of logical is *physical*, which refers to the real organization of a system. For example, a logical description of a file is that it is a collection of data stored together. This is the way files appear to users. Physically, however, a single file can be divided into many pieces scattered across a disk.

➠ See also *fragmentation; physical.*

logical operator: Same as *Boolean operator.*

log in: Same as *log on.*

log off: Same as *log out.*

log on: To make a computer system recognize you so that you can begin a computer session. Most personal computers have no log-on procedure—you just turn the machine on and begin working. For larger systems and networks, however, you usually need to enter a username and *password* before the computer system will allow you to execute programs.

➠ See also *password; username.*

log out: To end a session at the computer. For personal computers, you can log out simply by exiting applications and turning the machine off. On larger computers and networks, where you share computer resources with other users, there is generally an operating system command that lets you log off.

look-and-feel: Refers to the general appearance and operation of a user interface. This is a hot legal issue because some software companies are claiming that competitors who copy the look-and-feel of their products are infringing on their copyright protection. To date, the courts have not ruled definitively on this matter.

➠ See also *user interface.*

loop: In programming, a loop is a series of instructions that is repeated until a certain condition is met. Each pass through the loop is called an *iteration.* Loops constitute one of the most basic and powerful programming concepts.

➠ See also *iteration.*

lossless compression: Refers to data compression techniques in which no data is lost. The PKZIP compression technology is an example of lossless compression. For most types of data, lossless compression techniques can reduce the space needed by only about 50%. For greater compression, one must use a *lossy compression* technique.

➠ See also *data compression; lossy compression; PKZIP.*

lossy compression: Refers to data compression techniques in which some amount of data is lost. Lossy compression technologies attempt to eliminate redundant or unnecessary information. Most video compression technologies, such as JPEG, use a lossy technique.

➠ See also *data compression; JPEG.*

Lotus 1-2-3: A spreadsheet program designed for IBM-compatible personal computers by Lotus Corporation in 1982. Lotus 1-2-3 was the first publicly available program to combine graphics, spreadsheet functions and data management (three functions, hence the name). Its relative ease of use and flexibility made it an enormous success and contributed to the acceptance of personal computers in business.

➠ See also *spreadsheet.*

lowercase: Small letters, as opposed to capital letters. The word *yes,* for example, is in lowercase, while the word *YES* is in uppercase. For many programs, this distinction is very important. Programs that distinguish between lowercase and uppercase are said to be case sensitive.

➠ See also *case sensitivity; uppercase.*

low-level format: Hard disks must be formatted twice before they can be used. The first format, called a *low-level* or *physical* format, sets the interleave factor and prepares the disk for a particular type of disk controller. This is generally performed at the factory.

➡ See also *controller; format; interleaving.*

low-level language: A machine language or an assembly language. Low-level languages are closer to the hardware than are high-level programming languages, which are closer to human languages.

➡ See also *assembly language; high-level language; language; machine language; programming language.*

low resolution: See under *resolution.*

LPT: A name frequently used by operating systems to identify a printer. Although LPT originally stood for *line printer terminal*, it is now used more generally to identify any type of printer.

➡ See also *printer.*

LQ: See *letter quality.*

LSI: See *large-scale integration.*

luggable: Same as *transportable.*

M: Abbreviation for *mega* or megabyte.

Mac: Short for *Macintosh computer*.

machine address: Same as *absolute address*.

machine code: See under *machine language*.

machine dependent: Refers to a software application that runs only on a particular model of computer. Programs that run on a variety of computers are called *machine independent.*

Almost all programs have some machine dependencies (that is, they run somewhat differently on different computers), but the degree of independence can vary widely. Machine-independent programs give you more flexibility: if you buy a new computer, you can continue using the same software package instead of learning a new one. On the other hand, machine-dependent programs often take advantage of special hardware features of a particular computer, making the programs faster.

Another term for *machine dependent* is device dependent, but whereas *machine dependent* usually refers to the computer, device dependent can refer to a dependency on any device, like a printer.

➠ See also *application.*

machine independent: Able to run on a variety of computers.

➠ See also *machine dependent.*

machine language: The lowest-level programming language. Machine languages are the only languages understood by computers. While easily understood by computers, machine languages are almost impossible for humans to use because they consist entirely of numbers. Programmers, therefore, use either a high-level programming language or an assembly language. An assembly language contains the same instructions as a machine language, but the instructions and variables have names instead of being just numbers (see Figure 68 at *programming language*).

Programs written in high-level languages are translated into assembly language or machine language by a compiler. Assembly language programs are translated into machine language by a program called an *assembler.*

Every CPU has its own unique machine language. Programs must be rewritten or recompiled, therefore, to run on different types of computers.

➭ See assembler; *assembly language; compiler; CPU; high-level language; low-level language; programming language.*

machine readable: In a form that a computer can accept. Machine-readable data includes files stored on disk or tape, or data that comes from a device connected to a computer. Even typewritten pages can be considered machine-readable if you have an optical character recognition (OCR) system.

➭ See also *optical character recognition.*

Macintosh computer: A popular model of computer made by Apple Computer (Figure 49). Introduced in 1984, the Macintosh features a graphical user interface (GUI) that utilizes windows, icons, and a mouse to make it relatively easy for novices to use the computer productively. Rather than learning a complex set of commands, you need only point to a selection on a menu and click a mouse button.

Moreover, the GUI is embedded into the operating system. This means that all applications that run on a Macintosh computer have a similar user interface. Once a user has become familiar with one application, he or she can learn new applications relatively easily.

The Macintosh family of computers is not compatible with the IBM family of personal computers. They have different microprocessors and different file formats. This makes it difficult (though not impossible) to share data between the two types of computers.

Since the Macintosh interface's arrival on the marketplace and its enthusiastic acceptance by customers, numerous software producers have produced similar interfaces. For example, Microsoft offers a Mac-like GUI for PCs called *Windows*.

There are many different Macintosh models, with varying degrees of speed and power. All models are available in many different configurations—different monitors, disk drives, and memory. All older Macintosh computers use a microprocessor from the Motorola 68000 family, but in 1994 Apple switched to the PowerPC microprocessor. PowerMacs can also run programs written for the Motorola processors.

➠ See also *Apple Computer; graphical user interface; PowerPC.*

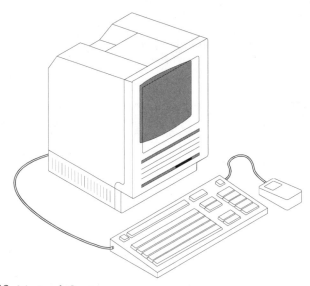

Figure 49: *Macintosh Computer*

macro: (1) A symbol, name, or key that represents a list of commands, actions, or keystrokes. Many programs allow you to create macros so that you can enter a single character or word to perform a whole series of actions. Suppose, for example, that you are editing a file and want to indent every third line five spaces. If your word processor supports macros, you can create one that consists of the following keystrokes:

Move Cursor to Beginning of Line
Move Cursor Down 1 Line
Move Cursor Down 1 Line
Move Cursor Down 1 Line
Insert 5 Spaces

Now you can enter the name of the macro, and the word processor will perform all these commands at once.

You can also use macros to enter words or phrases that you use frequently. For example, you could define a macro to contain all the keystrokes necessary to begin a letter—your name, address, and a code that inserts the current date. Then, whenever you write a letter, you just press the macro key to include the letter header.

In a way, macros are like simple programs or batch files. Some applications support sophisticated macros that even allow you to use variables and flow control structures such as loops.

➠ See also *batch file; command; loop; program.*

(2) In dBASE programs, a macro is a variable that points to another variable where the data is actually stored. In most other applications, this would be called a *link*.

➠ See also *dBASE; link.*

magnetic disk: See under *disk.*

magnetic tape: See under *tape.*

magneto-optical (MO) drive: A type of disk drive that combines magnetic disk technologies with CD-ROM technologies. Like magnetic disks, MO disks can be read and written to. And like floppy disks, they are removable. However, their storage capacity can be more than 200 megabytes, much greater than magnetic floppies. In terms of data access speed, they are faster than floppies and CD-ROMs, but not as fast as hard disk drives.

➠ See also *CD-ROM; hard disk; mass storage.*

mail: See *e-mail.*

mailbox: An area in memory or on a storage device where e-mail is placed. In e-mail systems, each user has a private mailbox. When the user receives e-mail, the mail system automatically puts it in the mailbox.

The mail system allows you to scan mail that is in your mailbox, copy it to a file, delete it, print it, or forward it to another user. If you want to save mail, it is a good idea to copy it to a file, because files tend to be more stable than mailboxes.

➠ See also *e-mail*.

mail merge: A feature supported by many word processors that enables you to generate form letters. To use a mail-merge system, you first store a set of information, like a list of names and addresses, in one file. In another file, you write a letter, substituting special symbols in place of names and addresses (or whatever other information will come from the first file). For example, you might write:

Dear NAME:

Our records show that your address is:

STREET
CITY, STATE ZIP

If this is incorrect, . . .

When you execute the merge command, the word processor automatically generates letters by replacing symbols (NAME, STREET, CITY, STATE, and ZIP) in the second file with the appropriate data from the first file (see Figure 53 at *merge*).

The power and flexibility of mail merge systems varies considerably from one word processor to another. Some word processors support a full set of logical operators that enable you to specify certain conditions under which information should be merged. Also, some merge systems allow you to merge data from several files at once.

Mail merge is sometimes called *print merge*.

➠ See also *merge*.

main memory: Refers to physical memory that is internal to the computer. The word *main* is used to distinguish it from external mass storage devices such as disk drives. Another term for main memory is RAM.

The computer can manipulate only data that is in main memory. Therefore, every program you execute and every file you access must be copied from a storage device into main memory. The amount of main memory on a computer is crucial because it determines how many programs can be executed at one time and how much data can be readily available to a program.

Because computers often have too little main memory to hold all the data they need, computer engineers invented a technique called *swapping,* in which portions of data are copied into main memory as they are needed. Swapping occurs when there is no room in memory for needed data. When one portion of data is copied into memory, an equal-sized portion is copied (swapped) out to make room. Another technique, called *virtual memory*, enables a computer to access larger amounts of data than main memory can hold at one time, but it is a relatively slow process. Therefore, the more memory a computer has and the more it can avoid swapping, the faster it will be able to execute large programs.

Now, most PCs come with a minimum of 4 megabytes of main memory. This is adequate for some applications, but you may need more memory to run sophisticated applications, particularly those that include graphics. You can usually increase the amount of memory by inserting extra memory in the form of chips or memory expansion boards.

➠ See also *chip; conventional memory; expanded memory; expansion board; extended memory; K; loader; megabyte; memory; RAM; swapping; user memory; virtual memory.*

mainframe: A very large and expensive computer capable of supporting hundreds, or even thousands, of users simultaneously. In the hierarchy that starts with a simple microprocessor (in watches, for example) at the bottom and moves to supercomputers at the top, mainframes are just below supercomputers. In some ways, mainframes are more powerful than supercomputers because they support more simultaneous programs. But supercomputers can execute a single program faster than a mainframe. The distinction between small mainframes and minicomputers is vague, depending really on how the manufacturer wants to market its machines.

Unisys and IBM are the largest manufacturers of mainframes.

➠ See also *computer; microprocessor; minicomputer; supercomputer.*

male connector: See under connector.

management information system: See under *MIS*.

manual recalculation: In spreadsheet programs, a mode in which formulas are not recalculated until you explicitly (manually) run the recalculation function. Compare with automatic recalculation, where cells containing formulas are automatically reevaluated whenever necessary.

➠ See also *recalculate*.

map: (n) A file showing the structure of a program after it has been compiled. The *map file* lists every variable in the program along with its memory address. This information is useful for debugging purposes. Normally a compiler will not produce a map file unless you explicitly ask for it by specifying the appropriate compiler option.

➠ See also *compile; debug; option*.

(v) (1) To make logical connections between two entities. Because programs cannot translate directly from human concepts to computer numbers, they translate incrementally through a series of layers. Each layer contains the same amount of information as the layer above but in a form somewhat closer to the form that the computer understands. This activity of translating from one layer to another is called *mapping.*

The term *map* is often used to describe programming languages. For example, C is an efficient programming language because it *maps well* onto the machine language. What this means is that it is relatively easy to translate from the C language to machine languages.

➠ See also *programming language*.

(2) To copy a set of objects from one place to another while preserving the objects' organization. For example, when loaded, programs on a disk are mapped into memory. Graphics images in memory are mapped onto a display screen.

➠ See also *load*.

map file: See under *map*.

MAPI: Abbreviation of *Messaging Application Programming Interface,* a system built into Microsoft Windows that enables different e-mail applications to work together to distribute mail. As long as both applications are *MAPI-enabled,* they can share mail messages with each other.

➠ See also *API; e-mail.*

margins: In word processing, the strips of white space around the edge of the paper. Most word processors allow you to specify the widths of margins. The wider the left and right margins, the narrower the page. The wider the top and bottom margins, the shorter the page.

If your word processor performs *word wrap,* it will automatically adjust the length of the lines when you change the widths of the margins.

➠ See also *word processing; word wrap.*

mask: A filter that selectively includes or excludes certain values. For example, when defining a database field, it is possible to assign a mask that indicates what sort of value the field should hold. Values that do not conform to the mask cannot be entered.

➠ See also *field.*

mass storage: Refers to various techniques and devices for storing large amounts of data. The earliest storage devices were punched paper cards, which were used as early as 1804 to control silk-weaving looms. Modern mass storage devices include all types of disk drives and tape drives. Mass storage is distinct from *memory,* which refers to temporary storage areas within the computer. Unlike main memory, mass storage devices retain data even when the computer is turned off.

The main types of mass storage are:

floppy disks: Relatively slow and have a small capacity, but they are portable, inexpensive, and reliable.

hard disks: Very fast and with more capacity than floppy disks, but also more expensive. Some hard disk systems are portable (removable cartridges), but most are not.

optical disks: Unlike floppy and hard disks, which use electromagnetism to encode data, optical disk systems use a laser to read and write data. Optical disks have very large storage capacity, but they are not as fast as hard disks. In addition, the inexpensive optical disk drives are read-only; read/write varieties are very expensive.

tapes: Relatively inexpensive and can have very large storage capacities, but they do not permit random access of data.

Mass storage is measured in kilobytes (1,024 bytes), megabytes (1,024 kilobytes), and gigabytes (1,024 megabytes).

➡ See also *disk; floppy disk; gigabyte; hard disk; K; main memory; megabyte; memory; optical disk; random access; tape.*

master/slave: Refers to an architecture in which one device (the master) controls one or more other devices (the slaves).

math coprocessor: See under *coprocessor.*

mathematical expression: Any expression that represents a numeric value.

➡ See also *expression.*

matrix: (1) A two-dimensional array; that is, an array of rows and columns.

➡ See also *array.*

(2) The background area of color display.

➡ See also *background.*

302

maximize: In graphical user interfaces, to enlarge a window to its maximum size. In Windows 3.x and Macintosh environments, the buttons for minimizing and maximizing windows are located in the top right corner of the window (Figure 50).

➠ See also *graphical user interface; window; zoom.*

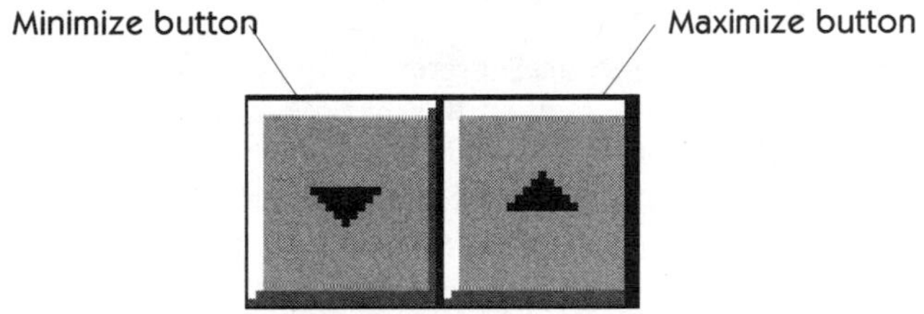

Minimize button   Maximize button

Figure 50: *Minimize and Maximize Buttons*

MB: Short for *megabyte* (1,048,576 bytes).

Mbyte: Short for *megabyte.*

MCA: See *Micro Channel architecture.*

MCGA: PC Abbreviation of *multicolor/graphics array* (or *memory controller gate array*), the graphics system built into some older PCs. It provides graphics capabilities equal to or greater than MDA and CGA, but it is not as powerful as EGA or VGA. Like VGA, MCGA uses analog signals.

➠ See also *CGA; EGA; graphics; MDA; monitor; VGA; video standards.*

MDA: PC Abbreviation of *monochrome display adapter,* an old monochrome video standard for PCs. MDA supports high-resolution monochrome text but does not support graphics or colors. The resolution for text is 720 by 350 pixels.

➠ See also *graphics; Hercules graphics; monitor; monochrome; pixel; resolution; VGA; video standards.*

mean time between failures: See *MTBF*.

media: (1) Objects on which data can be stored. These include hard disks, floppy disks, CD-ROMs, and tapes.

➠ See also *disk; mass storage.*

(2) In computer networks, *media* refers to the cables linking workstations together. There are many different types of transmission media, the most popular being twisted-pair wire (normal electrical wire), coaxial cable (the type of cable used for cable television), and fiber optic cable (cables made out of glass).

➠ See also *cable; fiber optics; local-area network; network.*

(3) The form and technology used to communicate information. Multimedia presentations, for example, combine sound, pictures, and videos, all of which are different types of media.

➠ See also *multimedia.*

meg: Short for *megabyte.*

mega: In decimal systems, the prefix *mega* means one million, but in binary systems, *mega* stands for 2 to the 20th power, or 1,048,576. One megabyte, therefore, is 1,048,576 bytes (this is equivalent to 1,024K).

➠ See also *giga; kilobyte; megabyte.*

megabyte: 1,048,576 (2^{20}) bytes. *Megabyte* is frequently abbreviated as M or *MB*.

megaflop: See *MFLOP.*

megahertz: See *MHz.*

membrane keyboard: A type of keyboard in which the keys are covered by a transparent, plastic shell. The keys have very little movement, but are sensitive to pressure applied on them. The advantage of membrane keyboards is that the covering protects the components from dirt, but it is difficult to type accurately and quickly.

➠ See also *keyboard*.

memory: Internal storage areas in the computer. The term *memory* identifies data storage that comes in the form of chips, and the word *storage* is used for memory that exists on tapes or disks. Moreover, the term *memory* is usually used as a shorthand for *physical memory*, which refers to the actual chips capable of holding data. Some computers also use virtual memory, which expands physical memory onto a hard disk.

Every computer comes with a certain amount of physical memory, usually referred to as *main memory* or *RAM.* You can think of main memory as an array of boxes, each of which can hold a single byte of information. A computer that has 1 megabyte of memory, therefore, can hold about 1 million bytes (or characters) of information.

There are several different types of memory:

RAM (random-access memory): This is the same as main memory. When used by itself, the term RAM refers to read and write memory; that is, you can both write data into RAM and read data from RAM. This is in contrast to ROM, which permits you only to read data. Most RAM is volatile, which means that it requires a steady flow of electricity to maintain its contents. As soon as the power is turned off, whatever data was in RAM is lost.

ROM (read-only memory): Computers almost always contain a small amount of read-only memory that holds instructions for starting up the computer. Unlike RAM, ROM cannot be written to.

PROM (programmable read-only memory): A PROM is a memory chip on which you can store a program. But once the PROM has been used, you cannot wipe it clean and use it to store something else. Like ROMs, PROMs are non-volatile.

EPROM (erasable programmable read-only memory): An EPROM is a special type of PROM that can be erased by exposing it to ultraviolet light.

EEPROM (electrically erasable programmable read-only memory): An EEPROM is a special type of PROM that can be erased by exposing it to an electrical charge.

➠ See also *chip; EEPROM; EPROM; main memory; PROM; RAM; ROM; virtual memory; VRAM.*

memory cache: See under cache.

memory controller gate array: See MCGA.

memory dump: See under *dump.*

memory effect: The property of nickel-cadmium (Nicad) batteries that causes them to lose their capacity for full recharging if they are recharged before they are fully drained. The term derives from the fact that the battery appears to have a *memory* for the amount of charging it can sustain. If it is recharged when it is already full, it will sustain only a small charge the next time as well, even if it is fully drained. Modern NiCad batteries do not suffer from the memory-effect problem as much as older ones do.

➠ See also *NiCad battery pack.*

memory resident: Permanently in memory. Normally, a computer does not have enough memory to hold all the programs you use. When you want to run a program, therefore, the operating system is obliged to free some memory by copying data or programs from main memory to a disk. This process is known as *swapping.*

Certain programs, however, can be marked as being *memory resident,* which means that the operating system is not permitted to swap them out to a storage device; they will always remain in memory.

The programs and data used most frequently are the ones that should be memory resident. This includes central portions of the operating system and special programs, such as calendars and calculators, that you want to be able to access immediately.

Another term for *memory resident* is *RAM resident*. In DOS systems, memory-resident programs are called *pop-up utilities* or *TSRs* (terminate and stay resident).

➠ See also *memory; operating system; swap; TSR.*

menu: A list of commands or options from which you can choose (Figure 51). Most applications now have a menu-driven component. You can choose an item from the menu by highlighting it and then pressing the Enter or Return key, or by simply pointing to the item with a mouse and clicking one of the mouse buttons.

The antithesis of a menu-driven program is a command-driven system, in which you must explicitly enter the command you want rather than choose from a list of possible commands. Menu-driven systems are simpler and easier to learn but are generally not as flexible as command-driven systems, which lend themselves more naturally to interaction with programs.

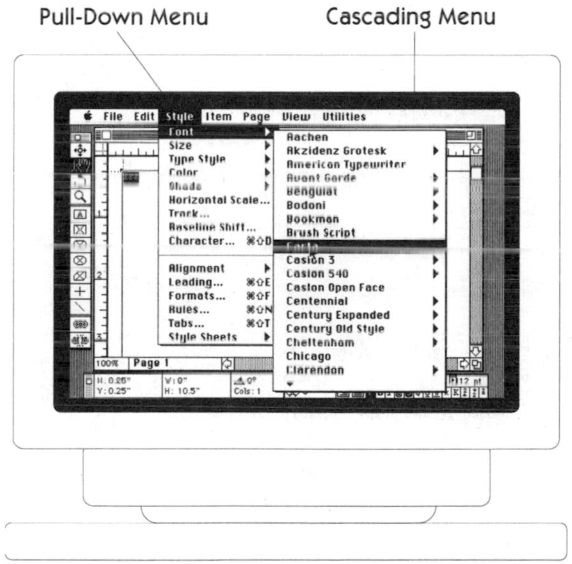

Figure 51: *Menus*

There are several different types of menus:

pop-up menu: A menu that appears temporarily when you click the mouse button on a selection. Once you make a selection from a pop-up menu, the menu usually disappears.

cascading menu: A submenu that opens when you select a choice from another menu.

pull-down menu: A special type of pop-up menu that appears directly beneath the command you selected.

moving-bar menu: A menu in which options are highlighted by a bar that you can move from one item to another. Most menus are moving-bar menus.

menu bar: A menu arranged horizontally. Each menu option is generally associated with another pull-down menu that appears when you make a selection.

tear-off menu: A pop-up menu that you can move around the screen like a window.

➠ See also *command driven; graphical user interface; user interface.*

menu bar: A horizontal menu that appears on top of a window (Figure 52). Usually, each option in a menu bar is associated with a pull-down menu.

➠ See also *menu; window.*

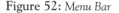

Figure 52: *Menu Bar*

menu driven: Refers to programs whose user interface employs menus. The antithesis of a menu-driven program is a command-driven program.

➡ See also *command driven; menu; user interface.*

merge: (1) To combine two files in such a way that the resulting file has the same organization as the two individual files (Figure 53). For example, if two files contain a list of names in alphabetical order, merging the two files results in one large file with all the names still in alphabetical order.

Note that *merge* is different from append. Append means to combine two files by adding one of them to the end of the other.

(2) In word processing, *mail merge* refers to generating form letters by combining one file containing a list of names, addresses, and other information with a second file containing the text of the letter.

➡ See also *mail merge.*

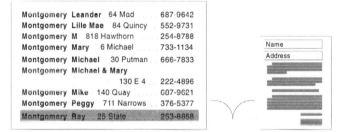

Figure 53: *Mail Merge*

message box: Same as alert box.

Messaging Application Programming Interface: See *MAPI*.

MFLOP: Short for *mega floating-point operations per second*, MFLOPs are a common measure of the speed of computers used to perform *floating-point* calculations. Another common measure of computer speed and power is *MIPS* (million *instructions* per second), which indicates integer performance.

➠ See also *floating-point number; MIPS.*

MFM: [PC] Abbreviation of *modified frequency modulation*, an encoding scheme used by some PC disk drives. A competing scheme, known as RLL (run length limited), produces faster data access speeds and can increase a disk's storage capacity by up to 50 percent.

Technically, any disk drive can use MFM or RLL. The one it uses depends on the disk controller.

➠ See also *controller; disk drive; RLL; ST-506 interface.*

MHz: Abbreviation for *megahertz*. One MHz represents one million cycles per second. The speed of microprocessors, called the *clock speed*, is measured in megahertz. For example, a microprocessor that runs at 66MHz executes 66 million cycles per second. Each computer instruction requires a fixed number of cycles, so the clock speed determines how many instructions per second the microprocessor can execute. To a large degree, this controls how powerful the microprocessor is. Another chief factor in determining a microprocessor's power is its data width (that is, how many bits it can manipulate at one time).

In addition to microprocessors, the speeds of buses are also measured in MHz.

➠ See also *bus; clock speed; microprocessor.*

micro: (1) Short for *microprocessor*.

(2) Short for *personal computer*.

(3) A prefix meaning *one millionth*. For example, a *microsecond* is one millionth of a second.

(4) Something very small. For example, a *microfloppy* is a small floppy disk.

➠ See also micro*floppy disk*.

Micro Channel Architecture (MCA): [PC] A bus architecture for older PCs. It is called a bus *architecture* because it defines how peripheral devices and internal components communicate across the computer's expansion bus. Introduced by IBM in 1987, MCA was designed to take the place of the older AT bus, the architecture used on IBM PC-ATs and compatibles. For a variety of reasons, however, the industry never accepted the new architecture.

➠ See also AT *bus; bus; local bus*.

Microcom Networking Protocol: See *MNP*.

microcomputer: Same as *personal computer*.

microfloppy disk: A small floppy disk (See Figure 33 at floppy disk). Microfloppy disks come enclosed in hard, 3s. Although smaller than older-style floppies, microfloppies have greater storage capacity.
　　[PC] PCs support two types of microfloppies:

■ double-density microfloppies hold 720K.
■ high-density microfloppies can store 1.44MB (megabytes).

[MAC] For Macintosh computers, which have always used microfloppies, there are three sizes:

■ Single-sided standard microfloppies hold 400K.
■ Double-sided standard microfloppies hold 800 K.
■ Double-sided, high-density microfloppies hold 1.44 megabytes.

➠ See also *density; disk; floppy disk*.

micro-justification: Refers to the use of microspacing to justify text.

➠ See also *microspacing.*

microprocessor: A silicon chip that contains a CPU. In the world of personal computers, the terms *microprocessor* and CPU are used interchangeably. At the heart of all personal computers and most workstations sits a microprocessor. Microprocessors also control the logic of almost all digital devices, from clock radios to fuel-injection systems for automobiles.

Two basic characteristics differentiate microprocessors:

bandwidth: The number of bits processed in a single instruction.

clock speed: Given in megahertz (MHz), the clock speed determines how many instructions per second the processor can execute.

In both cases, the higher the value, the more powerful the CPU. For example, a 32-bit microprocessor that runs at 50MHz is more powerful than a 16-bit microprocessor that runs at 25MHz.

In addition to bandwidth and clock speed, microprocessors are classified as being either RISC (reduced instruction set computer) or CISC (complex instruction set computer).

➠ See also *bandwidth; chip;* CISC; *clock speed;* CPU; *Intel microprocessors; Motorola microprocessors; PowerPC;* RISC.

Microsoft Windows: [PC] A family of operating systems for personal computers. Windows dominates the personal computer world, running, by some estimates, on 90% of all personal computers. The remaining 10% are mostly Macintosh computers. Like the Macintosh operating environment, Windows provides a graphical user interface (GUI), virtual memory management, multitasking, and support for many peripheral devices.

In addition to Windows 3.x and Windows 95, which run on Intel-based machines, Microsoft also sells Windows NT, a more advanced operating system that runs on a variety of hardware platforms.

➠ See also *graphical user interface; Intel microprocessors;* DOS; OS/2; *Windows 95; Windows NT.*

Figure 54: *MS-Windows*

microspacing: The insertion of variable-sized spaces between letters to justify text. For example, the following justified text uses microspacing:

> This text is right- and left-justified and is microspaced. Compare with the following example, which is not microspaced.

Without microspacing, the text would look like the following:

> This   text   is   right-   and
> left-justified   and   is   not
> microspaced.   Compare   with
> the   previous   example,   which
> is   microspaced.

To print microspaced text, you need an ink-jet or laser printer. Most daisy-wheel printers and inexpensive dot-matrix printers are not capable of microspacing (See Figure 69 at *proportional spacing*).

➡ See also *justification; printer.*

MIDI: Pronounced *middy*, an acronym for *musical instrument digital inter-face*, a standard adopted by the electronic music industry for repre-senting and transmitting sounds in a form that electronic devices can use. At minimum, a MIDI representation of a sound includes values for the note's pitch, length, and volume. It can also include additional characteristics, such as attack and delay time.

The MIDI standard is supported by most synthesizers, so sounds created on one synthesizer can be played and manipulated on another synthesizer. Computers that have a MIDI interface can record sounds created by a synthesizer and then manipulate the data to produce new sounds. For example, you can change the key of a composition with a single keystroke.

A number of software programs are available for composing and editing music that conforms to the MIDI standard. They offer a vari-ety of functions: for instance, when you play a tune on a keyboard connected to a computer, a music program can translate what you play into a written score.

➠ See also *Amiga; Macintosh computer; sound card.*

million instructions per second: See *MIPS*.

millisecond: One thousandth of a second. Access times of hard disk drives are measured in milliseconds, usually abbreviated as *ms*.

➠ See also *access time.*

mini: Short for *minicomputer.*

minicomputer: A midsized computer. In size and power, minicomputers lie between *workstations* and *mainframes*. In the past decade, the distinc-tion between large minicomputers and small mainframes has blurred, however, as has the distinction between small minicomputers and workstations. But in general, a minicomputer is a multiprocessing sys-tem capable of supporting from 4 to about 200 users simultaneously.

The most popular model of minicomputer is the VAX made by Dig-ital Equipment Corporation. Other large manufacturers of minicom-puters include IBM, Data General, and Prime Computer.

➠ See also *computer; mainframe; multi-user; workstation.*

minifloppy: A 5½-inch floppy disk.

⟶ See also *floppy disk.*

minimize: In graphical user interfaces, to convert a window into an icon.

⟶ See also *graphical user interface; icon; window.*

minitower: See under *tower model.*

MIPS: Acronym for *million instructions per second.* A common measure of a computer's speed and power, MIPS measures roughly the number of machine instructions that a computer can execute in one second. However, different instructions require more or less time than others, and there is no standard method for measuring MIPS. In addition, MIPS refers only to the CPU speed, whereas real applications are generally limited by other factors, such as I/O speed. A machine with a high MIPS rating, therefore, might not run a particular application any faster than a machine with a low MIPS rating.

Despite these problems, the MIPS rating can give you a general idea of a computer's speed. The IBM PC/XT computer, for example, is rated at m-based PCs run at over 100 MIPS.

⟶ See also *CPU; MFLOPS.*

MIS: Short for *management information system,* MIS refers to a class of software that provides managers with tools for organizing and evaluating their department. Typically, MIS systems are written in COBOL and run on mainframes or minicomputers.

⟶ See also *COBOL; mainframe; minicomputer.*

MNP: Abbreviation of *Microcom Networking Protocol,* a communications protocol developed by Microcom, Inc., that is used by many high-speed modems. MNP supports several different classes of communication, each higher class providing additional features. Modems can support one or more classes. Class 4 provides error detection and automatically varies the transmission speed based on the quality of the line. Class 5 provides data compression. Class 6 attempts to detect the highest transmission speed of the modem at the other end of the connect and transmit at that speed.

The most common levels of MNP support are Class 4 and Class 5, frequently called *MNP-4* and *MNP-5*. Using the data compression techniques provided by MNP-5, devices can double normal transmission speeds.

Because MNP is built into the modem hardware, it affects all data transmission. In contrast, software protocols, such as *Xmodem* and *Kermit*, affect only file transfer operations.

➡ See also *communications protocol; data compression; Kermit; modem; Xmodem*.

mode: The state or setting of a program or device. For example, when a word processor is in *insert mode*, characters that you type are inserted at the cursor position. In *overstrike mode*, characters typed replace existing characters.

The term *mode* implies a choice—that you can change the setting and put the system in a different mode.

➡ See also *insert mode; overstrike*.

modem: Acronym for *modulator-demodulator*. A modem is a device that enables a computer to transmit data over telephone lines (Figure 55). Computer information is stored digitally, whereas information transmitted over telephone lines is transmitted in the form of analog waves. A modem converts between these two forms. (Note that ISDN telephone lines send data digitally, so they do not require modems.)

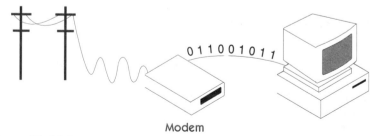

Modem

Figure 55: *Modem*

Fortunately, there is one standard interface for connecting external modems to computers called *RS-232*. Consequently, any external modem can be attached to any computer that has an RS-232 port, which almost all personal computers have. There are also modems that come as an expansion board that you can insert into a vacant expansion slot. These are sometimes called *onboard* or *internal modems* and are more machine specific.

While the modem interfaces are standardized, a number of different protocols for formatting data to be transmitted over telephone lines exist. Some, like CCITT V.34, are official standards, while others have been developed by private companies. Most modems have built-in support for the more common protocols—at slow data transmission speeds at least, most modems can communicate with each other. At high transmission speeds, however, the protocols are less standardized.

Aside from the transmission protocols that they support, the following characteristics distinguish one modem from another:

bps: How fast the modem can transmit and receive data. At slow rates, modems are measured in terms of baud rates. The slowest rate is 300 baud (about 25 cps). At higher speeds, modems are measured in terms of bits per second (bps). The fastest modems run at 28,800 bps, although they can achieve even higher data transfer rates by compressing the data. Obviously, the faster the transmission rate, the faster you can send and receive data. Note, however, that you cannot receive data any faster than it is being sent. If, for example, the device sending data to your computer is sending it at 2,400 bps, you must receive it at 2,400 bps. It does not always pay, therefore, to have a very fast modem. In addition, some telephone lines are unable to transmit data reliably at very high rates.

voice/data: Many modems support a switch to change between voice and data modes. In data mode, the modem acts like a regular modem. In voice mode, the modem acts like a regular telephone. Modems that support a voice/data switch have a built-in loudspeaker and microphone for voice communication.

auto-answer: An auto-answer modem enables your computer to receive calls in your absence. This is only necessary if you are offering some type of computer service that people can call in to use.

data compression: Some modems perform data compression, which enables them to send data at faster rates. However, the modem at the receiving end must be able to decompress the data using the same compression technique.

flash memory: Some modems come with flash memory rather than conventional ROM, which means that the communications protocols can be easily updated if necessary.

To get the most out of a modem, you should have a communications software *package*, a program that simplifies the task of transferring data.

➥ See also *bps*; *CCITT*; *communications*; *communications protocol*; *communications software*; *data compression*; *flash memory*; *Hayes compatible*; *MNP*; *RS-232C*

modified frequency modulation: See *MFM*.

modifier key: A key on a keyboard that only has a meaning when combined with another key. Examples of modifier keys include the Shift, Control, and Alt keys.

➥ See also *keyboard*.

MO drive: See *magneto-optical (MO) drive*.

modular architecture: Refers to the design of any system composed of separate components that can be connected together. The beauty of modular architecture is that you can replace or add any one component (module) without affecting the rest of the system. The opposite of a modular architecture is an *integrated* architecture, in which no clear divisions exist between components.

The term *modular* can apply to both hardware and software. *Modular software design*, for example, refers to a design strategy in which a system is composed of relatively small and autonomous routines that fit together.

➥ See also *architecture*; *integrated*; *module*.

Modula-2: A programming language designed by Niklaus Wirth, the author of Pascal. Wirth created Modula-2 in the late 1970s to answer many of the criticisms leveled at Pascal, which he had created ten years earlier. In particular, Modula-2 addresses Pascal's lack of support for separate compilation of modules and multitasking. Although Modula-2 found support in academia, it is not often used for applications.

➠ See also *compile; multitasking; Pascal; programming language.*

module: (1) In software, a module is a part of a program. Programs are composed of one or more independently developed modules that are not combined until the program is linked. A single module can contain one or several routines.

➠ See also *link; program; routine.*

(2) In hardware, a module is a self-contained component.

➠ See also *modular architecture.*

moiré: An undesirable pattern that appears when a graphic image is displayed or printed with an inappropriate resolution. Moiré patterns are difficult to predict because they result from a complex combination of parameters: the size of the image, resolution of the image, resolution of the output device, halftone screen angle, etc.

If you're planning to print a graphic image (particularly a bit-mapped image) on a high-resolution printer, it's a good idea to print a test page first to see if there are any moiré patterns. If there are, you can sometimes eliminate them by changing the resolution of the printout, resizing the image, or changing the angle of the halftone screen.

➠ See also *halftone.*

monitor: (1) Another term for display screen. The term *monitor*, however, usually refers to the entire box, whereas display screen can mean just the screen. In addition, the term *monitor* often implies graphics capabilities.

There are many ways to classify monitors. The most basic is in terms of color capabilities, which separates monitors into three classes:

monochrome: Monochrome monitors actually display two colors, one for the background and one for the foreground. The colors can be black and white, green and black, or amber and black.

gray-scale: A gray-scale monitor is a special type of monochrome monitor capable of displaying different shades of gray.

color: Color monitors can display anywhere from 16 to over 1 million different colors. Color monitors are sometimes called *RGB monitors* because they accept three separate signals—red, green, and blue.

Color and gray-scaling monitors are often classified by the number of bits they use to represent each pixel. For example, an 8-bit monitor represents each pixel with 8 bits. The more bits per pixel, the more colors and shades of gray the monitor can display.

After this classification, the most important aspect of a monitor is its screen size. Like televisions, screen sizes are measured in diagonal inches, the distance from one corner to the opposite corner diagonally. A typical size for *VGA* monitors is 14 inches. Monitors that are 16 or more inches diagonally are often called *full-page* monitors. In addition to their size, monitors can be either *portrait* (height greater than width) or *landscape* (width greater than height). Larger landscape monitors can display two full pages, side by side.

The resolution of a monitor indicates how densely packed the pixels are. In general, the more pixels (often expressed in dots per inch), the sharper the image. Most modern monitors can display 1024 by 768 pixels, the SVGA standard. Some high-end models can display 1280 by 1024, or even 1800 by 1200.

Another common way of classifying monitors is in terms of the type of signal they accept: analog or digital. Low-cost digital monitors are often called *TTL monitors*. Most monitors accept analog signals, which is required by the VGA, SVGA, 8514/A, and other high-resolution color standards. Some monitors are capable of accepting either type of signal.

Some monitors are *fixed frequency*, which means that they accept input at only one frequency. Another type of monitor, called a *multiscanning monitor*, automatically adjusts to the frequency of the signals being sent to it. This means that it can accept input from different types of video adapters. Like fixed-frequency monitors, multiscanning monitors accept TTL, analog, or both types of input.

Other factors that determine a monitor's quality include the following:

bandwidth: The range of signal frequencies the monitor can handle. This determines how much data it can process.

refresh rate: How many times per second the screen is refreshed (redrawn). To avoid flickering, the refresh rate should be at least 70 Hz.

interlaced or noninterlaced: Interlacing is a technique that enables a monitor to have more resolution, but it reduces the monitor's reaction speed.

dot pitch: The amount of space between each pixel. The smaller the dot pitch, the sharper the image. However, very small dot pitches may also translate into decreased brightness and contrast.

convergence: The clarity and sharpness of each pixel.

➡ See also *analog monitor; bandwidth; convergence; digital monitor; display screen; dot pitch; dots per inch; fixed-frequency monitor; gray scaling; interlacing; monochrome; multiscanning monitor; pixel; refresh; RGB monitor; SVGA; TTL monitor; VGA; video adapter.*

(2) A program that *observes* a computer. For example, some monitor programs report how often another program accesses a disk drive or how much CPU time it uses.

monochrome: One color. Monitors, for example, can be monochrome, grayscale or color. Monochrome monitors actually use two colors, one for the display image (the foreground) and one for the background. Graphic images can also be monochrome, grayscale, or color.

➡ See also *background; foreground; graphics; gray scaling; monitor.*

monochrome display adapter: See *MDA.*

monospacing: Refers to fonts in which each character has the same width. The opposite of monospacing is *proportional spacing, in which* different characters have different widths. For example, in a proportionally spaced font, the letter *o* would be wider than the letter *i*. Proportionally spaced fonts look more professional, but monospaced fonts are often superior for tabular data because the uniform width of each character makes alignment of columns easier.

Most printed matter, including this book, uses proportional spacing.

➠ See also *font; proportional spacing.*

morphing: Short for *metamorphosing*, morphing refers to an animation technique in which one image is gradually turned into another. Many advanced animation programs support some type of morphing feature.

Mosaic: An application that simplifies accessing documents on the World Wide Web. Originally produced by the National Center for Supercomputing Applications (NCSA), Mosaic has always been distributed as freeware. In 1994, however, the NCSA turned over commercial development of the program to a company called Spyglass, which was subsequently purchased by CompuServe. There are now several varieties of Mosaic, some free and some for sale.

➠ See also *Internet; World Wide Web.*

motherboard: The main circuit board of a microcomputer. The motherboard contains the connectors for attaching additional boards. Typically, the motherboard contains the CPU, BIOS, memory, mass storage interfaces, serial and parallel ports, expansion slots, and all the controllers required to control standard peripheral devices, such as the display screen, keyboard, and disk drive. Other circuit boards are called *add-ons* or *expansion boards*.

Because the motherboard contains the CPU, all other chips attached to the motherboard can access the CPU directly without going through the bus. For this reason, it is a good idea to fill up the motherboard completely before adding expansion boards. For example, to add memory to your system, you may be able to insert chips directly onto the motherboard instead of purchasing a separate memory board.

On most PCs, it is possible to replace the motherboard to upgrade to a faster microprocessor. Replacing the motherboard is somewhat more difficult and more expensive than adding an accelerator board, but it has two advantages:

- The motherboard contains the bus, ROM, and main memory. Replacing it, therefore, improves performance of all of these components in addition to adding a faster CPU. Also, by replacing everything at once, you can avoid potential compatibility problems.
- Replacing the motherboard avoids using up one of the expansion slots.

➠ See also *add-on; BIOS; bus; controller; CPU; expansion board; expansion slot; microprocessor; port; printed circuit board.*

motion-JPEG: JPEG stands for the *Joint Photographic Experts Group standard*, a standard for storing and compressing digital images. Motion-JPEG extends this standard by supporting videos. In motion-JPEG, each frame in the video is stored with the JPEG format.

➠ See also *JPEG; MPEG.*

Motion Picture Experts Group: See MPEG.

Motorola microprocessors: Motorola Corporation is one of the leading manufacturers of microprocessors. Until the early 1990s, Motorola microprocessors were used in all Apple Macintosh computers and in many workstations. Following the development of its 68040 chip in 1989, however, Motorola abandoned the 680x0 line of CISC chips in favor of RISC technologies. In 1993, Motorola joined Apple Computer and IBM in designing a new RISC architecture that would form the basis of the next generation of personal computers. This effort culminated in the introduction of the PowerPC architecture in 1994.

There are four main chips in the 680x0 family: the 6800, 68020, 68030, and 68040. Many people refer to them by their last three digits. For example, the "oh-forty" refers to the 68040 chip.

➠ See also *CISC; microprocessor; PowerPC; RISC.*

mount: (1) To make a mass storage device available. In Macintosh environments, for example, inserting a floppy disk into the drive is called *mounting* the floppy.

(2) To install a device, such as a disk drive or expansion board.

mouse: A device that controls the movement of the cursor or pointer on a display screen. A mouse is a small object you can roll along a hard, flat surface (Figure 56). Its name is derived from its shape, which looks a bit like a mouse, its connecting wire that one can imagine to be the mouse's tail, and the fact that one must make it scurry along a surface. As you move the mouse, the pointer on the display screen moves in the same direction. Mice contain at least one button and sometimes as many as three, which have different functions depending on what program is running.

Invented by Douglas Engelbart of Stanford Research Center in 1963, and pioneered by Xerox in the 1970s, the mouse is one of the great breakthroughs in computer ergonomics because it frees the user to a large extent from using the keyboard. In particular, the mouse is important for graphical user interfaces because you can simply point to options and objects and click a mouse button. Such applications are often called *point-and-click* programs. The mouse is also useful for graphics programs that allow you to draw pictures by using the mouse like a pen, pencil, or paintbrush.

There are three basic types of mice:

mechanical: Has a rubber or metal ball on its underside that can roll in all directions. Sensors within the mouse detect the direction the ball is rolling and move the screen pointer accordingly.

optical: Uses a laser to detect the mouse's movement. You must roll the mouse along a special mat with a grid so that the optical mechanism has a frame of reference. Optical mice respond more quickly and precisely than mechanical mice, but they are also more expensive.

optomechanical: Uses a combination of the mechanical and optical technologies. Unlike optical mice, however, optomechanical mice do not require gridded mats.

PC Mice connect to PCs in one of three ways:

Serial mice connect directly to an RS-232C serial port. This is the simplest type of connection.

Bus mice connect to the bus through an interface card. This is somewhat more complicated because you need to configure and install an expansion board.

Cordless mice aren't physically connected at all. Instead they rely on infrared or radio waves to communicate with the computer.

The choice between the first two connections depends on whether you have a free serial port. If you do, it is usually simpler to connect a serial mouse. Cordless mice are more expensive than both serial and bus mice, but they do eliminate the cord, which can sometimes get in the way.

⟨MAC⟩ Mice connect to Macintosh computers through the ADB (Apple Desktop bus) port.

➠ See also *ADB; bus; cursor; ergonomics; expansion board; graphical user interface; menu driven; pointer; serial port; trackball.*

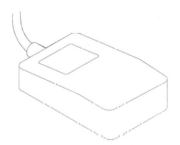

Figure 56: *Mouse*

mousepad: A pad over which you can move a mouse. Mousepads provide more traction than smooth surfaces such as glass and wood, so they make it easier to move a mouse accurately.

For mechanical mice, mousepads are optional. Optical mice, however, require special mousepads that have grids drawn on them.

➠ See also *mouse.*

mouse pointer: See under *pointer.*

325

moving-bar menu: A common type of menu in which options are selected by moving a highlighted bar over them. You can move the bar with a mouse or with arrow keys, or sometimes with the Tab key.

➡ See also *menu.*

MPC: PC Abbreviation of *Multimedia Personal Computer,* a software and hardware standard developed by a consortium of computer firms led by Microsoft. There are two MPC standards, called *MPC* and *MPC-2,* respectively. Each specifies a minimum hardware configuration for running multimedia software. To run MPC-2 software, you need at least an Intel 486SX microprocessor with a clock speed of 25MHz, 8MB (megabytes) of RAM, a VGA display, and a double-speed CD-ROM drive.

➡ See also *CD-ROM; Intel microprocessors; multimedia.*

MPEG: Short for *Motion Picture Experts Group,* one of the leading standards for compressing full-motion digital video. Unlike some competing standards, such as Video for Windows, Indeo and QuickTime, MPEG requires special hardware for decompression. However, it produces better results than these software-only solutions.

The MPEG-1 standard defines a video resolution of 352-by-240 at 30 frames per second (fps). This produces video quality slightly below the quality of conventional VCR videos.

➡ See also *data compression; fps; video.*

ms: Short for *millisecond,* one thousandth of a second. Access times of mass storage devices are often measured in milliseconds.

➡ See also *mass storage.*

MS-DOS: Pronounced *em-ess-doss.* See under *DOS.*

MS-Windows: Pronounced *emm-ess-windows.* See *Microsoft Windows.*

MTBF: Short for *mean time between failures*. MTBF ratings are measured in hours and indicate the sturdiness of hard disk drives and printers. Typical disk drives for personal computers have MTBF ratings of about 40,000 hours. This means that at least half of the disk drives with such a rating will fail once in the first 40,000 hours of operation. Most working conditions are not ideal, so MTBF ratings can be considered as only approximate guidelines for judging the hardiness of disk drives. The fact that MTBF ratings exist at all, however, underscores the fact that every disk drive will eventually fail if run long enough.

➡ See also *disk drive.*

multicolor/graphics array: See MCGA.

MultiFinder: MAC The multitasking version of *Finder* for Apple Macintosh computers. This is the part of the operating system responsible for managing the desktop locating documents and folders and handling the Clipboard and Scrapbook. For System 6, and earlier versions of the Macintosh operating system, MultiFinder was optional. Since System 7, MultiFinder has replaced the older Finder.

➡ See also *clipboard; desktop; Finder; Macintosh computer; multitasking; operating system.*

multifrequency monitor: A type of video monitor capable of accepting signals at more than one frequency range. This enables the monitor to support several different video standards. Typically, multifrequency monitors for PCs support MDA, Hercules, CGA, VGA, and sometimes SVGA.

Multifrequency monitors differ somewhat from *multiscanning monitors*. Multiscanning monitors can support video signals at any frequency level within its range, whereas multifrequency monitors support only a select number of frequency levels. However, because almost all video signals conform to one of a handful of video standards, the greater potential of multiscanning monitors is generally not utilized.

➡ See also *monitor; multiscanning monitor; video adapter.*

multimedia: The use of computers to present text, graphics, video, animation, and sound in an integrated way. Long touted as the future revolution in computing, multimedia applications were, until the mid-90s, uncommon due to the expensive hardware required. With recent increases in performance and decreases in price, however, multimedia is finally finding its way into the mainstream of personal computer applications. To date, most multimedia titles have been games or reference works, but we can expect other types of applications to use multimedia in the future.

Because of the storage demands of multimedia applications, the most effective media are CD-ROMs.

➠ See also *CD-ROM; hypertext; authoring tool.*

multimedia kit: A package of hardware and software that adds multimedia capabilities to a computer. Typically a multimedia kit includes a CD-ROM player, a sound card, speakers, and a bundle of CD-ROMs.

➠ See also *multimedia.*

Multimedia Personal Computer: See *MPC.*

multiprocessing: (1) Refers to a computer system's ability to support more than one process (program) at the same time. Multiprocessing operating systems enable several programs to run concurrently. UNIX is one of the most widely used multiprocessing systems, but there are many others, including OS/2 for high-end PCs. Multiprocessing systems are much more complicated than single-process systems because the operating system must allocate resources to competing processes in a reasonable manner.

➠ See also *multitasking; OS/2; process; UNIX.*

(2) Refers to the utilization of multiple CPUs in a single computer system. This is also called *parallel processing.*

➠ See also *CPU; distributed processing; parallel processing.*

multiscanning monitor: A type of monitor that automatically adjusts to the signal frequency of the video display board to which it is connected. Consequently, multiscanning monitors can display images based on almost any graphics display system, including MDA, Hercules, EGA, VGA, and SVGA.

In contrast, fixed-frequency monitors respond to only one, or a few, frequencies, so they can connect to a limited number of video display boards. However, fixed-frequency monitors are less expensive than multiscanning monitors and sometimes produce sharper images.

Multiscanning monitors are also called *multisync, multifrequency,* and *variable-frequency* monitors. Increasingly, however, the term *multifrequency monitor* is reserved for monitors that support a fixed number of video frequencies. In contrast, multiscanning monitors scan the incoming signals and set themselves to whatever frequency range they are receiving. In practice, there is little difference between the two types of monitors because most video signals conform to one of a handful of video standards.

➡ See also *analog monitor; digital monitor; fixed-frequency monitor; video adapter; video standards.*

multisync monitor: Same as *multiscanning monitor.*

multitasking: The ability to execute more than one *task* at the same time, a task being a program. The terms *multitasking* and *multiprocessing* are often used interchangeably, although multiprocessing sometimes implies that more than one CPU is involved.

In multitasking, only one CPU is involved, but it switches from one program to another so quickly that it gives the appearance of executing all of the programs at the same time.

There are two basic types of multitasking: *preemptive* and *cooperative.* In preemptive multitasking, the operating system parcels out CPU *time slices* to each program. In cooperative multitasking, each program can control the CPU for as long as it needs it. If a program is not using the CPU, however, it can allow another program to use it temporarily. OS/2 and UNIX use preemptive multitasking, whereas Microsoft Windows and the MultiFinder (for Macintosh computers) use cooperative multitasking.

➡ See also *MultiFinder; multiprocessing; operating system; OS/2; UNIX.*

multithreading: The ability of an operating system to execute different parts of a program, called *threads,* simultaneously. The programmer must carefully design the program in such a way that all the threads can run at the same time without interfering with each other.

➠ See also *multitasking.*

multi-user: Refers to computer systems that support two or more simultaneous users. All mainframes and minicomputers are multi-user systems, but most personal computers and workstations are not. Another term for *multi-user* is *time sharing.*

➠ See also *mainframe; minicomputer.*

musical instrument digital interface: See *MIDI.*

name: A sequence of one or more characters that uniquely identifies a
file, variable, account, or other entity. Computer systems impose various rules about naming objects. For example, there is often a limit to
the number of characters you can use, and not all characters are
allowed.

Names are sometimes called *identifiers*.

➠ See also *extension; filename; variable.*

nanosecond: A billionth of a second. Many computer operations, such
as the speed of memory chips, are measured in nanoseconds. *Nanosecond* is often abbreviated as *ns*.

➠ See also *access time.*

National Television Standards Committee: See *NTSC*.

native: Referring to an original form. For example, many applications
can work with files in a variety of formats, but an application's *native
file format* is the one it uses internally. For all other formats, the application must first convert the file to its native format.

natural language: A human language. For example, English, French,
and Chinese are natural languages. Computer languages, such as
FORTRAN and C, are not.

Probably the single most challenging problem in computer science is
to develop computers that can understand natural languages. So far,
the complete solution to this problem has proved elusive, although a

great deal of progress has been made. Fourth-generation languages are the programming languages closest to natural languages.

➠ See also *fourth-generation language; language.*

navigation keys: Same as *cursor control keys.*

near letter quality: A quality of print that is not quite letter quality, but is better than draft quality (see Figure 46 at *letter quality*). Many dot-matrix printers produce near letter quality print. Near letter quality is often abbreviated *NLQ.*

➠ See also *dot-matrix printer; draft quality; letter quality; printer.*

nesting: Embedding one object in another object of the same type. Nesting is quite common in programming. It also occurs in applications. For example, many word processing applications allow you to embed (nest) one document inside another.

Net: Short for *Internet,* as in *"I found this on file on the Net."*

➠ See also Internet.

NetBIOS: PC Short for *Network Basic Input Output System,* an application programming interface (API) that augments the DOS BIOS by adding special functions for local-area networks (LANs). Almost all LANs for PCs are based on the NetBIOS. Some LAN manufacturers have even extended it, adding additional network capabilities.

➠ See also *API; BIOS; local-area network.*

netiquette: The etiquette guidelines for posting messages to online services, and particularly Internet newsgroups. Netiquette covers not only rules to maintain civility in discussions (i.e., avoiding flames), but also special guidelines unique to the electronic nature of forum messages. For example, netiquette advises users to use simple formats because complex formatting may not appear correctly for all readers. In most cases, netiquette is enforced by fellow users who will vociferously object if you break a rule of netiquette.

➠ See also *forum; Internet.*

NetWare: A popular local-area network (LAN) operating system developed by Novell Corporation. NetWare is a software product that runs on a variety of different types of LANs, from Ethernets to IBM token-ring networks. It provides users and programmers with a consistent interface that is independent of the actual hardware used to transmit messages.

➠ See also *Ethernet; local-area network; operating system; token-ring network.*

network: A group of two or more computer systems linked together. There are many types of computer networks, including:

local-area networks (LANs): The computers are geographically close together (that is, in the same building).

wide-area networks (WANs): The computers are farther apart and are connected by telephone lines or radio waves.

In addition to these types, the following characteristics are also used to categorize different types of networks:

topology: The geometric arrangement of a computer system. Common topologies include a bus, star, and ring (see Figure 80 at *topology*).

protocol: The protocol defines a common set of rules and signals that computers on the network use to communicate. One of the most popular protocols for LANs is called *Ethernet.* Another popular LAN protocol for PCs is the IBM token-ring network.

architecture: Networks can be broadly classified as using either a peer-to-peer or client/server architecture.

Computers on a network are sometimes called *nodes*. Computers and devices that allocate resources for a network are called *servers*.

➤ See also *client/server architecture; Ethernet; local-area network; protocol; server; token-ring network; topology; wide-area network.*

Network Basic Input/Output System: See *NetBIOS.*

network interface card (NIC): A *expansion board* you insert into a computer so the computer can be connected to a network. Most NICs are designed for a particular type of network, protocol, and media, although some can serve multiple networks.

➤ See also *expansion board; local-area network; media; network; protocol.*

network operating system (NOS): An operating system that includes special functions for connecting computers and devices into a local-area network (LAN). Some operating systems, such as UNIX and the Mac OS, have networking functions built in. The term *network operating system*, however, is generally reserved for software that enhances a basic operating system by adding networking features. For example, some popular NOS's for DOS and Windows systems include Novell Netware, Artisoft's LANtastic, and Microsoft LAN Manager.

➤ See also *local-area network; operating system.*

neural network: A type of artificial intelligence that attempts to imitate the way a human brain works. Rather than using a digital model, in which all computations manipulate zeros and ones, a neural network works by creating connections between *processing elements*, the computer equivalent of neurons. The organization and weights of the connections determine the output.

Neural networks are particularly effective for predicting events when the networks have a large database of prior examples to draw on. Strictly speaking, a neural network implies a non-digital computer, but neural networks can be simulated on digital computers.

The field of neural networks was pioneered by Bernard Widrow of Stanford University in the 1950s. To date, there are very few commercial applications of neural networks, but the approach is beginning to prove useful in certain areas that involve recognizing complex patterns, such as voice recognition.

➠ See also *artificial intelligence; digital; voice recognition.*

newbie: Slang term for someone who is a new user on an online service, particularly the Internet.

➠ See also *online service.*

newsgroup: Same as *forum.*

NextStep: An object-oriented operating system developed by Next Inc., a company started in 1985 by Steven Jobs, one of the co-founders of Apple Computer. Although NextStep is considered by many experts to be a technical masterpiece, it has failed to gain significant market share.

➠ See also *Apple Computer; object oriented; operating system.*

NIC: See *network interface card.*

NiCad battery pack: NiCad stands for *nickel-cadmium*, the materials used in the battery packs for many notebook computers. NiCad batteries can provide considerable power, but they need to be recharged every three or four hours. Full recharging can take as much as twelve hours, although newer batteries can be recharged in just a few hours.

Older NiCad batteries suffer from a phenomenon known as the *memory effect.* If they were only partially drained and then recharged, they lost their capacity to be fully charged. This is not such a problem with modern NiCad batteries.

Even with full drainage (called *deep discharging*), all batteries have a limit to the number of times they can be recharged. The maximum for most NiCad batteries is about one thousand recharges.

➠ See also *battery pack; memory effect; NiMH battery pack; notebook computer.*

NiMH battery pack: NiMH stands for *Nickel-Metal Hydride,* the materials used in some battery packs. Unlike the more common Nicad batteries, NiMH batteries use heavy metals that may have toxic effects. However, they can store up to 50% more power than Nicad batteries and do not suffer from memory effects.

➠ See also *battery pack; memory effect; NiCad battery pack.*

NLQ: Stands for *near letter quality.*

node: (1) In networks, a processing location. A node can be a computer or some other device, such as a printer.

➠ See also *network.*

(2) In tree structures, a node is a point where two or more lines meet.

➠ See also *tree structure.*

noise: In communications, interference (static) that destroys the integrity of signals on a line. Noise can come from a variety of sources, including radio waves, nearby electrical wires, lightning, and bad connections. One of the major advantages of fiber optic cables over metal cables is that they are much less susceptible to noise.

➠ See also *communications; fiber optics.*

non-impact printer: A type of printer that does not operate by striking a head against a ribbon. Examples of nonimpact printers include laser and ink-jet printers. The term *nonimpact* is important primarily in that it distinguishes quiet printers from noisy (impact) printers.

➠ See also *impact printer; ink-jet printer; laser printer; printer.*

non-interlaced: Refers to monitors and video standards that do not use interlacing techniques to improve resolution. Although interlacing increases resolution, it also increases screen flicker and reduces reaction time.

➠ See also *screen flicker; interlacing; monitor.*

non-volatile memory: Types of memory that retain their contents when power is turned off. ROM is nonvolatile, whereas RAM is *volatile.*

➠ See also *memory; RAM; ROM.*

NOR operator: A Boolean operator that returns a value of TRUE only if both operands are FALSE.

➠ See also *Boolean operator.*

NOS: See *network operating system.*

notebook computer: An extremely lightweight personal computer. Notebook computers typically weigh less than 6 pounds and are small enough to fit easily in a briefcase. Aside from size, the principal difference between a notebook computer and a personal computer is the display screen. Notebook computers use a variety of techniques, known as *flat-panel technologies,* to produce a lightweight and non-bulky display screen..

The quality of notebook display screens varies considerably. In general, notebook display screens are limited to VGA resolution. Active-matrix screens produce very sharp images, but they do not refresh as rapidly as full-size monitors.

In terms of computing power, modern notebook computers are nearly equivalent to personal computers. They have the same CPUs, memory capacity, and disk drives. However, all this power in a small package is expensive. Notebook computers cost about twice as much as equivalent regular-sized computers.

Notebook computers come with battery packs that enable you to run them without plugging them in. However, the batteries need to be recharged every few hours.

➠ See also *active-matrix display; battery pack; hand-held computer; PDA; slate PC; subnotebook computer; VGA*

Figure 57: *Notebook Computer*

NOT operator: A Boolean operator that returns TRUE if its operand is FALSE, and FALSE if its operand is TRUE.

➠ See also *Boolean operator.*

Novell NetWare: See under *NetWare.*

ns: Short for *nanosecond.*

NSFnet: A wide-area network developed under the auspices of the National Science Foundation (NSF). NSFnet is replacing ARPANET as the main government network linking universities and research facilities.

➠ See also *ARPANET; network; wide-area network.*

NTSC: Abbreviation of *National Television Standards Committee.* The NTSC is responsible for setting television and video standards in the United States (in Europe and the rest of the world, the dominant television standards are PAL and SECAM). The NTSC standard for television defines a composite video signal with a refresh rate of 60 half-frames (interlaced) per second. Each frame can contain 16 million different colors.

The NTSC standard is incompatible with most computer video standards, which generally use *RGB* video signals. However, you can insert special video adapters into your computer that convert NTSC signals into computer video signals and vice versa.

➠ See also *composite video; interlacing; RGB monitor; video adapter.*

NuBus: ⎡MAC⎤ The expansion bus for all versions of the Macintosh computers starting with the Macintosh II. Apple has indicated that sometime in the future it may replace NuBus with PCI.

➠ See also *expansion bus; Macintosh computer; PCI.*

null character: A character that has all its bits set to 0. A null character, therefore, has a numeric value of 0, but it has a special meaning when interpreted as text. In some programming languages, notably C, a null character is used to mark the end of a character string. In database and spreadsheet applications, null characters are often used as padding and are displayed as spaces.

➠ See also *character string; padding.*

null-modem cable: A specially designed cable that allows you to connect two computers directly to each other via their communications ports (RS-232 ports). Null modems are particularly useful with portable computers because they enable the portable computer to exchange data with a larger system.

➠ See also *modem; port; RS-232C.*

number cruncher: (1) A computer whose dominant characteristic is its ability to perform large amounts of numerical computations quickly. Supercomputers, for example, are sometimes called number crunchers. In addition, the term *number cruncher* is often applied to powerful workstations.

➠ See also *supercomputer; workstation.*

(2) The term *number cruncher* is sometimes applied to programs. For example, statistical programs are number crunchers because their main task is to perform mathematical calculations.

(3) Less frequently, the term *number cruncher* refers to individuals who use a computer primarily for analyzing numbers.

numeric coprocessor: See under *coprocessor.*

numeric keypad: A separate set of keys on some keyboards that contain the numbers 0 through 9 and a decimal point arranged as on an adding machine (Figure 58). Numeric keypads make it easier to enter large amounts of numeric data.

Frequently, the keys on the numeric keyboard also serve as cursor control keys. Their meanings, therefore, depend on what mode the numeric keypad is in. In *numeric mode,* they represent numbers; in *cursor control mode,* they are like arrow keys. Keyboards that support these dual functions contain an additional key that enables you to switch modes. The name of this key varies—on many keyboards it is labeled *Num Lock.*

➠ See also *arrow keys; keyboard; mode; Num Lock key.*

Figure 58: *Numeric keypad*

Num Lock key: A key that switches the numeric keypad from numeric mode to cursor control mode, and vice versa. In numeric mode, the keys represent numbers even when they are combined with the Shift key, Function key, or Control key. Otherwise these combinations may have different meanings.

The Num Lock key is a toggle key, meaning that it changes the current mode. If the numeric keypad is already locked in numeric mode, pressing the Num Lock key releases it.

➠ See also *cursor control keys; numeric keypad; toggle.*

O

OA: Short for *office automation.*

object: Generally, any item that can be individually selected and manipulated. This can include shapes and pictures that appear on a display screen as well as less tangible software entities. In object-oriented programming, for example, an object is a self-contained entity that consists of both data and procedures to manipulate the data.

➧ See also *object oriented; object-oriented programming; object-oriented graphics; OLE.*

object code: The code produced by a compiler (see Figure 17 at *compiler*). Programmers write programs in a form called *source code.* The source code consists of instructions in a particular language, like C or FORTRAN. Computers, however, can only execute instructions written in a low-level language called *machine language.*

To get from source code to machine language, the programs must be transformed by a compiler. The compiler produces an intermediary form called *object code.* Object code is often the same as or similar to a computer's machine language. The final step in producing an executable program is to transform the object code into machine language, if it is not already in this form. This can be done by a number of different types of programs, called *assemblers, binders, linkers,* and *loaders.*

➧ See also *assembler; assembly language; code; compile; link; load; machine language.*

Object Linking and Embedding: See *OLE.*

object oriented: A popular buzzword that can mean different things depending on how it is being used. *Object-oriented programming (OOP)* refers to a special type of programming that combines data structures with functions to create re-usable objects (see under *object-oriented programming*). Object-oriented graphics is the same as *vector graphics*. Otherwise, the term *object-oriented* is generally used to describe a system that deals primarily with different types of objects, and where the actions you can take depend on what type of object you are manipulating. For example an object-oriented draw program might enable you to draw many types of objects, such as circles, rectangles, triangles, etc. Applying the same action to each of these objects, however, would produce different results. If the action is *Make 3D*, for instance, the result would be a sphere, box, and pyramid, respectively.

➥ See also *object-oriented programming; vector graphics.*

object-oriented graphics: The representation of graphical objects, such as lines, arcs, circles, and rectangles, with mathematical formulas. This method of describing objects enables the system to manipulate the objects more freely. In an object-oriented system, for example, you can overlap objects but still access them individually, which is difficult in a bit-mapped system. Also, object-oriented images profit from high-quality output devices. The higher the resolution of a monitor or printer, the sharper an object-oriented image will look. In contrast, bit-mapped images always appear the same regardless of a device's resolution.

One of the most widely used formats for object-oriented graphics is PostScript. PostScript is a page description language (PDL) that makes it possible to describe objects and manipulate them in various ways. For example, you can make objects smaller or larger, turn them at various angles, and change their shading and color. A font described in PostScript, therefore, can easily be transformed into another font by changing its size or weight. Object-oriented fonts are called *outline fonts, scalable fonts,* or *vector fonts.*

Object-oriented graphics is also called *vector graphics*, whereas bit-mapped graphics is sometimes called *raster graphics.*

➥ See also *bit-mapped graphics; graphics; PostScript; scalable font; vector graphics.*

object-oriented programming (OOP): A type of programming in which programmers define not only the data type of a data structure, but also the types of operations (functions) that can be applied to the data structure. In this way, the data structure becomes an *object* that includes both data and functions. In addition, programmers can create relationships between one object and another. For example, objects can *inherit* characteristics from other objects.

One of the principal advantages of object-oriented programming techniques over conventional programming techniques is that they enable programmers to create modules that do not need to be changed when a new type of object is added. A programmer can simply create a new object that inherits many of its features from existing objects. This makes object-oriented programs easier to modify.

To perform object-oriented programming, one needs an *object-oriented programming language (OOPL)*. C++ and Smalltalk are two of the more popular languages, and there are also object-oriented versions of Pascal.

➠ See also *C++; component software.*

OCR: See *optical character recognition.*

octal: Refers to the base-8 number system, which uses just eight unique symbols (0, 1, 2, 3, 4, 5, 6, and 7). Programs often display data in octal format because it is relatively easy for humans to read and can easily be translated into binary format, which is the most important format for computers (Table 21). By contrast, decimal format is the easiest format for humans to read because it is the one we use in everyday life, but translating between decimal and binary formats is relatively difficult.

In octal format, each digit represents three binary digits, as shown in Table 21. With this table it is easy to translate between octal and binary. For example, the octal number 3456 is 011 100 101 110 in binary.

➠ See also *binary; decimal; hexadecimal.*

ODBC: Abbreviation of *Open DataBase Connectivity*, a standard database access method developed by Microsoft Corporation. The goal of ODBC is to make it possible to access any data from any application, regardless of which database management system (DBMS) is handling the data. ODBC manages this by inserting a middle layer, called a *database driver*, between an application and the DBMS. The purpose

Table 21
OCTAL AND BINARY EQUIVALENTS

OCTAL	BINARY
0	000
1	001
2	010
3	011
4	100
5	101
6	110
7	111

of this layer is to translate the application's data queries into commands that the DBMS understands. For this to work, both the application and the DBMS must be *ODBC-compliant*—that is, the application must be capable of issuing ODBC commands and the DBMS must be capable of responding to them. Since version 2.0, the standard supports SAG SQL.

➠ See also *DBMS; driver; query; SQL.*

odd header: In word processing, a header that appears only on odd-numbered pages.

➠ See also *header.*

odd parity: The mode of parity checking in which each byte contains an odd number of set bits.

➠ See also *parity checking.*

OEM: (n) Stands for *original equipment manufacturer,* which is a misleading term for a company that has a special relationship with computer producers. OEMs buy computers in bulk and customize them for a particular application. They then sell the customized computer under their own name. The term is really a misnomer because OEMs are not the *original* manufacturers—they are the customizers.

Another term for OEM is *VAR (value-added reseller)*.

(v) To provide equipment to another company, an OEM, which customizes and markets the equipment.

office automation: The use of computer systems to execute a variety of office operations, such as word processing, accounting, and e-mail. Office automation almost always implies a network of computers with a variety of available programs.

➠ See also *e-mail; network; word processing.*

off-line: (1) Not connected. For example, all printers have a switch that allows you to turn them off-line. While the printer is off-line, you can perform certain commands like advancing the paper *(form feed)*, but you cannot print documents sent from the computer. The opposite of off-line is *on-line.*

➠ See also *form feed; on-line.*

(2) Aside from its technical meaning, off-line is used frequently in a more general sense to describe events that occur outside of a standard procedure. For example, if somebody at a meeting says "let's continue this discussion off-line," it means "let's discuss it informally at another time."

offset: (1) Refers to a value added to a base address to produce a second address. For example, if B represents address 100, then the expression,

    B+5

would signify the address 105. The 5 in the expression is the offset. Specifying addresses using an offset is called *relative addressing* because the resulting address is relative to some other point. Another word for *offset* is *displacement.*

➠ See also *address; base address; relative address.*

(2) In desktop publishing, the offset is the amount of space along the edge of the paper. Its purpose is to allow room for the binding. The offset is sometimes called the *gutter*.

➠ See also *desktop publishing; gutter.*

offset printing: A printing technique whereby ink is spread on a metal plate with etched images, and then transferred to paper by pressing the paper against the plate. Most print shops use offset printing to produce large volumes of high-quality documents. Although the equipment and set-up costs are relatively high, the actual printing process is relatively inexpensive.

Desktop publishing generally involves producing documents on the computer, printing out drafts on a laser printer, and then offset printing the final version. To produce the plates used in offset printing, a print shop requires either film or high-resolution paper output, which the printer can then photograph. You can obtain either by taking a PostScript file to a service bureau.

➠ See also *desktop publishing; PostScript; service bureau.*

OLE: Abbreviation of *Object Linking and Embedding,* pronounced *oh-leh.* OLE is a compound document *standard* developed by Microsoft Corporation. It enables you to create objects with one application and then link or embed them in a second application. Embedded objects retain their original format and links to the application that created them.

Support for OLE is built into the Windows and Macintosh operating systems. A competing compound document standard developed jointly by IBM, Apple Computer, and other computer firms is called *OpenDoc.*

➠ See also *component software; link; object oriented; OpenDoc.*

on-board: Literally, on a circuit board. *On-board memory,* for example, refers to memory chips on the motherboard. *On-board modems* are modems that are on expansion boards.

➠ See also *expansion board; motherboard; on-board modem; printed circuit board.*

on-board modem: Another term for an *internal modem*; that is, a modem that comes as an expansion board you can insert into a computer.

➠ See also *modem*.

1-2-3: See *Lotus 1-2-3*.

on-line: Turned on and connected. For example, printers are online when they are ready to receive data from the computer. You can also turn a printer *off-line*. While the printer is off-line, you can perform certain tasks such as advancing the paper, but you cannot send data to it. Most printers have an on-line button you can press to turn the machine on- or off-line.

Users are considered *on-line* when they are connected to a computer service through a modem. That is, they are actually *on the line*.

➠ See also *off-line; printer*.

online help: See under *help*.

online service: A business that provides its subscribers with a wide variety of data transmitted over telecommunications lines. Online services provide an infrastructure in which subscribers can communicate with one another, either by exchanging e-mail messages or by participating in online conferences (forums). In addition, the service can connect users with an almost unlimited number of third-party information providers. Subscribers can get up-to-date stock quotes, news stories hot off the wire, articles from many magazines and journals, in fact, almost any information that has been put in electronic form. Of course, all this data carries a price.

The difference between an online service and a bulletin board service is one of scale and profits. Online services provide a variety of information and services, whereas BBSs normally concentrate on a single theme. In addition, BBSs are often operated on a non-profit basis whereas online services are always for profit. Two of the largest online services are CompuServe and Prodigy.

One online service that defies classification is the Internet. In terms of users, it is the largest service, but it is not centrally controlled by any one organization, nor is it operated for profit.

➠ See also *bulletin board system; CompuServe; Internet.*

OOP: See *object-oriented programming.*

OOPL: Stands for *object-oriented programming language.*

➠ See also *object-oriented programming.*

open: (v) To make an object accessible. Whenever you access a file (that is, you edit a text file or run a program file), the operating system opens the file. Opening a file can be simple or complex depending on the operating system. For example, in a multiprocessing operating system, in which different users can share the same resources, the operating system must decide whether the file can be accessed simultaneously by more than one user, and if so, it must ensure that different users do not try to modify the file's contents at the same time.

➠ See also *close; file; operating system.*

(adj) Accessible. When used to describe designs or architectures, *open* means public. See under *open architecture.*

open architecture: An architecture whose specifications are public. This includes officially approved standards as well as privately designed architectures whose specifications are made public by the designers. The opposite of *open* is *closed* or *proprietary.*

The great advantage of open architectures is that anyone can design add-on products for it. By making an architecture public, however, a manufacturer allows others to duplicate its product. The IBM PC, for example, was based on open architectures, and has spawned an entire industry of IBM clones. In contrast, the Macintosh architecture and operating system was predominantly closed until recently.

➠ See also *add-on; architecture; clone; proprietary; standard.*

OpenDoc: A standard and application programming interface (API) that makes it possible to design independent programs (components) that can work together on a single document. OpenDoc is being developed by a loose alliance of companies, including Apple Computer, IBM, and Lotus. Notably absent from this list is Microsoft, which is pushing an alternative standard and API called *Object Linking and Embedding (OLE)*.

➠ See also *component software; OLE.*

operand: In all computer languages, expressions consist of two types of components: *operands* and *operators*. Operands are the objects that are manipulated and operators are the symbols that represent specific actions. For example, in the expression

$$5 + x$$

x and 5 are operands and + is an operator. All expressions have at least one operand.

➠ See also *expression; operator.*

operating environment: The environment in which users run programs. For example, the DOS environment consists of all the DOS commands available to users. The Macintosh environment, on the other hand, is a graphical user interface that uses icons and menus instead of commands.

There is a thin line between operating environments and shells. Historically, shells are the interfaces to operating systems. They do not actually add any new capabilities; they simply provide a better user interface. So-called intelligent shells, however, actually extend an operating system's capabilities, so there is little difference between intelligent shells and operating environments.

Operating environments are sometimes called *control programs*.

➠ See also *environment; graphical user interface; Microsoft Windows; operating system; shell.*

operating system: The most important program that runs on a computer. Every general-purpose computer must have an operating system to run other programs. Operating systems perform basic tasks,

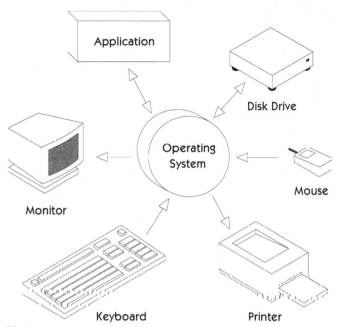

Figure 59: *Operating System*

such as recognizing input from the keyboard, sending output to the display screen, keeping track of files and directories on the disk, and controlling peripheral devices such as disk drives and printers (Figure 59).

For large systems, the operating system has even greater responsibilities and powers. It is like a traffic cop—it makes sure that different programs and users running at the same time do not interfere with each other. The operating system is also responsible for *security*, ensuring that unauthorized users do not access the system.

Operating systems can be classified as follows:

multi-user: Allows two or more users to run programs at the same time. Some operating systems permit hundreds or even thousands of concurrent users.

multiprocessing: Supports running a program on more than one CPU.

multitasking: Allows more than one program to run concurrently.

multithreading: Allows different parts of a single program to run concurrently.

real-time: Responds to input instantly. General-purpose operating systems, such as DOS and UNIX, are not real-time.

Operating systems provide a software platform on top of which other programs, called *application programs,* can run. The application programs must be written to run on top of a particular operating system. Your choice of operating system, therefore, determines to a great extent the applications you can run. For PCs, the most popular operating systems are DOS, OS/2, and Windows, but others are available, such as Xenix.

As a user, you normally interact with the operating system through a set of commands. For example, the DOS operating system contains commands such as COPY and RENAME for copying files and changing the names of files, respectively. The commands are accepted and executed by a part of the operating system called the *command processor* or *command line interpreter.* Graphical user interfaces allow you to enter commands by pointing and clicking at objects that appear on the screen.

➠ See also *BIOS; command processor; file management; DOS; multiprocessing; multitasking; multithreading; multi-user; OS/2; UNIX; Microsoft Windows*

operator: (1) A symbol that represents a specific action. For example, a plus sign (+) is an operator that represents addition. The basic mathematical operators are shown in Table 22.

In addition to these operators, many programs and programming languages recognize other operators that allow you to manipulate numbers and text in more sophisticated ways. For example, Boolean operators enable you to test the truth or falsity of conditions, and *relational operators* let you compare one value to another.

➠ See also *Boolean operator; expression; operand; precedence; relational operator.*

(2) A computer operator is an individual who is responsible for mounting tapes and disks, making backups, and generally ensuring that a computer runs properly.

Table 22
MATHEMATICAL OPERATORS

OPERATOR	ACTION
+	addition
-	subtraction
*	multiplication
/	division

optical character recognition: Often abbreviated OCR, optical character recognition refers to the branch of computer science that involves reading text from paper and translating the images into a form that the computer can manipulate (for example, into ASCII codes). An OCR system enables you to take a book or a magazine article and feed it directly into an electronic computer file.

All OCR systems include an optical scanner for reading text, and sophisticated software for analyzing images. Most OCR systems use a combination of hardware (specialized circuit boards) and software to recognize characters, although some inexpensive systems do it entirely through software. Advanced OCR systems can read text in large variety of fonts, but they still have difficulty with handwritten text.

The potential of OCR systems is enormous because they enable users to harness the power of computers to access printed documents. OCR is already being used widely in the legal profession, where searches that once required hours or days can now be accomplished in a few seconds.

➠ See also *ASCII; font; optical scanner; printed circuit board.*

optical disk: A storage medium from which data is read and to which it is written by lasers. Optical disks can store much more data—up to 6 gigabytes (6 billion bytes) than magnetic media, such as floppies and hard disks. There are three basic types of optical disks:

CD-ROM: Like audio CDs, CD-ROMs come with data already encoded onto them. The data is permanent and can be read any number of times, but CD-ROMs cannot be modified.

WORM: Stands for write-once, read-many. With a WORM disk drive, you can write data onto a WORM disk, but only once. After that, the WORM disk behaves just like a CD-ROM.

erasable: Optical disks that can be erased and loaded with new data, just like magnetic disks. These are often referred to as EO (erasable optical) disks.

These three technologies are not compatible with one another; each requires a different type of disk drive and disk. Even within one category, there are many competing formats, although CD-ROMs are relatively standardized.

➡ See *CD-ROM, disk, erasable optical disk, mass storage, ROM, WORM.*

optical fiber: See under *fiber optics.*

optical mouse: See under *mouse.*

optical scanner: A device that can read text or illustrations printed on paper and translate the information into a form the computer can use. A scanner works by digitizing an image—dividing it into a grid of boxes and representing each box with either a zero or a one, depending on whether the box is filled in. (For color and gray scaling, the same principle applies, but each box is then represented by up to 24 bits.) The resulting matrix of bits, called a *bit map,* can then be stored in a file, displayed on a screen, and manipulated by programs (Figure 60).

Optical scanners do not distinguish text from illustrations; they represent all images as bit maps. Therefore, you cannot directly edit text that has been scanned. To edit text read by an optical scanner, you need an *optical character recognition (OCR)* system to translate the image into ASCII characters. Most optical scanners sold today come with OCR packages.

Scanners differ from one another in the following respects:

scanning technology: Most scanners use charge-coupled device (CCD) arrays, which consist of tightly packed rows of light receptors that can detect variations in light intensity and frequency. The quality of the CCD array is probably the single most important factor affecting the

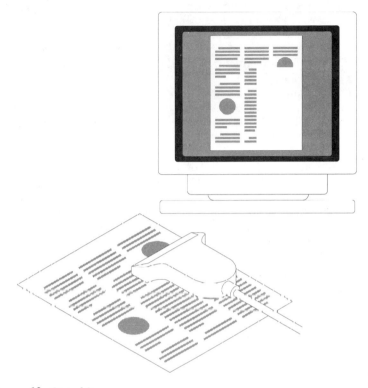

Figure 60: *Optical Scanner*

quality of the scanner. Industry-strength drum scanners use a different technology that relies on a photomultiplier tube (PMT), but this type of scanner is much more expensive than the more common CCD-based scanners.

resolution: The denser the bit map, the higher the resolution. Typically, scanners support resolutions of from 72 to 600 dpi.

bit depth: The number of bits used to represent each pixel. The greater the bit depth, the more colors or grayscales can be represented. For example, a 24-bit color scanner can represent 2^{24} (16.7 million) colors. Note, however, that a large color range is useless if the CCD arrays are capable of detecting only a small number of distinct colors.

size and shape: Some scanners are small hand-held devices that you move across the paper (Figure 60). These hand-held scanners are often called *half-page scanners* because they can only scan 2 to 5 inches at a time. Hand-held scanners are adequate for small pictures and photos, but they are difficult to use if you need to scan an entire page of text or graphics.

Larger scanners include machines into which you can feed sheets of paper. These are called *sheet-fed scanners.* Sheet-fed scanners are excellent for loose sheets of paper, but they are unable to handle bound documents.

A second type of large scanner, called a *flatbed scanner,* is like a photocopy machine. It consists of a board on which you lay books, magazines, and other documents that you want to scan.

Overhead scanners (also called *copyboard scanners*) look somewhat like overhead projectors. You place documents face-up on a scanning bed, and a small overhead tower moves across the page.

➡ See also *ASCII; bit map; CCD; fax machine; font; gray scaling; optical character recognition; resolution; TWAIN*

optimize: (1) In programming, to fine-tune a program so that it runs more quickly or takes up less space.

(2) When applied to disks, the term means the same as defragment. See under *fragmentation.*

option: (1) In command-driven interfaces, an option is an addition to a command that changes or refines the command in a specified manner. As the term implies, options are just that—they are not required.

In the DOS operating system, options are preceded by a slash (/). For example the DIR command supports the /P option, which causes the system to pause between screenfuls of data. Other operating systems and applications have different rules for specifying options. Another word for option is *switch.*

➡ See also *command; command driven.*

(2) In graphical user interfaces, an option is a choice in a menu or dialog box.

➡ See also *dialog box; graphical user interface; menu.*

Option key: MAC A key on Macintosh keyboards that you use in concert with other keys to generate special characters and commands. On PCs, the corresponding key is called an *Alt key.*

➠ See also *Alt key; keyboard; Macintosh computer.*

opto-mechanical mouse: See under *mouse.*

orientation: See under *landscape* and *portrait.*

original equipment manufacturer: See *OEM.*

OR operator: A Boolean operator that returns a value of TRUE if either of its operands is TRUE. This is called an *inclusive OR operator.* There is also an *exclusive OR operator* (often abbreviated *XOR*) that returns a value of TRUE only if both operands have different values.

➠ See also *Boolean operator.*

orphan: In word processing, an orphan is the first line of a paragraph that appears as the last line of a page, or the last line of a paragraph that appears as the first line of a page (this is sometimes called a *widow*). Orphans are considered bad form in page layout, so most word processors allow you to avoid them.

➠ See also *widow; word processing.*

OS/2: PC An operating system for PCs developed originally by Microsoft Corporation and IBM, but now sold and managed solely by IBM. OS/2 is compatible with DOS and Windows, which means that it can run all DOS and Windows programs. However, programs written specifically to run under OS/2 will not run under DOS or Windows.

Since its introduction in the late 80s, OS/2 has traveled a particularly rocky road. The first releases were hampered by a number of technical and marketing problems. Then Microsoft abandoned the project in favor of its own operating system solution, Microsoft Windows. That break spawned a feud between the two computer giants that is still being played out in many arenas.

In terms of technology, the latest versions of OS/2 and Windows are remarkably similar. Both are full 32-bit, multitasking operating systems that can run DOS and Windows applications. Microsoft Windows has the momentum, however, and it remains to be seen whether OS/2 will survive the 90s.

➠ See also *graphical user interface; Microsoft Windows; DOS; multitasking; operating system; PC.*

outline font: A *scalable font* in which the outlines of each character are geometrically defined. The most popular languages for defining outline fonts are *PostScript* and *TrueType.*

An outline font is *scalable* because, given a geometrical description of a typeface, a printer or other display device can generate the characters at any size (scale). Aside from offering innumerable sizes of each font, outline fonts have the added advantage that they make the most of an output device's resolution. The more resolution a printer or monitor offers, the better an outline font will look.

➠ See also *bit map; font; PostScript; resolution; scalable font; TrueType; typeface; vector graphics.*

output: (n) Anything that comes out of a computer. Output can be meaningful information or gibberish, and it can appear in a variety of forms—as binary numbers, as characters, as pictures, and as printed pages. Output devices include display screens, loudspeakers, and printers.

(v) To give out. For example, display screens output images, printers output print, and loudspeakers output sounds.

➠ See also *I/O.*

output device: Any machine capable of representing information from a computer. This includes display screens, printers, plotters, and synthesizers.

➠ See also *device; output.*

OverDrive: A user-installable microprocessor from Intel. Many PCs are built with an OverDrive socket, which allows the owner to upgrade to a faster microprocessor simply by inserting an OverDrive chip.

➠ See also *Intel microprocessors.*

overflow error: An error that occurs when the computer attempts to handle a number that is too large for it. Every computer has a well-defined range of values that it can represent. If during execution of a program it arrives at a number outside this range, it will experience an overflow error. Overflow errors are sometimes referred to as *overflow conditions.*

overlaid windows: Windows arranged so that they overlap each other. Overlaid windows resemble a stack of pieces of paper lying on top of one another; only the topmost window is displayed in full. You can move a window to the top or bottom of the stack by clicking one of the mouse buttons. This is known as *popping* or *pushing,* respectively.
Overlaid windows are also called *cascading windows.* Windows that do not overlap are called *tiled windows.*

➠ See also *pop; push; tiled windows; window*

overstrike: To print one character directly on top of another. In older printers, this was one way to create unusual characters, but it is not necessary with modern printers.

overwrite mode: Most word processors and text editors allow you to choose between two modes: *overwrite* and *insert.* In overwrite mode, every character you type is displayed at the cursor position. If a character is already at that position, it is replaced. In insert mode, each character you type is inserted at the cursor position. This means that existing characters are moved over to make room for the new character, but they are not replaced.
Overwrite mode is sometimes called *overtype mode.*

➠ See also *insert mode.*

P

pack: To compress data.

➡ See also *data compression; packed file.*

packed file: A file in a compressed format. Many operating systems and applications contain commands that enable you to pack a file so that it takes up less memory. For example, suppose you have a text file containing ten consecutive space characters. Normally, this would require ten bytes of storage. However, a program that packs files would replace the space characters by a special *space-series* character followed by the number of spaces being replaced. In this case, the ten spaces would require only two bytes. This is just one packing technique—there are many others. One disadvantage of packed files, however, is that they can be read only by the program that packed them because they contain special codes.

Some modems automatically pack data before transmitting it across communications lines. This can produce faster communication because fewer bytes need to be sent. However, the modem on the receiving side must be capable of *unpacking* the data.

Packing is often referred to as data compression, particularly when it involves data communications.

➡ See also *data compression; modem.*

pad character: A character used to fill empty space. Many applications have fields that must be a particular length. For example, in a database application, you may have a field that is ten characters in length. If you use only four of the allotted characters, the program itself must fill in the remaining six characters with pad characters.

Some applications allow you to choose the character to be used as padding.

➠ See also *database; field; null character.*

padding: Filling in unused space.

➠ See also *pad character.*

page: (n) (1) A fixed amount of data.

➠ See also *page-mode memory.*

(2) In word processing, a page of text. Most text-processing applications recognize a hierarchy of components, starting with a character at the lowest level, followed by a *word,* a *line,* a *paragraph,* and a *page.* Applications permit certain operations for each type of component; for example, you can delete a character, a word, a line, and sometimes an entire page. For pages, you can also specify formatting characteristics (for example, page size, margins, and number of columns).

(3) In virtual memory systems, a page is a fixed number of bytes recognized by the operating system.

(4) Short for web page.

➠ See also *main memory; paging; segment; swap; virtual memory.*

(v) (1) To display one page (or screenful) of a document at a time. To contrast, see *scroll.*

(2) To copy a page of data from main memory to a mass storage device, or vice versa. Paging is one form of swapping.

➠ See also *paging; swap; virtual memory.*

page break: The end of a page of text. In word-processing systems, you can enter special codes, called *hard page breaks* or *forced page breaks,* that cause the printer to advance to the next page. Without hard page breaks, the word processor automatically begins a new page after a page has been filled (this depends on the number of lines per page). In this case, the page break is called a *soft page break*.

➠ See also *hard; soft; word processing.*

Page Description Language (PDL): A language for describing the layout and contents of a printed page. The best-known PDLs are Adobe PostScript and Hewlett-Packard PCL (Printer Control Language), both of which are used to control laser printers.

Both PostScript and modern versions of PCL are *object-oriented*, meaning that they describe a page in terms of geometrical objects such as lines, arcs, and circles.

➠ See also *laser printer; object oriented; PCL; PostScript.*

Page Down key: Often abbreviated *PgDn*, the Page Down key is standard on PC and Macintosh keyboards. Its meaning differs from one program to another, but it usually moves the cursor down a set number of lines.

page eject: Same as *form feed.*

page fault: See under *paging.*

page layout program: A program that enables you to format pages of text and graphics. Many word-processing systems support their own page layout functions, but page layout applications designed specifically for this purpose generally give you more control over fine points such as text flow, kerning, and positioning of graphics.

➠ See also *desktop publishing; kerning; text flow; word processing.*

page-mode memory: A special type of RAM divided into discrete sections, called *pages.* Within any page of memory, the CPU can access memory quickly without resorting to wait states. Typically, a page is 2K bytes.

➠ See also *CPU; memory; RAM; wait state.*

page preview: See under *preview*.

page printer: Any printer that processes an entire page at one time. All laser and ink-jet printers are page printers, which means that they must have enough memory to store at least one page.

➡ See also *laser printer; page description language; printer*.

pages per minute: See *ppm*.

Page Up key: Often abbreviated *PgUp*, the Page Up key is standard on PC and Macintosh keyboards. Its meaning differs from one program to another, but it usually scrolls the document up one screenful.

page-white display: A special type of LCD display screen that uses supertwist technology to produce a high contrast between the foreground and background.

➡ See also *flat-panel display; LCD; supertwist*.

pagination: (1) Refers to numbering pages in a document.

(2) Refers to dividing a document into pages. Most word processors automatically paginate documents based on a page size that you specify. Some word processors enable you to avoid widows and orphans during pagination.

➡ See also *orphan; widow; word processing*.

paging: A technique used by virtual memory operating systems to help ensure that the data you need is available as quickly as possible. The operating system copies a certain number of pages from your storage device to main memory. When a program needs a page that is not in main memory, the operating system copies the required page into memory and copies another page back to the disk. One says that the operating system *pages* the data. Each time a page is needed that is not currently in memory, a *page fault* occurs.

This type of virtual memory is called *paged virtual memory*. Another form of virtual memory is *segmented virtual memory* (see **Figure 86** at *virtual memory*).

➡ See also *main memory; operating system; page; segment; swap; virtual memory*.

paint program: A graphics program that enables you to draw pictures on the display screen which are represented as bit maps (bit-mapped graphics). In contrast, *draw programs* use vector graphics (object-oriented images), which scale better.

Most paint programs provide the *tools* listed in Table 23 in the form of icons. By selecting an icon, you can perform functions associated with the tool.

In addition to these tools, paint programs also provide easy ways to draw common shapes such as straight lines, rectangles, circles, and ovals.

➡ See also *bit-mapped graphics; draw program; graphics; vector graphics*.

Table 23
PAINT TOOLS

ICON	TOOL	FUNCTION
	Brush	For freehand painting using the currently selected pattern and color. Most paint programs provide differently shaped brushes for different styles of painting.
	Eraser	For erasing selected areas of the display screen.
	Lasso	For selecting parts of an illustration.
	Pen	For drawing freehand lines.
	Scissors	For cutting a section of a painting.
	Spraycan	For spray painting in the current pattern and color.

palette: (1) In computer graphics, a palette is the set of available colors. For a given application, the palette may be only a subset of all the colors that can be physically displayed. For example, a SVGA system can display 16 million unique colors, but a given program may use only 256 of them at a time. The computer system's palette, therefore, would consist of the 16 million colors, but the program's palette would contain only the 256-color subset.

On monochrome systems, the term *palette* is sometimes used to refer to the available fill patterns.

➠ See also *EGA; graphics; video adapter.*

(2) In paint and illustration programs, a palette is a collection of symbols that represent drawing tools. For example, a simple palette might contain a paintbrush, a pencil, and an eraser.

➠ See also *draw program; graphics; paint program.*

palmtop: A small computer that literally fits in your palm. Compared to full-size computers, palmtops are severely limited, but they are practical for certain functions such as phone books and calendars. Palmtops that use a pen rather than a keyboard for input are often called *hand-held computers* or *PDAs.*

Because of their small size, most palmtop computers do not include disk drives. However, many contain PCMCIA slots in which you can insert disk drives, modems, memory, and other devices.

➠ See also *hand-held computer; notebook computer; PDA; portable computer.*

Pantone Matching System (PMS): A popular color matching system used by the printing industry to print spot colors. Most applications that support color printing allow you to specify colors by indicating the Pantone name or number. This assures that you get the right color when the file is printed, even though the color may not look right when displayed on your monitor.

PMS works well for spot colors but not for process colors, which are generally specified using the CMYK color model.

➠ See also *CMYK; process colors; spot color.*

paper feed: The mechanism or method that moves paper through a printer. For example, a *tractor-feed* mechanism is one that pulls the paper with a rotating wheel whose nubs catch in holes on either side of the paper.

➠ See also *printer; tractor feed.*

paperless office: The idealized office in which paper is absent because all information is stored and transferred electronically. With the ever-expanding application of computers into business areas as diverse as accounting, desktop publishing, billing, mail, and scheduling, it seemed in the early 80s that the real paperless office was just around the corner. Ironically, just the opposite has transpired. The ease with which computers enable people to print all sorts of documents has created a flood of new paper. Indeed, perhaps the most widespread computer application is the fax machine, which uses paper by the roll.

Some analysts believe that the paperless office is still an achievable and laudable goal, but that certain key technologies such as optical character recognition (OCR) must be improved. Others, however, argue that the tangibleness of paper documents yields certain benefits that will never disappear.

➠ See also *fax machine; optical character recognition; workgroup computing.*

paper-white display: A high-quality monochrome monitor that displays characters in black against a white background. Such monitors are popular for desktop publishing because they most closely mimic real paper with black type. Some manufacturers make a distinction between normal white-background monitors and paper-white monitors, where the background is slightly tinted to look more like bonded paper.

➠ See also *display screen; monitor.*

parallel: Refers to processes that occur simultaneously. Printers and other devices are said to be either *parallel* or *serial. Parallel* means the device is capable of receiving more than one bit at a time (that is, it receives several bits *in parallel*). Most modern printers are parallel.

➠ See also *parallel port; port; printer; serial.*

parallel interface: A channel capable of transferring more than one bit simultaneously. Almost all personal computers come with at least one parallel interface that is reserved for connecting a printer. The other type of interface is a *serial interface*.

➡ See also *channel; parallel; parallel port; serial port.*

parallel port: A parallel interface for connecting an external device such as a printer. Most personal computers have both a parallel port and at least one serial port.

[PC] On PCs, the parallel port uses a 25-pin connector (type DB-25) and is used almost exclusively to connect printers. It is often called a *Centronics interface* after the company that designed the original standard for parallel communication between a computer and printer. (The modern parallel interface is based on a design by Epson.)

A newer type of parallel port, which supports the same connectors as the Centronics interface, is the *EPP (Enhanced Parallel Port)* or *ECP (Extended Capabilities Port)*. Both of these parallel ports support bi-directional communication and transfer rates ten times as fast as the Centronics port.

[MAC] Macintoshes have SCSI and LocalTalk ports, which are parallel, but are more flexible. They are used for many types of communication in addition to connecting printers.

➡ See also *Centronics interface; LocalTalk; parallel; port; SCSI; serial port.*

parallel processing: The simultaneous use of more than one CPU to execute a program. Ideally, parallel processing makes a program run faster because there are more engines (CPUs) running it. In practice, it is often difficult to divide a program in such a way that separate CPUs can execute different portions without interfering with each other.

Most computers have just one CPU, but some models have several. There are even computers with thousands of CPUs. With single-CPU computers, it is possible to perform parallel processing by connecting the computers in a network. However, this type of parallel processing requires very sophisticated software called *distributed processing* software.

Note that parallel processing differs from multitasking, in which a single CPU executes several programs at once.

➡ See also *CPU; distributed processing; multitasking.*

parameter: (1) Characteristic. For example, *specifying parameters* means defining the characteristics of something. In general, parameters are used to customize a program. For example, filenames, page lengths, and font specifications could all be considered parameters.
(2) In programming, the term *parameter* is synonymous with argument, a value that is passed to a routine.

➧ See also *argument; routine.*

parameter RAM (PRAM): See *PRAM.*

parent directory: Refers to the directory above another directory. Every directory, except the root directory, lies beneath another directory. The higher directory is called the *parent directory*, and the lower directory is called a *subdirectory.* In DOS and UNIX systems, the parent directory is identified by two dots (..).

➧ See also *directory; root directory.*

parity: The quality of being either odd or even. The fact that all numbers have a parity is commonly used in data communications to ensure the validity of data. This is called *parity checking.*

➧ See also *parity checking.*

parity bit: See under *parity checking.*

parity checking: In communications, parity checking refers to the use of *parity bits* to check that data has been transmitted accurately. The parity bit is added to every seven bits that are transmitted. The parity bit for each byte (seven data bits plus a parity bit) is set so that all bytes have either an odd number or an even number of set bits.
   Assume, for example, that two devices are communicating with even parity (the most common form of parity checking). As the transmitting device sends data, it counts the number of set bits in each group of seven bits. If the number of set bits is even, it sets the parity bit to 0; if the number of set bits is odd, it sets the parity bit to 1. In this way, every byte has an even number of set bits. On the receiving side, the device checks each byte to make sure that it has an even

number of set bits. If it finds an odd number of set bits, the receiver knows there was an error during transmission.

The sender and receiver must both agree to use parity checking and to agree on whether parity is to be odd or even. If the two sides are not configured with the same *parity sense*, communication will be impossible.

Parity checking is the most basic form of error detection in communications. Although it detects many errors, it is not foolproof, because it cannot detect situations in which two or four consecutive bits are changed due to electrical noise. There are many other more sophisticated protocols for ensuring transmission accuracy, such as MNP and CCITT V.42.

Parity checking is used not only in communications but also to test memory storage devices. Many PCs, for example, perform a parity check on memory every time you boot the machine.

➡ See also *CCITT; communications; communications protocol; MNP; modem.*

park: To lock the *read/write head* of a hard disk drive in a safe position so that the disk will not be damaged while moving the drive. Parking the disk is particularly important for portable computers, which are moved frequently. The disk will automatically *unpark* itself once you turn the power on.

Most modern disk drives support *automatic head parking*, in which the drive automatically parks the head whenever the power is turned off.

➡ See also *disk drive; head; head crash.*

partition: (v) To divide memory or mass storage into isolated sections. In DOS systems, you can partition a disk, and each partition will behave like a separate disk drive. Partitioning is particularly useful if you run more than one operating system. For example, you might reserve one partition for DOS and another for UNIX.

MAC On Apple Macintosh computers, there are two types of partitioning: *hard* and *soft*. Hard partitioning is the same as DOS partitioning—the disk is physically divided into different sections. Soft partitioning, on the other hand, does not physically affect the disk at all, but it fools the Finder into believing that the disk is partitioned. The advantage of this is that you can partition the disk without affecting the data on it. With hard partitioning, it is usually necessary to reformat the entire disk.

➠ See also *disk drive; Finder.*

(n) A section of main memory or mass storage that has been reserved for a particular application.

Pascal: Pronounced *pass-kal,* a high-level programming language developed by Niklaus Wirth in the late 1960s. The language is named after Blaise Pascal, a seventeenth-century French mathematician who constructed one of the first mechanical adding machines.

Pascal is best known for its affinity to structured programming techniques. The nature of the language forces programmers to design programs methodically and carefully. For this reason, it is a popular teaching language.

Despite its success in academia, Pascal has had only modest success in the business world. Part of the resistance to Pascal by professional programmers stems from its inflexibility and lack of tools for developing large applications.

To address some of these criticisms, Wirth designed a new language called *Modula-2.* Modula-2 is similar to Pascal in many respects, but it contains additional features.

➠ See also *Modula-2; programming language.*

passive-matrix display: A common type of flat-panel display consisting of a grid of horizontal and vertical wires. At the intersection of each grid is an LCD element which constitutes a single pixel, either letting light through or blocking it. A higher quality and more expensive type of display, called an *active-matrix display,* uses a transistor to control each pixel.

➠ See also *active-matrix display; flat-panel display; LCD; pixel; TFT.*

password: A secret series of characters that enables a user to access a file, computer, or program. On multi-user systems, each user must enter his or her password before the computer will respond to commands. The password helps ensure that unauthorized users do not access the computer. In addition, data files and programs may require a password.

Ideally, the password should be something that nobody could guess. In practice, most people choose a password that is easy to remember, such as their name or their initials. This is one reason it is relatively easy to break into most computer systems.

➠ See also *log on; security.*

paste: To copy an object from a buffer (or clipboard) to a file. In word processing, blocks of text are moved from one place to another by cutting and pasting. When you cut a block of text, the word processor removes the block from your file and places it in a temporary holding area (a buffer). You can then paste the material in the buffer somewhere else.

Modern operating systems, such as Microsoft Windows, allow you to cut an object from one application and paste it into another. Depending on how the object is pasted, it can be either *linked* or *embedded.*

➠ See also *buffer; clipboard; cut; embedded object; link; OLE.*

patch: A temporary fix to a program bug. A patch is an actual piece of object code that is inserted into (*patched* into) an executable program.

➠ *See also bug; executable file; object code.*

path: (1) |PC| In DOS systems, a path is a list of directories where the operating system looks for executable files if it is unable to find the file in the working directory (Figure 61). You can specify the list of directories with the PATH command.

➠ See also *executable file; DOS; working directory.*

(2) Another name for *pathname.*

➠ See also *pathname.*

pathname: A sequence of symbols and names that identifies a file. Every file has a name, called a *filename,* so the simplest type of pathname is just a filename. If you specify a filename as the pathname, the operating system looks for that file in your current working directory.

However, if the file resides in a different directory, you must tell the operating system how to find that directory. You do this by specifying a path that the operating system must follow.

The pathname always starts from your working directory or from the root directory. Each operating system has its own rules for specifying paths. In DOS systems, for example, the root directory is named \, and each subdirectory is separated by an additional backslash. In UNIX, the root directory is named /, and each subdirectory is followed by a slash. In Macintosh environments, directories are separated by a colon.

➠ See also *directory; filename; root directory; working directory.*

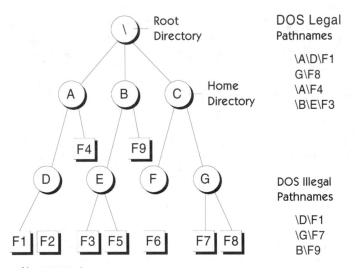

Figure 61: *DOS Paths*

pattern recognition: An important field of computer science concerned with recognizing patterns, particularly visual and sound patterns. It is central to optical character recognition (OCR), voice recognition, and handwriting recognition.

➠ See also *handwriting recognition; optical character recognition; voice recognition.*

Pause key: A key that you can use to temporarily halt the display of data. Generally, you use the Pause key to freeze data that is being scrolled on the display screen. To continue scrolling, you can press any key.

In DOS, an alternative to using the Pause key is to use the MORE command, which displays one screenful of data at a time.

➠ See also *scroll.*

PC: (1) Short for *personal computer* or *IBM PC.* The first personal computer produced by IBM was called the *PC,* and increasingly the term PC came to mean IBM or IBM-compatible personal computers, to the exclusion of other types of personal computers, such as Macintoshes.

In recent years, the term *PC* has become more and more difficult to pin down. In general, though, it applies to any personal computer based on an Intel microprocessor, or on an Intel-compatible microprocessor. For nearly every other component, including the operating system, there are several options, all of which fall under the rubric of PC:

expansion bus: ISA, EISA, or MCA

local bus: VL-Bus or PCI

mass storage interface: IDE, ESDI, or SCSI.

operating system: DOS, Windows, or OS/2.

video standard: VGA, SVGA, or 8514/A.

➠ See also *expansion bus; IBM PC; local bus; Macintosh computer; operating system; personal computer; video standard.*

(2) *PC* can stand for *printed circuit,* so a PC *board* is a printed circuit board.

➠ See also *printed circuit board.*

PC/AT: See under *AT.*

PCB: Short for *printed circuit board.*

PC card: A computer device packaged in a small card about the size of a credit card and conforming to the PCMCIA standard.

➠ See also *PCMCIA.*

PC-DOS: PC The name IBM uses to market the DOS operating system developed by Microsoft.

➠ See also *DOS*

PC fax: Same as *fax modem.*

PCI: Acronym for *Peripheral Component Interconnect,* a local bus standard developed by Intel Corporation. Most modern PCs include a PCI bus in addition to a more general ISA expansion bus. Many analysts, however, believe that PCI will eventually supplant ISA entirely. In addition, Apple computer has indicated that future versions of the PowerMac will use PCI.

PCI Version 1.0 is a 32-bit bus that runs at a clock speed of 33 MHz. This yields a throughput rate of 132 megabytes per second. PCI 2.0 is a 64-bit bus running at a clock speed of 66MHz.

Although it was developed by Intel, PCI is not tied to any particular family of microprocessors. In fact, in a strict sense, it is not a local bus at all because it does not connect directly with the microprocessor. For this reason, some people call it a *mezzanine bus.*

➠ See also expansion bus; *Industry Standard Architecture (ISA) bus; local bus.*

PCL: Abbreviation of *Printer Control Language*, the *page description language (PDL)* developed by Hewlett Packard and used in many of their laser and ink-jet printers. PCL 5 and later versions support a *scalable font* technology called *Intellifont.*

➠ See also *HP-compatible printer; Intellifont; laser printer; page description language; PostScript; scalable font.*

PCMCIA: Short for *Personal Computer Memory Card International Association,* and pronounced as separate letters, PCMCIA is an organization consisting of some 500 companies that has developed a standard for small, credit card-sized devices, called *PC Cards*. Originally designed for adding memory to portable computers, the PCMCIA standard has been expanded several times and is now suitable for many types of devices. There are in fact three types of PCMCIA cards. All three have the same rectangular size (85.6 by 54 millimeters), but different widths:

- Type I cards can be up to 3.3 mm thick, and are used primarily for adding additional ROM or RAM to a computer.
- Type II cards can be up to 5.5 mm thick. These cards are often used for modem and fax modem cards.
- Type III cards can be up to 10.5 mm thick, which is sufficiently large for portable disk drives.

As with the cards, PCMCIA slots also come in three sizes:

- A Type I slot can hold one Type I card
- A Type II slot can hold one Type II card or two Type I cards
- A Type III slot can hold one Type III card or a Type I and Type II card.

Ideally, you should be able to exchange PC Cards on the fly, without rebooting your computer. For example, you should be able to slip in a fax modem card when you want to send a fax and then, when you're done, replace the fax modem card with a memory card. Unfortunately, because of deficiencies in the initial standard and poor implementations by card manufacturers, this has sometimes not worked as planned. However, the standard appears to be reaching a level of maturity where such plug-and-play installation is becoming a reality.

Some analysts believe that the PC card has the potential to become the dominant expansion technology for desktop model computers as well as portable computers.

➠ See also *plug-and-play.*

PCX: Originally developed by ZSOFT for its PC Paintbrush program, PCX is a graphics file format for graphics programs running on PCs. It is supported by most optical scanners, fax programs, and desktop publishing systems. Files in the PCX format end with a ".pcx" (pronounced *dot-p-c-x*) extension. Two other common bit map formats are BMP and *TIFF*.

➠ See also *bit-mapped graphics; BMP; graphics file formats; TIFF.*

PDA: Short for *personal digital assistant*, a handheld device that combines computing, telephone/fax, and networking features. A typical PDA can function as a cellular phone, fax sender, and personal organizer. Unlike portable computers, most PDAs are pen-based, using a stylus rather than a keyboard for input. This means that they also incorporate handwriting recognition features. Some PDAs can also react to voice input by using voice recognition technologies.

The field of PDA was pioneered by Apple Computer, which introduced the Newton MessagePad in 1993. Shortly thereafter, several other manufacturers offered similar products. To date, PDAs have had only modest success in the marketplace, due to their high price tags and limited applications. However, many experts believe that PDAs will eventually become common gadgets.

➠ See also *Apple Computer; cellular phone; handheld computer; handwriting recognition; palmtop; voice recognition.*

PDL: See *page description language.*

peer-to-peer architecture: A type of network in which each workstation has equivalent capabilities and responsibilities. This differs from client/server architectures, in which some workstations are dedicated to serving the others. Peer-to-peer networks are generally simpler and less expensive, but they usually do not offer the same performance under heavy loads.

➠ See also *client/server architecture; local-area network.*

pel: Short for *pixel.*

pen computer: A computer that utilizes an electronic pen (called a *stylus*) rather than a keyboard for input. Pen computers require special operating systems that support handwriting recognition so that users can write on the screen or on a tablet instead of typing on a keyboard.

Most pen computers are hand-held devices, which are too small for a full-size keyboard.

➠ See also *hand-held computer; palmtop; PDA.*

Pentium microprocessor: See under *Intel microprocessors.*

peripheral: Short for peripheral device.

Peripheral Component Interconnect: See *PCI.*

peripheral device: Any external device attached to a computer. Examples of peripherals include printers, disk drives, display monitors, keyboards, and mice.

➠ See also *device.*

personal computer: A small, relatively inexpensive computer designed for an individual user. In price, personal computers range anywhere from a few hundred dollars to over five thousand dollars. All are based on the microprocessor technology that enables manufacturers to put an entire CPU on one chip. Businesses use personal computers for word processing, accounting, desktop publishing, and for running spreadsheet and database management applications. At home, the most popular use for personal computers is for playing games.

Personal computers first appeared in the late 1970s. One of the first and most popular personal computers was the Apple II, introduced in 1977 by Apple Computer. During the late 1970s and early 1980s, new models and competing operating systems seemed to appear daily. Then, in 1981, IBM entered the fray with its first personal computer, known as the *IBM PC.* The IBM PC quickly became the personal computer of choice, and most other personal computer manufacturers fell by the wayside. One of the few companies to survive IBM's onslaught was Apple Computer, which remains a major player in the personal computer marketplace.

Other companies adjusted to IBM's dominance by building IBM clones, computers that were internally almost the same as the IBM PC, but that cost less. Because IBM clones used the same microprocessors as IBM PCs, they were capable of running the same software. Over the years, IBM has lost much of its influence in directing the evolution of PCs. Many of its innovations, such as the MCA expansion bus and the OS/2 operating system, have not been accepted by the industry or the marketplace.

Today, the world of personal computers is basically divided between Apple Macintoshes and PCs. The principal characteristics of personal computers are that they are single-user systems and are based on microprocessors; however, although personal computers are designed as single-user systems, it is common to link them together to form a network. In terms of power, there is great variety. At the high end, the distinction between personal computers and workstations has faded. High-end models of the Macintosh and PC offer the same computing power and graphics capability as low-end workstations by Sun, Hewlett-Packard, and DEC.

➡ See also *Amiga; clone; Macintosh computer; microprocessor; PC; workstation.*

Personal Computer Memory Card International Association: See under *PCMCIA.*

Personal Digital Assistant: See *PDA.*

personal finance manager: A simple *accounting program* that helps individuals manage their finances. Personal finance managers help you balance your checkbook and keep track of investments. Some can even help you pay your bills by printing out checks or transferring money electronically from your bank account.

➡ See also *accounting software.*

personal information manager: See *PIM.*

PGA: Short for *pin grid array,* a type of chip in which the connecting pins are located on the bottom in concentric squares. PGA chips are particularly good for chips that have many pins, such as modern microprocessors. Compare with DIP and *SIP.*

➡ See also *chip.*

PgDn key: See *Page Down key.*

PgUp key: See *Page Up key.*

phase-change printer: Same as *solid ink-jet printer.*

Phoenix BIOS: PC Phoenix Corporation is the largest producer of BIOS chips for IBM PC clones.

➠ See also *BIOS; clone.*

photo illustration: A type of computer art that begins with a digitized photograph. Using special image enhancement software, the artist can then apply a variety of special effects to transform the photo into a work of art.

➠ See also *image enhancement software.*

PhotoCD: A file format for storing digital photographs developed by Eastman Kodak Co.

physical: Refers to anything pertaining to hardware. The opposite of physical is *logical* or *virtual*, which describe software objects. For example, *physical memory* refers to the actual RAM chips installed in a computer. *Virtual memory*, on the other hand, is an imaginary storage area used by programs.

A *physical data structure* refers to the actual organization of data on a storage device. The *logical data structure* refers to how the information appears to a program or user. For example, a data file is a collection of information stored together. This is its logical structure. Physically, however, a file could be stored on a disk in several scattered pieces.

➠ See also *fragmentation; hardware; logical; software; virtual memory.*

PIC: Short for *Lotus Picture File*, the graphics file format used to represent graphics generated by Lotus 1-2-3.

➠ See also *graphics; graphics file formats; Lotus 1-2-3.*

pica: In typesetting, a pica is a unit of measurement equal to 1/6 of an inch, or 12 points.

➠ See also *point*.

PICT file format: ⬛MAC⬛ A file format developed by Apple Computer in 1984. PICT files are encoded in QuickDraw commands and can hold both object-oriented images and bit-mapped images. It is supported by all graphics programs that run on Macintosh computers.

The original PICT format supports 8 colors. A newer version of PICT, called *PICT2*, supports up to 256 colors.

➠ See also *graphics; graphics file formats; Macintosh computer; object oriented; QuickDraw*.

pie chart: A type of presentation graphic in which percentage values are represented as slices of a pie (Figure 62).

➠ See also *presentation graphics*.

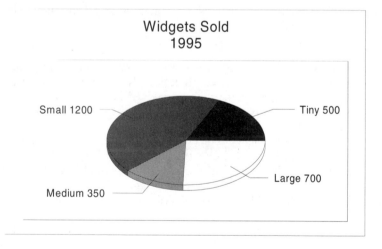

Figure 62: *Pie Chart*

PIM: Acronym for *personal information manager*, a type of software application designed to help users organize random bits of information.

Although the category is fuzzy, most PIMs enable you to enter various kinds of textual notes—reminders, lists, dates—and to link these bits of information together in useful ways. Many PIMs also include calendar, scheduling, and calculator programs.

➠ See also *calculator; calendar; scheduler.*

pin: (1) In dot-matrix printers, the devices that press on the ink ribbon to make dots on the paper. Printers are classified by how many pins they have on the printer head. The more pins a printer has, the higher-quality type it is capable of producing. Dot-matrix printers can have anywhere from 9 to 24 pins. A 24-pin printer can produce letter-quality print.

➠ See also *dot-matrix printer; letter quality; near letter-quality; printer.*

(2) A male lead on a connector.

➠ See also *connector.*

(3) Silicon chips have an array of thin metal feet (pins) on their underside that enables them to be attached to a circuit board. The pins are very delicate and easily bent. If they are damaged, the chip will not sit correctly and will malfunction.

➠ See also *chip.*

pin feed: Same as *tractor feed.*

pin grid array: See *PGA.*

pipe: A temporary software connection between two programs or commands. Normally, the operating system accepts input from the keyboard and sends output to the display screen. Sometimes, however, it is useful to use the output from one command as the input for a second command, without passing the data through the keyboard or display screen. Pipes were invented for these situations (Figure 63).

One of the best examples of pipe usage is linking the command that lists files in a directory to a command that sorts data. By piping the two commands together, you can display the files in sorted order. In

UNIX and DOS, the pipe symbol is a vertical bar (|). The DOS command to list files in alphabetical order, therefore, would be:
DIR | SORT

➠ See also *input; output.*

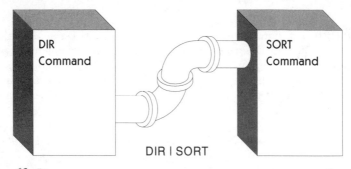

DIR I SORT

Figure 63: *Pipes*

pipelining: A technique used in advanced microprocessors where the microprocessor begins executing a second instruction before the first has been completed. That is, several instructions are in the "pipe" simultaneously, each at a different processing stage. Although formerly a feature only of high-performance and RISC-based microprocessors, pipelining is now common in microprocessors used in personal computers. Intel's Pentium chip, for example, uses pipelining to execute as many as four instructions simultaneously.

➠ See also *Intel microprocessors; microprocessor; RISC.*

piracy: See *software piracy.*

pitch: (1) For *fixed-pitch* (or *monospaced*) fonts, *pitch* refers to the number of characters printed per inch. Pitch is one characteristic of a monospaced font. Common pitch values are 10 and 12.
  In *proportional-pitch* fonts, different characters have different widths, depending on their size. For example, the letter *d* would be wider than the letter *l*. Proportional fonts, therefore, have no pitch value.

➠ See also *font; proportional pitch.*

(2) In graphics, *dot pitch* refers to the spacing between pixels on a monitor. The smaller the dot pitch, the sharper the image.

➠ See also *dot pitch; monitor.*

pixel: Short for *Picture Element,* a pixel is a single point in a graphic image. Graphics monitors display pictures by dividing the display screen into thousands (or millions) of pixels, arranged in rows and columns. The pixels are so close together that they appear connected. The number of bits used to represent each pixel determines how many colors or shades of gray can be displayed. For example, an 8-bit color monitor uses 8 bits for each pixel, making it possible to display 2^8 (256) different colors or shades of gray.

On color monitors, each pixel is actually composed of three dots—a red, a blue, and a green one. Ideally, the three dots should all converge at the same point, but all monitors have some convergence error that can make color pixels appear fuzzy.

The quality of a display monitor largely depends on its resolution, how many pixels it can display, and how many bits are used to represent each pixel. VGA monitors display 640 by 480, or about 300,000 pixels. In contrast, SVGA monitors display 1,024 by 768, or nearly 800,000 pixels. True Color monitors use 24 bits per pixel, allowing them to display more than 16 million different colors.

➠ See also *convergence; graphics; gray scaling; monitor; resolution; True Color.*

PKZIP: One of the most widely used file compression methods. PKZIP was developed by PKWARE, Inc. in 1989 and distributed as shareware. Files that have been compressed using PKWARE are said to be *zipped*. Decompressing them is called *unzipping*.

The *PK* stands for Phillip Katz, the author of the programs.

➠ See also *data compression; shareware; zip.*

plain text: Refers to textual data in ASCII format. Plain text is the most portable format because it is supported by nearly every application on every machine. It is quite limited, however, because it cannot contain any formatting commands.

➠ See also *ASCII file.*

plasma display: A type of flat-panel display that works by sandwiching an ionized gas between two wired panels. In one panel the wires are placed in vertical rows, and in the other they are placed in horizontal rows. Together, the two panels form a grid. An individual point (pixel) can then be charged by passing a current through the appropriate x-coordinate and y-coordinate wires. When the gas is charged, it glows a bright orange.

⊪ See also *flat-panel display; pixel.*

platform: The underlying hardware or software for a system. For example, the platform might be an Intel 80486 processor running DOS Version 6.0. The platform could also be UNIX machines on an Ethernet network.

The platform defines a standard around which a system can be developed. Once the platform has been defined, software developers can produce appropriate software and managers can purchase appropriate hardware and applications.

The term cross-platform refers to applications, formats, or devices that work on different platforms. For example, a *cross-platform programming environment* enables a programmer to develop programs for many platforms at once.

platter: A round magnetic plate that constitutes part of a hard disk. Hard disks typically contain two, four, or eight platters. Each platter requires two read/write heads, one for each side.

⊪ See also *hard disk.*

plot: To produce an image by drawing lines. You can program a computer to plot images on a display screen or on paper.

⊪ See also *plotter.*

plotter: A device that draws pictures on paper based on commands from a computer (Figure 64). Plotters differ from printers in that they draw lines using a pen. As a result, they can produce continuous lines, whereas printers can only simulate lines by printing a closely spaced series of dots. Multicolor plotters use different-colored pens to draw different colors.

In general, plotters are considerably more expensive than printers. They are used in engineering applications where precision is mandatory.

➠ See also *printer*.

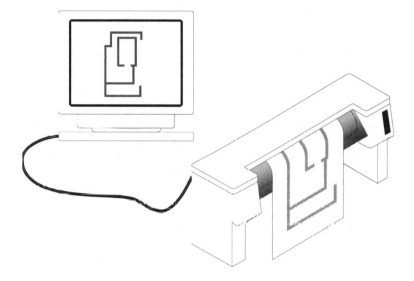

Figure 64: *Plotter*

plug: A connector used to link together devices.

➠ See also *connector*.

plug-and-play: Refers to the ability of a computer system to automatically configure expansion boards and other devices. You should be able to plug in a device and play with it, without worrying about setting DIP switches, jumpers, and other configuration elements. Since the introduction of the NuBus, the Apple Macintosh has been a plug-and-play computer, while the PC has not. This may change, however, as manufacturers adopt the new Plug and Play (PnP) specification created by Microsoft and Intel in 1993.

➠ See also *PnP*.

plug compatible: Refers to a device's ability to connect to other devices made by a different manufacturer without any alterations. For example, many companies sell plug-compatible expansion boards for PCs. These are circuit boards that you can insert without modification into a PC to give the computer added capabilities.

➡ See also *compatible; expansion board.*

PMS: See *Pantone Matching System (PMS).*

PnP: PC Short for *Plug and Play*, a technology developed by Microsoft and Intel that supports plug-and-play installation. PnP is built into the Windows 95 operating system, but to use it, the computer's BIOS and expansion boards must also support PnP.

➡ See also *BIOS; expansion board; plug and play.*

point: (v) To move the pointer on a display screen to select an item. Graphical user interfaces, such as the Macintosh interface, are often called *point-and-click* interfaces because a user typically points to an object on the screen and then clicks a button on the mouse.

➡ See also *graphical user interface; mouse; pointer.*

(n) In typography, a point is about 1/72 of an inch and is used to measure the height of characters. (Historically, a point was .0138 inches, a little less than 1/72 of an inch, but this has changed.) This paragraph, for example, is printed in 9-point type.

The height of the characters is one characteristic of fonts. Some fonts are referred to as *fixed-point fonts* because their representation allows for only one size. In contrast, a *scalable font* is one that is represented in such a way that the size can easily be changed.

➡ See also *font; leading; scalable font.*

pointer: (1) In graphical user interfaces, a pointer is a small arrow or other symbol (Figure 65) on the display screen that moves as you move the mouse. You can select commands and options by positioning the tip of the arrow over the desired choice and clicking a mouse button.

Many text processing programs use an *I-beam pointer*. Pointers are often referred to as *mouse pointers*.

➡ See also *graphical user interface; I-beam pointer*.

(2) In programming, a pointer is a special type of variable that holds a memory address (that is, it *points* to a memory location).

➡ See also *address; variable*.

Grabber pointer   I-beam pointer   Selection pointer

Figure 65: *Different Types of Pointers*

pointing device: A device with which you can control the movement of the pointer to select items on a display screen. Examples of pointing devices include mice, trackballs, joysticks, touchpads, and light pens.

➡ See also *input device; joystick; light pen; mouse; pointer; pointing stick; touchpad; trackball*.

pointing stick: A pointing device first developed by IBM for its notebook computers that consists of a miniature joystick, usually with a rubber eraser-head tip, positioned somewhere between the keys on the keyboard. Most pointing sticks are pressure-sensitive, so the pointer moves faster when more pressure is applied.

➡ See also *joystick; pointing device; trackball*.

Point-to-Point Protocol: See *PPP*.

polling: Making continuous requests for data from another device. For example, modems that support polling can call another system and request data.

➠ See also *modem*.

polyline: In computer graphics, a continuous line composed of one or more line segments. You can create a polyline by specifying the endpoints of each segment (Figure 66). In draw programs, you can treat a polyline as a single object, or divide it into its component segments.

➠ See also *draw program*.

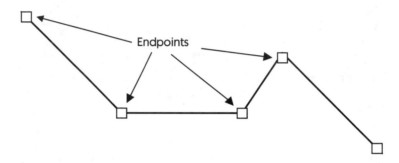

Figure 66: *Polyline*

pop: Given a stack of items, *popping* one of the items means to pull it off the stack. Although originally coined to describe manipulation of data stacks, the term is often used in connection with display windows. When two or more windows overlap, you can pop one of them so that it is the topmost window.

The opposite of pop is *push*, which means to move an object onto a stack.

➠ See also *pop-up window; push; stack; window*.

pop-up menu: See under *menu*.

pop-up utility: A program installed to be *memory resident* so that you can always execute it by pressing a special key, called a *hot key*. When you press the hot key, the pop-up utility appears, regardless of which application you are currently running. When you exit the pop-up utility, the system returns you to your previous program.

In DOS systems, pop-up utilities are also called *TSRs*.

➠ See also *hot key; memory resident; TSR*.

pop-up window: A window that suddenly appears (pops up) when you select an option with a mouse or press a special function key. Usually, the pop-up window contains a menu of commands and stays on the screen only until you select one of the commands. It then disappears. A special kind of pop-up window is a *pull-down menu*, which appears just below the item you selected, as if you had pulled it down.

➠ See also *graphical user interface; pull-down menu; window*.

port: (n) An interface on a computer to which you can connect a device. Personal computers have various types of ports. Internally, there are several ports for connecting disk drives, display screens, and keyboards. Externally, personal computers have ports for connecting modems, printers, mice, and other peripheral devices.

Almost all personal computers come with a serial RS-232C port or RS-422 port for connecting a modem or mouse and a parallel port for connecting a printer. On PCs, the parallel port is a Centronics interface that uses a 25-pin connector. SCSI (Small Computer System Interface) ports support higher transmission speeds than do conventional ports, and enable you to attach up to seven devices to the same port. All Apple Macintosh computers since the Macintosh Plus have a SCSI port.

➠ See also *Centronics parallel interface; interface; parallel port; serial port*.

(v) To move a program from one type of computer to another. To port an application, you need to rewrite sections that are machine dependent, and then recompile the program on the new computer. Programs that can be ported easily are said to be *portable*.

➠ See also *compile; machine dependent; portable*.

portable: (1) When used to describe hardware, *portable* means small and lightweight. A portable computer is a computer small enough to carry. Portable computers include notebook and subnotebook computers, hand-held computers, palmtops, and PDAs.

➠ See also *hand-held computer; notebook computer; palmtop; PDA; subnotebook computer.*

(2) When used to describe software, *portable* means that the software has the ability to run on a variety of computers. *Portable* and *machine independent* mean the same thing—that the software does not depend on a particular type of hardware.

➠ See also *machine independent.*

portrait: The terms *portrait* and *landscape* refer to different orientations of the paper—whether it is oriented vertically or horizontally (see Figure 45 at *landscape*). A page with portrait orientation, typical for letters, memos, and other text documents, is taller than it is wide.

Not all printers are capable of generating text in landscape mode. Orientation is also a characteristic of monitors. Portrait monitors are often called *full-page monitors.*

➠ See also *full-page monitor; monitor; landscape; printer.*

post: (v) To publish a message in an online forum or newsgroup.

➠ See also *forum; Usenet.*

(n) A message published in an online forum or newsgroup.

PostScript: A *page description language (PDL)* developed by Adobe Systems. PostScript is primarily a language for printing documents on laser printers, but it can be adapted to produce images on other types of devices. PostScript is the standard for desktop publishing because it is supported by *imagesetters,* the very high-resolution printers used by service bureaus to produce camera-ready copy.

PostScript is an *object-oriented language,* meaning that it treats images, including fonts, as collections of geometrical objects rather than as bit maps. PostScript fonts are called *outline fonts* because the outline of each character is defined. They are also called *scalable fonts* because their size can be changed with PostScript commands. Given a single typeface definition, a PostScript printer can thus produce a multitude of fonts. In contrast, many non-PostScript printers represent fonts with bit maps. To print a bit-mapped typeface with different sizes, these printers require a complete set of bit maps for each size.

The principal advantage of object-oriented (*vector*) graphics over bit-mapped graphics is that object-oriented images take advantage of high-resolution output devices whereas bit-mapped images do not. A PostScript drawing looks much better when printed on a 600-dpi printer than on a 300-dpi printer. A bit-mapped image looks the same on both printers.

Every PostScript printer contains a built-in interpreter that executes PostScript instructions. If your laser printer does not come with PostScript support, you may be able to purchase a cartridge that contains PostScript.

There are two basic versions of PostScript: Level 1 and Level 2. Level 2 PostScript, which was released in 1992, has better support for color printing.

➠ See also *desktop publishing; EPS; laser printer; object-oriented graphics; page description language; service bureau.*

POTS: Short for *plain old telephone service,* and refers to the standard telephone service that most homes use. In contrast, telephone services based on high-speed, digital communications lines, such as ISDN and FDDI, are not POTS. The main distinctions between POTS and non-POTS services are speed and bandwidth. POTS is generally restricted to about 28.8 kbps (28,800 bits per second).

➠ See also *communications; ISDN.*

power down: To turn a machine off.

PowerPC: A RISC-based computer architecture developed jointly by IBM, Apple Computer, and Motorola Corporation. The name is derived from IBM's name for the architecture, *Performance Optimization With Enhanced RISC.*

The first computers based on the PowerPC architecture were the Power Macs, which appeared in 1994. Since then, other manufacturers, including IBM, have built PCs based on the PowerPC. Although the initial reviews have been good, it remains to be seen whether this new architecture can eventually supplant, or even coexist, with the huge number of Intel-based computers in use and on the market.

There are already a number of different operating systems that run on PowerPC-based computers, including the Macintosh operating system (System 7.5 and higher), Windows NT, and OS/2.

➧ See also *Intel microprocessor; microprocessor; Motorola microprocessors; RISC.*

power supply: The component that supplies power to a computer. Most personal computers can be plugged into standard electrical outlets. The power supply then pulls the required amount of electricity and converts the AC current to DC current. It also regulates the voltage to eliminate spikes and surges common in most electrical systems. Not all power supplies, however, do an adequate voltage-regulation job, so a computer is always susceptible to large voltage fluctuations.

Power supplies are rated in terms of the number of watts they generate. The more powerful the computer, the more watts it can provide to components. In general, 200 watts should be sufficient.

➧ See also *UPS.*

power up: To turn a machine on.

power user: A sophisticated user of personal computers. A power user is typically someone who has considerable experience with computers and utilizes the most advanced features of applications.

➧ See also *user.*

ppm: Stands for *pages per minute* and is used to measure the speed of certain types of printers, particularly laser printers. An average speed for laser printers printing text is 8 ppm.

Note that the ppm advertised for printers applies only to text. Complex graphics can slow a printer down considerably. Increasingly, the abbreviation *gppm* is being used for graphics pages per minute.

➧ See also *laser printer; printer.*

PPP: Short for *Point-to-Point Protocol,* a method of connecting a computer to the Internet. PPP is more stable than the older SLIP protocol and provides error checking features.

➠ See also *Internet; protocol; SLIP.*

PRAM: MAC Pronounced *pee-ram,* short for *parameter* RAM. On Macintosh computers, PRAM is a small portion of RAM used to store information about the way the system is configured. For example, parameter RAM holds the date and time, desktop pattern, mouse settings, volume settings, and other control data set with control panels. Parameter RAM is powered by a battery, so it does not lose its contents when the power is turned off.

➠ See also *configure; control panel; Macintosh computer; memory; RAM.*

precedence: A characteristic of operators that indicates when they will be evaluated when they appear in complex expressions. Operators with high precedence are evaluated before operators with low precedence. For example, the multiplication operator (*) has higher preference than the addition operator (+), so the expression

    2+3*4

equals 14, not 20.
　　You can override precedence rules by surrounding parts of an expression with parentheses. For example,

    (2+3)*4

would evaluate to 20.

➠ See also *expression; operand; operator.*

precision: When used to describe floating-point numbers, *precision* refers to the number of bits used to hold the fractional part. The more precision a system uses, the more exactly it can represent fractional quantities.
　　Floating-point numbers are often classified as *single precision* or *double precision.* A double-precision number uses twice as many bits as a

393

single-precision value, so it can represent fractional quantities much more exactly.

➠ See also *double precision; floating-point number.*

preemptive multitasking: See under *multitasking.*

prepress service bureau: See under *service bureau.*

presentation graphics: A type of business software that enables users to create highly stylized images for slide shows and reports. The software includes functions for creating various types of charts and graphs and for inserting text in a variety of fonts. Most systems enable you to import data from a spreadsheet application to create the charts and graphs.
Presentation graphics is often called *business graphics.*

➠ See also *bar chart; graphics; line graph; pie chart; spreadsheet.*

preview: In word processing, *previewing* refers to formatting a document for the printer, but then displaying it on the display screen instead of printing it (see Figure 37 at *greeking*). Previewing allows you to see exactly how the document will appear when printed. If you have a WYSIWYG, previewing is unnecessary because the display screen always resembles the printed version. For word processors that are not WYSIWYGs, however, previewing is the next-best thing. If your word processor does not support previewing, you may be able to buy a separate program that allows you to preview documents.

➠ See also *greeking; thumbnail; word processing; WYSIWYG.*

primary cache: A memory cache built into the microprocessor.

➠ See also *cache.*

primary storage: A somewhat dated term for *main memory.* Mass storage devices, such as disk drives and tapes, are sometimes called *secondary storage.*

➠ See also *main memory; mass storage.*

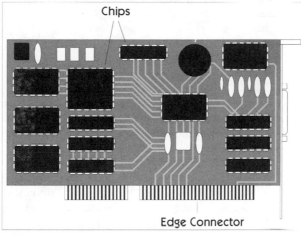

Figure 67: *Printed Circuit Board*

printed circuit board: Sometimes abbreviated *PCB*, a thin, rectangular plate on which chips and other electronic components are placed (Figure 67). Computers consist of one or more boards, often called *cards* or *adapters*. Circuit boards fall into the following categories:

motherboard: The principal board that has connectors for attaching devices to the bus. Typically, the mother board contains the CPU, memory, and basic controllers for the system. On PCs, the motherboard is often called the *system board.*

expansion board: Any board that plugs into one of the computer's expansion slots. Expansion boards include controller boards, LAN cards, and video adapters.

daughterboard: Any board that attaches directly to an expansion board.

controller board: A special type of expansion board that contains a controller for a peripheral device. When you attach new devices, such as a disk drive or graphics monitor, to a computer, you often need to add a controller board.

Network Interface Card (NIC): An expansion board that enables a PC to be connected to a local-area network (LAN).

video adapter: An expansion board that contains a controller for a graphics monitor.

➠ See also *controller; expansion board; expansion slot; local-area network; motherboard; video adapter*

printer: A device that prints text or illustrations on paper. There are many different types of printers. In terms of the technology utilized, printers fall into the following categories:

daisy-wheel: Similar to a ball-head typewriter, this type of printer has a plastic or metal wheel on which the shape of each character stands out in relief. A hammer presses the wheel against a ribbon, which in turn makes an ink stain in the shape of the character on the paper. Daisy-wheel printers produce letter-quality print but cannot print graphics.

dot-matrix: Creates characters by striking pins against an ink ribbon. Each pin makes a dot, and combinations of dots form characters and illustrations.

ink-jet: Sprays ink at a sheet of paper. Ink-jet printers produce high-quality text and graphics.

laser: Uses the same technology as copy machines. Laser printers produce very high quality text and graphics.

LCD & LED: Similar to a laser printer, but uses liquid crystals or light-emitting diodes rather than a laser to produce an image on the drum.

line printer: Contains a chain of characters or pins that print an entire line at one time. Line printers are very fast, but produce low-quality print.

thermal printer: An inexpensive printer that works by pushing heated pins against heat-sensitive paper. Thermal printers are widely used in calculators and fax machines.

Printers are also classified by the following characteristics:

quality of type: The output produced by printers is said to be either letter quality (as good as a typewriter), near letter quality, or draft quality. Only daisy-wheel, ink-jet, and laser printers produce letter-quality type. Some dot-matrix printers claim letter-quality print, but if you look closely, you can see the difference. ·

speed: Measured in characters per second (cps) or pages per minute (ppm), the speed of printers varies widely. Daisy-wheel printers tend to be the slowest, printing about 30 cps. Line printers are fastest (up to 3,000 lines per minute). Dot-matrix printers can print up to 500 cps, and laser printers range from about 4 to 20 text pages per minute.

impact or non-impact: Impact printers include all printers that work by striking an ink ribbon. Daisy-wheel, dot-matrix, and line printers are impact printers. Non-impact printers include laser printers and ink-jet printers. The important difference between impact and non-impact printers is that impact printers are much noisier.

graphics: Some printers (daisy-wheel and line printers) can print only text. Other printers can print both text and graphics.

fonts: Some printers, notably dot matrix printers, are limited to one or a few fonts. In contrast, laser and ink-jet printers are capable of printing an almost unlimited variety of fonts. Daisy-wheel printers can also print different fonts, but you need to change the daisy wheel, making it difficult to mix fonts in the same document.

➡ See also *daisy-wheel printer; dot-matrix printer; draft quality; font; graphics; impact printer; ink-jet printer; laser printer; LCD; LED; letter quality; line printer; LCD printer; near letter quality; non-impact printer; printer driver; printer engine; thermal printer.*

Printer Control Language: See *PCL.*

printer driver: A program that controls a printer. Whenever you print a document, the printer driver takes over, feeding data to the printer with the correct control commands. Most modern operating systems come with printer drivers for the most common types of printers, but you must install them before you can use the printer.

➡ See also *driver.*

printer engine: The main component of a printer that actually performs the printing. The printer engine determines how fast and at what resolution the printer can print. Although there are many manufacturers of printers, many use the same printer engines. The difference between printers using the same printer engine revolves around other features, such as paper handling abilities and the console.

➠ See also *printer*.

print merge: Same as *mail merge*.

printout: A printed version of text or data. Another term for printout is *hard copy*.

Print Screen key: [PC] Often abbreviated *Prt Scr*, the Print Screen key is a useful key supported on most PCs. In DOS, pressing the Print Screen key causes the computer to send whatever images and text are currently on the display screen to the printer. Some graphics applications, including Windows, use the Print Screen key to obtain screen captures.

➠ See also *capture; hardcopy*.

print server: See under *server*.

print spooling: See under *spooling*.

procedure: (1) Same as *routine*, *subroutine*, and *function*. A procedure is a section of a program that performs a specific task.

➠ See also *routine*.

(2) An ordered set of tasks for performing some action.

process: (n) An executing program. The term is used loosely as a synonym of *task*.

➠ See also *task*.

(v) To perform some useful operations on data.

process colors: Refers to the CMYK color model used in offset printing.

➠ See also CMYK *color model; color separation; offset printing.*

processor: Short for *microprocessor* or CPU.

➠ See also *CPU; microprocessor.*

Prodigy: One of the largest online services, developed jointly by IBM and Sears. Prodigy is targeted particularly at home users, and sports an attractive graphical interface.

➠ See also *online service.*

program: (n) An organized list of instructions that, when executed, causes the computer to behave in a predetermined manner. Without programs, computers are useless.
  A program is like a recipe. It contains a list of ingredients (called *variables*) and a list of directions (called *statements*) that tell the computer what to do with the variables. The variables can represent numeric data, text, or graphical images.
  There are many programming languages—C, C++, Pascal, BASIC, FORTRAN, COBOL, and LISP are just a few. These are all high-level languages. One can also write programs in *low-level languages* called *assembly languages,* although this is more difficult. Low-level languages are closer to the language used by a computer, while high-level languages are closer to human languages.
  Eventually, every program must be translated into a *machine language* that the computer can understand. This translation is performed by compilers, *interpreters,* and assemblers.
  When you buy software, you normally buy an executable version of a program. This means that the program is already in machine lan-

guage—it has already been compiled and assembled and is ready to execute.

➠ See also *assembler; assembly language; compiler; executable file; high-level language; instruction; interpreter; language; low-level language; machine language; programming language; software.*

(v) To write programs.

programmable read-only memory: See *PROM.*

programmer: (1) An individual who writes programs.

➠ See also *program.*

(2) A device that writes a program onto a PROM chip.

➠ See also *PROM.*

programming language: A vocabulary and set of grammatical rules for instructing a computer to perform specific tasks. The term *programming language* usually refers to high-level languages, such as BASIC, C, C++, COBOL, FORTRAN, and Pascal. Each language has a unique set of keywords (words that it understands) and a special syntax for organizing program instructions.

High-level programming languages, while simple compared to human languages, are more complex than the languages the computer actually understands, called *machine languages.* Each different type of CPU has its own unique machine language.

Lying between machine languages and high-level languages are languages called *assembly languages* (Figure 63). Assembly languages are similar to machine languages, but they are much easier to program in because they allow a programmer to substitute names for numbers. Machine languages consist of numbers only.

Lying above high-level languages are languages called *fourth-generation languages* (usually abbreviated 4GL). 4GLs are far removed from machine languages and represent the class of computer languages closest to human languages.

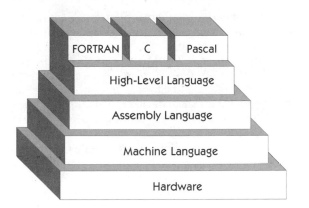

Figure 68: *Hierarchy of Programming Languages*

Regardless of what language you use, eventually you need to convert your program into machine language so that the computer can understand it. There are two ways to do this:

- *compile* the program
- *interpret* the program

See *compile* and *interpreter* for more information about these two methods.

The question of which language is best is one that consumes a lot of time and energy among computer professionals. Every language has its strengths and weaknesses. For example, FORTRAN is a particularly good language for processing numerical data, but it does not lend itself very well to organizing large programs. Pascal is very good for writing well-structured and readable programs, but it is not as flexible as the C programming language. C++ embodies powerful object-oriented features, but it is complex and difficult to learn.

The choice of which language to use depends on the type of computer the program is to run on, what sort of program it is, and the expertise of the programmer.

➡ See also *assembly language; BASIC; C; C++; compiler; fourth-generation language; high-level language; FORTRAN; interpreter; language; machine language; LISP; object-oriented programming; Pascal; syntax.*

PROM: Pronounced *prom*, an acronym for *programmable read-only memory.* A PROM is a memory chip on which data can be written only once. Once a program has been written onto a PROM, it remains there forever. Unlike main memory, PROMs retain their contents when the computer is turned off.

The difference between a PROM and a ROM (read-only memory) is that a PROM is manufactured as blank memory, whereas a ROM is programmed during the manufacturing process. To write data onto a PROM chip, you need a special device called a *PROM programmer* or *PROM burner*. The process of programming a PROM is sometimes called *burning* the PROM.

An *EPROM* (erasable programmable read-only memory) is a special type of PROM that can be erased by exposing it to ultraviolet light. Once it is erased, it can be reprogrammed. An EEPROM is similar to a PROM, but requires only electricity to be erased.

➡ See also *EEPROM; EPROM; main memory; memory; ROM.*

prompt: A symbol on a display screen indicating that the computer is waiting for input. Once the computer has displayed a prompt, it waits for you to enter some information. Generally, it will wait forever, but some programs have built-in time-outs that cause the program to continue execution after it has waited a specified amount of time.

property: Characteristic of an object. In many programming languages, including Visual Basic, the term property is used to describe attributes associated with a data structure.

proportional font: A font in which different characters have different *pitches* (widths). Proportional fonts are also called *proportional-pitch fonts*. The opposite of a proportional font is a *fixed-pitch* font.

➡ See also *font; pitch; proportional pitch.*

proportional pitch: Same as *proportionally spaced.* See under *proportional spacing.*

proportional spacing: Using different widths for different characters. In a proportionally spaced font, the letter *I* is narrower than the letter *q* and the letter *m* wider. This book uses a proportionally spaced font, as do most books, magazines, and newspapers.

The opposite of proportional spacing is *monospacing.* In a monospaced font, each character has the same width. Non-graphics display screens, display text in a monospaced font. (See Figure 69 for an example of both types of fonts.) Almost all printers, with the exception of line printers, are able to print with either proportionally spaced or monospaced fonts.

➠ See also *fixed pitch; font; pitch.*

windows

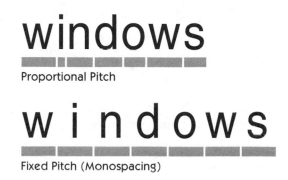

Proportional Pitch

w i n d o w s

Fixed Pitch (Monospacing)

Figure 69: *Proportional Pitch vs. Fixed Pitch*

proprietary: Privately owned and controlled. In the computer industry, *proprietary* is the opposite of *open.* A proprietary design or technique is one that is owned by a company. It also implies that the company has not divulged specifications that would allow other companies to duplicate the product.

Increasingly, proprietary architectures are seen as a disadvantage. Consumers prefer open and standardized architectures, which allow them to mix and match products from different manufacturers.

➠ See also *architecture; open architecture; standard*

protected mode: A type of memory utilization available on Intel 80286 and later model microprocessors. In protected mode, these processors provide the following features:

protection: Each program can be allocated a certain section of memory. Other programs cannot use this memory, so each program is protected from interference from other programs.

extended memory: Enables a single program to access more than 640K of memory.

virtual memory: Expands the address space to over 1GB.

multitasking: Enables the microprocessor to switch from one program to another so the computer can execute several programs at once.

Unfortunately, the DOS operating system is not designed to take advantage of these features. To run programs in protected mode, you need a more sophisticated operating system, such as OS/2, Windows, or UNIX.

➠ See also *extended memory; Intel microprocessors; Microsoft Windows; DOS; multitasking; OS/2; UNIX; virtual memory.*

protocol: An agreed-upon format for transmitting data between two devices. The protocol determines the following:

- the type of error checking to be used
- data compression method, if any
- how the sending device will indicate that it has finished sending a message
- how the receiving device will indicate that it has received a message

There are a variety of standard protocols from which programmers can choose. Each has particular advantages and disadvantages; for example, some are simpler than others, some are more reliable, and some are faster.

From a user's point of view, the only interesting aspect about protocols is that your computer or device must support the right ones if you want to communicate with other computers. The protocol can be implemented either in hardware or in software.

➠ See also *communications; communications protocol; modem.*

Prt Scr key: See *Print Screen key.*

public carrier: A government-regulated organization that provides telecommunications services to the public. This includes AT&T, MCI, and Western Union. Most public carriers provide *electronic mail* services that enable you to send messages and documents over a telephone line to other computer users.

➠ See also *e-mail.*

public-domain software: Refers to any program that is not copyrighted. Public-domain software is free and can be used without restrictions. The term *public-domain software* is often used incorrectly to include *freeware*, free software that is nevertheless copyrighted.

➠ See also *freeware; shareware.*

puck: A pointing device used with digitizing tablets. See under *digitizing tablet.*

pull-down menu: A menu of commands or options that appears when you select an item with a mouse. The item you select is generally at the top of the display screen, and the menu appears just below it, as if you had pulled it down.

➠ See also *command; menu; option; pop-up window.*

punctuation: Like punctuation in human languages, punctuation in programming languages serves to separate words and phrases. But unlike human punctuation, which is often optional, computer punctuation is strictly required.

purge: To systematically and permanently remove old and unneeded data. The term purge is stronger than delete. It is often possible to regain deleted objects by *undeleting* them, but purged objects are gone forever.

➠ See also *delete.*

push: In programming, to place a data item onto a stack. The opposite of push is *pop*, which means to remove an object from a stack.

➠ See also *pop; stack.*

push-button: A button in a dialog box. See under *button.*

➠ See also *dialog box.*

QBE: See *query by example.*

QIC: The abbreviation for *quarter-inch cartridge.* QIC tapes are among the most popular tapes used for backing up personal computers. There are many different types of QIC tapes, as shown in Table 24. They are divided into two general classes: full-size and minicartridge. The full-size cartridges are often referred to as *DC 6000* cartridges, and mini-cartridges are called *DC 2000* cartridges.

The QIC-40 and QIC-80 standards are sometimes referred to as *floppy tape* standards because they are designed to use a personal computer's existing floppy disk drive controller instead of requiring a customized controller.

The various QIC standards are controlled by a consortium of manufacturers called the *Quarter-Inch Cartridge Drive Standards, Inc.* The term *QIC,* therefore, is used to refer both to the type of tape and to the standards-producing organization.

➡ See also *mass storage; tape.*

quad-speed CD-ROM drive: A CD-ROM drive designed to run four times as fast as original models. Often denoted as *4X CD players,* they provide data transfer rates of 600K per second and data access times— as low as 125 milliseconds (ms).

➡ See also *CD-ROM player.*

quarter-inch cartridge: See *QIC.*

Table 24
QIC STANDARDS

QIC TYPE	CAPACITY	CARTRIDGE SIZE
QIC-24	60MB	Full
QIC-40	40MB	Mini
QIC-80	80MB 120MB	Mini
QIC-100	20MB 40MB	Mini
QIC-120	125MB	Full
QIC-128	86MB 128MB	Mini
QIC-150	150MB 250MB	Full
QIC-380	380MB	Mini
QIC-525	320MB 525MB	Full
QIC-1000	1.01GB	Full
QIC-1350	1.35GB	Full
QIC-2000	2GB	Mini
QIC-3010	340MB	Mini
QIC-3020	680MB	Mini

query: (n) A request for information from a database. There are three general methods for posing queries:

choosing parameters from a menu: In this method, the database system presents a list of parameters from which you can choose. This is perhaps the easiest way to pose a query because the menus guide you, but it is also the least flexible.

query by example (QBE): In this method, the system presents a blank record and lets you specify the fields and values that define the query.

query language: Many database systems require you to make requests for information in the form of a stylized query that must be written in a special query language. This is the most complex method because it forces you to learn a specialized language, but it is also the most powerful.

➦ See also *database management system; field; menu; query language; query by example; record.*

(v) To make a request for information from a database.

query by example: In database management systems, *query by example* (QBE) refers to a method of forming queries in which the database program displays a blank record with a space for each field. You can then enter conditions for each field that you want to be included in the query. For example, if you wanted to find all records where the AGE field is greater than 65, you would enter >65 in the AGE field blank.

QBE systems are considered easier to learn than formal query languages.

➦ See also *database management system; field; query language; query; record.*

query language: A specialized language for requesting information from a database. For example, the query

SELECT ALL WHERE age > 30 AND name = "Smith"

requests all records in which the name-field is "Smith" and the Age field has a value greater than 30. The de facto standard for query languages is *SQL.*

➦ See also *database management system; query; SQL.*

queue: (v) To line up. In computer science, *queuing* refers to lining up jobs for a computer or device. For example, if you want to print a number of documents, the operating system (or a special print spooler) queues the documents by placing them in a special area called a *print buffer* or *print queue.* The printer then pulls the documents off the queue one at a time. Another term for this is *print spooling.*

The order in which a system executes jobs on a queue depends on the priority system being used. Most commonly, jobs are executed in the same order that they were placed on the queue, but in some schemes certain jobs are given higher priority.

➠ See also *buffer*; *job*; *operating system*; *spooling*.

(n) (1) A group of jobs waiting to be executed.

(2) In programming, a queue is a data structure in which elements are removed in the same order they were entered. This is often referred to as FIFO (first in, first out). In contrast, a *stack* is a data structure in which elements are removed in the reverse order from which they were entered. This is referred to as LIFO (last in, first out).

➠ See also *data structure*; *stack*.

QuickDraw: MAC The underlying graphics display system for Apple Macintosh computers. The QuickDraw system enables programs to create and manipulate graphical objects. Because all Macintosh programs use QuickDraw, they all share a common look.

There are several versions of QuickDraw that offer different color capabilities and other features. The newest, called *QuickDraw GX*, supports 16.7 million colors.

QuickDraw is currently used primarily for displaying images on monitors, but some printers use it as well.

➠ See also *graphics*; *Macintosh computer*; *pixel*; *PostScript*; *scalable font*.

QuickTime: A video and animation system developed by Apple Computer. QuickTime is built into the Macintosh operating system and is used by most Mac applications that include video or animation. PCs can also run files in QuickTime format, but they require a special QuickTime driver. On the PC side, QuickTime is competing with a number of other standards, including AVI, Indeo, and Cinepak.

➠ See also *animation*; *AVI*; *Cinepak*; *Indeo*; *multimedia*; *video*.

quit: To exit a program in an orderly way. Compare with *abort*, which exits a program in an unorderly fashion.

QWERTY keyboard: Pronounced *kwer-tee,* refers to the arrangement of keys on a standard English computer keyboard or typewriter. The name derives from the first six characters on the top alphabetic line of the keyboard.

The arrangement of characters on a QWERTY keyboard was designed in 1868 by Christopher Sholes, the inventor of the typewriter. According to popular myth, Sholes arranged the keys in their odd fashion to prevent jamming on mechanical typewriters by separating commonly used letter combinations. However, there is no evidence to support this assertion, except that the arrangement does, in fact, inhibit fast typing.

With the emergence of ball-head electric typewriters and computer keyboards, on which jamming is not an issue, new keyboards designed for speed typing have been invented. The best-known is called a *Dvorak keyboard.* Despite their more rational designs, these new keyboards have not received wide acceptance.

➡ See also *Dvorak keyboard; keyboard.*

radio buttons: In graphical user interfaces, groups of buttons, of which only one can be on at a time (Figure 70). When you select one button, all the others are automatically deselected. Compare with check box, which allows you to select any combination of options.

➠ See also *button; check box; graphical user interface; select.*

Figure 70: *Radio Buttons*

ragged: In text processing, *ragged* means not aligned along a margin. The opposite of ragged is *flush* or *justified*. For example, the following text has a *ragged right* margin:

> This text has ragged right
> margin because each
> line ends at a different
> spot.

Most word processors allow you to choose between ragged and justified margins.

➠ See also *flush; justify.*

RAM: Pronounced *ramm,* acronym for *random access memory,* a type of computer memory that can be accessed randomly; that is, any byte of memory can be accessed without touching the preceding bytes. RAM is the most common type of memory found in computers and other devices, such as printers.

There are two basic types of RAM:

- dynamic RAM (DRAM)
- static RAM (SRAM)

The two types differ in the technology they use to hold data, dynamic RAM being the more common type. Dynamic RAM needs to be refreshed thousands of times per second. Static RAM needs to be refreshed less often, which makes it faster; but it is also more expensive than dynamic RAM. Both types of RAM are *volatile,* meaning that they lose their contents when the power is turned off.

In common usage, the term *RAM* is synonymous with *main memory,* the memory available to programs. For example, a computer with 8M RAM has approximately 8 million bytes of memory that programs can use. In contrast, *ROM (read-only memory)* refers to special memory used to store programs that boot the computer and perform diagnostics. Most personal computers have a small amount of ROM (a few thousand bytes). In fact, both types of memory (ROM and RAM) allow random access. To be precise, therefore, RAM should be referred to as *read/write RAM* and ROM as *read-only RAM.*

➡ See also *main memory; memory; ROM; SRAM; VRAM.*

RAM cache: (1) Same as *processor cache.*

➡ See also *cache.*

(2) ⃞MAC⃞ On Apple Macintosh computers, the term *RAM cache* refers to a disk cache.

➡ See also *disk cache.*

RAM disk: Refers to RAM that has been configured to simulate a disk drive. You can access files on a RAM disk as you would access files on a real disk. RAM disks, however, are approximately a thousand times faster than hard disk drives. They are particularly useful, therefore, for applications that require frequent disk accesses.

Because they are made of normal RAM, RAM disks lose their contents once the computer is turned off. To use a RAM disk, therefore, you need to copy files from a real hard disk at the beginning of the session and then copy the files back to the hard disk before you turn the computer off. Note that if there is a power failure, you will lose whatever data is on the RAM disk. (Some RAM disks come with a battery backup to make them more stable.)

➠ See also *disk; extended memory; RAM.*

RAM resident: Same as *memory resident.*

random access: Refers to the ability to access data at random. The opposite of *random access* is *sequential access.* To go from point A to point Z in a sequential-access system, you must pass through all intervening points. In a random-access system, you can jump directly to point Z (Figure 71). Disks are random access media, whereas tapes are sequential access media.

The terms *random access* and *sequential access* are often used to describe data files. A random-access data file enables you to read or write information anywhere in the file. In a sequential-access file, you can only read and write information sequentially, starting from the beginning of the file.

Both types of files have advantages and disadvantages. If you are always accessing information in the same order, a sequential-access file is faster. If you tend to access information randomly, random access is better.

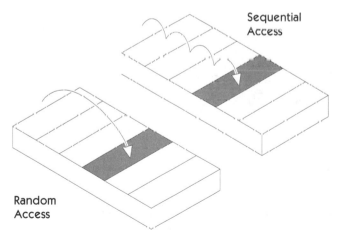

Sequential
Access

Random
Access

Figure 71: *Random Access*

Random access is sometimes called *direct access.*

➠ See also *access; RAM; sequential access.*

random-access memory: See *RAM.*

range: In spreadsheet applications, one or more contiguous cells. For example, a range could be an entire row or column, or multiple rows or columns. The only restrictions on ranges is that all the cells of the range must be contiguous and the entire range must be rectangular in shape; that is, you cannot have a range consisting of three cells in one column and four cells in the next.

Once you have defined a range, you can perform operations on it. This is a powerful feature because it allows you to manipulate a set of cells with one expression.

➠ See also *cell; expression; function; spreadsheet.*

raster graphics: See under *bit-mapped graphics.*

raster image processor (RIP): A hardware-software combination that converts a vector image into a bit-mapped image. All PostScript printers contain a RIP that converts the PostScript commands into bit-mapped pages that the printer can output.

➠ See also *bit map; PostScript; vector graphics.*

raw data: Information that has not been organized, formatted, or analyzed.

➠ See also *data.*

ray tracing: In computer graphics, an advanced technique for adding realism to an image by including variations in shade, color intensity, and shadows that would be produced by having one or more light sources. Ray tracing software works by simulating the path of a single light ray as it would be absorbed or reflected by various objects in the image. To work properly, the artist must specify parameters of the light source (intensity, color, etc.) as well as all the objects (how reflective or absorbent the materials are).

Ray tracing requires enormous computational resources, and is supported by only the most advanced graphics systems.

➠ See also *graphics.*

RDBMS: Short for *relational database management system* and pronounced as separate letters.

➠ See also *database management system; relational database.*

read: (v) To copy data from a storage medium, such as a disk, to main memory, where it can be utilized by a program.

(n) The act of reading. For example, *a fast disk drive performs 100 reads per second.*

readme file: A small text file that comes with many software packages and contains information not included in the official documentation. Typically, readme files contain late-breaking information that could not be included in the printed documentation.

read-only: Capable of being displayed, but not modified or deleted. All operating systems allow you to protect objects (disks, files, directories) with a *read-only attribute* that prevents other users from modifying the object.

➠ See also *attribute; CD-ROM; read/write; ROM.*

read-only memory: See *ROM.*

read/write: Capable of being displayed (read) and modified (written to). Most objects (disks, files, directories) are read/write, but operating systems also allow you to protect objects with a *read-only attribute* that prevents other users from modifying the object.

➠ See also *read-only.*

read/write head: See *head*.

real address: Same as *absolute address*.

real mode: [PC] An execution mode supported by the Intel 80286 and later processors. In real mode, these processors imitate the Intel 8088 and 8086 microprocessors, although they run much faster. The other mode available is called *protected mode*. In protected mode, programs can access extended memory and virtual memory. Protected mode also supports multitasking. The 80386 and later microprocessors support a third mode called *virtual 8086 mode*. In virtual mode, these microprocessors can run several real-mode programs at once.

   The DOS operating system was not designed to take advantage of protected mode, so it always executes programs in real mode.

➠ See also *extended memory; Intel microprocessors; Microsoft Windows; DOS; multitasking; OS/2; protected mode; virtual memory.*

real time: Occurring immediately. The term is used to describe a number of different computer features. For example, real-time operating systems are systems that respond to input immediately. They are used for such tasks as navigation, in which the computer must react to a steady flow of new information without interruption. Most general-purpose operating systems are not real-time because they can take a few seconds, or even minutes, to react.

   Real time can also refer to events simulated by a computer at the same speed that they would occur in real life. In graphics animation, for example, a real-time program would display objects moving across the screen at the same speed that they would actually move.

➠ See also *operating system.*

real-time clock: A clock that keeps track of the time even when the computer is turned off. Real-time clocks run on a special battery that is not connected to the normal power supply. In contrast, clocks that are not real-time do not function when the computer is off.

   Do not confuse a computer's real-time clock with its CPU clock. The CPU clock regulates the execution of instructions.

➠ See also *clock speed; CPU.*

reboot: To restart a computer. On a PC, you can reboot by pressing the Alt, Control and Delete keys simultaneously. This is called a *warm boot*. You can also perform a cold boot by turning the computer off and then on again.

[MAC] On Macs, you reboot by selecting the "Restart" option from the Special menu.

➡ See also *boot*.

recalculate: In spreadsheet programs, *recalculation* refers to computing the values of cells in a spreadsheet. Recalculation is necessary whenever you change a formula or enter new data into one or more cells. Depending on the size and complexity of your spreadsheet, recalculation can be a time-consuming process. One criterion for evaluating spreadsheet programs, therefore, is how fast they recalculate.

To make recalculation faster, many spreadsheet programs support *minimal recalculation* (also called *optimal recalculation*), in which the program calculates only the values of cells that will change. In addition, some spreadsheets support background *recalculation*, which allows you to perform other operations while a recalculation is in progress.

➡ See also *background; cell; formula; spreadsheet*.

record: (1) In database management systems, a complete set of information. Records are composed of *fields*, each of which contains one item of information. A set of records constitutes a *file*. For example, a personnel file might contain records that have three fields: a name field, an address field, and a phone number field (see Figure 21 at database).

➡ See also *database management system; field; file*.

(2) Some programming languages allow you to define a special data structure called a *record*. Generally, a record is a combination of other data objects. For example, a record might contain three integers, a floating-point number, and a character string.

➡ See also *data structure; data type*.

record locking: See under *lock*.

417

recursion: A programming method in which a routine calls itself. Recursion is an extremely powerful concept, but it can strain a computer's memory resources. Some programming languages, such as LISP and Prolog, are specifically designed to use recursive methods.

➥ See *programming; programming language.*

red-green-blue monitor: See *RGB monitor.*

redirection: In operating system shells, *redirection* refers to directing input and output to files and devices other than the default I/O devices. By default, input generally comes from the keyboard or mouse, and output goes to the display monitor. With a redirection operator, you can override these defaults so that a command or program takes input from some other device and sends output to a different device.

In DOS and UNIX systems, the redirection operators are < for input and > for output. For example, the DOS command

    sort < c:\list > c:\sorted

takes input from a file called *list*, sorts it, and sends output to a file called *sorted.*

➥ See also *default; device; DOS; file; I/O; operating system; operator; shell; UNIX.*

redlining: In word processing, *redlining* refers to marking text that has been edited. Typically, redlining is used when two or more people are working on a document together; each individual can *redline* the text he or she has added or edited. The redlined text will then appear in a special color (or as bold) so that others can see the changes that have been made.

➥ See also *word processing.*

reduced instruction set computer: See *RISC.*

refresh: To recharge a device with power or information. For example, *dynamic RAM* needs to be refreshed thousands of times per second or it will lose the data stored in it.

Similarly, display monitors must be refreshed many times per second. The *refresh rate* for a monitor is measured in hertz (Hz) and is also called the *vertical frequency*. The old standard for monitor refresh rates was 60Hz, but a new standard developed by VESA sets the refresh rate at 72Hz for VGA and SVGA monitors. The faster the refresh rate, the less the monitor flickers.

➠ See also *dynamic RAM; interlacing; monitor; screen flicker.*

register: (n) A storage area within the CPU. All data must be represented in a register before it can be processed. For example, if two numbers are to be multiplied, both numbers must be in registers, and the result is also placed in a register. (The register can contain the address of a memory location where data is stored rather than the actual data itself.)

The number of registers that a CPU has and the size of each (number of bits) help determine the power and speed of a CPU. For example a 32-bit CPU is one in which each register is 32 bits wide. Therefore, each CPU instruction can manipulate 32 bits of data.

Usually, the movement of data in and out of registers is completely transparent to users, and even to programmers. Only assembly language programs can manipulate registers. In high-level languages, the compiler is responsible for translating high-level operations into low-level operations that access registers.

➠ See also *compiler; CPU; microprocessor.*

(v) To notify a manufacturer that you have purchased its product. Registering a product is often a prerequisite to receiving customer support, and it is one of the ways that software producers control software piracy.

➠ See also *software piracy.*

relational database: A type of database that stores data in the form of a table. Relational databases are powerful because they require few assumptions about how data is related or how it will be extracted from the database. As a result, the same database can be viewed in many different ways.

Another feature of relational systems is that a single database can be spread across several tables. This differs from flat-file databases, in which each database is self-contained in a single table.

Almost all full-scale database systems for personal computers use a relational database. Small database systems, however, use other designs that provide less flexibility in posing queries.

➠ See also *database management system; flat-file database; query.*

relational expression: See under *relational operator.*

relational operator: An operator that compares two values. Table 25 lists the most common relational operators.

For example, the expression

$$x < 5$$

means *x is less than 5.* This expression will have a value of TRUE if the variable x is less than 5; otherwise the value of the expression will be FALSE.

Relational operators are sometimes called *comparison operators.* Expressions that contain relational operators are called *relational expressions.*

➠ See also *Boolean logic; expression; operator.*

Table 25
RELATIONAL OPERATORS

SYMBOL	MNEMONIC	MEANING
=	EQ	Equal to
<> (or !=)	NE	Not equal to
>	GT	Greater than
>=	GE	Greater than or equal to
<	LT	Less than
<=	LE	Less than or equal to

relative address: An address specified by indicating its distance from another address, called the *base address*. For example, a relative address might be B+15, B being the base address and 15 the distance (called the *offset*).

There are two types of addressing: *relative addressing* and *absolute addressing*. In absolute addressing, you specify the actual address (called the *absolute address*) of a memory location (see Figure 1 at *address*).

Relative and absolute addressing are used in a variety of circumstances. In programming, you can use either mode to identify locations in main memory or on mass storage devices. In spreadsheet applications, you can use either mode to designate a particular cell.

➠ See also *absolute address; address; base address; cell; memory; offset.*

relative cell reference: In spreadsheet applications, a reference to a cell or group of cells by indicating how far away it is from some other cell. For example, in Lotus 1-2-3 and many other spreadsheet programs, the cell reference "C2" is relative. Initially it points to the cell in the third column and second row, but it does this by specifying how far away this cell is from some other cell. For example, if you insert this reference in cell A1, the program will translate it to "2 columns right and 1 row down." If you then copy the reference to cell B4, it will now point to cell D5.

In contrast, an absolute cell reference always points to the same cell, no matter where the reference appears.

➠ See also *absolute cell reference; cell; spreadsheet.*

remote: In networks, *remote* refers to files, devices, and other resources that are not connected directly to your workstation. Resources at your workstation are considered local.

➠ See also *local-area network; local; network; workstation.*

remote control: Refers to a program's ability to access a computer system from a remote location. Remote-control programs for PCs enable you to access data stored on your home system even when you are traveling.

➠ See also *host; local; remote.*

removable cartridge: Same as *removable hard disk*.

removable hard disk: A type of disk drive system in which hard disks are enclosed in plastic or metal cartridges so that they can be removed like floppy disks. Removable disk drives combine the best aspects of hard and floppy disks. They are as fast as hard disks and have the portability of floppy disks. The storage capacity of a typical removable hard disk can range from 60MB (megabytes) to 250MB, much more than the capacity of floppy disks.

➠ See also *cartridge; disk; hard disk; mass storage*.

rendering: Refers to the process of adding realism to a computer graphics by adding three-dimensional qualities such as shadows and variations in color and shade. One technique for rendering graphics is called *ray tracing*.

➠ See also *ray tracing*.

repaginate: To recalculate page breaks. Word processing and desktop publishing systems decide where to end one page and begin the next based on a set of parameters including the page size, margin size, and widow and orphan settings. Most systems automatically repaginate whenever you modify a document. However, repagination can be time-consuming, so some systems allow you temporarily turn off automatic repagination until you're ready.

➠ See also *orphan; page break; widow*.

replace: To insert a new object in place of an existing object. The term is used most often in connection with search and replace operations, in which you search for one word or phrase and replace all occurrences with a new word or phrase.

report: A formatted and organized presentation of data. Most database management systems include a report writer that enables you to design and generate reports.

➠ See also *report writer*.

report generator: Same as *report writer.*

report writer: A program, usually part of a database management system, that extracts information from one or more files and presents the information in a specified format. Most report writers allow you to select records that meet certain conditions and to display selected fields in rows and columns. You can also format data into pie charts, bar charts, and other diagrams. Once you have created a format for a report, you can save the format specifications in a file and continue reusing it for new data.

The report writer is one of the most important components of a database management system because it determines how much flexibility you have in outputting data.

➠ See also *database management system; field; record.*

reserved word: A special word reserved by a programming language or by a program. You are not allowed to use reserved words as variable names. For example, in BASIC and COBOL, the word *IF* is reserved because it has a special meaning.

Reserved words are sometimes called *keywords.*

➠ See also *keyword; variable.*

reset button: A button or switch on many computers that allows you to reset the computer. When you press the reset button, the computer will enter its start-up procedure as if you had turned the power off and then on again. Generally, you would use the reset button only when a program error has caused your computer to *hang.*

[PC] Note that on PCs, pressing the reset button is somewhat different from performing a reboot by pressing the Ctrl+Alt I Del reboot keys. When you perform a warm reboot, the system does not repeat the initial start-up stages during which memory is checked.

➠ See also *boot; hang; reboot.*

resident: (1) See *memory resident.*

(2) See *resident font.*

resident font: Also called an *internal font* or *built-in font,* a resident font is a font built into the hardware of a printer. All dot-matrix and laser printers come with one or more resident fonts. You can add additional fonts by inserting font cartridges or downloading soft fonts.

➡ See also *download; font; font cartridge; printer; soft font.*

resize: See under *size.*

resolution: Refers to the sharpness and clarity of an image. The term is most often used to describe monitors, printers, and bit-mapped graphic images. In the case of dot-matrix and laser printers, the resolution indicates the number of dots per inch. For example, a 300-dpi (dots per inch) printer is one that is capable of printing 300 distinct dots in a line 1 inch long. This means it can print 90,000 dots per square inch.

For graphics monitors, the resolution signifies the number of dots (pixels) on the entire screen. For example, a 640-by-480 pixel screen is capable of displaying 640 distinct dots on each of 480 lines, or about 300,000 pixels. This translates into different dpi measurements depending on the size of the screen. For example, a 15-inch VGA monitor (640x480) displays about 50 dots per inch.

Printers, monitors, scanners, and other I/O devices are often classified as *high resolution, medium resolution,* or *low resolution* (Figure 72). The actual resolution ranges for each of these grades is constantly shifting as the technology improves.

➡ See also *dots per inch; monitor; pixel; printer; video adapter.*

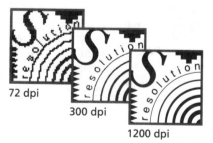

Figure 72: *Resolution*

72 dpi
300 dpi
1200 dpi

resolution enhancement: A collection of techniques used in many laser printers to enable the printer to print at a higher resolution than normal. Most laser printers have printer engines that print at either 300 dpi (dots per inch) or 600 dpi. Using clever algorithms that rec-

ognize curved lines, a printer with resolution enhancement can produce output whose resolution appears to be much higher than the
print engine's rated resolution. This is why many printer manufacturers characterize their printers with two resolution ratings: the *engine
resolution* and the *effective resolution.*

A common resolution enhancement technique is to vary the size of
the dots.

➠ See also *laser printer; printer engine; resolution.*

resource: (1) Generally, any item that can be used. Devices such as
printers and disk drives are resources, as is memory.

(2) In many operating systems, including Microsoft Windows and the
Macintosh operating system, the term *resource* refers specifically to
data or routines that are available to programs.

restore: In graphical user interfaces, to *restore* means to return a window to its original size.

➠ See also *graphical user interface; size; window; zoom.*

return: A *return* is a special code that causes a word processor or other
application to advance to the beginning of the next line. A *soft return*
is a return that the application inserts automatically when you reach
the end of a line. A *hard return* is a return that you explicitly enter by
pressing the Return or Enter key.

➠ See also *hard return; Return key; soft return.*

Return key: Almost all computer keyboards have a key marked *Return*
or *Enter;* the two names are synonymous. The Return key moves the
cursor (or insertion point) to the beginning of the next line. But more
important, it returns control to whatever program is currently running. After a program requests information from you (by displaying a
prompt), it will usually not respond to your input until you have
pressed the Return key. This allows you to correct typing mistakes or
to reconsider your entry before it is too late. In many applications,
pressing the Return key moves the cursor to the next field.

In word-processing programs, pressing the Return key inserts a hard return into a document.

In technical documentation, the Return key is sometimes signified by a ↵ symbol.

➠ See also *cursor; hard return; insertion point; keyboard; prompt.*

reverse engineering: The process of recreating a design by analyzing a final product. Reverse engineering is common in both hardware and software. Several companies have succeeded in producing Intel-compatible microprocessors through reverse engineering. Whether reverse engineering is legal or not depends on who you ask. The courts have not yet made a definitive ruling.

reverse video: A display method that causes a portion of the display to appear like a negative of the regular display. If the display screen normally displays light images against a dark background, putting it in *reverse video mode* will cause it to display dark images against a light background.

Many programs use reverse video to highlight items, such as selected text or menu options. Also, some systems allow you to change the mode for all displays, so you can choose the display that is most comfortable for you. Some people prefer dark images on a light background, while others prefer light images on a dark background.

➠ See also *background; display screen; foreground.*

RGB monitor: Short for *red, green, blue monitor,* a monitor that requires separate signals for each of the three colors. This differs from color televisions, for example, which use composite video signals, in which all the colors are mixed together. All color computer monitors are RGB monitors.

An RGB monitor consists of a vacuum tube with three electron guns—one each for red, green, and blue—at one end and the screen at the other end. The three electron guns fire electrons at the screen, which contains a phosphorous coating. When the phosphors are excited by the electron beams, they glow. Depending on which beam excites them, they glow either red, green, or blue. Ideally, the three beams should converge for each point on the screen so that each pixel is a combination of the three colors.

➠ See also *composite video; convergence; monitor.*

rich text format (RTF): A standard developed by Microsoft Corporation for specifying formatting of documents. RTF files are actually ASCII files with special commands to indicate formatting information, such as fonts and margins. Microsoft has tried to make RTF the universal document formatting language, but up till now it has not been successful. Other document formatting languages that are gaining ground are the Hypertext Markup Language (HTML), which is used to define documents on the World Wide Web, and the Standard Generalized Markup Language (SGML), which is a more robust version of HTML.

➠ *See also HTML; SGML; World Wide Web.*

right justify: See under *justify.*

ring network: A local-area network (LAN) whose topology is a ring. That is, all of the nodes are connected in a closed loop. Messages travel around the ring, with each node reading those messages addressed to it. One of the advantages of ring networks is that they can span larger distances than other types of networks, such as bus networks, because each node regenerates messages as they pass through it.

➠ See also *local-area network; token-ring network; topology.*

RIP: Pronounced *rip,* acronym for *raster image processor.* See *raster image processor (RIP).*

RISC: Pronounced *risk,* acronym for *reduced instruction set computer,* a type of microprocessor that recognizes a relatively limited number of instructions. Until the mid-1980s, the tendency among computer manufacturers was to build increasingly complex CPUs that had ever-larger sets of instructions. At that time, however, a number of computer manufacturers decided to reverse this trend by building CPUs capable of executing only a very limited set of instructions. One advantage of reduced instruction set computers is that they can execute their instructions very fast because the instructions are so simple. Another, perhaps more important advantage, is that RISC chips require fewer transistors, which makes them cheaper to design and produce. Since the emergence of RISC computers, conventional computers have been referred to as CISCs (*complex instruction set computers*).

There is still considerable controversy among experts about the ultimate value of RISC architectures. Its proponents argue that RISC machines are both cheaper and faster, and are therefore the machines of the future. Skeptics note that by making the hardware simpler, RISC architectures put a greater burden on the software. They argue that this is not worth the trouble because conventional microprocessors are becoming increasingly fast and cheap anyway.

To some extent, the argument is becoming moot because CISC and RISC implementations are becoming more and more alike. Many of today's RISC chips support as many instructions as yesterday's CISC chips. And today's CISC chips use many techniques formerly associated with RISC chips.

➠ See also *CPU; instruction; microprocessor.*

RLL: PC Abbreviation of *run length limited*, an encoding scheme used to store data on some PC hard disks. Although RLL produces fast data access times and increases a disk's storage capacity, it is not as prevalent as another encoding scheme called *MFM (modified frequency modulation)*.

Technically, any disk drive can use either encoding method. The one used depends on the disk controller.

➠ See also *controller; disk drive; MFM.*

robotics: The field of computer science and engineering concerned with creating robots, devices that can move and react to sensory input. Robotics is one branch of artificial intelligence.

Robots are now widely used in factories to perform high-precision jobs such as welding and riveting. They are also used in special situations that would be dangerous for humans—for example, in cleaning toxic wastes or defusing bombs.

Although great advances have been made in the field of robotics during the last decade, robots are still not very useful in everyday life, as they are too clumsy to perform ordinary household chores.

➠ See also *artificial intelligence.*

ROM: Pronounced *rahm*, acronym for *read-only memory*, computer memory on which data has been prerecorded. Once data has been written onto a ROM chip, it cannot be removed and can only be read.

Unlike main memory (RAM), ROM retains its contents even when the computer is turned off. ROM is referred to as being *nonvolatile*, whereas RAM is *volatile*.

Most personal computers contain a small amount of ROM that stores critical programs such as the program that boots the computer. In addition, ROMs are used extensively in calculators and peripheral devices such as laser printers, whose fonts are often stored in ROMs.

A variation of a ROM is a *PROM (programmable read-only memory)*. PROMs are manufactured as blank chips on which data can be written with a special device called a *PROM programmer*.

➡ See also BIOS; *boot; firmware; memory; PROM; RAM.*

roman: In typography, *roman* refers to fonts with characters that are straight up and down rather than slanted. A font designed with characters slanted to the right is *italic*.

➡ See also *font; italic.*

ROM-BIOS: See *BIOS.*

root directory: The top directory in a file system (see Figure 26 at *directory*). The root directory is provided by the operating system and has a special name; for example, in DOS systems the root directory is called \. The root directory is sometimes referred to simply as the *root*.

➡ See also *directory; file management; hierarchical.*

router: A device that connects two LANs of the same type. Routers are similar to bridges, but provide additional functionality, such as the ability to filter messages and forward them to different places based on various criteria.

➡ See also *gateway.*

routine: A section of a program that performs a particular task. Programs consist of *modules*, each of which contains one or more routines. The term *routine* is synonymous with *procedure, function,* and *subroutine.*

➠ See also *module; program.*

RS-232C: A standard interface (*RS* stands for *recommended standard*) approved by the Electronics Industry Association (EIA) for connecting serial devices (see Figure 19 at *connector*). Almost all modems conform to the RS-232C standard and most personal computers have an RS-232C *port* for connecting a modem or other device. In addition to modems, many display screens, mice, and serial printers are designed to connect to a RS-232C *port.*

The RS-232C standard supports two types of connectors—a 25-pin D-type connector (DB-25) and a 9-pin D-type connector (DB-9). The type of serial communications used by PCs requires only 9 pins so either type of connector will work equally well.

Although RS-232C is still the most common standard for serial communication, the EIA has recently defined successors to RS-232C called *RS-422* and *RS-423.* The new standards are backward compatible so that RS-232 devices can connect to an RS-422 port.

In 1987, the EIA upgraded and changed the named of RS-232C. The new name is EIA-232D, but the standard is generally still referred to by its old name.

➠ See also *connector; interface; modem; RS-422 and RS-423; serial port.*

RS-422 and RS-423: Standard interfaces approved by the Electronics Industry Association (EIA) for connecting serial devices. The RS-422 and RS-423 standards are designed to replace the older RS-232C standard because they support higher data rates and greater immunity to electrical interference. All Apple Macintosh computers contain an RS-422 port that can also be used for RS-232C communication.

➠ See also *communications; connector; interface; modem; port; RS-232C.*

RTF: See *rich text format (RTF).*

rule: (1) In word processing and desktop publishing, a straight line that separates columns of text or illustrations.

(2) In expert systems, a conditional statement that tells the system how to react to a particular situation.

➠ See also *expert system*.

ruler: In word processing, a line running across the display screen (Figure 73). It measures the page layout in points, picas, inches, or centimeters. It is sometimes called the *ruler line* and is particularly useful for setting margins and tabs. Sophisticated desktop publishing systems and page layout programs sometimes support *movable rulers* that you can move around the display screen to measure particular items of text or graphics.

➠ See also *desktop publishing; margins; page layout program*.

Figure 73: *Ruler*

run: (1) To execute a program.

(2) To operate. For example, a device that is *running* is one that is turned on and operating properly.

run length limited: See *RLL*.

running head: See under *header*.

runtime error: An error that occurs during the execution of a program. In contrast, *compile-time* errors occur while a program is being compiled. Runtime errors indicate bugs in the program or problems that the designers had anticipated but could do nothing about. For example, running out of memory will often cause a runtime error.

    Note that runtime errors differ from bombs or crashes in that you can often recover gracefully from a runtime error.

➠ See also *bug; compiler; crash; bomb*.

runtime version: A limited version of one program that enables you to run another program. To run a program written in Visual BASIC, for example, you need the runtime version of Visual Basic. This allows you to run Visual Basic programs but not to develop them yourself. Many other development applications, particularly database applications, require a runtime version to execute.

    Software companies have different approaches to runtime versions. Some allow you to distribute the runtime version freely, while others require that you pay a license fee.

sampling: A technique used to capture continuous phenomena, whereby periodic snapshots are taken. If the sampling rate is fast enough, the human sensory organs cannot discern the gaps between each snapshot when they are played back. This is the principle behind motion pictures.

Sampling is the key technique used to digitize analog information. For example, music CDs are produced by sampling live sound at frequent intervals and then digitizing each sample. The term *sampling* is also used to describe a similar process in digital photography.

➠ See also *analog; digital camera; digital; digitize.*

sans serif: Pronounced *san-serr-if*, refers to a category of typefaces that do not use *serifs*, small lines at the ends of characters. Popular sans serif fonts include Helvetica, Avant Garde, Arial, and Geneva. Serif fonts include Times Roman, Courier, New Century Schoolbook, and Palatino (see Figure 85 at *typeface*).

According to most studies, sans serif fonts are more difficult to read. For this reason, they are used most often for short text components such as headlines or captions.

➠ See also *font.*

save: To copy data from a temporary area to a more permanent storage medium. When you edit a file with a word processor, for example, the word processor copies the entire file, or portions of the file, into an area of main memory called a *buffer*. Any changes you make to the file are made to the copy in the buffer, not to the real file on the disk. The buffer is temporary—as soon as you exit the program or turn off the computer, the buffer disappears. To record your modifications to the file on the disk, you must save the file. When you do this, the word processor copies the contents of the buffer back to the file on the disk, replacing the previous version of the file.

Because computers can break down at any moment, it is a good idea to save your files periodically. Otherwise, you will lose all the work you have done during an editing session. Many applications automatically save files at regular intervals, which you can specify. These intermediate saves are sometimes called *snapshots*.

➠ See also *autosave*.

scalable font: A font represented in an object-oriented graphics language such as PostScript or TrueType. Such fonts are called *scalable* because the representation of the font defines the shape of each character (the typeface) but not the size. Given a typeface definition, a scalable-font system can produce characters at any size (or *scale*).

Aside from offering innumerable sizes of each font, scalable fonts have an added advantage in that they make the most of an output device's resolution. The more resolution a printer or monitor has, the better a scalable font will look.

Scalable fonts are often called *outline fonts* because the most common method of representing scalable fonts is to define the outline of each character. Scalable fonts are also called *object-oriented fonts* or *vector fonts*.

➠ See also *font; outline font; PostScript; TrueType; typeface; vector graphics*.

scale: To change the size of an object while maintaining its shape. Most graphics software, particularly vector-based packages, allow you to scale objects freely.

➠ See also *graphics; scalable font; vector graphics*.

scan: To digitize an image by passing it through an optical scanner. See under *optical scanner*.

scanner: See *optical scanner*.

scatter diagram: A type of diagram used to show the relationship between data items that have two numeric properties. One property is represented along the x-axis and the other along the y-axis. Each item is then represented by a single point.

Scatter diagrams are used frequently by computer publications to compare categories of hardware and software products. One axis represents price, while the other represents performance. Typically, all compared products fall near an imaginary diagonal line—that is, performance and price rise together. However, the scatter diagram makes it easy to see items that do not fall near this line, items that are expensive but offer poor performance or items that are inexpensive but provide good performance.

scheduler: (1) A software product designed to help a group of colleagues schedule meetings and other appointments. The scheduler program allows members of a group to view each others' calendars so that they can choose a convenient time. Once a time has been selected, the scheduler can automatically send out reminders through e-mail and can even reserve resources such as conference rooms and overhead projectors.

➠ See also *workgroup computing.*

(2) In operating systems, a scheduler is a program that coordinates the use of shared resources, such as a printer.

➠ See also *operating system.*

scientific notation: A format for representing real (floating-point) numbers. Instead of writing the full number, scientific notation represents values as a number between 1 and 10 multiplied by 10 to some power. The 10 is often replaced by an uppercase or lowercase *E.* Table 26 shows some examples.

Scientific notation is much simpler for very large and very small numbers, such as the second and fourth examples. Most programming languages, and many numeric applications, allow you to enter and display numbers using scientific notation.

➠ See also *floating-point number.*

scissoring: Same as *clipping.* See under *clip.*

Table 26
SCIENTIFIC NOTATION

NUMBER IN NORMAL NOTATION	SCIENTIFIC NOTATION (1)	SCIENTIFIC NOTATION (2)
0.0004	4.0^{-4}	4.0E-4
1,000,000,000.0	1.0^9	1.0E9
-37.456	-3.7456^2	-3.7456E2
-0.000000349	-3.49^{-7}	-3.49E-7

Scrapbook: MAC In Macintosh environments, a desk accessory (DA) that enables you to store objects for future use. The Scrapbook is similar to the clipboard, but it allows more than one item to be stored in it at once. Also, it retains its contents when the computer is turned off.

➠ See also *clipboard; desk accessory.*

screen: (1) Short for display screen.

(2) In offset printing, a mesh used to create halftones. See under *halftone.*

screen capture: Refers to the act of copying what is currently displayed on a screen to a file or printer. If the system is in graphics mode, the screen capture will result in a graphics file containing a bit map of the image. If the system is in text mode, the screen capture will normally load a file with ASCII codes.

➠ See also *Print Screen key.*

screen dump: Same as *screen capture.*

screen flicker: The phenomenon whereby a display screen appears to flicker. Screen flicker results from a variety of factors, the most important of which is the monitor's *refresh rate*, the speed with which the screen is redrawn. If the refresh rate is too slow, the screen will appear to glimmer. Another factor that affects screen flicker is the persistence of the screen phosphors. Low-persistence phosphors fade more quickly than high-persistence monitors, making screen flicker more likely. Screen flicker can also be affected by lighting. Finally, screen flicker is a subjective perception that affects people differently. Some people perceive screen flicker where others do not.

➡ See also *interlacing; monitor; refresh.*

screen font: A font designed especially for a display screen. Typically, display fonts are bit-mapped, and must be specially designed to compensate for the relatively low resolution of display screens.

➡ See also *font; resolution.*

screen saver: A small program that takes over the display screen if there are no keystrokes or mouse movements for a specified duration. Screen savers were originally developed to prevent *ghosting*, the permanent etching of a pattern on a display screen. For older monochrome monitors, ghosting often occurred if the same pattern was displayed on a display screen for a long period of time. Screen savers would prevent this by either blanking out the screen entirely or by displaying a constantly moving image.

Modern display screens do not suffer so much from this problem. Today, therefore, screen savers are mostly an adornment, a way to liven up the computer. Many screen savers provide another benefit, hiding a user's work from would-be snoopers. These screen savers fill the display with an image or animation until the user enters a password.

➡ See also *display screen; monitor.*

screen shot: Same as *screen capture.*

script: Another term for *macro* or batch file, a script is a list of commands that can be executed without user interaction. A *script language* is a simple programming language with which you can write scripts.

Apple Computer uses the term *script* to refer to programs written in its HyperCard language.

➠ See also *batch file; HyperCard software; macro.*

scroll: To view consecutive lines of data on the display screen. The term *scroll* means that once the screen is full, each new line appears at the edge of the screen and all other lines move over one position. For example, when you scroll down, each new line appears at the bottom of the screen and all the other lines move up one row, so that the top line disappears.

The term *vertical scrolling* refers to the ability to scroll up or down. *Horizontal scrolling* means that the image moves sideways. In theory, the display should move smoothly, as if it were a piece of paper being moved up, down, or sideways. In practice, however, scrolling is not always so smooth.

The scrolling method of viewing documents does not recognize page boundaries. One advantage to scrolling, therefore, is that you can look at the end of one page and the beginning of the next page at the same time.

Another method of viewing data is called *paging*, whereby an entire page is displayed at once. Each subsequent page replaces the previous page on the screen.

➠ See also *page; scroll bar.*

scroll bar: A bar that appears on the side or bottom of a window to control which part of a list or document is currently in the window's frame. The scroll bar makes it easy to move to any part of a file.

Typically, a scroll bar has arrows at either end, a gray or colored area in the middle, and a *scroll box* (or *elevator*) that moves from one end to the other to reflect your position in the document. Clicking on the arrows causes the document to scroll in the indicated direction. You can also quickly move to any part of a document by dragging the scroll box to the corresponding part of the scroll bar.

Many windowing systems support both horizontal and vertical scroll bars, as shown in Figure 74.

➠ See also *click; drag; graphical user interface; window.*

scroll box: See under *scroll bar.*

Scroll Bar   Scroll Arrow

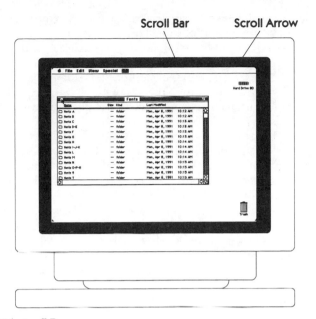

Figure 74: *Scroll Bar*

Scroll Lock key: A key on PC and enhanced Macintosh keyboards that controls the way the cursor control keys work for some programs. Many applications ignore the Scroll Lock setting.

➠ See also *cursor control keys; scroll.*

SCSI: Abbreviation of small computer system interface. Pronounced scuzzy, SCSI is a parallel interface standard used by Apple Macintosh computers, some PCs, and many UNIX systems for attaching peripheral devices to computers. All Apple Macintosh computers starting with the Macintosh Plus come with a SCSI port for attaching devices such as disk drives and printers.

SCSI interfaces provide for faster data transmission rates (up to 4 megabytes per second) than standard serial and parallel ports. In addition, you can attach up to seven devices to a single SCSI port, so that SCSI is really an I/O bus rather than simply an interface.

Although SCSI is an ANSI standard, there are many variations of it, so two SCSI interfaces may be incompatible. For example, SCSI supports several types of connectors.

While SCSI is the only standard interface for Macintoshes, PCs support a variety of interfaces in addition to SCSI. These include *IDE, enhanced IDE* and *ESDI* for mass storage devices, and *Centronics* for printers. You can, however, attach SCSI devices to a PC by inserting a SCSI board in one of the expansion slots. Many high-end new PCs come with SCSI built in. Note, however, that the lack of a single SCSI standard means that some devices may not work with some SCSI boards.

A new ANSI standard, called *SCSI-2*, widens the data bus from 8 to either 16 or 32 bits and provides a burst mode for transferring data to and from disk drives. SCSI-2 can support data rates as fast as 10 megabytes per second (Mbps). SCSI-2 is sometimes called *Fast SCSI, Wide SCSI, Fast/Wide SCSI* or *Fast SCSI-2*.

Yet a third SCSI variation, known as *SCSI-3*, is expected to be ratified by ANSI in 1996. SCSI-3, also known as *UltraSCSI*, will support data transfer rates as fast as 40 Mbps.

➠ See also *bus; daisy chain; interface; port.*

search and replace: A feature supported by most word processors that lets you replace a character string (a series of characters) with another string wherever the first string appears in the document. Most word processors have two search and replace modes. In the first mode, the word processor automatically makes all the replacements in the file. In the second mode, the word processor requires you to approve each replacement. This is safer because you may not want to make the change everywhere.

Search and replace is sometimes called *find and replace.*

➠ See also *character string; word processing.*

secondary cache: Cache memory that is external to the microprocessor.

➠ See also *cache.*

secondary storage: Same as *mass storage.*

sector: The smallest unit that can be on a disk. When you format a disk, the operating system divides it into tracks and sectors (Figure

75). The tracks are concentric circles around the disk and the sectors are segments within each circle. For example, a formatted disk might have 40 tracks, with each track divided into 10 sectors. The operating system and disk drive keep tabs on where information is stored on the disk by noting its track and sector number (see Figure 39 at *interleaving*).

Generally, every track has the same number of sectors, but some high-capacity hard disk drives use a technique called *zoned-bit recording* in which tracks on the outside of the disk contain more sectors than those on the inside.

A sector that cannot be used due to a physical flaw on the disk is called a *bad sector*.

➠ See also *bad sector; disk; format; interleaving; track.*

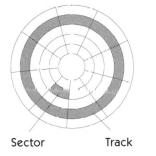 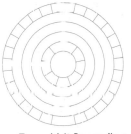

Sector　　　　Track　　　　Zoned-bit Recording

Figure 75: *Disk Sectors*

security: Refers to techniques for ensuring that data stored in a computer cannot be read or compromised. Most security measures involve data encryption and passwords. Data encryption is the translation of data into a form that is unintelligible without a deciphering mechanism. A password is a secret word or phrase that gives a user access to a particular program or system.

➠ See also *encryption; password.*

seek time: Refers to the time a program or device takes to locate a particular piece of data. For disk drives, the terms *seek time* and *access time* are often used interchangeably.

➠ See also *access time; disk drive.*

segment: (1) In virtual memory systems, a segment is a variable-sized portion of data that is swapped in and out of main memory. Contrast with *page*, which is a fixed-sized portion of data.

➠ See also *main memory; page; swap; virtual memory.*

(2) A piece of a polyline. See under *polyline.*

select: To choose an object so that you can manipulate it in some way. In graphical user interfaces, you usually need to select an object—an icon, file, folder, and so on—before you can do anything with it. To select an object, you move the pointer to the object and click a mouse button. In many applications, you can select blocks of text by positioning the pointer at an end-point of the block and then dragging the pointer over the block.

➠ See also *drag; graphical user interface; icon; pointer.*

semantics: In linguistics, the study of meanings. In computer science, the term is frequently used to differentiate the meaning of an instruction from its format. The format, which covers the spelling of language components and the rules controlling how components are combined, is called the language's *syntax.* For example, if you misspell a command, it is a syntax error. If, on the other hand, you enter a legal command that does not make any sense in the current context, it is a semantic error.

➠ See also *programming language; syntax.*

semiconductor: A material that is neither a good conductor of electricity (like copper) nor a good insulator (like rubber). The most common semiconductor materials are silicon and geranium. Computer chips, both for CPU and memory, are composed of semiconductor materials. Semiconductors make it possible to miniaturize electronic components. Not only does miniaturization mean that the components take up less space, it also means that they are faster and require less energy.

➠ See also *chip.*

sequential access: Refers to reading or writing data records in sequential order, that is, one record after the other. To read record 10, for example, you would first need to read records 1 through 9. This differs from *random access*, in which you can read and write records in any order (See Figure 71 at *random access*).

Some programming languages and operating systems distinguish between sequential-access data files and random-access data files, allowing you to choose between the two types. Sequential-access files are faster if you always access records in the same order. Random-access files are faster if you need to read or write records in a random order.

Devices can also be classified as sequential access or random access. For example, a tape drive is a sequential-access device because to get to point q on the tape, the drive needs to pass through points a through p. A disk drive, on the other hand, is a random-access device because the drive can access any point on the disk without passing through all intervening points.

➠ See also *random access*.

serial: One by one. Serial data transfer refers to transmitting data one bit at a time. The opposite of serial is *parallel*, in which several bits are transmitted concurrently.

➠ See also *communications; parallel; serial port*.

serial interface: Same as *serial port*.

Serial Line Internet Protocol: See *SLIP*.

serial mouse: A mouse that connects to a computer via a serial port. The other type of mouse is a bus mouse, which attaches to a computer via an expansion board. Serial mice are easier to install, but they require an unused serial port.

➠ See also *mouse; port; serial; serial port*.

serial port: A port, or *interface*, that can be used for serial communication, in which only 1 bit is transmitted at a time.

Most serial ports on personal computers conform to the RS-232C or RS-422 standards. A serial port is a general-purpose interface that can be used for almost any type of device, including modems, mice, and printers (although most printers are connected to a parallel port).

➠ See also *communications; interface; parallel port; port; RS-232C; RS-422 and 423.*

serif: A small decorative line added as embellishment to the basic form of a character. Typefaces are often described as being *serif* or *sans serif* (without serifs). The most common serif typeface is Times Roman. A common sans serif typeface is Helvetica (See Figure 85 at *typeface*).

➠ See also *font; sans serif; typeface.*

server: A computer or device on a network that manages network resources. For example, a *file server* is a computer and storage device dedicated to storing files. Any user on the network can store files on the server. A *print server* is a computer that manages one or more printers, and a *network server* is a computer that manages network traffic. A database *server* is a computer system that processes database queries.

Servers are often dedicated, meaning that they perform no other tasks besides their server tasks. On multiprocessing operating systems, however, a single computer can execute several programs at once. A server in this case could refer to the program that is managing resources rather than the entire computer.

➠ See also *client/server architecture; local-area network; network.*

service: (1) See *customer support.*

(2) See *online service.*

service bureau: Short for *prepress service bureau,* a company that provides a variety of desktop publishing services. In particular, service bureaus have imagesetters that can produce high-resolution output on paper or film. This is a necessary step before printing a document with offset printing.

In addition to providing high-resolution output, many service bureaus also offer scanning services, as well as general consultancy. Some service bureaus have computers equipped with desktop publishing software which you can rent by the hour.

➠ See also *desktop publishing; imagesetter; offset printing; PostScript.*

service provider: A company that provides access to the Internet. For a monthly fee, the service provider gives you a software package, username, password and access phone number. Equipped with a modem, you can then log on to the Internet and browse the World Wide Web and USENET, and send and receive e-mail.

➠ See also *e-mail; Internet; USENET; World Wide Web.*

setup: (v) To install and configure hardware or software. Most Windows applications come with a program called *SETUP.EXE*, which installs the software on the computer's hard disk.

(n) The configuration of hardware or software.

SGML: Abbreviation of *Standard Generalized Markup Language*, a system for organizing and tagging elements of a document. SGML was developed and standardized by the International Organization for Standards (ISO) in 1986. SGML itself does not specify any particular formatting; rather, it specifies the rules for tagging elements. These tags can then be interpreted to format elements in different ways.

SGML is used widely to manage large documents that are subject to frequent revisions and need to be printed or delivered in different formats. Because it is a large and complex system, it is not yet widely used on personal computers. However, the growth of Internet, and especially the World Wide Web, is creating renewed interest in SGML because the World Wide Web uses HTML, which is one way of defining and interpreting tags according to SGML rules.

➠ See also *HTML; hypertext; ISO; Rich Text Format; World Wide Web.*

shadowing: A technique used to increase a computer's speed by using high-speed RAM memory in place of slower ROM memory. On PCs, for example, all code to control hardware devices, such as keyboards, is normally executed in a special ROM chip called the *ROM-BIOS*. However, this chip is slower than the general-purpose RAM that comprises main memory. Many PC manufacturers, therefore, copy the BIOS code into RAM when the computer boots. The RAM used to hold the BIOS code is called *shadow RAM*.

➠ See also *BIOS; boot; main memory; RAM; ROM.*

shareware: Software distributed on the basis of an honor system. Most shareware is delivered free of charge, but the author usually requests that you pay a small fee if you like the program and use it regularly. By sending the small fee, you become registered with the producer so that you can receive service assistance and updates. You can copy shareware and pass it along to friends and colleagues, but they too are expected to pay a fee if they use the product.

Shareware is inexpensive because it is usually produced by a single programmer and is offered directly to customers. Thus, there are practically no packaging or advertising expenses.

Shareware is available from a number of sources, including bulletin board services and online services. Note that shareware differs from public-domain software in that shareware is copyrighted. This means that you cannot sell a shareware product as your own.

➠ See also *bulletin board system; freeware; online service; public-domain software; software piracy.*

sheet feeder: Also called *cut-sheet feeder*, a mechanism that holds a stack of paper and feeds each sheet into a printer one at a time. Sheet feeders are built into laser printers and are optional components for dot-matrix printers. Many fax machines also come with sheet feeders, as do some optical scanners.

➠ See also *dot-matrix printer; fax machine; laser printer; optical scanner; printer.*

shell: (1) The outermost layer of a program. *Shell* is another term for *user interface.* Operating systems and applications sometimes provide an alternative shell to make interaction with the program easier. For example, if the application is usually command driven, the shell might be a menu-driven system that translates the user's selections into the appropriate commands.

➠ See also *command driven; menu driven; user interface.*

(2) Sometimes called *command shell,* a shell is the command processor interface. The command processor is the program that executes operating system commands. The shell, therefore, is the part of the command processor that accepts commands. After verifying that the commands are valid, the shell sends them to another part of the command processor to be executed.

UNIX systems offer a choice between several different shells, the most popular being the *Cshell,* the *Bourne shell,* and the *Korn shell.* Each offers a somewhat different command language.

➠ See also *command language; command processor; interface; operating environment; operating system; UNIX.*

shift clicking: Clicking a mouse button while holding the Shift key down. In Microsoft Windows and Macintosh systems, shift clicking enables you to select multiple items. Normally, when you select an item, the system deselects the previously selected item. However, if you shift click an item, the previously selected item(s) remain selected.

➠ See also *click; graphical user interface; Macintosh computer; Microsoft Windows; mouse; select.*

Shift key: A key on computer keyboards that gives the other keys an alternate meaning. When combined with alphabetic keys, the Shift key causes the system to output a capital letter. The Shift key can also be combined with other keys to produce program-dependent results.

➠ See also *Alt key; Control key; keyboard.*

shortcut key: A special key combination that causes a specific command to be executed. Typically, shortcut keys combine the Ctrl or Alt keys with some other keys. In Windows environments, for example, Ctrl+C is used as the shortcut key to copy. On PCs, the function keys are also often used as shortcut keys.

Most applications come with some shortcut keys already defined. Many, however, allow you to define your own shortcut keys for frequently-used commands.

➠ See also *Alt key; command; Control key;*

shut down: (1) To turn the power off.

(2) MAC Macintoshes have a "Shut Down" option in the Special menu. On newer Macs, selecting this option actually turns the computer off. On older Macs, it just prepares the computer to be manually turned off.

SIG: Acronym for *special interest group*, a group of users interested in a particular subject who discuss the subject at meetings or via an online service. SIGs exist for almost every conceivable subject. Online SIGs are sometimes called *forums* or *conferences.*

➠ See also *bulletin board system; forum; online service.*

sign: A symbol that identifies a number as being either positive or negative. A positive sign is +; a negative sign is -. These two signs are also used to indicate addition and subtraction, respectively.

➠ See also *operators.*

Silicon Valley: A nickname for the region north of San Francisco that contains an unusually high concentration of computer companies. Silicon is the most common semiconductor material used to produce chips.

➠ See also *chip; semiconductor.*

SIMM: Acronym for *single in-line memory module*, a small circuit board that can hold a group of memory chips. Typically, SIMMs hold up to 8 (on Macintoshes) or 9 (on PCs) RAM chips. On PCs, the ninth chip is for parity error checking. Unlike memory chips, SIMMs are measured in bytes rather than bits. In today's SIMMs, each chip holds

2MB, so a single SIMM holds 16MB. SIMMs are easier to install than individual memory chips.

➠ See also *chip; RAM.*

simulation: The process of imitating a real phenomenon with a set of mathematical formulas. Advanced computer programs can simulate weather conditions, chemical reactions, atomic reactions, even biological processes. In theory, any phenomena that can be reduced to mathematical data and equations can be simulated on a computer. In practice, however, simulation is extremely difficult because most natural phenomena are subject to an almost infinite number of influences. One of the tricks to developing useful simulations, therefore, is to determine which are the most important factors.

In addition to imitating processes to see how they behave under different conditions, simulations are also used to test new theories. After creating a theory of causal relationships, the theorist can codify the relationships in the form of a computer program. If the program then behaves in the same way as the real process, there is a good chance that the proposed relationships are correct.

single-density disk: A low-density floppy disk. All modern floppies are double-density or high-density.

➠ See also *floppy disk.*

single in-line memory module: See *SIMM.*

single in-line package: See *SIP.*

single-sided disk: A floppy disk with only one side prepared for storing data. Single-sided disks have half as much storage capacity as double-sided disks. Most floppies are double-sided.

➠ See also *floppy disk.*

SIP: Abbreviation of *single in-line package,* a type of housing for electronic components in which the connecting pins protrude from one side. Compare with DIP and *PGA.*

➡ See also *DIP; PGA.*

680x0: See under *Motorola microprocessors.*

size: To make an object larger or smaller. In graphical user interfaces, you can size windows to make them larger or smaller.

Other terms for *size* are *resize* and *scale.*

➡ See also *graphical user interface; scale; window.*

slate PC: A class of notebook computer that accepts input from an electronic pen rather than from a keyboard. Slate PCs are particularly useful in situations where keyboards are awkward or unnecessary. Typically, slate PCs can decipher clearly written block letters and translate them into their ASCII equivalents. To date, however, they cannot handle script, although the technology of handwriting recognition is progressing rapidly.

➡ See also *handwriting recognition; hand-held computer; notebook computer; PDA.*

slave: Any device that is controlled by another device, called the *master.*

sleep mode: An energy-saving mode of operation in which all unnecessary components are shut down. Many battery-operated devices, such as notebook computers, support a sleep mode. When a notebook computer goes into sleep mode, it shuts down the display screen and disk drive. Once awakened, the computer returns to its former operating status.

slimline model: A small desktop model computer. See under *desktop model computer.*

SLIP: Short for *Serial Line Internet Protocol,* one of two methods for connecting to the Internet. The other method is PPP (Point-to-Point Protocol). SLIP is an older and simpler protocol, but from a practical perspective, there's not much difference between connecting to the Internet via SLIP or PPP. In general, service providers offer only one protocol although some support both protocols.

➠ See also *Internet; PPP; protocol; service provider.*

slot: An opening in a computer where you can insert a printed circuit board. Slots are often called *expansion slots* because they allow you to expand the capabilities of a computer. The boards you insert in expansion slots are called *expansion boards* or *add-on boards.*
   Do not confuse slots with bays. Bays are sites within the computer where you can install disk drives.

➠ See also *bay; expansion board; expansion slot; printed circuit board.*

small computer system interface: See *SCSI.*

smart battery: See under *battery pack.*

smart terminal: A terminal that has some processing capabilities, but not as many as an *intelligent terminal.* Smart terminals have built-in logic for performing simple display operations, such as blinking and boldface. In contrast, a *dumb terminal* has no processing capabilities at all.

➠ See also *dumb terminal; intelligent terminal; terminal.*

smiley: Same as *emoticon.*

smoothing: A technique used by some printers to make curves look smoother (See Figure 4 at *antialiasing*). Most printers that support smoothing implement it by reducing the dot size of the dots that make up a curved line. In addition, some printers can alter the horizontal alignment of dots to minimize jaggies.

➠ See also *antialiasing; jaggies; laser printer.*

soft: In computer science, *soft* is used to describe things that are intangible. For example, you cannot touch *software*. It's like music—you can see musical scores and touch CDs and tapes, but the music itself is intangible. Similarly, you can see software instructions (programs), and touch floppy disks on which the programs are stored, but the software itself is intangible.

Soft is also used to describe things that are easily changed or impermanent. In contrast, *hard* is used to describe things that are immutable.

➡ See also *hard; hardware; software.*

soft font: A font that is copied from a computer's disk to a printer's memory. Soft fonts can be erased, unlike *resident fonts* (fonts that are built into the printer) or font cartridges.

Soft fonts are generated by a font program in the computer. You can control the program to specify the font size and other characteristics. The disadvantages of soft fonts are that they require a lot of disk space and printer memory (from 10K to over 200K for a single font), and it takes time to download the fonts to the printer.

Soft fonts are also called *downloadable fonts.*

➡ See also *download; font; font cartridge; laser printer; resident font.*

soft hyphen: See under *hyphenation.*

soft return: The term *return* refers to moving to the beginning of the next line in a text document. Word processors utilize two types of returns: *hard* and *soft*. In both cases, the return consists of special codes inserted into the document to cause the display screen, printer, or other output device to advance to the next line.

The difference between the two types of returns is that soft returns are inserted automatically by the word processor as part of its word wrap capability. Whenever too little room remains on the current line for the next word, the word processor inserts a soft return. The position of soft returns automatically changes, however, if you change the length of a line by adding or deleting words, or if you change the margins.

A hard return, on the other hand, always stays in the same place unless you explicitly delete it. Whenever you press the Return or

Enter key, the word processor inserts a hard return. Hard returns are used to create new paragraphs or to align items in a table.

➡ See also *hard return; margins; word wrap.*

software: Computer instructions or data. Anything that can be stored electronically is software. The storage devices and display devices are hardware.

The terms *software* and *hardware* are used as both nouns and adjectives. For example, you can say: "The problem lies in the software," meaning that there is a problem with the program or data, not with the computer itself. You can also say: "It's a software problem."

The distinction between software and hardware is sometimes confusing because they are so integrally linked. Clearly, when you purchase a program, you are buying software. But to buy the software, you need to buy the disk (hardware) on which the software is recorded.

Software is often divided into two categories:

systems software: Includes the operating system and all the utilities that enable the computer to function.

applications software: Includes programs that do real work for users.

For example, word processors, spreadsheets, and database management systems fall under the category of applications software.

➡ See also *application; data; hardware; program; systems software.*

software piracy: The unauthorized copying of software. Most retail programs are licensed for use at just one computer site or for use by only one user at any time. By buying the software, you become a *licensed user* rather than an owner. You are allowed to make copies of the program for backup purposes, but it is against the law to give copies to friends and colleagues.

Software piracy is all but impossible to stop, although software companies are launching more and more lawsuits against major infractors. Originally, software companies tried to stop software piracy by copy-protecting their software. This strategy failed, however, because it was inconvenient for users and was not 100 percent foolproof.

An entirely different approach to software piracy, called *shareware,* acknowledges the futility of trying to stop people from copying software and instead relies on people's honesty. Shareware publishers encourage users to give copies of programs to friends and colleagues but ask everyone who uses a program regularly to pay a registration fee to the program's author directly.

➠ See also *copy protection; register; shareware; software.*

SOHO: Acronym for *Small Office/Home Office*, the fastest growing market for computer hardware and software. So-called SOHO products are specifically designed to meet the needs of professionals who work at home or in small offices.

solid ink-jet printer: A type of color printer that works by melting wax-based inks and then spraying them on paper. Solid ink-jet printers produce very vivid colors and can print on nearly any surface, but they are relatively slow and expensive.
Solid ink-jet printers are also called *phase-change printers.*

➠ See also *color printer; ink-jet printer.*

sound card: An expansion board that enables a computer to manipulate and output sounds. Sound cards are necessary for nearly all CD-ROMs and have become commonplace on modern personal computers. Sound cards enable the computer to output sound through speakers connected to the board, to record sound input from a microphone connected to the computer, and manipulate sound stored on a disk.
Nearly all sound cards support MIDI, a standard for representing music electronically. In addition, most sound cards are Sound Blaster-compatible, which means that they can process commands written for a Sound Blaster card, the de facto standard for PC sound.
Sound cards use two basic methods to translate digital data into analog sounds:

FM synthesis mimics different musical instruments according to built-in formulas.

wavetable synthesis relies on recordings of actual instruments to produce sound. Wavetable synthesis produces more accurate sound, but is also more expensive.

➠ See also *CD-ROM; MIDI; multimedia.*

source: A place from which data is taken. Many computer commands involve moving data. The place from which the data is moved is called the *source*, whereas the place it is moved to is called the *destination* or *target*. If you copy a file from one directory to another, for example, you copy it from the *source directory* to the destination *directory*. The source and destination can be files, directories, or devices (that is, printers or storage devices).

➠ See also *copy; destination.*

source code: Program instructions in their original form. The word *source* differentiates code from various other forms that it can have (for example, object code and *executable code*).

Initially, a programmer writes a program in a particular programming language. This form of the program is called the *source program,* or more generically, *source code.* To execute the program, however, the programmer must translate it into machine language, the language that the computer understands. The first step of this translation process is usually performed by a utility called a *compiler* (see Figure 17 at *compiler*). The compiler translates the source code into a form called *object code.* Sometimes the object code is the same as machine code; sometimes it needs to be translated into machine language by a utility called an *assembler.*

Source code is the only format that is readable by humans. When you purchase programs, you usually receive them in their machine-language format. This means that you can execute them directly, but you cannot read or modify them. Some software manufacturers provide source code, but this is useful only if you are an experienced programmer.

➠ See also *assembler; code; compiler; machine language, object code, program; programming language.*

special character: A character that is not a letter, number, symbol, or punctuation mark. Control characters, for example, are special characters, as are special formatting characters such as paragraph marks.

➠ See also *control character.*

special interest group: See *SIG.*

speech recognition: Same as *voice recognition*.

speech synthesis: Refers to a computer's ability to produce sound that resembles human speech. Although they can't imitate the full spectrum of human cadences and intonations, speech synthesis systems can read text files and output them in a very intelligible, if somewhat dull, voice. Many systems even allow the user to choose the type of voice—for example, male or female. Speech synthesis systems are particularly valuable for seeing-impaired individuals.

➡ See also *voice recognition*.

spell checker: A program that checks the spelling of words in a text document. Spell checkers are particularly valuable for catching typos, but they do not help when your misspelling creates another valid word; for example, you type *too* instead of *to*.
   Many word processors come with a built-in spell checker, but you can also purchase stand-alone utilities.

➡ See also *word processing*.

spelling checker: See *spell checker*.

split screen: Division of the display screen into separate parts, each of which displays a different document, or different parts of the same document.

➡ See also *window*.

spooler: A program that controls spooling—putting jobs on a queue and taking them off one at a time. Most operating systems come with one or more spoolers, such as a print spooler for spooling documents. In addition, some applications include spoolers. Many word processors, for example, include their own print spooler.
   A good print spooler should allow you to change the order of documents in the queue and to cancel specific print jobs.

➡ See also *queue; spooling*.

spooling: Acronym for *simultaneous peripheral operations on-line, spooling* refers to putting jobs in a buffer, a special area in memory or on a disk where a device can access them when it is ready. Spooling is useful because devices access data at different rates. The buffer provides a waiting station where data can rest while the slower device catches up.

The most common spooling application is *print spooling*. In print spooling, documents are loaded into a buffer (usually an area on a disk), and then the printer pulls them off the buffer at its own rate. Because the documents are in a buffer where they can be by the printer, you can perform other operations on the computer while the printing takes place in the background. Spooling also lets you place a number of print jobs on a queue instead of waiting for each one to finish before specifying the next one.

➠ See also *background; buffer; queue.*

spot color: Refers to a method of specifying and printing colors in which each color is printed with its own ink. In contrast, *process color* printing uses four inks (cyan, magenta, yellow, and black) to produce all other colors. Spot color printing is effective when the printed matter contains only one to three different colors, but it becomes prohibitively expensive for more colors.

Most desktop publishing and graphics applications allow you to specify spot colors for text and other elements. There are a number of color specification systems for specifying spot colors, but Pantone is the most widely used.

➠ See also *color separation, Pantone Matching System; process colors.*

spreadsheet: A table of values arranged in rows and columns. Each value can have a predefined relationship to the other values. If you change one value, therefore, you may need to change other values as well..

Spreadsheet applications (often referred to simply as *spreadsheets*) are computer programs that let you create and manipulate spreadsheets electronically (Figure 76). In a spreadsheet application, each value sits in a cell. You can define what type of data is in each cell and how different cells depend on one another. The relationships between cells are called *formulas*, and the names of the cells are called *labels.*

Once you have defined the cells and the formulas for linking them together, you can enter your data. You can then modify selected val-

Figure 76: *Spreadsheet Application*

ues to see how all the other values change accordingly. This enables you to study various what-if scenarios.

A simple example of a useful spreadsheet application is one that calculates mortgage payments for a house. You would define five cells:

1. total cost of the house
2. down payment
3. mortgage rate
4. mortgage term
5. monthly payment

Once you had defined how these cells depend on one another, you could enter numbers and play with various possibilities. For example, keeping all the other values the same, you could see how different mortgage rates would affect your monthly payments.

There are a number of spreadsheet applications on the market, Lotus 1-2-3 and Excel being among the most famous. The more powerful spreadsheet applications support graphics features that enable you to produce charts and graphs from the data.

Some spreadsheets are *multidimensional,* meaning that you can link one spreadsheet to another. A three-dimensional spreadsheet, for example, is like a stack of spreadsheets all connected by formulas. A change made in one spreadsheet automatically affects other spreadsheets.

➠ See also *cell; Excel; formula; label; Lotus 1-2-3; three-dimensional spreadsheet*

SQL: Abbreviation of *structured query language*, and pronounced as separate letters. SQL is a standardized query language for requesting information from a database. The original version called *SEQUEL* (*structured English query language*) was designed by an IBM research center in 1974 and 1975. SQL was first introduced as a commercial database system in 1979 by Oracle Corporation.

Historically, SQL has been the favorite database management system for minicomputers and mainframes. Increasingly, however, SQL is being supported by PC database systems because it supports distributed databases (databases that are spread out over several computer systems). This enables several users on a local-area network to access the same database simultaneously.

Although there are different dialects of SQL, it is nevertheless the closest thing to a standard query language that currently exists. In 1986, ANSI approved a rudimentary version of SQL as the official standard, but most versions of SQL since then have included many extensions to the ANSI standard. In 1991, ANSI updated the standard. The new standard is known as SAG SQL.

➠ See also *database management system; distributed database; query; query language.*

SRAM: Short for *static random access memory*, and pronounced *ess-ram.* SRAM is a type of memory that is faster and more reliable than the more common DRAM (dynamic RAM). The term *static* is derived from the fact that it needs to be refreshed less often than dynamic RAM.

While DRAM supports access times of about 70 nanoseconds, SRAM can give access times as low as 10 nanoseconds. In addition, its cycle time is much shorter than that of DRAM because it does not need to pause between accesses. Unfortunately, it is also much more expensive to produce than DRAM. Due to its high speed, SRAM is often used as a memory cache.

➠ See also *access time; cache; cycle time; dynamic RAM; RAM.*

stack: (1) In programming, a special type of data structure in which items are removed in the reverse order from that in which they are added, so the most recently added item is the first one removed. This is also called *last-in, first-out (LIFO)*.
Adding an item to a stack is called *pushing*. Removing an item from a stack is called *popping*.

➠ See also *data structure; pop; push; queue.*

(2) In Apple Computer's HyperCard software system, a stack is a collection of cards.

➠ See also *HyperCard.*

stand-alone: Refers to a device that is self-contained, one that does not require any other devices to function. For example, a fax machine is a stand-alone device because it does not require a computer, printer, modem, or other device. A printer, on the other hand, is not a stand-alone device because it requires a computer to feed it data.

➠ See also *fax machine.*

standard: A definition or format that has been approved by a recognized standards organization or is accepted as a de facto standard by the industry. Standards exist for programming languages, operating systems, data formats, communications protocols, and electrical interfaces.
From a user's standpoint, standards are extremely important in the computer industry because they allow the combination of products from different manufacturers to create a customized system. Without standards, only hardware and software from the same company could be used together. In addition, standard user interfaces can make it much easier to learn how to use new applications.
Most official computer standards are set by one of the following organizations:

- ANSI (American National Standards Institute)
- CCITT (Comité Consultatif Internationale Télégraphique et Téléphonique)
- IEEE (Institute of Electrical and Electronic Engineers)
- ISO (International Standards Organization)
- VESA (Video Electronics Standards Association)

IEEE sets standards for most types of electrical interfaces. Its most famous standard is probably RS-232C, which defines an interface for serial communication. This is the interface used by most modems, and a number of other devices, including display screens and mice. IEEE is also responsible for designing floating-point data formats. While IEEE is generally concerned with hardware, ANSI is primarily concerned with software. ANSI has defined standards for a number of programming languages, including C, COBOL, and FORTRAN. CCITT defines international standards, particularly communications protocols. It has defined a number of standards, including V.22, V.32, V.34 and V.42, that specify protocols for transmitting data over telephone lines.

In addition to standards approved by organizations, there are also de facto standards. These are formats that have become standard simply because a large number of companies have agreed to use them. They have not been formally approved as standards, but they are standards nonetheless. PostScript is a good example of a de facto standard.

➤ See also *ANSI; architecture; CCITT; compatible; de facto standard; IEEE; ISO; open architecture; VESA.*

Standard Generalized Markup Language: See *SGML.*

standard input: The place from which input comes unless you specify a different input device. The standard input device is usually the keyboard.

➤ See also *input.*

standard output: The place where output goes unless you specify a different output device. The standard output device is usually the display screen.

➤ See also *output.*

star network: A local-area network (LAN) that uses a star topology in which all nodes are connected to a central computer (see Figure 80 at *topology*). The main disadvantage of star networks is that they require more cabling than other topologies, such as a bus or ring networks. In addition, if the central computer fails, the entire network becomes unusable.

➠ See also *local-area network (LAN)*; *topology*.

start bit: In asynchronous communications, the bit that signals the receiver that data is coming. Every byte of data is preceded by a start bit and followed by a stop bit.

➠ See also *asynchronous*; *bit*; *byte*.

start-stop transmission: See under *asynchronous*.

statement: An instruction written in a high-level language. A statement directs the computer to perform a specified action. A single statement in a high-level language can represent several machine-language instructions. Programs consist of statements and *expressions*. An expression is a group of symbols that represent a value.

➠ See also *expression*; *programming language*.

static RAM: See *SRAM*.

static variable: A variable that retains the same data throughout the execution of a program. In contrast, a *dynamic variable* can have different values during the course of a program.

➠ See also *dynamic variable*; *variable*.

station: Short for *workstation*.

ST-412 interface: Same as *ST-506 interface*.

ST-506 interface: PC A standard interface for connecting hard disk drives to PCs. Newer standards, such as enhanced IDE and SCSI, support faster data transfer rates.

ST-506 is sometimes referred to as *MFM*, which is the most prevalent encoding scheme used on ST-506 disk drives. ST-506 also supports the RLL encoding format.

➠ See also *hard disk; IDE interface; interface; MFM; RLL; SCSI.*

stop bit: In asynchronous communications, a bit that indicates that a byte has just been transmitted. Every byte of data is preceded by a start bit and followed by a stop bit.

➠ See also *asynchronous; bit; byte.*

storage: The capacity of a device to hold and retain data.

➠ See also *mass storage.*

storage device: A device capable of storing data. The term usually refers to mass storage devices, such as disk and tape drives.

➠ See also *disk drive; mass storage; tape drive.*

store: To copy data from a CPU to memory, or from memory to a mass storage device.

streamer: Same as *tape.*

strikeout: A method of highlighting text by drawing a horizontal line through the characters. ~~This text, for example, has strikeout formatting.~~

Many word processors support edit modes in which deleted sections are displayed with strikeouts. This is particularly effective in workgroups where two or more people are editing the same document.

Strikeout is also called *strikethrough.*

➠ See also *workgroup computing.*

strikethrough: Same as *strikeout*.

string: See character string.

Structured Query Language: See *SQL*.

style: In word processing, a named set of formatting parameters. By applying the style name to a section of text, you can change many formatting properties at once.

➠ See also *format; style sheet.*

style sheet: In word processing and desktop publishing, a style sheet is a file or form that defines the layout of a document. When you fill in a style sheet, you specify such parameters as the page size, margins, and fonts. Style sheets are useful because you can use the same style sheet for many documents. For example, you could define one style sheet for personal letters, another for official letters, and a third for reports.
Stylesheets are also called *templates*.

➠ See also *desktop publishing; font; layout; margins; style; word processing.*

stylus: A pointing and drawing device shaped like a pen. You use a stylus with a graphics tablet or touch screen.

➠ See also *digitizing tablet; touch screen.*

subdirectory: A directory below another directory. Every directory except the root directory is a subdirectory (see Figure 26 at *directory*). On Macintosh computers, subdirectories are called *folders*.

➠ See also *directory; folder; root directory.*

subnotebook computer: A portable computer that is slightly lighter and smaller than a full-sized notebook computer. Typically, subnotebook computers have a smaller keyboard and screen, but are otherwise equivalent to notebook computers.

➠ See also *hand-held computer; notebook computer; portable computer.*

subroutine: Same as *routine.*

subscript: (1) In programming, a symbol or number used to identify an element in an array. Usually, the subscript is placed in brackets following the array name. For example, AR[5] identifies element number 5 in an array called AR.

If the array is multidimensional, you must specify a subscript for each dimension. For example, MD[5][3][9] identifies an element in a three-dimensional array called MD.

Different programming languages have different rules for specifying subscripts. For example, the BASIC language uses parentheses in place of brackets.

➠ See also *array.*

(2) In word processing, a character that appears slightly below the line, as in this example: H_2O. A *superscript* is a character that appears slightly above the line.

➠ See also *superscript; word processing.*

supercomputer: The fastest type of computer. Supercomputers are very expensive and are employed for specialized applications that require immense amounts of mathematical calculations. For example, weather forecasting requires a supercomputer. Other uses of supercomputers include animated graphics, fluid dynamic calculations, nuclear energy research, and petroleum exploration.

The chief difference between a supercomputer and a mainframe is that a supercomputer channels all its power into executing a few programs as fast as possible, whereas a mainframe uses its power to execute many programs concurrently.

➠ See also *computer; mainframe.*

SuperDrive: MAC The common name for the *FDHD (floppy disk, high density)* disk drive that comes with all models of the Apple Macintosh computer. The SuperDrive can read and write to all three Macintosh disk sizes (400K, 800K, and 1.2MB) as well as the two IBM 3½-inch disk formats: 720K and 1.44MB.

➠ See also *FDHD*; *floppy disk*; *Macintosh computer*.

superscript: A symbol or character that appears slightly above a line, as in this example:

$$area = 2\pi r^2$$

Footnote numbers appearing in text are also superscripts. A symbol or character that appears slightly below a line is called a *subscript*.

➠ See also *subscript*; *word processing*.

supertwist: A technique for improving LCD display screens by twisting light rays. In addition to normal supertwist displays, there also exist *double supertwist* and *triple supertwist* displays. In general, the more twists, the higher the contrast.

➠ See also *background*; *backlighting*; *flat-panel display*; *LCD*; *notebook computer*.

Super VGA: See *SVGA*.

support: (v) To have a specific functionality. For example, a word processor that *supports* graphics is one that has a graphics component. The word *support*, however, is vague. It could mean that the word processor enables you to create graphics illustrations, that you can insert graphics created by another program, or something entirely different.

As another example, an operating system that supports multiple users is one that enables several users to run programs at the same time.

(n) Short for customer support, the assistance that a vendor offers to customers. Support can vary widely, from nothing at all to a phone hotline to house calls.

➠ See also *customer support*.

surge protector: A device that protects a power supply from electrical surges. All computers come with some surge protection built into the power supply, but it is a good idea to purchase a separate device. A more robust form of protection from electrical disturbances is called an *uninterruptible power supply* (UPS).

➠ See also *UPS*.

SVGA: Short for *Super VGA*, a set of graphics standards designed to offer greater resolution than VGA. There are several varieties of SVGA, each providing a different resolution:

- 800 by 600 pixels
- 1024 by 768 pixels
- 1280 by 1024 pixels
- 1600 by 1200 pixels

All SVGA standards support a palette of 16 million colors, but the number of colors that can be displayed simultaneously is limited by the amount of video memory installed in a system. One SVGA system might display only 16 simultaneous colors while another displays the entire palette of 16 million colors. The SVGA standards are developed by a consortium of monitor and graphics manufacturers called *VESA*.

➠ See also *palette; resolution; VESA; VGA; video standards*.

swap: (1) To replace pages or segments of data in memory. Swapping is a useful technique that enables a computer to execute programs and manipulate data files larger than main memory. The operating system copies as much data as possible into main memory, and leaves the rest on the disk. When the operating system needs data from the disk, it exchanges a portion of data (called a *page* or *segment*) in main memory with a portion of data on the disk.

DOS does not perform swapping, but most other operating systems, including OS/2, Windows, and UNIX, do.

Swapping is often called *paging*.

➠ See also *memory; operating system; page; segment; virtual memory*.

(2) In UNIX systems, *swapping* refers to moving entire processes in
and out of main memory.

➠ See also *main memory; process; UNIX.*

swap file: PC In Windows environments, a hidden file used by the
operating system for swapping.

➠ See also *swap.*

switch: (1) A small lever or button. The switches on the back of printers and on expansion boards are called *DIP switches.* A switch that has
just two positions is called a *toggle switch.*

➠ See also *DIP switch; toggle.*

(2) Another word for *option* or *parameter*—a symbol that you add to a
command to modify the command's behavior.

➠ See also *option; parameter.*

synchronous: Occurring at regular intervals. The opposite of *synchronous* is asynchronous. Most communication between computers and
devices is asynchronous—it can occur at any time and at irregular
intervals. Communication within a computer, however, is usually
synchronous and is governed by the microprocessor clock. Signals
along the bus, for example, can occur only at specific points in the
clock cycle (See Figure 6 at *asynchronous*).

➠ See also *asynchronous; bus; clock speed.*

syntax: Refers to the spelling and grammar of a programming language.
Computers are inflexible machines that understand what you type
only if you type it in the exact form that the computer expects. The
expected form is called the *syntax.*
  Each program defines its own syntactical rules that control which
words the computer understands, which combinations of words are
meaningful, and what punctuation is necessary.

➠ See also *language; semantics.*

sysop: Pronounced *siss-op,* short for *system operator,* an individual who manages a bulletin board system (BBS), *online service,* or *special interest group (SIG).*

➠ See also *bulletin board system; network; SIG.*

system: (1) Refers to a combination of components working together. For example, a *computer system* includes both hardware and software. A *Windows system* is a personal computer running the Windows operating system. A *desktop publishing system* is a computer running desktop publishing software.

(2) Short for *computer system.*

(3) Short for *operating system.*

(4) An organization or methodology. The binary numbering system, for instance, is a way to count using only two digits.

System: MAC On Macintoshes, *System* is short for *System file,* an essential program that runs whenever you start up a Macintosh. The System provides information to all other applications that run on a Macintosh. The System and Finder programs together make up the Macintosh operating system.

➠ See also *Finder; Macintosh; operating system.*

system board: Same as *motherboard.*

system call: The invocation of an operating system routine. Operating systems contain sets of routines for performing various low-level operations. For example, all operating systems have a routine for creating a directory. If you want to execute an operating system routine from a program, you must make a system call.

➠ See also *invoke; operating system; routine.*

System folder: MAC A standard folder on Macintoshes that contains the System and Finder programs, as well as other resources needed by the operating system.

➠ See also *Finder; folder; Macintosh; System.*

system prompt: See under *prompt.*

system unit: The main part of a personal computer. The system unit includes the chassis, microprocessor, main memory, bus, and ports, but does not include the keyboard or monitor, or any peripheral devices.

systems analyst: A programmer or consultant who designs and manages the development of business applications. Typically, systems analysts are more involved in design issues than in day-to-day coding. However, *systems analyst* is a somewhat arbitrary title, so different companies define the role differently.

➠ See also *programmer.*

systems software: Refers to the operating system and all utility programs that manage computer resources at a low level. Software is generally divided into systems software and applications software. Applications software comprises programs designed for an end user, such as word processors, database systems, and spreadsheet programs. Systems software includes compilers, loaders, linkers, and debuggers (See Figure 5 at *application*).

➠ See also *application; end user; software; utility.*

tab character: A special character that can be inserted into a text document.

Different programs react to tab characters in different ways. Most word processors, for example, move the cursor or insertion point to the next *tab stop*, and most printers move the print head to the next tab stop as well. Some programs, however, simply ignore tabs.

➡ See also *Tab key; tab stop.*

Tab key: A key on computer keyboards that inserts a tab character or moves the insertion point to the next tab stop. Some applications respond to the tab key by inserting spaces up to the next tab stop. This is often called a *soft tab*, whereas a real tab character is called a *hard tab*.

Spreadsheet and database management applications usually respond to the Tab key by moving the cursor to the next field or cell. In dialog boxes and menus, pressing the Tab key highlights the next button or option.

➡ See also *cell; cursor; field; insertion point; tab character; tab stop.*

table: Refers to data arranged in rows and columns. A *spreadsheet*, for example, is a table. In relational database management systems, all information is stored in the form of tables.

➡ See also *database management system; relational database; spreadsheet.*

tablet: Short for *graphics tablet*, digitizing tablet, or *electronic tablet*.

➡ See also *digitizing tablet.*

tab stop: A stop point for tabbing. In word processing, each line contains a number of tab stops placed at regular intervals (for example,
every half inch). They can be changed, however, as most word processors allow you to set tab stops wherever you want. When you press
the Tab key, the cursor or insertion point jumps to the next tab stop,
which itself is invisible. Although tab stops do not exist in the text
file, the word processor keeps track of them so that it can react correctly to the Tab key.

➡ See also *tab character; Tab key.*

Tagged Image File Format: See *TIFF.*

tape: A magnetically coated strip of plastic on which data can be
encoded. Tapes for computers are similar to tapes used to store
music. Some personal computers, in fact, enable you to use normal
cassette tapes.
  Storing data on tapes is considerably cheaper than storing data on
disks. Tapes also have large storage capacities, ranging from a few
hundred kilobytes to several gigabytes. Accessing data on tapes, however, is much slower than data on disks. Tapes are *sequential-access*
media, which means that to get to a particular point on the tape, the
tape must go through all the preceding points. In contrast, disks are
random-access media because a disk drive can access any point at random without passing through intervening points.
  Because tapes are so slow, they are generally used only for long-
term storage and backup. Data to be used regularly is almost always
kept on a disk. Tapes are also used for transporting large amounts of
data.
  Tapes come in a variety of sizes and formats. The most common are
listed in Table 27.
  Tapes are sometimes called *streamers* or *streaming tapes.*

➡ See also *backup; DAT; disk drive; mass storage; QIC; sequential access.*

tape drive: A device, like a tape recorder, that reads data from and
writes it onto a tape. Tape drives have data capacities of anywhere
from a few hundred kilobytes to several gigabytes. Their transfer
speeds also vary considerably. Fast tape drives can transfer as much as
20MB (megabytes) per minute.

Table 27
TAPES

TYPE	CAPACITY	NOTES
Half-inch	60MB to 400MB	Half-inch tapes come both as 9-track reels and as cartridges. The tapes themselves are relatively cheap but they require expensive tape drives.
Quarter-inch	40MB to 5GB	Quarter-inch cartridges (QIC tapes) are relatively inexpensive and support fast data transfer rates. Quarter-inch minicartridges are even less expensive, but their data capacities are smaller and their transfer rates are slower.
8-mm Helical-scan	1GB to 5GB	8-mm helical-scan cartridges use the same technology as VCR tapes and have the greatest capacity (along with DAT cartridges), but they require relatively expensive tape drives. They also have relatively slow data transfer rates.
4-mm DAT	1.3GB	DAT (Digital Audio Tape) cartridges have the greatest capacity (along with 8-mm helical-scan cartridges) but they require relatively expensive tape drives. They also have relatively slow data transfer rates.

The disadvantage of tape drives is that they are *sequential-access* devices, which means that to read any particular block of data, you need to read all the preceding blocks. This makes them much too slow for general-purpose storage operations. However, they are the least expensive media for making backups.

➠ See also *backup; tape.*

target: Synonymous with destination, a target is a file or device to which data is moved or copied. Many computer commands involve copying data from one place to another. One says that the computer copies from the source to the target (or destination).

➠ See also *source.*

task: An operating system concept that refers to the combination of a program being executed and bookkeeping information used by the operating system. Whenever you execute a program, the operating system creates a new task for it. The task is like an envelope for the program: it identifies the program with a *task number* and attaches other bookkeeping information to it.

Many operating systems, including UNIX, OS/2, and Windows, are capable of running many tasks at the same time and are called *multitasking* operating systems.

In most operating systems, there is a one-to-one relationship between the task and the program, but some operating systems allow a program to be divided into multiple tasks. Such systems are called *multithreading* operating systems.

➠ See also *multithreading; multitasking; operating system.*

task switching: Refers to operating systems or operating environments that enable you to switch from one program to another without losing your spot in the first program. Many utilities are available that add task switching to DOS systems.

Note that task switching is not the same as *multitasking.* In multitasking, the CPU switches back and forth quickly between programs, giving the appearance that all programs are running simultaneously. In task switching, the CPU does not switch back and forth, but executes only one program at a time. Task switching does allow you to switch smoothly from one program to another.

Task switching is sometimes called *context switching.*

➠ See also *DOS; multitasking; operating environment; operating system.*

TCP/IP: Acronym for *Transport Control Protocol/Internet Protocol,* a communications protocol developed by the Department of Defense. TCP/IP is actually two protocols—TCP and IP—but they are almost always used together. TCP/IP is built into the UNIX operating system and is used by the Internet, making it the de facto standard for transmitting data over networks. Even network operating systems that have their own protocols, such as Netware, also support TCP/IP.

➠ See also *communications; Internet; Netware; Protocol.*

tear-off menu: A pop-up menu that you can move around the screen like a window. Regular pop-up menus are attached to the menu selection that caused them to pop up.

➠ See also *menu.*

technical support: See customer support.

telecommunications: Refers to all types of data transmission, from voice to video.

➠ See also *communications.*

telecommuting: A term coined by Jack Nilles in the early 1970s to describe a geographically dispersed office where workers can work at home on a computer and transmit data and documents to a central office via telephone lines. A major argument in favor of telecommuting over vehicular commuting is that it does not produce air pollution. In addition, many people are more productive working at home than in an office. For others, however, the contrary holds true.

➠ See also *e-mail; network; workgroup computing.*

telecopy: To send a document from one place to another via a fax machine.

➠ See also *fax machine.*

Telenet: One of the largest public data networks (PDNs) in the United States. Telenet is owned by U.S. Sprint Communications Corporation. A competing network, called *Tymnet,* is owned by McDonnell Douglas. Telenet serves as the communications backbone for many online services.

➠ See also *online service; wide-area network.*

template: (1) A plastic or paper diagram that you can put on your keyboard to indicate the meanings of different keys for a particular program (Figure 77).

(2) A sheet of plastic with menus and command boxes drawn on it that you place on top of a digitizing tablet. You can select commands by pressing the digitizing tablet's pen against a command box or by positioning the cursor over a box and pressing one of the cursor keys.

➠ See also *cursor; digitizing tablet.*

(3) In spreadsheet and database applications, a template is a blank form that shows which fields exist, their locations, and their length. In spreadsheet applications, for example, a template is a spreadsheet in which all the cells have been defined but no data has yet been entered.

(4) In some word processing applications, *template* is used in place of *style sheet.*

(5) PC DOS uses the term *template* to mean command buffer.

➠ See also *command buffer.*

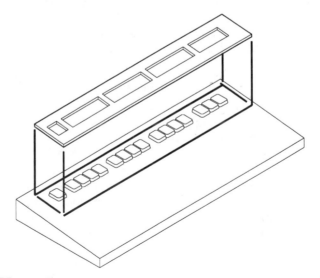

Figure 77: *Template*

terabyte: 2^{40} (1,099,511,627,776) bytes. This is approximately 1 trillion bytes.

➠ See also *gigabyte; megabyte.*

terminal: (1) A device that enables you to communicate with a computer. Generally, a terminal is a combination of keyboard and display screen.
Terminals are sometimes divided into three classes based on how much processing power they contain:

intelligent terminal: A stand-alone device that contains main memory and a CPU.

smart terminal: Contains some processing power, but not as much as an intelligent terminal.

dumb terminal: Has no processing capabilities. It relies entirely on the computer's processor.

➠ See also *display screen; dumb terminal; intelligent terminal; keyboard; monitor; smart terminal.*

(2) In networking, a terminal is a personal computer or workstation connected to a mainframe. The personal computer usually runs terminal emulation software that makes the mainframe think it is like any other mainframe terminal.

➠ See also *emulation; network.*

terminal emulation: Refers to making a computer respond like a particular type of terminal. Terminal emulation programs allow you to access a mainframe computer or bulletin board service with a personal computer.

➠ See also *bulletin board service; emulation; mainframe; terminal.*

terminate and stay resident: See *TSR.*

Texas Instruments Graphics Architecture (TIGA): A high-resolution graphics specification designed by Texas Instruments. Unlike other graphics standards, TIGA does not specify a particular resolution or number of colors. Instead, it defines an interface between software and graphics processors. Programs written for TIGA, therefore, should be able to run on future systems that conform to the TIGA standard, regardless of resolution and color specifics.

Currently, the only graphics standard that conforms to TIGA is TI 34010, which defines a resolution of 1,024 by 768, with 256 simultaneous colors. Two competing standards with the same resolution are 8514/A from IBM and SVGA from VESA.

➠ See also *8514/A; graphics; SVGA; TI 34010; VESA; video standards; XGA.*

text: Words, sentences, paragraphs. This book, for example, consists of text. *Text processing* refers to the ability to manipulate words, lines, and pages. Typically, the term *text* refers to text stored as ASCII codes (that is, without any formatting). Objects that are *not* text include graphics, numbers (if they're not stored as ASCII characters), and program code.

➠ See also *ASCII.*

text editor: See *editor.*

text file: A file that holds text. The term *text file* is often used as a synonym for ASCII file, a file in which characters are represented by their ASCII codes.

➠ See also *ASCII; file; text.*

text flow: Same as *text wrap.*

text mode: A video mode in which a display screen is divided into rows and columns of boxes. Each box can contain one character. Text mode is also called *character mode.*

All video standards for the PC, including VGA, support a text mode that divides the screen into 25 rows and 80 columns. In addition to text mode, most video adapters support a *graphics mode*, in which the display screen is divided into an array of *pixels*.

Whereas character-based programs run in text mode, all graphics-based programs run in graphics mode.

➠ See also *character based; graphics based; graphics mode; video mode; video standards.*

text wrap: A feature supported by many word processors that enables you to surround a picture or diagram with text (Figure 78). The text wraps around the graphic. Text wrap is also called *text flow.*

➠ See also *word processing.*

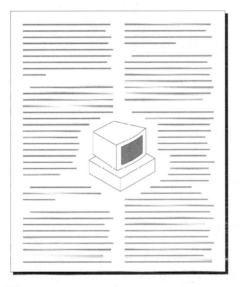

Figure 78: *Text Wrap*

TFT: Abbreviation of *thin film transistor*, a type of LCD flat-panel display screen, in which each pixel is controlled by from one to four transistors. The TFT technology provides the best resolution of all the flat-panel techniques, but it is also the most expensive. TFT screens are sometimes called *active-matrix LCDs.*

➠ See also *active-matrix display; flat-panel display; LCD.*

thermal printer: A type of printer that produces images by pushing electrically heated pins against special heat-sensitive paper. Thermal printers are inexpensive and are used in most calculators and many fax machines. They produce low-quality print, and the paper tends to curl and fade after a few weeks or months.

➠ See also *fax machine; printer.*

thin film transistor: See *TFT*.

thread: (1) In online discussions, a series of messages that have been posted as replies to each other. A single forum or conference typically contains many threads covering different subjects. By reading each message in a thread, one after the other, you can see how the discussion has evolved. You can start a new thread by posting a message that is not a reply to an earlier message.

➠ See also *forum; online service.*

(2) In programming, a part of a program that can execute independently of other parts. Operating systems that support multithreading enable programmers to design programs whose threaded parts can execute concurrently.

➠ See also *multithreading.*

3-D spreadsheet: See *three-dimensional spreadsheet.*

three-dimensional spreadsheet: A spreadsheet program that allows you to arrange data as a stack of tables, each of which has the same shape and size. You can analyze a single table or an entire group of tables.

➠ See also *spreadsheet.*

3DO: A technology that supports photo-realistic graphics, full-motion video, and CD-quality sound. The first applications of this technology were stand-alone devices used for playing games, but the technology is beginning to find its way into PCs in the form of expansion boards.

➡ See also *expansion board; multimedia.*

386: Short for the *Intel 80386 microprocessor.*

➡ See also *bus; Intel microprocessors; main memory; register; virtual memory.*

386SX: Short for the *Intel 80386SX microprocessor.*

➡ See also *Intel microprocessors.*

throughput: The amount of data transferred from one place to another or processed in a specified amount of time. Data transfer rates for disk drives and networks are measured in terms of throughput. Typically, throughputs are measured in bits per second *(bps).*

➡ See also *disk drive; network.*

thumbnail: A miniature display of a page to be printed. Thumbnails enable you to see the layout of many pages on the screen at once. Generally, thumbnails are too small to show the actual text, so *greeking* is used to indicate how the text will look (See Figure 37 at *greeking*).

➡ See also *desktop publishing; greeking; layout.*

TIFF: Acronym for *tagged image file format,* one of the most widely supported file formats for storing bit-mapped images on personal computers (both PCs and Macintosh computers). Other popular formats are BMP and *PCX.*

TIFF graphics can be any resolution, and they can be black and white, gray-scaled, or color.

➡ See also *bit map; graphics; graphics file formats; gray scaling; PCX.*

TIGA: See *Texas Instruments Graphics Architecture.*

tiled windows: Windows arranged so that they do not overlap each other. Overlapping windows are often called *overlaid* or cascading windows.

➡ See also *cascading windows; overlaid windows; window.*

time-out: An interrupt signal generated by a program that has waited a certain length of time for some input but has not received it. Many programs perform time-outs so that the program does not sit idle waiting for input that may never come. For example, automatic bankteller machines perform a time-out if you do not enter your password quickly enough.

➡ See also *interrupt.*

time sharing: Refers to the concurrent use of a computer by more than one user—users *share* the computer's time. *Time sharing* is synonymous with *multi-user.* Almost all mainframes and minicomputers are time-sharing systems, but most personal computers and workstations are not.

➡ See also *mainframe; minicomputer; multi-user.*

TI 34010: A video standard from Texas Instruments that supports a resolution of 1,024 by 768. TI 34010 conforms to TI's Graphics Architecture (TIGA). Unlike IBM's 8514/A, which supports the same resolution, TI 34010 is noninterlaced.

➡ See also *8514/A; interlacing; TIGA; video standards.*

title bar: A bar on top of a window. The title bar contains the name of the file or application. In many graphical user interfaces, including the Macintosh and Microsoft Windows interfaces, you move (*drag*) a window by grabbing the title bar.

➡ See also *drag; window.*

toggle: To switch from one setting to another. The term *toggle* implies that there are only two possible settings and that you are switching from the current setting to the other setting.

A *toggle switch* is a switch that has just two positions. For example, light switches that turn a light on or off are toggle switches. On computer keyboards, the Caps Lock key is a toggle switch because pressing it can have two meanings depending on what the current setting is. If Caps Lock is already on, then pressing the Caps Lock key turns it off. If Caps Lock is off, pressing the Caps Lock key turns it on.

➡ See also *switch; keyboard.*

token: (1) In programming languages, a single element of a programming language. For example, a token could be a keyword, an operator, or a punctuation mark.

➡ See also *keyword; operator; programming language.*

(2) In networking, a token is a special series of bits that travels around a token-ring network. As the token circulates, computers attached to the network can capture it. The token acts like a ticket, enabling its owner to send a message across the network. There is only one token for each network, so there is no possibility that two computers will attempt to transmit messages at the same time (see Figure 79 at *token-ring network*).

➡ See also *token-ring network.*

token-ring network: (1) A type of computer network in which all the computers are arranged (schematically) in a circle (Figure 79). A *token*, which is a special bit pattern, travels around the circle. To send a message, a computer catches the token, attaches a message to it, and then lets it continue to travel around the network.

➡ See also *local-area network; network; token.*

(2) When capitalized, *Token Ring* refers to the PC network protocol developed by IBM. The IBM Token-Ring specification has been standardized by the IEEE as the IEEE 802.5 standard.

➡ See also *IEEE; local-area network.*

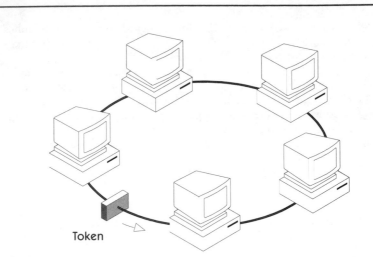

Token

Figure 79: *Token-ring Network*

toner: A special type of ink used by copy machines and laser printers. Toner consists of a dry, powdery substance that is electrically charged so that it adheres to a drum, plate, or piece of paper charged with the opposite polarity.

For most laser printers, the toner comes in a cartridge that you insert into the printer. When the cartridge is empty, you can replace it or have it refilled. Typically, you can print thousands of pages with a single cartridge.

➡ See also *laser printer*.

topology: The shape of a local-area network (LAN). There are three principal topologies used in LANs (Figure 80).

bus topology: All devices are connected to a central cable, called the *bus* or *backbone*. Bus networks are relatively inexpensive and easy to install. Ethernet systems use a bus topology.

ring topology: All devices are connected to one another in the shape of a closed loop, so that each device is connected directly to two other devices, one on either side of it. Ring topologies are relatively expensive and difficult to install, but they are robust (one failed device does not usually make the entire network fail).

star topology: All devices are connected to a central hub. Star networks are relatively easy to install and manage, but bottlenecks can occur because all data must pass through the hub.

➠ See also *Ethernet; local-area network.*

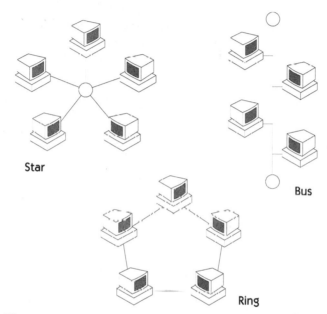

Figure 80: *Topologies*

TOPS: Acronym for *transparent operating system*, a type of local-area network designed by Sun Microsystems that can combine Apple Macintosh computers, PCs, and Sun workstations on the same network. A particular strength of TOPS is that the networking software is *transparent*, meaning that users do not need to adjust to a new operating environment. PC users see their PC interface and Mac users see the Mac interface.

TOPS uses the Macintosh computer's built-in AppleTalk protocol. It is a peer-to-peer network, which means that it does not require any computers to be set aside as file servers. Authorized users can access files from any disk drive connected to the network.

➠ See also *AppleTalk; local-area network; peer-to-peer architecture.*

touchpad: A small, touch-sensitive pad used as a pointing device on some portable computers. By moving a finger or other object along the pad, you can move the pointer on the display screen.

➡ See also *digitizing tablet; pointing device.*

touch screen: A type of display screen that has a touch-sensitive transparent panel covering the screen. Instead of using a pointing device such as a mouse or light pen, you can use your finger to point directly to objects on the screen.

Although touch screens provide a natural interface for computer novices, they are unsatisfactory for most applications because the finger is such a relatively large object. It is impossible to point accurately to small areas of the screen. In addition, most users find touch screens tiring to the arms after long use.

➡ See also *display screen; light pen; mouse; point.*

touch tablet: Same as *digitizing tablet.*

tower model: Refers to a computer in which the power supply, motherboard, and mass storage devices are stacked on top of each other in a cabinet (Figure 81). This is in contrast to desktop models, in which these components are housed in a more compact box.

The main advantage of tower models is that there are fewer space constraints, which makes installation of additional storage devices easier. Traditional tower models are about 21 inches tall. Many computer manufacturers now offer *minitower* models, which are about 14 inches tall, and *mid-sized* tower models, which are about 16 inches tall.

➡ See also *chassis; desktop model computer.*

TPI: Short for *tracks per inch*, the density of tracks on a disk. For example, double-density 5.25-inch floppies have a TPI of 48, while high-density floppies record 96 TPI. High-density 3.25-inch diskettes are formatted with 135 TPI.

➡ See also *disk; track.*

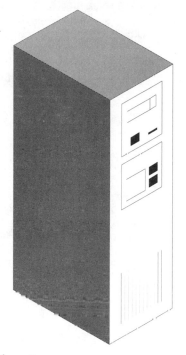

Figure 81: *Tower Configuration*

track: A ring on a disk where data can be written. A typical floppy disk has 80 (double-density) or 160 (high-density) tracks. For hard disks, each *platter* is divided into tracks, and a single track location that cuts through all platters is called a *cylinder.* Hard disks can have anywhere from 400 to more than 1000 cylinders.

Each track is further divided into a number of *sectors.* The operating system and disk drive remember where information is stored by noting its track and sector numbers (see Figure 39 at *interleaving*).

The density of tracks (how close together they are) is measured in terms of tracks per inch (TPI).

➡ See also *cylinder; format; hard disk; sector.*

trackball: A pointing device (Figure 82). Essentially, a trackball is a mouse lying on its back. To move the pointer, you rotate the ball with your thumb, your fingers, or the palm of your hand. There are usually one to three buttons next to the ball, which you use just like mouse buttons.

The advantage of trackballs over mice is that the trackball is stationary so it does not require much space to use it. In addition, you can place a trackball on any type of surface, including your lap. For both these reasons, trackballs are popular pointing devices for portable computers.

➠ See also *mouse; pointing device.*

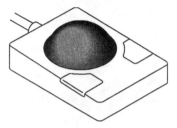

Figure 82: *Trackball*

tracks per inch: See *TPI.*

tractor feed: A method of feeding paper through a printer. Tractor-feed printers have two sprocketed wheels on either side of the printer that fit into holes in the paper (Figure 83). As the wheels revolve, the paper is pulled through the printer. Tractor feed is also called *pin feed*.

The other principal form of feeding paper into a printer is *friction feed*, which utilizes plastic or rubber rollers to squeeze a sheet of paper and pull it through the printer.

Tractor-feed printers require special paper (with holes), whereas friction feed printers can handle most types of cut-sheet paper, including envelopes. Some printers support both types of feeding mechanisms.

➠ See also *friction feed; printer.*

traffic: The load on a communications device or system. One of the principal jobs of a system administrator is to monitor traffic levels and take appropriate actions when traffic becomes heavy.

➠ See also *load.*

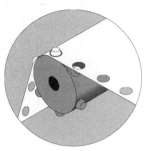 

Tractor Feed   Friction Feed

Figure 83: *Tractor Feed vs. Friction Feed*

transaction processing: A type of computer processing in which the computer responds immediately to user requests. Each request is considered to be a *transaction*. Automatic teller machines for banks are an example of transaction processing.

The opposite of transaction processing is batch processing, in which a batch of requests is stored and then executed all at one time. Transaction processing requires interaction with a user, whereas batch processing can take place without a user being present.

➡ See also *batch processing.*

Transfer Control Protocol/Internet Protocol: See *TCP/IP.*

transparent: Invisible. In computer software, an action is transparent if it takes place without any visible effect. Transparency is usually considered to be a good characteristic of a system because it shields the user from the system's complexity.

transportable: A large portable computer (over 15 pounds). Another term for *transportable* is *luggable.*

➡ See also *laptop computer; notebook computer; portable.*

tree structure: A type of data structure in which each element is attached to one or more elements directly *beneath* it. The connections between elements are called *branches*. Trees are often called *inverted trees* because they are normally drawn with the *root* at the top (Figure 84).

The elements at the very bottom of an inverted tree (that is, those that have no elements below them) are called *leaves*. Inverted trees are the data structures used to represent hierarchical file structures. In this case, the leaves are files and the other elements above the leaves are directories.

A binary *tree* is a special type of inverted tree in which each element has only two branches below it.

➠ See also *data structure; directory; hierarchical; leaf.*

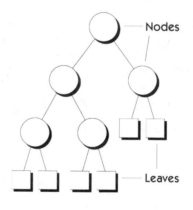

Binary Tree

Figure 84: *Tree Structure*

true color: Refers to any graphics device or software that uses at least 24 bits to represent each dot or pixel. Using 24 bits means that more than 16 million unique colors can be represented. Since humans can only distinguish a few million colors, this is more than enough to accurately represent any color image.

TrueType: An outline font technology developed jointly by Microsoft and Apple. Because TrueType support is built into all Windows and Macintosh operating systems, anyone using these operating systems can create documents using TrueType fonts.

Since being introduced in 1991, TrueType has quickly become the dominant font technology for everyday use, and is even displacing PostScript in many publishing environments.

➠ See also *font; outline font; PostScript.*

truncate: To cut off the end of something. Usually, the term is used to describe a type of rounding of floating-point numbers. If there are too few spaces for a long floating-point number, a program may truncate the number by lopping off the decimal digits that do not fit. For example, 3.14126 might be truncated to 3.14. Note that truncation always rounds the number down. If the number 1.19999 is truncated to one decimal digit, it becomes 1.1, not 1.2.

➠ See also *floating-point number.*

TSR: Abbreviation of *terminate and stay resident.* Refers to DOS programs that can be *memory resident* (remaining in memory at all times once they are loaded). Calendars, calculators, spell checkers, thesauruses, and notepads are often set up as TSRs so that you can instantly access them from within another program. TSRs are sometimes called *pop-up programs* because they can pop up in applications.

When you install a TSR, you define a special key sequence (usually a control character) that will invoke the TSR program. You can then press this *hot key* from within any application to run the TSR program. Many programs can be installed as a TSR, but TSRs reduce the amount of memory available to other programs. In addition, not all TSRs interact well with each other. You may have difficulties, therefore, if you try to keep too many TSRs in main memory at once.

TSRs are unnecessary with multitasking operating systems such as Windows, OS/2, and the Mac OS.

➠ See also *hot key; memory resident; multitasking; operating system.*

TTL monitor: TTL stands for *transistor-transistor logic* and refers to a special type of digital circuit. More commonly, however, *TTL* is used to designate any type of digital input or device. A TTL monitor, therefore, is a monitor that accepts digital input. TTL monitors are consistent with older graphics standards such as MDA, but all newer graphics standards, including VGA, require analog signals. Some monitors can accept both types of signal.

➡ See also *analog monitor; digital monitor; MDA.*

turnkey system: A computer system that has been customized for a particular application. The term derives from the idea that the end user can just turn a key and the system is ready to go. Turnkey systems include all the hardware and software necessary for the particular application. They are usually developed by OEMs *(original equipment manufacturers)* who buy a computer from another company and then add software and devices themselves.

➡ See also *OEM.*

TWAIN: Acronym for *Technology Without An Interesting Name,* the de facto interface standard for scanners. Nearly all scanners come with a TWAIN driver, which makes them compatible with any TWAIN-supporting software. Unfortunately, not all scanner software is TWAIN-compatible.

➡ See also *driver; optical scanner.*

tweak: To make small changes that fine-tune a piece of software or hardware. Tweaking sometimes refers to changing the values of underlying variables slightly to make the results of a program coincide with desired results. In this case, tweaking is not always a good thing since it undermines the integrity of the program.

twisted-pair cable: A type of cable that consists of two independently insulated wires twisted around one another. One wire carries the signal while the other wire is grounded and absorbs signal interference. Twisted-pair cable is used by older telephone networks and is the least expensive type of local-area network (LAN) cable. Other types of cables used for LANs include coaxial cables and fiber optic cables.

➡ See also *coaxial cable; fiber optic cable; local-area network.*

286: Short for the Intel 80286 microprocessor.

➠ See also *Intel microprocessors.*

Tymnet: One of the largest public data networks (PDNs) in the United States. Tymnet is owned by McDonnell Douglas Corporation. A competing network, called *Telenet*, is owned by U.S. Sprint Communications Corporation.

➠ See also *network.*

type: (v) (1) To enter characters by pressing keys on the keyboard.

(2) In DOS, OS/2, and many other operating systems, the TYPE command causes a file to appear on the display screen.

(n) Short for data type.

typeface: A design for a set of characters (Figure 85). Popular typefaces include Times Roman, Helvetica, and Courier. The typeface represents one aspect of a *font*. The font also includes such characteristics as size, weight, italics, and so on.

There are two general categories of typefaces: *serif* and *sans serif*. Sans serif typefaces are composed of simple lines, whereas serif typefaces use small decorative marks to embellish characters. Helvetica is a sans serif type and Times Roman is a serif type.

➠ See also *font.*

Serif   Sans Serif

Figure 85: *Typefaces*

typesetter: Same as *imagesetter.*

U

UART: Pronounced *u-art*, and short for *universal asynchronous receiver-transmitter*, the UART is a computer component that handles asynchronous serial communication. Every computer contains a UART to manage the serial ports, and all internal modems have their own UART.

As modems have become increasingly fast, the UART has come under greater scrutiny as the cause of transmission bottlenecks. If you are purchasing a fast external modem, make sure that the computer's UART can handle the modem's maximum transmission rate. The newer 16550 UART contains a 16-bit buffer, enabling it to support higher transmission rates than the older 8250 UART.

➠ See also *asynchronous; serial port.*

ultra large scale integration: See *ULSI.*

ULSI: Abbreviation of ultra large scale integration, which refers to placing more than one million circuit elements on a single chip. The Intel 486 and Pentium microprocessors, for example, use ULSI technology.

➠ See also *chip; Pentium microprocessor.*

underflow: Refers to the condition that occurs when a computer attempts to represent a number that is too small for it. Programs respond to underflow conditions in different ways. Some report an error, while others approximate as best they can and continue processing.

➠ See also *floating point; overflow error.*

undo: To return to a previous state by *undoing* the effects of one or more commands. The undo command is a valuable feature supported by many software products. It lets you try unknown commands with less risk, because you can always return to the previous state. Also, if you accidentally press the wrong function key, you can undo your mistake.

Many programs allow you to undo an unlimited number of commands. Each time you press the undo key, the previous command is undone. You can roll back an entire editing session this way. Other programs impose a limit on the number of commands you can undo.

➠ See also *command.*

undocumented: Refers to features that are not described in the official documentation of a product. This lack of documentation can occur for a variety of reasons, including oversight. More often, though, undocumented features are features that were included because they were useful to the programmers developing the product but were deemed either unnecessary or potentially dangerous to end users. Undocumented features can also include untested features that will be officially supported in a future release of the product.

➠ See also *documentation.*

Unicode: A standard for representing characters as integers. Unlike ASCII, which uses 8 bits for each character, Unicode uses 16 bits, which means that it can represent more than 65,000 unique characters. This is a bit of overkill for English and European languages, but it is necessary for some other languages, such as Chinese and Japanese. Many analysts believe that as the software industry becomes increasingly global, Unicode will eventually supplant ASCII as the standard character coding format.

➠ See also *ASCII; character.*

Uniform Resource Locator: See *URL.*

uninterruptible power supply: See *UPS.*

universal asynchronous receiver-transmitter: See *UART*.

UNIX: Pronounced *yoo-niks*, a popular *multi-user, multitasking* operating system developed at Bell Labs in the early 1970s. Created by just a handful of programmers, UNIX was designed to be a small, flexible system used exclusively by programmers. Although it has matured considerably over the years, UNIX still betrays its origins by its cryptic command names and its general lack of user-friendliness. This is changing, however, with graphical user interfaces such as MOTIF.

UNIX was one of the first operating systems to be written in a high-level programming language, namely C. This meant that it could run on virtually any computer that had a C compiler. This natural portability combined with its low price made it a popular choice among universities. (It was inexpensive because antitrust regulations prohibited Bell Labs from marketing it as a full-scale product.)

Bell Labs distributed the operating system in its source language form, so anyone who obtained a copy could modify and customize it for his own purposes. By the end of the 1970s, dozens of different versions of UNIX were running at various sites.

After its breakup in 1982, AT&T began to market UNIX in earnest. It also began the long and difficult process of defining a standard version of UNIX. To date, there are two main dialects of UNIX; one produced by AT&T known as *System V* and one developed at Berkeley University and known as *BSD4.x*, x being a number from 1 to 3.

Due to its portability, flexibility, and power, UNIX has become the leading operating system for workstations. It is less popular in the personal computer market, where it is known as *Xenix* or AIX (for PCs) and A/UX operating system (for Macintosh computers). Until recently, most personal computers did not have enough power to take advantage of UNIX. Now UNIX must compete with OS/2 and Windows NT, which offer many of the same features as UNIX while remaining compatible with DOS and Windows.

➠ See also *C; multitasking; operating system; OS/2.*

unpack: To convert a packed file into its original form. A packed file is a file that has been compressed to take up less storage area.

➠ See also *data compression.*

upgrade: A new version of a software or hardware product designed to replace an older version of the same product. Typically, software companies sell upgrades at a discount to prevent users from switching to other products. In most cases, you must prove you own an older version of the product to qualify for the upgrade price. In addition, the installation routines for upgrades often check to make sure that an older version is already installed on your computer; if not, you cannot install the upgrade.

In the 90s, software companies began offering *competitive upgrades,* which means that you can buy a program at a discount if you can prove that you own a competing program.

upload: To transmit data from a computer to a bulletin board service, mainframe, or network. For example, if you use a personal computer to log on to a network and you want to send files across the network, you must upload the files from your PC to the network.

➠ See also *bulletin board service; download; online service; network.*

uppercase: Uppercase characters are capital letters; *lowercase characters* are small letters. For example, *box* is in lowercase while *BOX* is in uppercase. The term is a vestige of the days when typesetters kept capital letters in a box above the lowercase letters.

A program that distinguishes between uppercase and lowercase is said to be case sensitive.

➠ See also *case sensitive.*

upper memory area: Same as *high memory.*

UPS: Abbreviation of *uninterruptible power supply,* a power supply that includes a battery to maintain power in the event of a power outage. Typically, a UPS keeps a computer running for several minutes after a power outage, enabling you to save data that is in RAM and shut down the computer gracefully. Many UPSs now offer a software component that enables you to automate backup and shut down procedures in case there's a power failure while you're away from the computer.

There are two basic types of UPS systems: *standby power systems (SPSs)* and *on-line* UPS systems. An SPS monitors the power line and switches to battery power as soon as it detects a problem. The switch to battery, however, can require several milliseconds, during which time the computer is not receiving any power.

An on-line UPS avoids these momentary power lapses by constantly providing power from its own inverter, even when the power line is functioning properly. In general, on-line UPSs are much more expensive than SPSs.

➠ See also *power supply*.

upward compatible: Refers to software that runs not only on the computer for which it was designed, but also on newer and more powerful models. For example, a program designed to run on an Intel 386 microprocessor, which also runs on a Pentium, is upward compatible. Upward compatibility is important because it means you can move to a newer, larger, and more sophisticated computer without converting your data.

In contrast to upward compatibility, *downward (backward) compatible* means that a program runs not only on the computer for which it was designed, but also on smaller and older models. For example, a program designed to run under MS-DOS 6.0, which also works under MS-DOS 5.0, is downward compatible.

➠ See also *compatible; downward compatible; DOS.*

URL: Abbreviation of *Uniform Resource Locator,* the global address of documents and other resources on the Internet.

➠ See also *Internet; World Wide Web.*

USENET: A worldwide bulletin board system that can be accessed through the Internet or through many online services. The USENET contains nearly two thousand forums, called *newsgroups,* that cover every imaginable interest group. It is used daily by millions of people around the world.

➠ See also *bulletin board service; forum; Internet.*

user: An individual who uses a computer. This includes expert programmers as well as novices. An *end user* is any individual who runs an application program.

➠ See also *application; end user.*

user-friendly: Refers to anything that makes it easier for novices to use a computer. Menu-driven programs, for example, are considered more user-friendly than command-driven systems. Graphical user interfaces (GUIs) are also considered user-friendly. Online help systems are another feature of user-friendly programs.

Although the term *user-friendly* represents an important concept, it has been so overused that it has become something of a cliché.

➠ See also *graphical user interface.*

user group: A group of individuals with common interests in some aspect of computers. Some user groups cover nearly everything with subgroups (called *SIGs*) for more specialized interests, while others concentrate on a particular area, such as computer graphics, or a particular application.

Nearly every major city in the U.S. has many user groups that meet to share ideas. Joining a local user group is a particularly good way for computer novices to get free expert advice.

➠ See also *SIG.*

user interface: The junction between a user and a computer program. An interface is a set of commands or menus through which a user communicates with a program. A command-driven interface is one in which you enter commands. A *menu-driven* interface is one in which you select command choices from various menus displayed on the screen.

The user interface is one of the most important parts of any program because it determines how easily you can make the program do what you want. A powerful program with a poorly designed user interface has little value. Graphical user interfaces (GUIs) that use windows, icons, and pop-up menus have become standard on personal computers.

➠ See also *graphical user interface.*

username: A name used to gain access to a computer system. Usernames, and often passwords, are required in multi-user systems. In most such systems, users can choose their own usernames and passwords.

Usernames are also required to access some bulletin board and online services.

➠ See also *bulletin board service; multi-user; online service; password.*

utility: A program that performs a very specific task, usually related to managing system resources. Operating systems contain a number of utilities for managing disk drives, printers, and other devices.

Utilities differ from applications mostly in terms of size and complexity. For example, word processors, spreadsheet programs, and database applications are considered applications because they are large programs that perform a variety of functions not directly related to managing computer resources.

Utilities are sometimes installed as *memory-resident* programs. On DOS systems, such utilities are called *TSRs.*

➠ See also *application; TSR.*

V.22: Pronounced *V-dot-twenty-two*, V.22 is short for the CCITT *V.22* communications standard. See under CCITT.

V.22bis: Pronounced *V-dot-twenty-two-biss*, V.22bis is short for the CCITT *V.22bis* communications standard. See under CCITT.

V.32: Pronounced *V-dot-thirty-two*, V.32 is short for the CCITT *V.32* communications standard. See under CCITT.

V.34: Pronounced *V-dot-thirty-four*, V.34 is short for the CCITT V.34 communications standard. See under CCITT.

V.42: Pronounced *V-dot-forty-two*, V.42 is short for the CCITT *V.42* communications standard. See under CCITT.

value-added reseller: See VAR.

vanilla: Without added features. A "vanilla PC," for example, would be a PC with all standard components.

vaporware: A sarcastic term used to designate software products that have been announced but are not yet available.

VAR: Acronym for *value-added reseller*. Same as *OEM* (*original equipment manufacturer*).

variable: A symbol or name that stands for a value. For example, in the expression

x+y

x and *y* are variables. Variables can represent numeric values, characters, character strings, or memory addresses.

Variables play an important role in computer programming because they enable programmers to write flexible programs. Rather than entering data directly into a program, a programmer can use variables to represent the data. Then, when the program is executed, the variables are replaced with real data. This makes it possible for the same program to process different sets of data.

Every variable has a name, called the *variable name*, and a data type. A variable's data type indicates what sort of value the variable represents, such as whether it is an integer, a floating-point number, or a character.

The opposite of a *variable* is a constant. Constants are values that never change. Because of their inflexibility, constants are used less often than variables in programming.

➠ See also *character string; constant; data; data type; expression.*

variable length: Refers to anything whose length can vary. For example, in databases, a *variable-length field* is a field that does not have a fixed length. Instead, the field length varies depending on what data is stored in it.

Variable-length fields are useful because they save space. Suppose, for example, that you want to define a NAME field. The length of each NAME field will vary according to the data placed in it. For example, *John Smith* is 10 characters long, but *Thomas Horatio Jefferson* is 24 characters long. With fixed-length fields, you would need to define each field to be long enough to hold the longest name. This would be a waste of space for records that had short names. With variable-length fields, the NAME field in each record would be just long enough to hold its data.

The opposite of *variable length* is *fixed length*.

➠ See also *database management system; field; fixed length; record.*

variable-length record: A record that has at least one variable-length field. The length of the entire record, therefore, varies according to what data is placed in the variable-length field.

➠ See also *field; fixed length; record; variable length.*

VDT: Short for *video display terminal.* See under *monitor.*

VDT radiation: The radiation emitted by video display terminals. Like televisions, computer monitors emit various types of radiation. Since the late 1980s, there has been a public debate about whether this radiation poses a health problem. To date, however, there is no conclusive evidence to settle the question once and for all.

➠ See also *ELF emission; monitor.*

vector: (1) In computer programming, a one-dimensional array.

➠ See also *array.*

(2) In computer graphics, a line that is defined by its start and end point.

➠ See also *vector graphics.*

vector font: Same as *scalable font.*

vector graphics: Same as *object-oriented graphics,* refers to software and hardware that use geometrical formulas to represent images. The other method for representing graphical images is through bit maps, in which the image is composed of a pattern of dots. This is sometimes called *raster graphics.* Programs that enable you to create and manipulate vector graphics are called *draw programs,* whereas programs that manipulated bit-mapped images are called *paint programs.*
Vector-oriented images are more flexible than bit maps because they can be resized and stretched. In addition, images stored as vectors look better on devices (monitors and printers) with higher resolution, whereas bit-mapped images always appear the same regardless of a device's resolution. Another advantage of vector graphics is that

representations of images often require less memory than bit-mapped images do.

Almost all sophisticated graphics systems, including CADD systems and animation software, use vector graphics. In addition, many printers (PostScript printers, for example) use vector graphics. Fonts represented as vectors are called *vector fonts, scalable fonts, object-oriented fonts,* and *outline fonts.*

Note that most output devices, including dot-matrix printers, laser printers, and display monitors, are raster devices (plotters are the notable exception). This means that all objects, even vector objects, must be translated into bit maps before being output. The difference between vector graphics and raster graphics, therefore, is that vector graphics are not translated into bit maps until the last possible moment, after all sizes and resolutions have been specified. PostScript printers, for example, have a raster image processor (RIP) that performs the translation within the printer. In their vector form, therefore, graphics representations can potentially be output on any device, with any resolution, and at any size.

➠ See also *autotracing; bit map; bit-mapped graphics; graphics; graphics file formats; object oriented; PostScript; raster image processor; scalable font.*

vertical justification: A feature supported by some word processors and desktop publishing systems in which the system automatically adjusts the vertical space between lines (the *leading*) so that columns and pages have an even top and bottom margin. This is also called *feathering.*

➠ See also *justification; leading; word processing.*

vertical scrolling: See *scroll.*

very large-scale integration: See *VLSI.*

VESA: Short for *Video Electronics Standards Association,* a consortium of video adapter and monitor manufacturers whose goal is to standardize video protocols. VESA has developed a family of video standards that offer greater resolution and more colors than VGA. These standards are known collectively as Super VGA (SVGA).

➠ See also *SVGA; VL-Bus.*

VESA Local Bus: See *VL-Bus.*

VGA: PC Abbreviation of *video graphics array,* a graphics display system for PCs developed by IBM. VGA has become one of the de facto standards for PCs. In text mode, VGA systems provide a resolution of 720 by 400 pixels. In graphics mode, the resolution is either 640 by 480 (with 16 colors) or 320 by 200 (with 256 colors). The total palette of colors is 262,144.

Unlike earlier graphics standards for PCs—MDA, CGA, and EGA—VGA uses analog signals rather than digital signals. Consequently, a monitor designed for one of the older standards will not be able to use VGA.

Since its introduction in 1987, several other standards have been developed that offer greater resolution and more colors (see *SVGA, 8514/A graphics standard,* and *XGA*), but VGA remains the lowest common denominator. All PCs made today support VGA, and possibly some other more advanced standard.

➠ See also *SVGA; video adapter.*

VGA Plus: See under *SVGA.*

video accelerator: Same as *graphics accelerator.*

video adapter: A board that plugs into a personal computer to give it display capabilities. The display capabilities of a computer, however, depend on both the logical circuitry (provided in the video adapter) and the display monitor. A monochrome monitor, for example, cannot display colors no matter how powerful the video adapter.

Many different types of video adapters are available for PCs. Most conform to one of the video standards defined by IBM or VESA. Each adapter offers several different video modes. The two basic categories of video modes are *text* and *graphics.* In text mode, a monitor can display only ASCII characters. In graphics mode, a monitor can display any bit-mapped image. Within the text and graphics modes, some monitors also offer a choice of resolutions. At lower resolutions a monitor can display more colors.

Most modern video adapters contain memory, so that the computer's RAM is not used for storing displays. In addition, some adapters have their own graphics coprocessor for performing graphics calculations. These adapters are often called *graphics accelerators*. Video adapters are also called *video cards, video boards,* and *video display boards.*

➠ See also *monitor; video mode; video standards;* VRAM.

video capture: Converting analog video signals, such as those generated by a video camera, into a digital format and then storing the digital video on a computer's mass storage device. Video capture requires a special video capture card that converts the analog signals into digital form and compresses the data.

video card: Same as *video adapter.*

videoconferencing: Conducting a conference between two or more participants at different sites by using computer networks to transmit audio and video data. For example, a *point-to-point* (two-person) video conferencing system works much like a video telephone. Each participant has a video camera, microphone, and speakers mounted on his or her computer. As the two participants speak to one another, their voices are carried over the network and delivered to the other's speakers, and whatever images appear in front of the video camera appear in a window on the other participant's monitor.

Multipoint videoconferencing allows three or more participants to sit in a virtual conference room and communicate as if they were sitting right next to each other. Until the mid 90s, the hardware costs made videoconferencing prohibitively expensive for most organizations, but that situation is changing rapidly. Many analysts believe that videoconferencing will be one of the fastest-growing segments of the computer industry in the latter half of the decade.

➠ See also *workgroup computing.*

video display board: Same as *video adapter.*

Video Electronics Standards Association: See VESA.

Video for Windows: [PC] A format developed by Microsoft Corporation for storing video and audio information. Files in this format have a .AVI extension. AVI files are limited to 320 x 240 resolution, and 15 frames per second, neither of which is adequate for full-screen, full-motion video. However, Video for Windows does not require any special hardware, making it the lowest common denominator for multimedia application. Many multimedia producers use this format because it allows them to sell their products to the largest base of users.

A competing software-only video format is QuickTime. Although QuickTime and Video for Windows are widely used, they may eventually succumb to technologies such as MPEG that use hardware to compress and decompress data.

➠ See also MPEG; QuickTime.

Video Graphics Array: See VGA.

video mode: The setting of a video adapter. Most video adapters can run in either *text mode* or *graphics mode.* In text mode, a monitor can display only ASCII characters. In graphics mode, a monitor can display any bit-mapped image. In addition to the text and graphics modes, some video adapters offer different resolution modes.

➠ See also *graphics mode; text mode; video adapter.*

video RAM: See VRAM.

video standards: There are a variety of video standards that define the resolution and colors for displays (Table 28). Support for a graphics standard is determined both by the monitor and by the video adapter. The monitor must be able to show the resolution and colors defined by the standard, and the video adapter must be capable of transmitting the appropriate signals to the monitor.

Listed here, in approximate order of increasing power and sophistication, are the more popular video standards for PCs. Note that many of these numbers represent only the minimums specified in the standards. Many suppliers of video adapters provide greater resolution and more colors. For more information, refer to the entries for the specific graphics systems.

➠ See also *8514/A; SVGA; TI 34010; VGA; video adapter; XGA.*

Table 28
POPULAR VIDEO STANDARDS FOR PCS

VIDEO STANDARD	RESOLUTION	SIMULTANEOUS COLORS
VGA (Video Graphics Array)	640 by 480	16
	320 by 200	256
SVGA	800 by 600	16
	1,024 by 768	256
	1,280 by 1,024	256
	1,600 by 1,200	256
8514/A	1,024 by 768	256
XGA (Extended Graphics Array)	640 by 480	65,536
	1,024 by 768	256
TI 34010	1,024 by 768	256

view: In database management systems, a view is a particular way of looking at a database. A single database can support numerous different views. Typically, a view arranges the records in some order and makes only certain fields visible. Note that different views do not affect the physical organization of the database.

➡ See also *database; database management system; field.*

viewer: A utility program that enables you to read a file in its *native format.* A Lotus 1-2-3 viewer, for example, enables you to read Lotus 1-2-3 files. Many shell utilities and file managers include viewers so that you can display different types of files.

➡ See also *file management; format; shell.*

virtual: Not real. The term *virtual* is popular among computer scientists and is used in a wide variety of situations. In general, it distinguishes something that is merely conceptual from something that has physical reality. For example, *virtual memory* refers to an imaginary set of locations, or addresses, where you can store data. It is imaginary in the sense that the memory area is not the same as the real physical memory composed of transistors. The difference is a bit like the difference between an architect's plans for a house and the actual house. A computer scientist might call the plans a *virtual house*. Another analogy is the difference between the brain and the mind. The mind is a *virtual brain*. It exists conceptually, but the actual physical matter is the brain.

The opposite of virtual is *real, absolute,* or *physical.*

➠ See also *virtual memory.*

virtual disk: Same as *RAM disk.*

virtual memory: An imaginary memory area supported by some operating systems (for example, Windows but not DOS) in conjunction with the hardware (Figure 86). You can think of virtual memory as an alternate set of memory addresses. Programs use these *virtual addresses* rather than real addresses to store instructions and data. When the program is actually executed, the virtual addresses are converted into real memory addresses.

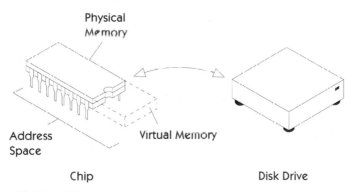

Figure 86: *Virtual Memory*

The purpose of virtual memory is to enlarge the *address space,* the set of addresses a program can utilize. For example, virtual memory might contain twice as many addresses as main memory. A program using all of virtual memory, therefore, would not be able to fit in main memory all at once. Nevertheless, the computer could execute such a program by copying into main memory those portions of the program needed at any given point during execution.

To facilitate copying virtual memory into real memory, the operating system divides virtual memory into *pages*, each of which contains a fixed number of addresses. Each page is stored on a disk until it is needed. When the page is needed, the operating system copies it from disk to main memory, translating the virtual addresses into real addresses.

The process of translating virtual addresses into real addresses is called *mapping*. The copying of virtual pages from disk to main memory is known as *paging* or *swapping*.

➡ See also *address space; main memory; operating system; page; paging; swap; virtual*

virtual reality: An artificial environment created with computer hardware and software and presented to the user in such a way that it appears and feels like a real environment. To "enter" a virtual reality, a user dons special gloves, earphones, and goggles, all of which receive their input from the computer system. In this way, at least three of the five senses are controlled by the computer. In addition to feeding sensory input to the user, the devices also monitor the user's actions. The goggles, for example, track how the eyes move and respond accordingly by sending new video input.

To date, virtual reality systems require extremely expensive hardware and software and are confined mostly to research laboratories.

➡ See also *cyberspace; virtual.*

virus: A piece of code that can replicate itself. All computer viruses are man-made. A simple virus that can make a copy of itself over and over again is relatively easy to produce. Even such a simple virus is dangerous because it will quickly use all available memory and bring the system to a halt. An even more dangerous type of virus is one capable of transmitting itself across networks and bypassing security systems.

Since 1987, when a virus infected ARPANET, a large network used by the Defense Department and many universities, many antivirus programs have become available. These programs periodically check your computer system for the best-known types of viruses. However, if you receive your software from reliable sources and you are not attached to a network, there is little chance that your system will be infected.

Some people distinguish between general viruses and *worms*. A worm is a special type of virus that can replicate itself and use memory, but cannot attach itself to other programs.

➠ See also ARPANET; *hacker; network.*

VL-Bus: Short for *VESA Local-Bus*, a local bus architecture created by the Video Electronics Standards Association (VESA). Although it was quite popular in PCs made in 1993 and 1994, it has been overshadowed by a competing local bus architecture called *PCI.*

➠ See also *expansion bus; local bus; PCI.*

VLSI: Abbreviation of *very large-scale integration,* the process of placing thousands (or hundreds of thousands) of electronic components on a single chip. Nearly all modern chips employ VLSI architectures, or ULSI (ultra large scale integration).

➠ See also *chip; integrated circuit; ULSI.*

voice mail: Refers to e-mail systems that support audio. Users can leave spoken messages for one another and listen to the messages by executing the appropriate command in the e-mail system.

➠ See also *e-mail.*

voice recognition: The field of computer science that deals with designing computer systems that can recognize spoken words. Note that voice recognition implies only that the computer can take dictation, not that it *understands* what is being said. Comprehending human languages falls under a different field of computer science called *natural language processing.*

A number of voice recognition systems are available on the market. The most powerful can recognize thousands of words. However, they require an extended training session during which the computer system becomes accustomed to a particular voice and accent. Such systems are said to be *speaker dependent.*

Most systems also require that the speaker speak slowly and distinctly and separate each word with a short pause. These systems are called *discrete speech* systems. It will be many years before voice recognition systems support *continuous speech* so that users can speak naturally.

Because of their limitations and high cost, voice recognition systems are used only in a few specialized situations. For example, such systems are useful in instances when the user is unable to use a keyboard to enter data because his or her hands are occupied or disabled. Instead of typing commands, the user can simply speak into a headset.

➠ See also *artificial intelligence; natural language.*

volatile memory: Memory that loses its contents when the power is turned off. All RAM, for example, is volatile. ROM, on the other hand, is *nonvolatile.*

➠ See also *memory; RAM; ROM.*

volume: A fixed amount of storage on a disk or tape. The term *volume* is often used as a synonym for the storage medium itself, but it is possible for a single disk to contain more than one volume or for a volume to span more than one disk.

➠ See also *disk; mass storage.*

volume label: PC In DOS systems, the name of a volume (that is, the name of a disk or tape). Specifying a volume label makes it easier to keep track of what data is stored on each medium.

➠ See also *disk; label; volume.*

VRAM: Short for *video* RAM, and pronounced *vee-ram.* VRAM is special-purpose memory used by video adapters. Unlike conventional RAM, VRAM can be accessed by two different devices simultaneously. This enables a monitor to access the VRAM for screen updates at the same time that a graphics processor provides new data. VRAM yields better graphics performance but is more expensive than normal RAM.

➠ See also *graphics; memory; monitor; processor; RAM.*

WAIS: Short for *Wide Area Information Server*, and pronounced *ways*, a program for finding documents on the Internet. WAIS is rather primitive in its search capabilities.

➧ See also *Gopher; Internet.*

wait state: A time-out period during which a CPU or bus lies idle. Wait states are sometimes required because different components function at different clock speeds. For example, if the CPU is much faster than the memory chips, it may need to sit idle during some clock cycles so that the memory chips can catch up. Likewise, buses sometimes require wait states if expansion boards run slower than the bus.

A *zero wait state* microprocessor is one that runs at the maximum speed without any time-outs to compensate for slow memory. Wait states can be avoided by using a variety of techniques, including page-mode memory, interleaved memory, and memory caches.

➧ See also *cache; clock speed; interleaving; page-mode memory.*

WAN: See *wide-area network.*

warm boot: Refers to resetting a computer that is already turned on. Resetting it returns the computer to its initial state, and any data or programs in main memory are erased. A warm boot is sometimes necessary when a program encounters an error from which it cannot recover. On PCs, you can perform a warm boot by pressing the Control, Alt, and Delete keys simultaneously. On Macs, you can perform a warm boot by pressing the Restart button.

A cold boot refers to turning a computer on from an off position.

➠ See also *boot; cold boot.*

web page: A document on the World Wide Web. Every web page is identified by a unique URL (Uniform Resource Locator).

➠ See also home page; URL; World Wide Web.

web site: A site (location) on the World Wide Web. Each web site contains a home page, which is the first document users see when they enter the site. The site might also contain additional documents and files. Each site is owned and managed by an individual, company or organization.

➠ See also *home page; World Wide Web.*

what-you-see-is-what-you-get: See *WYSIWYG.*

whitespace: Refers to all characters that appear as blanks on a display screen or printer. This includes the space character, the tab character, and sometimes other special characters that do not have a visual form (for example, the bell character and null character).

➠ See also *null character.*

Wide Area Information Server: See *WAIS.*

wide-area network (WAN): A computer network that spans a relatively large geographical area. Computers connected to a wide-area network are connected through telephone lines or radio waves.

➠ See also *Internet; network.*

wide SCSI: See under *SCSI.*

widow: (1) In word processing, the last line of a paragraph that appears as the first line of a page. Widows are considered bad form in page layout, so many word processors allow you to avoid them. When the word processor detects a widow, it can end the page one or more lines early so that at least the last two lines from the paragraph start the next page. Some word processors avoid widows by moving all the lines on the page closer together so that the last line can fit on the same page.

The converse of a widow is an *orphan*, the first line of a paragraph appearing as the last line of a page.

➡ See also *orphan; word processing.*

(2) The last line of a paragraph that is much shorter than all the other lines in the paragraph.

wild card: A special symbol that stands for one or more characters. Many operating systems and applications support wild cards for identifying files and directories. This enables you to select multiple files with a single specification. For example, in DOS and Windows, the asterisk (*) is a wild card that stands for any combination of letters. The file specification

m*

therefore, refers to all files that begin with *m*. Similarly, the specification

m*.doc

refers to all files that start with *m* and end with *.doc*.

Many word processors also support wild cards for performing text searches.

Winchester disk drive: Another term for *hard disk drive*. The term *Winchester* comes from an early type of disk drive developed by IBM that stored 30MB (megabytes) and had a 30-millisecond access time; so its inventors called it a Winchester in honor of the .30-caliber rifle of the same name. Although modern disk drives are faster and hold more data, the basic technology is the same, so *Winchester* has become synonymous with *hard*.

➠ See also *disk drive; hard disk.*

window: (1) An enclosed, rectangular area on a display screen. Most modern operating systems and applications have graphical user interfaces that let you divide your display into several windows. Within each window, you can run a different program or display different data.

Windows are particularly valuable in *multitasking environments*, which allow you to execute several programs at once. By dividing your display into windows, you can see the output from all the programs at the same time. To enter input into a program, you simply click on the desired window to make it the foreground process.

Graphical user interfaces, such as the one supported by the Apple Macintosh or Windows, enable you to set the dimensions and position of each window by moving the mouse and clicking appropriate buttons. Windows can be arranged so that they do not overlap (*tiled windows*) or so they do overlap (*overlaid windows*). Overlaid windows (also called *cascading windows*) resemble a stack of pieces of paper lying on top of one another; only the topmost window is displayed in full. You can move a window to the top of the stack by positioning the pointer in the portion of the window that is visible and clicking the mouse buttons. This is known as *popping*. You can expand a window to fill the entire screen by selecting the window's *zoom box*.

In addition to moving windows, changing their size, popping and zooming them, you can also replace an entire window with an icon (this is sometimes called *minimizing*). An icon is a small picture that represents the program running in the window. By converting a window into an icon, you can free up space on the display screen without erasing the window entirely. It is always possible to reconvert the icon into a window whenever you want.

➠ See also *graphical user interface; icon; Microsoft Window.*

(2) A window can also be a logical view of a file. By moving the window, you can view different portions of the file.

Windows: [PC] When spelled with a capital W, Windows is short for *Microsoft Windows.*

Windows Metafile Format: See *WMF.*

Windows 95: PC A major release of the Microsoft Windows operating system released in 1995. Windows 95 represents a significant advance over its precursor, Windows 3.1. In addition to sporting a new user interface, Windows 95 also includes a number of important internal improvements. Perhaps most important, it supports 32-bit applications, which means that future applications written specifically for this operating system should run much faster. And although Windows 95 can run older Windows and DOS applications, it has essentially removed DOS as the underlying platform. This has meant removal of many of the old DOS limitations, such as 640K of main memory and 8-character filenames.

➡ See also *Microsoft Windows.*

Windows NT: PC The most advanced version of the Windows operating system. Windows NT is a 32-bit operating system that supports preemptive multitasking

There are actually two versions of Windows NT: Windows NT Server, designed to act as a server in networks, and Windows NT Workstation for stand-alone or client workstations.

➡ See also *multitasking; preemptive multitasking; operating system; Windows.*

wizard: (1) A utility within an application that helps you use the application to perform a particular task. For example, a "letter wizard" within a word processing application would lead you through the steps of producing different types of correspondence.

(2) An outstanding programmer. Also called a *super-programmer.* Common wisdom holds that one wizard is worth ten average programmers.

WMF: PC Short for *Windows Metafile Format,* graphics file format used to exchange graphics information between Microsoft Windows applications. WMF files can hold both vector and bit-mapped images.

➡ See also *graphics; graphics file formats.*

word: (1) In word processing, any group of characters separated by spaces or punctuation on both sides. Whether it is a real word or not is unimportant to the word processor.

(2) In programming, the natural data size of a computer. The size of a word varies from one computer to another, depending on the CPU. For computers with a 16-bit CPU, a word is 16 bits (2 bytes). On large mainframes, a word can be as long as 64 bits (8 bytes).

Some computers and programming languages distinguish between *shortwords* and *longwords*. A shortword is usually 2 bytes long, while a longword is 4 bytes.

➠ See also *bit; byte; CPU.*

Word: When spelled with a capital *W*, Word refers to *Microsoft Word*, a powerful word processor.

WordPerfect: One of the most popular word processors for PCs and Apple Macintoshes.

➠ See also *word processing.*

word processing: Using a computer to create, edit, and print documents. Of all computer applications, word processing is the most common. To perform word processing, you need a computer, a special program called a *word processor*, and a printer. A word processor enables you to create a document, store it electronically on a disk, display it on a screen, modify it by entering commands and characters from the keyboard, and print it on a printer.

The great advantage of word processing over using a typewriter is that you can make changes without retyping the entire document. If you make a typing mistake, you simply back up the cursor and correct your mistake. If you want to delete a paragraph, you simply remove it, without leaving a trace. It is equally easy to insert a word, sentence, or paragraph in the middle of a document. Word processors also make it easy to move sections of text from one place to another within a document, or between documents. When you have made all the changes you want, you can send the file to a printer to get a hardcopy.

Word processors vary considerably, but all word processors support the following basic features:

insert text: Allows you to insert text anywhere in the document.

delete text: Allows you to erase characters, words, lines, or pages as easily as you can cross them out on paper.

cut and paste: Allows you to remove (cut) a section of text from one place in a document and insert (paste) it somewhere else.

copy: Allows you to duplicate a section of text.

page size and margins: Allows you to define various page sizes and margins, and the word processor will automatically readjust the text so that it fits.

search and replace: Allows you to direct the word processor to search for a particular word or phrase. You can also direct the word processor to replace one group of characters with another everywhere that the first group appears.

word wrap: The word processor automatically moves to the next line when you have filled one line with text, and it will readjust text if you change the margins.

print: Allows you to send a document to a printer to get hardcopy.

Word processors that support only these features (and maybe a few others) are called *text editors*. Most word processors, however, support additional features that enable you to manipulate and format documents in more sophisticated ways. These more advanced word processors are sometimes called *full-featured word processors*. Full-featured word processors usually support the following features:

file management: Many word processors contain file management capabilities that allow you to create, delete, move, and search for files.

font specifications: Allows you to change fonts within a document. For example, you can specify bold, italics, and underlining. Most word processors also let you change the font size and even the typeface.

footnotes and cross-references: Automates the numbering and placement of footnotes and enables you to easily cross-reference other sections of the document.

graphics: Allows you to embed illustrations and graphs into a document. Some word processors let you create the illustrations within the word processor; others let you insert an illustration produced by a different program.

headers, footers, and page numbering: Allows you to specify customized headers and footers that the word processor will put at the top and bottom of every page. The word processor automatically keeps track of page numbers so that the correct number appears on each page.

layout: Allows you to specify different margins within a single document and to specify various methods for indenting paragraphs.

macros: A macro is a character or word that represents a series of keystrokes. The keystrokes can represent text or commands. The ability to define macros allows you to save yourself a lot of time by replacing common combinations of keystrokes.

merges: Allows you to merge text from one file into another file. This is particularly useful for generating many files that have the same format but different data. Generating mailing labels is the classic example of using merges.

spell checker: A utility that allows you to check the spelling of words. It will highlight any words that it does not recognize.

tables of contents and indexes: Allows you to automatically create a table of contents and index based on special codes that you insert in the document.

thesaurus: A built-in thesaurus that allows you to search for synonyms without leaving the word processor.

windows: Allows you to edit two or more documents at the same time. Each document appears in a separate window. This is particularly valuable when working on a large project that consists of several different files.

WYSIWYG (what you see is what you get): With WYSIWYG, a document appears on the display screen exactly as it will look when printed.

The line dividing word processors from desktop publishing systems is constantly shifting. In general, though, desktop publishing applications support finer control over layout, and more support for full-color documents.

➠ See also *copy; cut; delete; desktop publishing; editor; font; footer; graphics; header; hyphenation; insert; justify; layout; macro; margins; merge; paste; spell checker; word wrap; WYSIWYG.*

word processor: A program or computer that enables you to perform word processing functions.

➠ See also *word processing.*

word wrap: In word processing, a feature that causes the word processor to force all text to fit within the defined margins. When you fill one line with text, the word processor automatically jumps to the next line so that you are not required to keep track of line lengths and to press the Return key after each line. The word processor divides lines in such a way that a word is never split between two lines (unless the word processor supports *hyphenation*).

Word wrap also occurs if you change the margins. In this case, the word processor readjusts all the text so that it fits within the new margins.

Note that word wrap inserts a *soft return* at the end of each line, not a *hard return.* Soft returns are invisible codes that the word processor utilizes. Hard returns are real characters inserted into the document.

Some word processors allow you to turn off the word-wrap feature. This is useful for writing programs and other types of formatted text where you want complete control over new lines.

➠ See also *hard return; hyphenation; margins; soft return; word processing.*

workgroup computing: A *workgroup* is a collection of individuals working together on a task. Workgroup computing occurs when all the individuals have computers connected to a network that allows them to send e-mail to one another, share data files, and schedule meetings.

workgroup productivity package: Software packages that include e-mail, calendar programs, scheduling programs, and other utilities that promote communication between users on a local-area network.

➠ See also *calendar; e-mail; local-area network; scheduler; workgroup computing.*

working directory: The directory in which you are currently working. Pathnames that do not start with the root directory are assumed by the operating system to start from the working directory.

➠ See also *directory; pathname; root directory.*

worksheet: Same as *spreadsheet.*

workstation: (1) A type of computer used for engineering applications (CAD/CAM), desktop publishing, software development, and other types of applications that require a moderate amount of computing power and relatively high quality graphics capabilities.

Workstations generally come with a large, high-resolution graphics screen, at least 16MB (megabytes) of RAM, built-in network support, and a graphical user interface. Most workstations also have a mass storage device such as a disk drive, but a special type of workstation, called a *diskless workstation,* comes without a disk drive. The most common operating system for workstations is UNIX.

In terms of computing power, workstations lie between personal computers and minicomputers, although the line is fuzzy on both ends. High-end personal computers such as the PowerMac are equivalent to low-end workstations. And high-end workstations are equivalent to minicomputers.

Like personal computers, most workstations are single-user computers. However, workstations are typically linked together to form a local-area network, although they can also be used as stand-alone systems.

The leading manufacturers of workstations are Sun Computer, Hewlett-Packard Corporation, and Digital Electronics Corporation.

➠ See also *CAD/CAM; computer; desktop publishing; diskless workstation; local-area network; minicomputer; personal computer; UNIX.*

(2) In networking, *workstation* refers to any computer connected to a local-area network. It could be a workstation or a personal computer.

➠ See also *local-area network; network; personal computer.*

World Wide Web: A system of Internet servers that support specially formatted documents. The documents are formatted in a language called *HTML (HyperText Markup Language)* that supports links to other documents, as well as graphics, audio, and video files. This means you can jump from one document to another simply by clicking on hot spots. Not all Internet servers are part of the World Wide Web.

There are several applications that make it easy to access the World Wide Web, two of the most popular being Mosaic and Netscape.

➠ See also *hypertext; Internet; Mosaic; web site.*

WORM (write-once, read-many): Refers to an optical disk technology that allows you to write data onto a disk just once. After that, the data is permanent and can be read any number of times. A single WORM disk can store from 600MB megabytes to over 3GB (gigabytes) of data.

Unlike CD-ROMs, there is no single standard for WORM disks, which means that they can only be read by the same type of drive that wrote them. This has hampered their acceptance, although they have found a niche market as an archival media.

➠ See also *CD-ROM; erasable optical disk; mass storage; optical disk.*

write: To copy data from main memory to a storage device, such as a disk.

➠ See also *read.*

write once, read many: See *WORM.*

write-protect: To mark a file or disk so that its contents cannot be modified or deleted. When you want to make sure that neither you nor another user can destroy data, you can write-protect it. Many operating systems include a command to write-protect files. You can also write-protect diskettes. 3½-inch diskettes have a small switch that you can set to turn on write-protection (see Figure 33 at *floppy disk*). You can write-protect 5¼-inch diskettes by covering the *write-protect notch* with tape.

Write-protected files and media can only be read; you cannot write
to them, edit them, append data to them, or delete them.

➠ See also *diskette*.

WWW: See *World Wide Web*.

WYSIWYG: Pronounced *wizzy-wig*, stands for *what you see is what you
get*. A WYSIWYG is a word processor that enables you to see on the
display screen exactly what the text will look like when printed. This
differs from other word processors, which are incapable of displaying
different fonts and graphics on the display screen even though the
formatting codes have been inserted into the file. WYSIWYGs are
especially popular for desktop publishing.

Note that the WYSIWYGness of an application is relative. Originally, WYSIWYG referred to any word processor that could accurately show line breaks on the display screen. Later WYSIWYGs had
to be able to show different font sizes, even if the screen display was
limited to one typeface. Now, a word processor must be able to display many different typefaces to be considered a WYSIWYG.

Still, some WYSIWYGs are more WYSIWYG than others. For
example, many desktop publishing systems print text using outline
fonts (PostScript fonts, for example). Many of these systems, however, use corresponding bit-mapped fonts to display documents on a
monitor. What you see on the display screen, therefore, is not exactly
what you see when you print out the document. In addition, standard
laser printers have a resolution of at least 300 dpi, whereas even the
best graphics monitors have resolutions of only 100 dpi. Graphics and
text, therefore, always look sharper when printed than they do on the
display screen. And colors often appear differently on a monitor than
they do when printed out.

➠ See also *color matching; desktop publishing; font; PostScript; resolution;
word processing; WYSIWYP*.

WYSIWYP: Short for *What You See Is What You Print*, and pronounced
wizzy-whip, refers to the ability of a computer system to print colors
exactly as they appear on a monitor. WYSIWYP printing requires a
special program, called a *color management system (CMS)* to calibrate
the monitor and printer.

➠ See also *color management system; color matching; WYSIWYG*.

X.25: See under *CCITT*.

X.400: See under *CCITT*.

X.500: See under *CCITT*.

Xenix: A version of UNIX that runs on PCs. Xenix was developed by Microsoft Corporation and is compatible with AT&T's System V definition.

➠ See also *operating system*; *UNIX*.

XGA: Short for *extended graphics array*, a high-resolution graphics standard introduced by IBM in 1990. XGA was designed to replace the older 8514/A video standard. It provides the same resolutions (640 by 480 or 1024 by 768 pixels), but supports more simultaneous colors (65 thousand compared to 8514/A's 256 colors). In addition, XGA allows monitors to be non-interlaced.

➠ See also *8514/A*; *interlacing*; *resolution*; *SVGA*; *VGA*; *video standards*.

x-height: In typography, the height of a lowercase *x* in a specific font. This is also called the *body height*, as it represents the height of a lowercase character, excluding ascenders and descenders.

➠ See also *ascender*; *baseline*; *descender*; *typeface*.

Xmodem: Originally developed in 1977 by Ward Christiansen, Xmodem is one of the most popular file-transfer protocols. Although Xmodem is a relatively simple protocol, it is fairly effective at detecting errors. It works by sending blocks of data together with a checksum and then waiting for acknowledgment of the block's receipt. The waiting slows down the rate of data transmission considerably, but it ensures accurate transmission.

Xmodem can be implemented either in software or in hardware. Many modems, and almost all communications software packages, support Xmodem. However, it is useful only at relatively slow data transmission speeds (less than 4,800 bps).

Enhanced versions of Xmodem that work at higher transmission speeds are known as *Ymodem* and *Zmodem.*

➠ See also *checksum; communications protocol; communications software; modem; protocol; Ymodem; Zmodem.*

XMS: PC Stands for *Extended Memory Specification*, a procedure developed jointly by AST Research, Intel Corporation, Lotus Development, and Microsoft Corporation for using extended memory and DOS's *high memory area*, a 64K block just above 1MB.

➠ See also *expanded memory; extended memory; high memory area.*

XOR operator: Known as the *exclusive OR* operator, a Boolean operator that returns a value of TRUE only if its two operands have different values.

➠ See also *Boolean operator.*

X-Windows: A windowing and graphics system developed at the Massachusetts Institute of Technology (MIT). MIT has placed the X-Windows source code in the public domain, making it a particularly attractive system for UNIX vendors. Almost all UNIX graphical interfaces, including Motif and OpenLook, are based on X-Windows.

➠ See also *graphical user interface; public-domain software; UNIX.*

Ymodem: An asynchronous communications protocol designed by Chuck Forsberg that extends Xmodem by increasing the transfer block size and by supporting batch file transfers. This enables you to specify a list of files and send them all at one time. With Xmodem, you can send only one file at a time.

➠ See also *batch processing; communications protocol; Xmodem; Zmodem.*

Zero Insertion Force (ZIF) socket: A chip socket that allows you to insert and remove a chip without special tools.

➠ See also *chip.*

zero wait state: Refers to microprocessors that have no *wait states*; that is, they run at their maximum speed without waiting for slower memory chips.

➠ See also *wait state.*

ZIF socket: See *Zero Insertion Force (ZIF) socket.*

ZIP: PC A popular data compression format for PCs. The actual utilities for compressing and expanding files according to the ZIP format are called *PKZIP* and *PKUNZIP,* respectively. Files that have been compressed with PKZIP usually end with a *.ZIP* extension.

A special kind of zipped file is a *self-extracting file,* which ends with a *.EXE* extension. You can *unzip* a self-extracting file by simply executing it.

➠ See also *data compression.*

Zmodem: An asynchronous communications protocol that provides faster data transfer rates and better error detection than Xmodem. In particular, Zmodem supports larger block sizes and enables the transfer to resume where it left off following a communications failure.

➠ See also *communications protocol; Xmodem; Ymodem.*

zoom: In graphical user interfaces, to make a window larger. Typically, there is a *zoom box* in one corner of the window. When you select the zoom box the first time, the system expands the window to fill the entire screen. (This is sometimes called *maximizing*.) When you select it again, the window shrinks to its original size. (This is sometimes called *restoring*.)

Many applications also provide a zoom feature, which enlarges the view of an object enabling you to see more detail.

➠ See also *box*; *maximize*; *graphical user interface*; *window*.